Eighth SIGHAN Workshop on Chinese Language Processing 2015

Co-located with ACL-IJCNLP 2015

Beijing, China
30 - 31 July 2015

ISBN: 978-1-5108-0949-9

Printed from e-media with permission by:

Curran Associates, Inc.
57 Morehouse Lane
Red Hook, NY 12571

Some format issues inherent in the e-media version may also appear in this print version.

Printed by Curran Associates, Inc. (2015)

For permission requests, please contact the Association for Computational Linguistics at the address below.

Association for Computational Linguistics
209 N. Eighth Street
Stroudsburg, Pennsylvania 18360

Phone: 1-570-476-8006
Fax: 1-570-476-0860

acl@aclweb.org

Additional copies of this publication are available from:

Curran Associates, Inc.
57 Morehouse Lane
Red Hook, NY 12571 USA
Phone: 845-758-0400
Fax: 845-758-2634
Email: curran@proceedings.com
Web: www.proceedings.com

ACL-IJCNLP 2015

The 53rd Annual Meeting of the Association for Computational Linguistics and the 7th International Joint Conference on Natural Language Processing

Proceedings of the Eighth SIGHAN Workshop on Chinese Language Processing

July 30-31, 2015
Beijing, China

Preface

Welcome to the Eighth SIGHAN Workshop on Chinese Language Processing! Sponsored by the Association for Computational Linguistics (ACL) Special Interest Group on Chinese Language Processing (SIGHAN), this year's SIGHAN-8 workshop is being held in Beijing, China, on July 30-31, 2015, and is co-located with ACL-IJCNLP 2015. The workshop program includes three keynote speeches, research paper presentations and two Bake-offs. We hope that these events will bring together researchers and practitioners to share ideas and developments in various aspects of Chinese language processing.

We have received 17 valid submissions, each of which has been assigned to three reviewers. After a rigorous review process, we have accepted 5 papers for oral presentations (30% acceptance rate) and 6 papers for poster presentations, representing a global acceptance rate of 65%.

We are honored to welcome our distinguished speakers: Dr. Min Zhang (Distinguished Professor, Soochow University, China) and Rou Song (Professor, Beijing Language and Culture University, China) will give the first keynote speech "Discourse and Machine Translation." Yanxiong Lu and Lianqiang Zhou (WeChat Pattern Recognition Center at Tencent) will speak on "Intelligent Q&A System and NLP Open Platform." Finally, Dr. Lun-Wei Ku (Assistant Research Fellow, Academia Sinica, Taiwan) will speak on "From Lexical to Compositional Chinese Sentiment Analysis."

We would also like to thank the Bake-off organizers. The first task Chinese Spelling Check task was organized by Dr. Yuen-Hsien Tseng (National Taiwan Normal University), Dr. Lung-Hao Lee (National Taiwan Normal University), Dr. Li-Ping Chang (National Taiwan Normal University), and Dr. Hsin-Hsi Chen (National Taiwan University). The second Topic-Based Chinese Message Polarity Classification task is organized by Dr. Xiangwen Liao (Fuzhou University, China), Dr. Ruifeng Xu (Harbin Institute of Technology, China), Dr. Li Binyang (University of International Relation, China), and Dr. Liheng Xu (Institute of Automation, Chinese Academy of Sciences, China). A total of sixteen teams participated in these two tasks and have achieved good results.

Finally, we would like to thank all authors for their submissions. We appreciate your active participation and support to ensure a smooth and successful conference. The publication of these papers represents the joint effort of many researchers, and we are grateful to the efforts of the review committee for their work, and to the SIGHAN committee for their continuing support. We wish all a rewarding and eye-opening time at the workshop.

SIGHAN-8 Workshop Co-organizers
Liang-Chih Yu, Yuan Ze University
Zhifang Sui, Peking University
Yue Zhang, Singapore University of Technology and Design
Vincent Ng, University of Texas at Dallas

Organizing Committee

Organizers:

Liang-Chih Yu, Yuan Ze University
Zhifang Sui, Peking University
Yue Zhang, Singapore University of Technology and Design
Vincent Ng, University of Texas at Dalles

SIGHAN Committee:

Chengqing Zong, Chinese Academy of Science
Min Zhang, Soochow University
Gina-Anne Levow, University of Washington
Nianwen Xue, Brandeis University

Program Committee:

Chia-Hui Chang, National Central University
Li-Ping Chang, National Taiwan Normal University
Wangxiang Che, Harbin Institute of Technology
Hsin-Hsi Chen, National Taiwan University
Kuan-hua Chen, National Taiwan University
Xiangyu Duan, Soochow University
Xianpei Han, Chinese Academy of Science
Xungjing Huang, Fudan University
Jing Jiang, Singapore Management University
Chunyu Kit, City University of Hong Kong
Wai Lam, Chinese University of Hong Kong
Chao-Hong Liu, Dublin City University
Lung-Hao Lee, National Taiwan University
Haizhou Li, Institute of Infocomm Research
Jyun-Jie Lin, Yuan Ze University
Yang Liu, Tsinghua University
Xiangwen Liao, Fuzhou University
Jianyun Nie, University of Montreal
Likun Qiu, Ludong University
Fuji Ren, The University of Tokoshima
Weiwei Sun, City University of Hong Kong
Yuen-Hsien Tseng, National Taiwan Normal University
Hsin-Min Wang, Academia Sinica
Kun Wang, Chinese Academy of Science
Derek F. Wong, University of Macau
Chung-Hsien Wu, National Chen Kung University
Ruifeng Xu, Harbin Institute of Technology
Chin-Sheng Yang, Yuan Ze University
Jui-Feng Yeh, National Chiayi University
Guodong Zhou, Soochow University
Qiang Zhou, TsingHua University
Jingbo Zhu, Northeastern University

Invited Talk: Discourse and Machine Translation

ZHANG Min, Soochow University, China
SONG Rou, Beijing Language and Culture University, China

Abstract

Discourse in linguistics refers to a unit of language longer than a single sentence. It has not been well studied in the research community of computational linguistics, but it has attracted more and more attention in very recent years. This talk consists of two parts, i.e., discourse and machine translation. We will first give an overview about discourse and review the research state-of-the-art of discourse from both linguistics and computational viewpoints, and then discuss how machine translation can benefit from discourse-level information. Finally, we conclude the talk with some future direction discussions.

Biography

ZHANG Min: a distinguished professor and vice dean of the school of computer science and technology, director of the research Institute for Human Language Technology at Soochow University (China), received his Ph.D. degree in computer science from Harbin Institute of Technology (China) in 1997. He has studied and worked oversea in industry and academy at South Korea and Singapore since 1997 to 2013. His current research interests include machine translation and natural language processing. He has co-authored 2 Springer books and more than 130 papers in leading journals and conferences, and co-edited 13 books published by Springer and IEEE. He is an associate editor of IEEE T-ASLP (2015-2017).

SONG Rou: a professor and Ph.D. supervisor at Applied Linguistics and Computer Application in Beijing Language and Culture University, received his Bachelor degree in mathematics and mechanics from Beijing University in 1968 and his mater Master degree in computer science from Beijing University in 1981. He has been working on Chinese Information Processing study for tens of years as the PIs of more than 10 national-level projects with the research focuses on discourse analysis, Chinese word segmentation, Computer-aided proofreading, Chinese word attribute, Chinese Orthographic Computing and Chinese POS and so on. He has published more than 100 papers at leading journals and conferences in computer science and linguistics. He has developed and commercialized several softwares with two patents. He has received several awards from Beijing City and MOE, China. He has been appointed as guest professors in a few domestic and oversea universities and research institutes.

Invited Talk: Intelligent Q&A System and NLP Open Platform

LU Yanxiong and ZHOU Lianqiang
WeChat Pattern Recognition Center, Tencent

Abstract

Building a general Q&A system that can handle any subject is a very challenging AI task. Internet social platforms accumulate large amount of active users and UGC (User Generate Content) data, which become valuable crowdsourcing resources. In this talk, we will discuss the opportunity of using WeChat crowdsourcing resources to build an intelligent Q&A systems as well as some open questions and challenges under this topic.

Tencent Open Platform "Wen Zhi" provides comprehensive natural language processing APIs, including the modules of Lexical, Syntax, Semantics and Paragraph. It also provides the web crawling, data extraction and transcoding services. In this talk we will give an overview of Tencent NLP open platform as well as the techniques behind.

Biography

LU Yanxiong is the senior researcher of WeChat Pattern Recognition Center, Tencent. He has been working on search query analysis, Q&A system and NLP related projects in Tencent. His current work focus on WeChat semantic analysis. His research interests include search engine, machine learning, NLP and big data analysis. Before joining in Tencent, Yanxiong worked in Baidu and graduated from Xidian University with master degree.

ZHOU Lianqiang has been working in the field of NLP and machine learning in Tencent, such as search query re-write, user interests mining, word segmentation, etc. He is now the senior researcher and team leader of NLP research group in Tencent Intelligent Computing and Search Lab. Before joining Tencent Lianqiang worked in several Internet companies and got his master degree from Harbin Institute of Technology.

Invited Talk: From Lexical to Compositional Chinese Sentiment Analysis

KU Lun-Wei
Academia Sinica, Taiwan

Abstract

Sentiment analysis determines the polarities and strength of sentiment-bearing expressions, and it has been an important and attractive research area due to its close affinity to applications. In the past research, sentiment analysis depended highly on lexical semantics. However, sentiment analysis is eager for the understanding of the context, and shallow features such as bag of words cannot fulfill this need. As a result, compositional semantics, which concerns the construction of meaning based on syntax, has been applied to sentiment analysis through different approaches. In the Chinese language, as morphological structures may represent the compositional semantics inside Chinese words, the compositional sentiment analysis can even start from determining the sentiment of morphemes, which will be touched in this talk.

This talk will begin from some background knowledge of sentiment analysis, such as how sentiment are categorized, where to find available corpora and which models are commonly applied, especially for the Chinese language. I will describe our work on compositional Chinese sentiment analysis from words to sentences. All our involved and recently developed related resources, including Chinese Morphological Dataset, Augmented NTU Sentiment Dictionary (aug-NTUSD), E-hownet with sentiment information, and Chinese Opinion Treebank, will also be introduced in this talk. I'll end by describing how we have begun to test our compositional model with word embeddings.

Biography

KU Lun-Wei received her Ph.D. degree in Computer Science and Information Engineering from National Taiwan University. Then she joined the Department of Computer Science and Information Engineering, National Yunlin University of Science and Technology (Yuntech), Taiwan, as an assistant professor. Since Aug. 2012, she joined the Institute of Information Science, Academia Sinica as an assistant research fellow. Previously, she was a postdoctoral researcher at the Department of Computer Science and Information Engineering, National Taiwan University, working on the project "Machine learning methods for ranking problems in multilingual information retrieval". She was a project researcher in Acer Product Value Lab, Taiwan, between Apr. 2003 and May 2004. At that time, she joined the project in speech recognition services for home media center. She was a software engineer/project manager in NaturalTel, a platform service provider of carriers, where she joined the development of speech entertainment service platform for Fareastone (Fetnet), Taiwan. Her international recognition includes CyberLink Technical Elite Fellowship in 2007, IBM Ph.D. Fellowship in 2008, ROCLING Doctorial Dissertation Distinction Award in 2009, and Good Design Award selected in 2012. Her research interests include natural language processing, information retrieval, sentiment analysis, and computational linguistics. She has been working on Chinese sentiment analysis since year 2005 and was the co-organizer of NTCIR MOAT Task (Multilingual Opinion Analysis Task, traditional Chinese side) from year 2006 to 2010. She is also one of the organizers of the SocialNLP workshop, which has been held jointly in IJCNLP 2013, Coling 2014, WWW 2015 and NAACL 2015. This year, she serves as the area chair of the sentiment analysis and opinion mining track in The 53rd Annual Meeting of the Association for Computational Linguistics and The 7th International Joint Conference on Natural Language Processing (ACL-IJCNLP 2015), as well as in The 2015 Conference on Empirical Methods on Natural Language Processing (EMNLP 2015). Other professional international activities she involved include The Publication Co-Chair, The 6th International Joint Conference on Natural Language Processing (IJCNLP-2013), Publicity Chair, The Twenty-fourth Conference on Computational Linguistics and Speech Processing (Rocling 2012), and Finance Chair, The Sixth Asia Information Retrieval Societies Conference (AIRS 2010).

This page intentionally left blank.

Table of Contents

Workshop Program

Thursday, July 30, 2015

09:00–09:10 **Opening Session**

09:10–10:30 **Invited Talk**

Discourse and Machine Translation
Min Zhang and Rou Song

10:30–10:50 **Coffee Break**

10:50–12:30 **Workshop Session**

10:50–11:10 *Sequential Annotation and Chunking of Chinese Discourse Structure*
Frances Yung, Kevin Duh and Yuji Matsumoto

11:10–11:30 *Create a Manual Chinese Word Segmentation Dataset Using Crowdsourcing Method*
Shichang Wang, Chu-Ren Huang, Yao Yao and Angel Chan

11:30–11:50 *Chinese Named Entity Recognition with Graph-based Semi-supervised Learning Model*
Aaron Li-Feng Han, Xiaodong Zeng, Derek F. Wong and Lidia S. Chao

11:50–12:10 *Sentence selection for automatic scoring of Mandarin proficiency*
Jiahong Yuan, Xiaoying Xu, Wei Lai, Weiping Ye, Xinru Zhao and Mark Liberman

12:10–12:30 *ACBiMA: Advanced Chinese Bi-Character Word Morphological Analyzer*
Ting-Hao Huang, Yun-Nung Chen and Lingpeng Kong

12:30–14:30 Lunch

14:30–15:30 Invited Talk

From Lexical to Compositional Chinese Sentiment Analysis
Lun-Wei Ku

15:30–16:00 Coffee Break

16:00–17:20 Bake-off Task 1: Chinese Spelling Check

16:00–16:20 *Introduction to SIGHAN 2015 Bake-off for Chinese Spelling Check*
Yuen-Hsien Tseng, Lung-Hao Lee, Li-Ping Chang and Hsin-Hsi Chen

16:20–16:40 *HANSpeller++: A Unified Framework for Chinese Spelling Correction*
Shuiyuan Zhang, Jinhua Xiong, Jianpeng Hou, Qiao Zhang and Xueqi Cheng

16:40–17:00 *Word Vector/Conditional Random Field-based Chinese Spelling Error Detection for SIGHAN-2015 Evaluation*
Yih-Ru Wang and Yuan-Fu Liao

17:00–17:20 *Introduction to a Proofreading Tool for Chinese Spelling Check Task of SIGHAN-8*
Tao-Hsing Chang, Hsueh-Chih Chen and Cheng-Han Yang

Friday, July 31, 2015

09:00–10:30 Invited Talk

Intelligent Q&A System and NLP Open Platform
Yanxiong Lu and Lianqiang Zhou

10:30–11:00 Coffee Break

11:00–12:20 Bake-off Task 2: Topic-Based Chinese Message Polarity Classification

11:00–11:20 *Overview of Topic-based Chinese Message Polarity Classification in SIGHAN 2015*
Xiangwen Liao, Binyang Li and Liheng Xu

11:20–11:40 *A Joint Model for Chinese Microblog Sentiment Analysis*
Yuhui Cao, Zhao Chen, Ruifeng Xu, Tao Chen and Lin Gui

11:40–12:00 *Learning Salient Samples and Distributed Representations for Topic-Based Chinese Message Polarity Classification*
Xin Kang, Yunong Wu and Zhifei Zhang

12:00–12:20 *An combined sentiment classification system for SIGHAN-8*
Qiuchi Li, Qiyu Zhi and Miao Li

Friday, July 31, 2015 (continued)

12:20–14:00 Lunch

14:00–15:20 Poster Session

Linguistic Knowledge-driven Approach to Chinese Comparative Elements Extraction
MinJun Park and Yulin Yuan

A CRF Method of Identifying Prepositional Phrases in Chinese Patent Texts
Hongzheng Li and Yaohong Jin

Emotion in Code-switching Texts: Corpus Construction and Analysis
Sophia Lee and Zhongqing Wang

Chinese in the Grammatical Framework: Grammar, Translation, and Other Applications Anonymous
Aarne Ranta, Tian Yan and Haiyan Qiao

KWB: An Automated Quick News System for Chinese Readers
Yiqi Bai, Wenjing Yang, Hao Zhang, Jingwen Wang, Ming Jia, Roland Tong and Jie Wang

Chinese Semantic Role Labeling using High-quality Syntactic Knowledge
Gongye Jin, Daisuke Kawahara and Sadao Kurohashi

Chinese Spelling Check System Based on N-gram Model
Weijian Xie, Peijie Huang, Xinrui Zhang, Kaiduo Hong, Qiang Huang, Bingzhou Chen and Lei Huang

NTOU Chinese Spelling Check System in Sighan-8 Bake-off
Wei-Cheng Chu and Chuan-Jie Lin

Topic-Based Chinese Message Sentiment Analysis: A Multilayered Analysis System
hongjie li, zhongqian sun and wei yang

Rule-Based Weibo Messages Sentiment Polarity Classification towards Given Topics
Hongzhao Zhou, Yonglin Teng, Min Hou, Wei He, Hongtao Zhu, Xiaolin Zhu and Yanfei Mu

Topic-Based Chinese Message Polarity Classification System at SIGHAN8-Task2
Chun Liao, Chong Feng, Sen Yang and Heyan Huang

Friday, July 31, 2015 (continued)

CT-SPA: Text sentiment polarity prediction model using semi-automatically expanded sentiment lexicon
Tao-Hsing Chang, Ming-Jhih Lin, Chun-Hsien Chen and Shao-Yu Wang

Chinese Microblogs Sentiment Classification using Maximum Entropy
Dashu Ye, Peijie Huang, Kaiduo Hong, Zhuoying Tang, Weijian Xie and Guilong Zhou

NDMSCS: A Topic-Based Chinese Microblog Polarity Classification System
Yang Wang, Yaqi Wang, Shi Feng, Daling Wang and Yifei Zhang

NEUDM: A System for Topic-Based Message Polarity Classification
Yaqi Wang, Shi Feng, Daling Wang and Yifei Zhang

15:20–15:30 Closing Session

Sequential Annotation and Chunking of Chinese Discourse Structure

Frances Yung **Kevin Duh** **Yuji Matsumoto**
Nara Institute of Science and Technology
8916-5 Takayama, Ikoma, Nara, 630-0192 Japan
{pikyufrances-y, kevinduh, matsu}@is.naist.jp

Abstract

We propose a linguistically driven approach to represent discourse relations in Chinese text as *sequences*. We observe that certain surface characteristics of Chinese texts, such as the order of clauses, are overt markers of discourse structures, yet existing annotation proposals adapted from formalism constructed for English do not fully incorporate these characteristics. We present an annotated resource consisting of 325 articles in the Chinese Treebank. In addition, using this annotation, we introduce a discourse chunker based on a cascade of classifiers and report 70% top-level discourse sense accuracy.

1 Introduction

Discourse relations refer to the relations between units of text at document level. As a key for language processing, they are used in tasks such as automatic summerization, sentiment analysis and text coherence assessment (Lin et al., 2011; Trivedi and Eisenstein, 2013; Yoshida et al., 2014). While discourse-annotated English resources are available, resources in other languages are limited. In this work, we present the linguistic motivation behind the Chinese discourse annotated corpus we constructed, and preliminary experiments on discourse chunking of Chinese.

1.1 Related Work

Major discourse annotated resources in English include the RST Treebank (Carlson et al., 2001) and the Penn Discourse Treebank (PDTB) (Prasad et al., 2008). The RST Treebank represents discourse relations in a tree structure, where a *satellite* text span is related to a *nucleus* text span. On the other hand, the Penn Discourse Treebank represents discourse structure in a predicate-argument-like structure, where discourse connectives (DCs) relates two text spans (*Arg1* and *Arg2*). Under this framerodk, covert discourse relations are represented by implicit DCs.

PDTB's annotation scheme is adapted by the recently released Chinese Discourse Treebank (CDTB) (Zhou and Xue, 2015). Other efforts to exploit Chinese discourse relations include cross-lingual annotation projection based on machine translation or word-aligned parallel corpus (Zhou et al., 2012; Li et al., 2014). Combinition of the RST and PDTB formalisms is also proposed. Zhou et al. (2014) adds the distinction of *satellite* and *nucleus* to PDTB-style annotation, and Li et al. (2014b) labels the connectives in an RST tree.

1.2 Motivation

Interpretation of discourse relations, as of other linguistic structures, is subject to the surface form of the text. We notice that Chinese discourse structures are expressed by certain surface features that do not exist in English.

First of all, Chinese sentences are sequences of clauses, typically separated by punctuations. Each clause can be considered a discourse argument. Above the clause level, Chinese sentences (marked by '。') are also units of discourse (Chu, 1998). When presented with texts where periods and commas are removed, native Chinese speakers disagree with where to restore them (Bittner, 2013). The actual sentence segmentation of the text thus represents the spans of discourse arguments intended by the writer and should be taken into account.

Secondly, it is well known that syntactical structure is presented by word order in Chinese - so is

Proceedings of the Eighth SIGHAN Workshop on Chinese Language Processing (SIGHAN-8), pages 1–6,
Beijing, China, July 30-31, 2015.

discourse. While the *Arg1* can occur before or after *Arg2* in English, arguments predominantly occur in fixed order in Chinese, depending on the logical relation. For example, the same concession relation can be expressed by both constructions (1) and (2) in English, but only construction (1) is acceptable in Chinese.

1. 虽然 (*suiran*, although) [*Arg2*] , [*Arg1*].
2. [*Arg1*], 虽然 (*suiran* ,although) [*Arg2*].

According to Chinese linguistics, adjunct clauses and discourse adverbials always precede the main clauses (Gasde and Paul, 1996; Chu and Ji, 1999). The clauses are semantically arranged in a topic-comment sequence following the writer's conceptual mind (Tai, 1985; Bittner, 2013). When the arguments are not arranged in the standard order, the sense of the DC is altered. For example, when '虽然' (*suiran*, although' is used in construction (2), it represents an 'expansion' relation (Huang et al., 2014). Therefore, discourse relations should be defined given the order of the arguments.

Lastly, parallel DCs are frequent in Chinese discourse, yet usually either one DC of the pair occurs to signify the same relation (Zhou et al., 2014). For example, (3) and (4) are grammatical alternatives to (1).

3. 虽然 (*suiran*, although) [*Arg1*] , 但是 (*danshi*, but) [*Arg2*].
4. [*Arg1*], 但是 (*danshi*, but) [*Arg2*].

Instead of viewing '虽然 (*suiran*, although) - 但是 (*danshi*, but)' as a pair of parallel DCs, they can be regarded individually as a forward-linking (fw-linking) DC and a backing linking (bw-linking) DC. A fw-linking DC relates its attached discourse unit to a later coming unit, while a bw-linking DC relates its attached discourse unit to a previous unit. Findings in linguistic studies also show that fw-linking DCs only link discourse units within the sentence boundary. On the other hand, bw-linking DCs can link a discourse unit to a preceding unit within or outside the sentence boundary, except when it is paired with a fw-linking DC (Eifring, 1995).

To summarize, in contrast with the ambiguous arguments in English, punctuations and limitations on DC usage explicitly mark certain discourse structure in Chinese. Section 2 illustrates the design of our annotation scheme driven by these constraints.

2 Sequential discourse annotation

We propose to follow the natural discourse chains in Chinese and annotate discourse structure as a sequence of alternating arguments and DCs. This section highlights the main differences of our scheme comparing with other frameworks.

2.1 Arguments

Each clause separated by punctuations except quotation marks is treated as a candidate argument. Clauses that do not function as discourse units are classified into 3 types - *attribution*, *optional punctuation* and *non-discourse adverbial*.

The main difference of our annotation scheme is that the the order of the arguments for each DC is defined by default. Since the arguments of a particular discourse relation occur in fixed order and are always adjacent, each argument is related to the immediately preceding argument by a bw-linking DC. In turn, the DC in the first clause of a sentence links the sentence to the previous one, preserving the 2 layer structure denoted by punctuations. An implicit bw-linking DC is inserted if the clause does not contain an explicit DC.

Another characteristic of our annotation is that 'parallel DCs' are annotated separately as one fw-linking DC and one bw-linking DC. Implicit bw-linking DCs are inserted , if possible, even the relation is already marked by a fw-linking DC in the previous argument [1]. In other words, duplicated annotation of one relation is allowed. This helps create more valid samples to capture various combinations of Chinese DCs. When an argument spans more than one discourse units, a fw-linking DC is used to mark the start of the span. Similarly, an implicit DC is inserted if necessary.

2.2 Connectives

There is a large variety of DCs in Chinese and their syntactical categories are controversial. Huang et al. (2014) reports a lexicon of 808 DCs, 359 of which found in the data. Since many DCs signal the same relation, we adopt a functionalist approach to label DC senses.

In this approach, a DC does not limit to any syntactical category. Annotators are asked to perform

[1]Temporal relations are often marked by one fw-linking DC alone and it is not acceptable to insert an implicit bw-linking DC. In this case, the 'redundant' tag is used.

a linguistic test by replacing a candidate expression with an unambiguous and preferably frequent DC of similar sense, which we call a 'main DC'. If the replacement is acceptable, then the expression is identified as a DC and the sense is categorized under the 'main DC'.

For example, '尤为' and '特别是' (*youwei, tebieshi*, in particular / especially) are categorized under '尤其 ' (*youqi*, in particular), if the annotator agrees that they are interchangeable in the context. The list of main DCs is not pre-defined but is constructed in the course of annotation. Based on the assigned 'main DC', each DC instant is categorized into the 4 main senses defined in PDTB: *contingency*, *comparison*, *temporal*, and *expansion*.

The discourse and syntactical limitations of the DCs are considered in the replaceability test. For example, the following pairs are not labeled the same 'main DC' even the signaled discourse relation is the same:

- Fw v.s. bw-linking DCs:
  虽然 (*suiran*, although), 但是 (*danshi*, but)
- *Cause-result* v.s. *result-cause* order:
  因为...所以... (*yinwei...suoyi...*, because... therefore...) and
  之所以...是因为... (*zhisuoyi...shiyinwei...*, the reason why...is because...) [2]
- Placed before v.s. after subject:
  却 (*Que* but) and 但是 (*danshi* but)

The list of 'main DCs' is not pre-defined but is constructed in the course of annotation; an expression is registered as another 'main DC' if it cannot be replaced. Note that expressions that are considered as 'alternative lexicalizations' in PDTB or CDTB are also categorized as explicit connectives, if they pass the replaceability test. Otherwise, an implicit DC, chosen from the list of 'main DCs', is inserted.

2.3 Annotation results

Materials of the corpus are raw texts of 325 articles (2353 sentences) from the Chinese Treebank (Bies et al., 2007) . Errors that affect the annotation process, namely punctuation errors that lead to wrong segmentation, have been corrected.

201 DCs are identified in our data, of which 66 are fw-linking DCs. The DCs are categorized into 73 'main DCs' and 22 have ambiguous senses (labelled with more than one 'main DCs'). The distribution of the tags is shown in Table 1. Note that some of the *'implicit'* relations we define belongs to *'explicit'* in other annotation schemes since 'double annotation' occurs in our annotation.

	CON	COM	TEM	EXP	total
Explicit	380	248	521	683	1832
Implicit	1551	446	164	3022	5183
	ADV	ATT	OPT		total
Non-discourse	630	783	336		1749

Table 1: Distribution of various tags in the annotated corpus (4 senses: CONtingency, COMparison, TEMporal, EXPansion; 3 types of non-discourse-unit segments: ATTRibution, OPTional punctuation, and non-discourse ADVerbial)

3 End-to-end discourse chunker

Our linguistically driven annotation of discourse structure takes the surface discourse features as ground truth. In particular, we define discourse relations based on default argument order and span. We demonstrate its learnability by building a discourse chunker in the form of a classifier cascade as used in English discourse parsing(Lin et al., 2010). Features are extracted from the default arguments of each relation. We evaluate the accuracy of each component and the overall accuracy of the final output, classifying up to the 4 main senses. The pipeline consists of 5 classifiers, as shown in Figure 1, each of which is trained with the relevant samples, e.g. only arguments annotated with explicit DCs are used to train the explicit DC classifier. 289 and 36 articles are used as training and testing data respectively.

Features include lexical and syntactical features (bag of words, bag of POS, word pairs and production rules) that have been used in classifying implicit English DCs (Pitler et al., 2009; Lin et al., 2010), and probability distribution of senses for explicit DC classification. The extraction of features is based on automatic parsing by the Stanford Parser (Levy and Manning, 2003). We also use the surrounding discourse relations as features, hypothesizing that certain relation sequences are more likely than others. The classifiers are trained by SVM with a linear kernel using the LIBSVM package(Chang and Lin, 2011).

[2] the 2 pairs are treated as 4 different DCs.

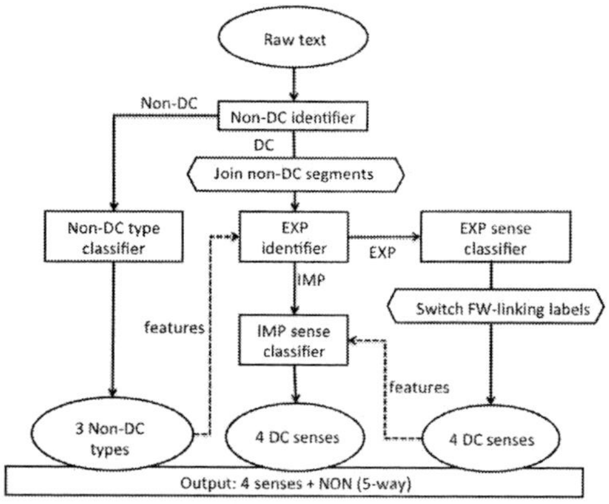

Figure 1: Cascade of discourse relation classifiers.

3.1 Results per component

Table 2 shows the accuracies of individual classifiers tested on relevant samples. Results based on predictions by the most frequent class are listed as baseline (BL). As expected, implicit relations (IMP) are much harder to classify than explicit relations (EXP). The classification result of non-discourse-unit segments (Non-dis or not) is similar to the preliminary report of Li et al. (2014b)(averaged F1 88.8%, accuracy 89.0%).

Step	classifiers	Test F1/Acc	BL F1/Acc
1	Non-dis or not	.91/.94	.44/.80
2	EXP identifier	.92/.93	.39/.65
3	EXP 4 senses	.90/.92	.15/.58
4	Non-dis 3 types	.86/.88	.17/.35
5	IMP 4 senses	.41/.61	.18/.58

Table 2: Accuracies of individual classifiers on 'gold' test samples. F1 is the average of the F1 for each class.

3.2 End-to-end evaluation

We run the classifiers from Steps 1-5. After Step 1, identified non-discourse-unit segments are joined as one argument and features are updated. The discourse context features are also updated after each step based on last classifier's output. The tag of a fw-linking DC is switched to the next segment, as a relation connecting the next segment to the current one. The current segment is thus passed to the implicit classifier, given that there is not any bw-linking DCs.

For applications that need discourse, it may not be necessary to distinguish between explicit and implicit relations. Thus, we combine the outputs of the explicit and implicit classifiers when evaluating the end-to-end outputs. Specifically, the pipeline outputs one of the 4 discourse senses or 'non-discourse-unit' across a segment boundary, while the reference can be more than one, since duplicated annotation is allowed. The system prediction is considered correct if it is included in the gold tag set. The combined outputs are evaluated in terms of accuracy.

Table 3 shows the classification accuracies evaluated by the above principle under different error propagation settings. For example, given gold identification of non-discourse segments (Step 1) and explicit DC classifier (Step 2), classification of the 4 main explicit sense reaches accuracy of 0.854, but is dropped to 0.800 if step 1 and step 2 are automatic [3]. It is observed that errors are generally propagated along the pipeline. Similar to the finding in English (Pitler et al., 2009), the discourse context as predicted by earlier classifiers does not affect the later steps - the results are the same based on gold or automatic outputs. The end-to-end accuracy of the proposed pipeline is 65.7% and the baseline (classify all as 'expansion') is 50.0%.

	Accuracies					
Step	non-dis or not 2-way	exp/imp /non-dis 3-way	explicit senses 4-way	non-dis types 3-way	implicit senses 4-way	over -all 5-way
4	Gold	Gold	Gold	Gold	.670	.706
3	Gold	Gold	Gold	.879	.670	.706
2	Gold	Gold	.854	.879	.670	.703
1	Gold	.888	.800	.865	.665	.697
-	.862	.847	.800	.836	.657	.657

Table 3: Accuracies at each stage under different error propagation settings.

Finally, we experimented with different variations of the pipeline, as shown in Table 4. The best result (70.1% accuracy), is obtained by classifying implicit DCs and non-discourse units in one step. For comaprison, Huang and Chen (2011) reports an accuracy of 88.28% on 4-way classification of inter-sentential discourse senses, and Huang and Chen (2012) reports an accuracy of 81.63% on 2-way classification of intra-sentential contingency vs comparison senses.

[3]Note that the results under the complete gold settings do not necessarily echo the results of the individual components, where duplicated outputs are counted individually.

Note that the result is much degraded if we train one 5-way classifier to classify all relations. This shows that explicit and implicit DCs ought to be treated separately, even though we do not concern about distinguishing them in the final output.

Pipeline variations	Overall 5-way acc.
steps 1-5	.657
combine steps 1-5	.549
switch steps 1 & 2	.697
switch steps 1 & 2 + combine steps 4&5	**.701**

Table 4: 5-way accuracies of modified pipelines

4 Conclusion

This work presents the annotation principles of our Chinese discourse corpus based on linguistics analysis. We propose to embrace the overt sequential features as ground truth discourse structures, and categorize DCs by their discourse functions. Based on the manually annotated corpus, we built and evaluate a classifier cascade that classifies explicit and implicit relations and the results support that our annotation is tractably learnable. The annotation is available at http://cl.naist.jp/nldata/zhendisco/.

References

Ann Bies, Martha Palmer, Justin Mott, and Colin Warner. 2007. English chinese translation treebank v 1.0.

Maria Bittner. 2013. Topic states in mandarin discourse. *Proceedings of the North American Conference on Chinese Linguistics.*

Lynn Carlson, Daniel Marcu, and Mary Ellen Okurowski. 2001. Building a discourse-tagged corpus in the framework of rhetorical structure theory. *Proceedings of the SIGdial Workshop on Discourse and Dialogue.*

Chihchung Chang and Chihjen Lin. 2011. Libsvm : a library for support vector machines. *ACM Transactions on Intelligent Systems and Technology.*

Chauncey Chenghsi Chu and Zongren Ji. 1999. *A Cognitive-Functional Grammar of Mandarin Chinese.* Crane.

Chauncey Chenghsi Chu. 1998. *A discourse grammar of Mandarin Chine.* P. Lang.

Halvor Eifring. 1995. *Clause Combination in Chinese.* BRILL.

Horst-Dieter Gasde and Waltraud Paul. 1996. Funcional categories, topic prominence, and complex sentences in mandarin chinese. *Linguistics*, 34.

Hen-Hsen Huang and Hsin-Hsi Chen. 2011. Chinese discourse relation recognition. *Proceedings of the International Joint Conference on Natural Language Processings.*

Hen-Hsen Huang and Hsin-Hsi Chen. 2012. Contingency and comparison relation labeling and structure predictuion in chinese sentences. *Proceedings of the Annual Meeting of SIGDIAL.*

Hen-Hsen Huang, Tai-Wei Chang, Huan-Yuan Chen, and Hsin-Hsi Chen. 2014. Interpretation of chinese discourse connectives for explicit discourse relation recognition. *Proceedings of the International Conference on Computational Linguistics.*

Roger Levy and Christopher Manning. 2003. Is it harder to parse chinese, or the chinese treebank. *Proceedings of the Annual Meeting of the Association for Computational Linguistics.*

Junyi Jessy Li, Marine Carpuat, and Ani Nenkova. 2014. Cross-lingual discourse relation analysis: A corpus study and a semi-supervised classifacation system. *Proceedings of the International Conference on Computational Linguistics.*

Yancui Li, Wenhi Feng, Jing Sun, Fang Kong, and Guodong Zhou. 2014b. Building chinese discourse corpus with connective-driven dependency tree structure. *Proceedings of the Conference on Empirical Methods on Natural Language Processing.*

Ziheng Lin, Hwee Tou Ng, , and Min Yen Kan. 2010. A pdtb-styled end-to-end discourse parser. *Technical report, National University of Singapore.*

Ziheng Lin, Hwee Tou Ng, and Minyen Kan. 2011. Automatic evaluating text coherence using discourse relations. *Proceedings of the Annual Meeting of the Association for Computational Linguistics.*

Emily Pitler, Annie Louis, and Ani Nenkova. 2009. Automatic sense prediction for implicit discourse relations in text. *Proceedings of the Annual Meeting of the Association for Computational Linguistics and the International Joint Conference on Natural Language Processing.*

Rashmi Prasad, Nikhit Dinesh, Alan Lee, Eleni Miltsakaki, Livio Robaldo, Aravind Joshi, and Bonnie Webber. 2008. The penn discourse treebank 2.0. *Proceedings of the Language Resource and Evaluation Conference.*

James HY Tai. 1985. Temporal sequence and chinese word order. *Iconicity in Syntax.*

Rakshit Trivedi and Jacob Eisenstein. 2013. Discourse connectors for latent subjectivity in sentiment analysis. *Proceedings of the North American Chapter of the Association for Computational Linguistics.*

Yasuhisa Yoshida, Jun Suzuki, Tsutomu Hirao, and Masaaki Nagata. 2014. Dependency-based discourse parser for single-document summarization. *Proceedings of the Conference on Empirical Methods on Natural Language Processing.*

Yuping Zhou and Nianwen Xue. 2015. The chinese discourse treebank: a chinese corpus annotated with discourse relations. *Language Resources and Evaluation*, 49(2).

Lan Jun Zhou, Wei Gao, Binyang Li, Zhongyu Wei, and Kam-Fat Wong. 2012. Cross-lingual identification of ambiguous discourse connectives for resource-poor language. *Proceedings of the International Conference on Computational Linguistics.*

Lan Jun Zhou, Binyang Li, Zhongyu Wei, and Kam-Fai Wong. 2014. The cuhk discourse treebank for chinese: Annotating explicit discourse connectives for the chinese treebank. *Proceedings of the Language Resource and Evaluation Conference.*

Create a Manual Chinese Word Segmentation Dataset Using Crowdsourcing Method

Shichang Wang, Chu-Ren Huang, Yao Yao, Angel Chan
Department of Chinese and Bilingual Studies
The Hong Kong Polytechnic University
Hung Hom, Kowloon, Hong Kong
shi-chang.wang@connect.polyu.hk
{churen.huang, y.yao, angel.ws.chan}@polyu.edu.hk

Abstract

The manual Chinese word segmentation dataset *WordSegCHC 1.0* which was built by eight crowdsourcing tasks conducted on the Crowdflower platform contains the manual word segmentation data of 152 Chinese sentences whose length ranges from 20 to 46 characters without punctuations. All the sentences received 200 segmentation responses in their corresponding crowdsourcing tasks and the numbers of valid response of them range from 123 to 143 (each sentence was segmented by more than 120 subjects). We also proposed an evaluation method called *manual segmentation error rate* ($MSER$) to evaluate the dataset; the $MSER$ of the dataset is proved to be very low which indicates reliable data quality. In this work, we applied the crowdsourcing method to Chinese word segmentation task and the results confirmed again that the crowdsourcing method is a promising tool for linguistic data collection; the framework of crowdsourcing linguistic data collection used in this work can be reused in similar tasks; the resultant dataset filled a gap in Chinese language resources to the best of our knowledge, and it has potential applications in the research of word intuition of Chinese speakers and Chinese language processing.

1 Introduction

Chinese word segmentation which can be conducted by human or computer in the form of written or oral, is a hot topic receiving great interest from several branches of linguistics especially from theoretical, computational and psychological linguistics, simply because it relates to or perhaps is the key to several critical theoretical and applicational issues, for example word definition, word intuition and Chinese language processing.

However in the traditional laboratory setting, limited by budget and/or the difficulty of large scale subject recruitment, etc., it is very difficult or even impossible to build large manual Chinese word segmentation dataset (the defining feature of this kind of dataset is that each sentence must be segmented by a large group of people in order to measure word intuition of Chinese speakers) and this hinders the availability of such language resource. Fortunately, the crowdsourcing method perhaps can help us to solve this problem. Being aware of this background, the crowdsourced manual Chinese word segmentation dataset *WordSegCHC 1.0* was built with multiple purposes in our mind.

The first purpose is to further explore the application of crowdsourcing method in language resource building and linguistic studies in the context of the Chinese language. Crowdsourcing method is a promising tool to solve the linguistic data bottleneck problem which widely happens in various linguistic studies; it is efficient and economic and can help us realize much higher randomness and much larger scale in sampling; in annotation tasks we can also get much higher redundancy to help us make decisions on ambiguous cases with more confidence; although its signal-to-noise ratio (SNR) is usually lower than the traditional laboratory method, it can yield high quality data as good as or even better than the traditional method when combined with several data quality control measures including parameter optimization, screening questions, performance monitoring, data valida-

Proceedings of the Eighth SIGHAN Workshop on Chinese Language Processing (SIGHAN-8), pages 7–14,
Beijing, China, July 30-31, 2015. ©2015 Association for Computational Linguistics and Asian Federation of Natural Language Processing

tion, data cleansing, majority voting, peer review, spammer monitor, etc (Crump et al., 2013; Allahbakhsh et al., 2013; Mason and Suri, 2012; Behrend et al., 2011; Buhrmester et al., 2011; Callison-Burch and Dredze, 2010; Paolacci et al., 2010; Ipeirotis et al., 2010; Munro et al., 2010; Snow et al., 2008).

We have already successfully applied crowdsourcing method to the semantic transparency of compound rating task and built a semantic transparency dataset which contains the semantic transparency rating data of about 1,200 disyllabic Chinese nominal compounds (Wang et al., 2014a); we want to further extend the application of crowdsourcing method to Chinese word segmentation task to further evaluate the crowdsourcing method and to build new language resource.

The second purpose is to support the studies on word intuition of Chinese speakers in general and to examine the effect of semantic transparency on word intuition in particular. Word intuition is speakers' intuitive knowledge on wordhood, i.e., what a word is. Laymen's word segmentation behavior is not instructed by linguistic theories on word, but by their word intuition, hence reflects their word intuition; because of this, the word segmentation task has been used to measure and study word intuition (王立, 2003; Hoosain, 1992). The basic idea is like this: if a Chinese sentence is segmented by, for example, 100 subjects, we can then observe what slices of the sentence are consistently treated as words by these subjects, what slices are consistently treated as non-words, and what slices are not so consistent by being treated as words by some and non-words by others. This kind of segmentation consistency can be a convenient measurement of Chinese speakers' word intuition.

Word intuition per se is an important issue awaiting more research which can contribute to the investigation of cognitive mechanism of humans' language competence and shed new light on the theoretical problem of word definition for the theoretical definition of word should generally accord with the speakers' word intuition (王洪君, 2006; 王立, 2003; 胡明扬, 1999; 陆志韦, 1964).

Semantic transparency/compositionality of a multi-morphemic form, simply speaking, is the extent to which the lexical meaning of the whole form can be derived from the lexical meanings of its constituents. More accurately speaking, this definition is merely the definition of overall semantic transparency (OST) of a multi-morphemic form; besides that, there is constituent semantic transparency (CST) too which means the extent to which the lexical meaning of each constituent as a independent lexical form retains itself in the lexical meaning of the whole form.

In the context of theoretical linguistics, semantic transparency is used as an empirical criterion of wordhood (Duanmu, 1998; 吕叔湘, 1979; Chao, 1968), but for Chinese disyllabic forms this criterion seems to be ignored to some extent by some linguists based on word intuition (王洪君, 2006; 冯胜利, 2004; 王立, 2003; 冯胜利, 2001; 胡明扬, 1999; 冯胜利, 1996; 吕叔湘, 1979); it is also treated as an indicator of lexicalization (Packard, 2000; 董秀芳, 2002; 李晋霞 and 李宇明, 2008). In the context of psycholinguistics, it is an "extremely important factor" (Libben, 1998) affecting the mechanism of mental lexicon, for example the representation, processing/recognition, and memorizing of multi-morphemic words (Han et al., 2014; Mok, 2009; 王春茂 and 彭聃龄, 2000; 王春茂 et al., 2000; 王春茂 and 彭聃龄, 1999; Libben, 1998; Tsai, 1994). Following this line of investigations, it is significant to examine the role semantic transparency plays in Chinese speakers' word intuition towards Chinese disyllabic forms. When we build the dataset, we carefully select sentence stimuli which contain word stimuli that cover all possible kinds of semantic transparency types to enable us to examine the role semantic transparency plays in word intuition of Chinese speakers.

The widely used Chinese segmented corpora, for example, the Sinica corpus (Chen et al., 1996), are usually segmented firstly by segmentation programs and then revised by experts according to certain word segmentation standard. From the inconsistent segmentation cases we can find plenty useful information to explore word intuition. But from the perspective of the measurement of Chinese speakers' word intuition, the data are biased by segmentation programs and word segmentation standards, so they are not so suitable and reliable for this purpose.

In order to better serve the studies of word intuition of Chinese speakers, we need manual word segmentation datasets. In such a dataset, each and every sentence is segmented manually by a large group of laymen, say 100, without the influence of any linguistic theory or any Chinese word segmentation standard. This kind of dataset which is both large and publicly accessible, to the best of our knowledge, is still a gap in Chinese language resources.

And the third purpose is that the resultant manual Chinese word segmentation dataset may have potential applications in the studies of Chinese language processing especially in the studies of automatic Chinese word segmentation and cognitive models of Chinese language processing.

2 Construction

2.1 Materials

The stimuli of word segmentation tasks are at least phrases, but we prefer naturally occurred sentences. In order to cover more linguistic phenomena to better support the studies of word intuition, we decide to use more than 150 long sentences (the crowdsourcing method makes this possible). Meanwhile, the resultant dataset must be able to support the examination of the effect of semantic transparency on word intuition; so these sentence stimuli should also contain the words which cover all the word stimuli to be used in the examination of semantic transparency effect. So the stimuli selection procedure consists of two steps: (1) word selection, i.e., to select an initial set of word which covers all the word stimuli would be used in the examination of semantic transparency effect, and (2) sentence selection, i.e., to select a set of sentences which contains the words selected in step 1 (each sentence carries one word) and at the same time satisfy other requirements.

Word Selection

We have already created a crowdsourced semantic transparency dataset *SimTransCNC 1.0* which contains the overall and constituent semantic transparency rating data of about 1,200 Chinese bimorphemic nominal compounds which have mid-range word frequencies (Wang et al., 2014a). Based on this dataset, 152 words are selected, for the distribution of these words, see Table 1.

	Word Structure		
Transaprency Type	NN	AN	VN
TT	20	10	10
TO	20	6	10
OT	20	10	10
OO	20	10	6

Table 1: Distribution of types of selected words.

These words are bimorphemic nominal compounds of the structure modifier-head, and cover three substructures: NN, AN, and VN. Following (Libben et al., 2003), we differentiate four transparency types: TT, TO, OT, and OO; "T" means "transparent", and "O" means "opaque". TT words show the highest OST scores and the most balanced CST scores, e.g., "江水"; OO words have the lowest OST scores and the most balanced CST scores, e.g., "脾气"; TO and OT words bear mid-range OST scores and the most imbalanced CST scores, e.g., "音色" (TO) and "贵人" (OT).

Sentence Selection

The words selected in step 1 are used as indexes, and all the sentences carrying them in Sinica corpus 4.0 are extracted. One sentence is selected for each word roughly according to the following criteria: (1) the length of sentence should be between 20 to 50 characters (punctuations excluded); (2) the sentence should not contain too many punctuations; (3) prefer concrete and narrative sentences to abstract ones which are difficult to understand; (4) if we cannot find proper sentences from Sinica corpus for some words, we will use other corpora (only 5 sentences). In this way, a total of 152 sentences are selected, for the length (in character) distribution, see Table 2.

	Length of Sentence
Min	20
Max	46
Sum	4,946
Mean	32.54
SD	5.46

Table 2: Length distribution of selected sentences.

2.2 Crowdsourcing Task Design

These 152 sentence stimuli are evenly and randomly divided into eight sentence groups; each sentence group has 19 sentences. We created one crowdsourcing task for each sentence group on *Crowdflower*; according to our previous studies, compared to *Amerzon Mechanical Turk* (MTurk), *Crowdflower* is a more feasible platform for Chinese linguistic data collection (Wang et al., 2014b; Wang et al., 2014a).

Questionnaires

The core of each crowdsourcing task is a questionnaire. Each questionnaire consists of five sections: (1) title, (2) instructions, (3) demographic questions, (4) screening questions, and (5) segmentation task; both simplified and traditional Chinese character versions are provided. Section 3, demographic questions, asks the on-line subjects to provide their identity information on gender, age, level of education, email address (optional). Section 4, screening questions, consists of four simple questions on the Chinese language which can be used to test if a subject is a Chinese speaker or not; the first two questions are open-ended Chinese character identification questions, each question shows a picture containing a simple Chinese character and asks the subject to identify that character and type it in the text-box blow it; the third question is a close-ended homophonic character identification question, it shows the subject a character and asks him/her to identify its homophonic character in 10 different characters; the fourth one is a close-ended antonymous character identification question, asks the subject to identify the antonymous character of the given one from 10 different characters. The section 4s of the eight crowdsourcing tasks share the same question types but have different question instances. Section 5, the segmentation task, shows the subjects 19 sentence stimuli and asks them to insert a word boundary symbol ("/") at each word boundary they perceive; the subjects are required to insert a "/" behind each punctuation and the last character of a sentence; the subjects are also informed that they need not to care about right or wrong, but just follow their intuition.

Parameters of Tasks

These eight crowdsourcing tasks are created with the following parameters: (1) each worker account can only submit one response to one task; (2) each IP address can only submit one response to one task; (3) we only accept the responses from mainland China, Hong Kong, Macao, Taiwan, Singapore, Indonesia, Malaysia, Thailand, Australia, Canada, Germany, United States, and New Zealand; (4) we pay 0.25USD for one response.

Quality Control Measures

The following quality control measures are used: (1) the section 4, screening questions, is used to discriminate Chinese speakers from non-Chinese speakers and to block bots; (2) the section 5, the segmentation task, will keep invisible unless the first two screening questions are correctly answered; (3) the answers to the segmentation questions in section 5 must comply with prescribed format to prevent random string: a) the segmentation answer to each sentence must be only composed by the original sentence with one or zero "/" behind each Chinese character and each punctuation, b) in the answers behind each punctuation there must be a "/", c) the end of an answer must be a "/"; (4) the submission attempts will be blocked unless all the required questions are answered and the answers satisfy the above conditions; (5) data cleansing will be conducted after data collection to rule out invalid responses.

2.3 Procedure

We firstly ran a small pretest task to test if the tasks were correctly designed, and it turned out that the pretest task could run smoothly. Then we launched the first task and let it run alone for about two days to further test the task design. After we finally confirmed that the tasks could really run smoothly, we launched the other seven tasks and let them run concurrently. Our aim was to collect 200 responses for each task; the speed was amazingly fast in the beginning, and all eight tasks received their first 100 responses in the first three to six days; then the speed became slower and slower, it eventually took us about 1.3 months to reach our aim; after all, *Crowdflower* is not a Chinese native crowdsourcing platform, this kind of speed is understandable.

2.4 Data Cleansing

All tasks successfully obtained 200 responses, however not all responses are valid. Compared to the laboratory setting, the crowdsourcing environment is quite noisy by nature, so before the newly collected data can be used in any seriously analysis to draw reliable conclusions, data cleansing must be conducted.

The raw responses underwent rule-based data cleansing. A response is considered invalid if it has at least one of the following five features: (1) at least one of the four screening questions are incorrectly answered; (2) the lengths of the resultant segments of at least one of its 19 sentences are all one character; (3) at least one segment longer than seven characters is observed in the resultant segments of its 19 sentences; (4) the completion time of the response is shorter than five minutes; (5) the completion time of the response is longer than one hour. Invalid responses were ruled out; the numbers of valid response of the eight tasks are listed in Table 3.

2.5 Results

The resultant dataset contains the manual Chinese word segmentation data of 152 sentences whose length ranges from 20 to 46 characters ($M = 32.54, SD = 5.46$), and each sentence is segmented by at least 123 and at most 143 subjects ($M = 133.5, SD = 7.37$).

Task	Valid Response	%
1	142	71
2	143	71.5
3	138	69
4	135	67.5
5	133	66.5
6	127	63.5
7	123	61.5
8	127	63.5
Min	123	61.5
Max	143	71.5
Mean	133.5	66.75
SD	7.37	3.68

Table 3: Numbers of valid response of the tasks.

3 Evaluation

Although Fleiss' kappa can be used to measure the agreement between raters, high agreement does not necessarily means high data quality especially in the situation of intuition measurement where variations among subjects are expected. And it cannot show directly how many errors the resultant dataset actually contains either. Knowing how many errors the dataset contains is very important to assess the reliability of the conclusions drawn from the dataset. We firstly define two kinds of manual segmentation errors, and based on that, a evaluation method called manual segmentation error rate (MSER) is proposed to evaluate the resultant dataset.

3.1 Types of Manual Segmentation Errors

In Chinese phrases/sentences, there are three types of non-monosyllabic segments from the point of view of manual word segmentation: ridiculous segments, indivisible segments, and modest segments. A ridiculous segment usually cannot be treated as one valid unit/word, because it makes no sense in the context of the phrase/sentence; for example, in the phrase "这是好东西", the segment "好东" cannot be treated as one unit/word, because it is incomprehensible. An indivisible segment usually cannot be divided, because it is an fixed unit and its lexical meaning cannot be derived easily from the lexical meanings of its constituents (or semantically opaque); it will become incomprehensible if it is divided; for example, in the phrase example, the segment "东西" is of this type. A modest segment can be either treated as one unit/word or divided into two or more units/words, because it is equally comprehensible no matter divided or not; the segment "这是" in the phrase example is of this type.

Two circumstances can be treated as errors of manual word segmentation; firstly, if a ridiculous segment appears in segmentation results, it can be treated as an error (type I error); and secondly, if an indivisible segment is divided in segmentation results, it can also be treated as an error (type II error). These two circumstances are not compatible with our general word intuition even to the least extent because they are simply incomprehensible; and they cannot be explained by variations of word intuition among speakers; normally, when the subjects do word segmentation tasks carefully according to their word intuition, these would not occur; so we can treat them as errors. Human word segmentation errors will occur when the subjects try to cheat by segmenting randomly or make accidental mistakes.

3.2 Manual Segmentation Error Rate

A subject divides the phrase/sentence S into n ($n \in \mathbb{N}^+$) segments by n segmentation operations (not $n-1$; the subject left the remaining segment at the tail as one word, it means the subject had "confirmed" that; this is a segmentation operation too). A segmentation operation can only yield one of the following four possible results: one type I error, one type II error, one type I error plus one type II error (two errors; e.g., "好东/西"), or no error. Suppose $e^{'}$ ($e^{'} \in \mathbb{N}$) is the number of times the type I error occurred during the segmentation process, and $e^{''}$ ($e^{''} \in \mathbb{N}$), the number of times the type II error occurred, then we can define manual segmentation error rate ($MSER$):

$$MSER = (e^{'} + e^{''})/n$$

In extreme cases, $MSER$ could be greater than one, for example, in the segmentation result "去哈/尔滨/", $e' = 2$, $e'' = 1$, $n = 2$, so $MSER = 3/2$. If this happens, we just assume that $MSER = 1$. $MSER$ can be used to evaluate manual word segmentation results; lower $MSER$ means better data quality. Let's consider its collective form; if S is segmented by m $(m \in \mathbb{N}^+)$ subjects, and the ith $(1 \leqslant i \leqslant m)$ subject's type I error count, type II error count, and segmentation operation count are e'_i, e''_i, n_i respectively, then the collective form of $MSER$ is:

$$MSER = \frac{\sum_{i=1}^{m}(e'_i + e''_i)}{\sum_{i=1}^{m} n_i}$$

As a convenient way, we can find type I errors and their counts in the unigram frequency list of the segmentation results, and find type II errors and their counts in the bigram frequency list of the segmentation results.

3.3 Evaluation Procedure and Results

Among the 19 sentences of each task, three sentences were sampled for evaluation: the first sentence, the middle (10th) sentence, and the last (19th) sentence. We calculated the $MSER$ for each of them, see Table 4 for details. The $MSERs$ of the segmentation results of these sentences are all very low ($< .05$), and the mean is only .013 ($SD = .004$); this means the resultant dataset only contains few error and indicates that the data quality is good.

Task	Sentence	$\sum n$	$\sum e'$	$\sum e''$	$MSER$
1	S_1	2864	13	20	.012
	S_{10}	3904	18	16	.009
	S_{19}	4046	12	7	.005
2	S_1	2993	29	19	.016
	S_{10}	2000	9	6	.008
	S_{19}	2529	19	26	.018
3	S_1	6634	32	27	.009
	S_{10}	2834	21	14	.012
	S_{19}	2894	43	22	.022
4	S_1	2612	24	22	.018
	S_{10}	1836	14	8	.012
	S_{19}	2640	26	20	.017
5	S_1	2361	15	14	.012
	S_{10}	2829	14	7	.007
	S_{19}	2489	14	15	.012
6	S_1	2906	35	22	.020
	S_{10}	2758	21	8	.011
	S_{19}	1711	20	13	.019
7	S_1	1857	19	11	.016
	S_{10}	3125	35	14	.016
	S_{19}	2808	28	10	.014
8	S_1	2465	23	14	.015
	S_{10}	3238	23	11	.011
	S_{19}	2042	15	7	.011
	Min	1711	9	6	.005
	Max	6634	43	27	.022
	Sum	68375	522	353	
	Mean	2848.96	21.75	14.71	.013
	SD	989.76	8.51	6.3	.004

Table 4: Segmentation error rates ($MSER$) of the segmentation results of the eight tasks.

4 Conclusion

We created the manual Chinese word segmentation dataset *WordSegCHC 1.0* using the crowdsourcing method; to the best of our knowledge, there is no publicly available resources of this kind; it can support the studies of word intuition especially the effect of semantic transparency on word intuition and has potential applications in Chinese language processing.

We also proposed an evaluation method called manual segmentation error rate ($MSER$) to evaluate manual word segmentation dataset. The error rate of the dataset is proved to be very low, and this indicates that its data quality is reliable.

This work also confirmed again that the crowdsourcing method is a feasible, convenient, and reliable tool to collect linguistic data. And through this work, a reusable general framework of crowdsourcing linguistic data collection is also presented. Following this framework, larger similar Chinese language resources can be constructed.

We will use this dataset to examine the role of semantic transparency in word intuition of Chinese speakers and to induce the factors affecting word intuition. The consequent discoveries will deepen our understanding of the word definition problem in the Chinese language which has both theoretical and applicational significance.

In the future, once the factors modulating Chinese Speakers' word intuition are clear, perhaps a computational cognitive model of Chinese word segmentation (Wu, 2011) can be proposed and we believe that this could be an interesting new direction of Chinese word segmentation research.

Acknowledgments

The work described in this paper was supported by a grant from the Research Grants Council of the Hong Kong SAR, China (Project No. 544011).

References

M Allahbakhsh, B Benatallah, A Ignjatovic, HR Motahari-Nezhad, E Bertino, and S Dustdar. 2013. Quality control in crowdsourcing systems: Issues and directions. *IEEE Internet Computing*, 17(2):76–81.

Tara S Behrend, David J Sharek, Adam W Meade, and Eric N Wiebe. 2011. The viability of crowdsourcing for survey research. *Behavior research methods*, 43(3):800–813.

Michael Buhrmester, Tracy Kwang, and Samuel D Gosling. 2011. Amazon's mechanical turk a new source of inexpensive, yet high-quality, data? *Perspectives on Psychological Science*, 6(1):3–5.

Chris Callison-Burch and Mark Dredze. 2010. Creating speech and language data with amazon's mechanical turk. In *Proceedings of the NAACL HLT 2010 Workshop on Creating Speech and Language Data with Amazon's Mechanical Turk*, pages 1–12. Association for Computational Linguistics.

Yuen Ren Chao. 1968. *A grammar of spoken Chinese*. University of California Pr.

Keh-Jiann Chen, Chu-Ren Huang, Li-Ping Chang, and Hui-Li Hsu. 1996. Sinica corpus: Design methodology for balanced corpora. In B.-S. Park and J.B. Kim, editors, *Proceeding of the 11th Pacific Asia Conference on Language, Information and Computation*, pages 167–176. Seoul:Kyung Hee University.

Matthew JC Crump, John V McDonnell, and Todd M Gureckis. 2013. Evaluating amazon's mechanical turk as a tool for experimental behavioral research. *PloS one*, 8(3):e57410.

San Duanmu. 1998. Wordhood in chinese. *New approaches to Chinese word formation: Morphology, phonology and the lexicon in modern and ancient Chinese*, pages 135–196.

Yi-Jhong Han, Shuo-chieh Huang, Chia-Ying Lee, Wen-Jui Kuo, and Shih-kuen Cheng. 2014. The modulation of semantic transparency on the recognition memory for two-character chinese words. *Memory & Cognition*, pages 1–10.

Rumjahn Hoosain. 1992. Psychological reality of the word in chinese. *Advances in psychology*, 90:111–130.

Panagiotis G Ipeirotis, Foster Provost, and Jing Wang. 2010. Quality management on amazon mechanical turk. In *Proceedings of the ACM SIGKDD workshop on human computation*, pages 64–67. ACM.

Gary Libben, Martha Gibson, Yeo Bom Yoon, and Dominiek Sandra. 2003. Compound fracture: The role of semantic transparency and morphological headedness. *Brain and Language*, 84(1):50 – 64.

Gary Libben. 1998. Semantic transparency in the processing of compounds: Consequences for representation, processing, and impairment. *Brain and Language*, 61(1):30 – 44.

Winter Mason and Siddharth Suri. 2012. Conducting behavioral research on amazon' s mechanical turk. *Behavior research methods*, 44(1):1–23.

Leh Woon Mok. 2009. Word-superiority effect as a function of semantic transparency of chinese bimorphemic compound words. *Language and Cognitive Processes*, 24(7-8):1039–1081.

Robert Munro, Steven Bethard, Victor Kuperman, Vicky Tzuyin Lai, Robin Melnick, Christopher Potts, Tyler Schnoebelen, and Harry Tily. 2010. Crowdsourcing and language studies: the new generation of linguistic data. In *Proceedings of the NAACL HLT 2010 Workshop on Creating Speech and Language Data with Amazon's Mechanical Turk*, pages 122–130. Association for Computational Linguistics.

Jerome L Packard. 2000. *The morphology of Chinese: A linguistic and cognitive approach*. Cambridge University Press.

Gabriele Paolacci, Jesse Chandler, and Panagiotis G Ipeirotis. 2010. Running experiments on amazon mechanical turk. *Judgment and Decision making*, 5(5):411–419.

Rion Snow, Brendan O'Connor, Daniel Jurafsky, and Andrew Y Ng. 2008. Cheap and fast—but is it good?: evaluating non-expert annotations for natural language tasks. In *Proceedings of the conference on empirical methods in natural language processing*, pages 254–263. Association for Computational Linguistics.

Chih-Hao Tsai. 1994. Effects of semantic transparency on the recognition of chinese two-character words: Evidence for a dual-process model. Master's thesis, Graduate Institute of Psychology, National Chung Cheng University, Chia-Yi, Taiwan.

Shichang Wang, Chu-Ren Huang, Yao Yao, and Angel Chan. 2014a. Building a semantic transparency dataset of chinese nominal compounds: A practice of crowdsourcing methodology. In *Proceedings of Workshop on Lexical and Grammatical Resources for Language Processing*, pages 147–156, Dublin, Ireland, August. Association for Computational Linguistics and Dublin City University.

Shichang Wang, Chu-Ren Huang, Yao Yao, and Angel Chan. 2014b. Exploring mental lexicon in an efficient and economic way: Crowdsourcing method for linguistic experiments. In *Proceedings of the 4th Workshop on Cognitive Aspects of the Lexicon (CogALex)*, pages 105–113, Dublin, Ireland, August. Association for Computational Linguistics and Dublin City University.

Zhijie Wu. 2011. A cognitive model of chinese word segmentation for machine translation. *Meta : journal des traducteurs / Meta: Translators' Journal*, 56(3):631–644, 9.

冯胜利. 1996. 论汉语的“韵律词”. *中国社会科学*, (1):161–176.

冯胜利. 2001. 从韵律看汉语“词”“语”分流之大界. *中国语文*, (1):27–37.

冯胜利. 2004. 论汉语“词”的多维性. *当代语言学*, 3(3):161–174.

吕叔湘. 1979. *汉语语法分析问题*. 商务印书馆.

李晋霞 and 李宇明. 2008. 论词义的透明度. *语言研究*, (3):60–65.

王春茂 and 彭聃龄. 1999. 合成词加工中的词频, 词素频率及语义透明度. *心理学报*, 31(3):266–273.

王春茂 and 彭聃龄. 2000. 多词素词的通达表征: 分解还是整体. *心理科学*, 23(4):395–398.

王春茂, 彭聃龄, et al. 2000. 重复启动作业中词的语义透明度的作用. *心理学报*, 32(2):127–132.

王洪君. 2006. 从本族人语感看汉语的“词”. *语言科学*.

王立. 2003. *汉语词的社会语言学研究*. 商务印书馆.

胡明扬. 1999. 说“词语”. *语言文字应用*, 3.

董秀芳. 2002. *词汇化: 汉语双音词的衍生和发展*. 四川民族出版社.

陆志韦. 1964. *汉语的构词法*. 科学出版社.

Chinese Named Entity Recognition with Graph-based Semi-supervised Learning Model

Aaron Li-Feng Han* Xiaodong Zeng+ Derek F. Wong+ Lidia S. Chao+

* Institute for Logic, Language and Computation, University of Amsterdam
Science Park 107, 1098 XG Amsterdam, The Netherlands
+ NLP2CT Laboratory/Department of Computer and Information Science
University of Macau, Macau S.A.R., China
l.han@uva.nl nlp2ct.samuel@gmail.com derekfw@umac.mo lidiasc@umac.mo

Abstract

Named entity recognition (NER) plays an important role in the NLP literature. The traditional methods tend to employ large annotated corpus to achieve a high performance. Different with many semi-supervised learning models for NER task, in this paper, we employ the graph-based semi-supervised learning (GBSSL) method to utilize the freely available unlabeled data. The experiment shows that the unlabeled corpus can enhance the state-of-the-art conditional random field (CRF) learning model and has potential to improve the tagging accuracy even though the margin is a little weak and not satisfying in current experiments.

1. Introduction

Named entity recognition (NER) can be regarded as a sub-task of the information extraction, and plays an important role in the natural language processing literature. The NER challenge has attracted a lot of researchers from NLP, and some successful NER tasks have been held in the past years. The annotations in MUC-7[1] Named Entity tasks (Marsh and Perzanowski, 1998) consist of entities (organization, person, and location), times and quantities such as monetary values and percentages, etc. among the languages of English, Chinese and Japanese.

The entity categories in CONLL-02 (Tjong Kim Sang, 2002) and CONLL-03 (Tjong Kim Sang and De Meulder, 2003) NER shared tasks consist of persons, locations, organizations and names of miscellaneous entities, and the languages span from Spanish, Dutch, English, to German.

The SIGHAN bakeoff-3 (Levow, 2006) and bakeoff-4 (Jin and Chen, 2008) tasks offer standard Chinese NER (CNER) corpora for training and testing, which contain the three commonly used entities, i.e., personal names, location names, and organization names. The CNER task is generally more difficult than the western languages due to the lack of word boundary information in Chinese expression.

Traditional methods used for the entity recognition tend to employ external annotated corpora to enhance the machine learning stage, and improve the testing scores using the enhanced models (Zhang et al., 2006; Mao et al., 2008; Yu et al., 2008). The conditional random filed (CRF) models have shown advantages and good performances in CNER tasks as compared with other machine learning algorithms (Zhou et al., 2006; Zhao and Kit, 2008), such as ME, HMM, etc. However, the annotated corpora are generally very expensive and time consuming.

On the other hand, there are a lot of freely available unlabeled data in the internet that can be used for our researches. Due to this reason, some researchers begin to explore the usage of the unlabeled data and the semi-supervised learning methods based on labeled training data and unlabeled external data have shown their advantages (Blum and Chawla, 2001; Shin et al., 2006; Zha et al., 2008; Zhang et al., 2013).

[1] http://www-nlpir.nist.gov/related_projects/muc/proceedings/ne_task.html

Proceedings of the Eighth SIGHAN Workshop on Chinese Language Processing (SIGHAN-8), pages 15–20,
Beijing, China, July 30-31, 2015.

2. Semi-supervised Learning

In the semi-supervised learning model, a sample $\{Z_i = (X_i, Y_i)\}_{i=1}^{n_l}$ is usually observed with labeling $Y_i \in \{-1,1\}$, in addition to independent unlabeled samples $\{X_j\}_{j=n_l+1}^{n}$ with the $n = n_l + n_u$. The $X_k = (X_{k1}, X_{k2}, \dots, X_{kp})\ k \in (1, n)$ is a p-dimentional input (Wang and Shen, 2007). The labeled samples are independently and identically distributed according to an unknown joint distribution $P(x, y)$, and the unlabeled samples are independently and identically distributed from distribution $P(x)$. Many semi-supervised learning models are designed through some assumptions relating $P(x)$ to the conditional distribution, which cover EM method, Bayesian network, etc. (Zhu, 2008).

The graph-based semi-supervised learning (GBSSL) methods have been successfully employed by many researchers. For instance, Goldberg and Zhu (2006) design the GBSSL model for sentiment categorization; Celikyilmaz et al. (2009) propose a GBSSL model for question-answering; Talukdar and Pereira (2010) use the GBSSL methods for class-Instance acquisition; Subramanya et al. (2010) utilize the GBSSL model for structured tagging models; Zeng et al., (2013) use the GBSSL method for the joint Chinese word segmentation and part of speech (POS) tagging and result in higher performances as compared with previous works. However, as far as we know, the GBSSL method has not been employed into the CNER task. To testify the effectiveness of the GBSSL model in the traditional CNER task, this paper utilizes some unlabeled data to enhance the CRF learning through GBSSL method.

3. Designed Models

To briefly introduce the GBSSL method, we assume $D_l = \{(x_j, r_j)\}_{j=1}^{l}$ denote l annotated data and the empirical label distribution of x_j is r_j. Assume the unlabeled data types are denoted as $D_u = \{x_i\}_{i=l+1}^{m}$. Then, the entire dataset can be represented as $D = D_u \cup D_l$. Let $G = (V, E)$ corresponds to an undirected graph with V as the vertices and E as the edges. Let V_l and V_u represent the labeled and unlabeled vertices respectively. One important thing is to select a proper similarity measure to calculate the similarity between a pair of vertices (Das and Smith, 2012). According to the smoothness assumption, if two instances are similar according to the graph, then the output labels should also be similar (Zhu, 2005).

There are mainly three stages in the designed models, i.e., graph construction, label propagation and CRF learning. Graph construction is performed on both labeled and unlabeled data, and the unlabeled data is automatically tagged through the label propagation stage. Then, the tagged external data will be added into the manually annotated training corpus to enhance the CRF learning model.

3.1 Graph Construction & Label Propagation

We follow the research of Subramanya et al. (2010) to represent the vertices using character trigrams in labeled and unlabeled sentences for graph construction.

A symmetric k-NN graph is utilized with the edge weights calculated by a symmetric similarity function designed by Zeng et al. (2013).

The feature set we employed to measure the similarity of two vertices based on the co-occurrence statistics is the optimized one by Han et al. (2013) for CNER tasks, as denoted in Table 1.

Feature	Meaning
$U_n, n \in (-4,2)$	Unigram, from previous 4th to following 2nd character
$B_{n,n+1}, n \in (-2,1)$	Bigram, 4 pairs of features, from previous 2nd to following 2nd character

Table 1: Feature set for measuring vertices similarity in graph construction and training CRF model.

After the graph construction on both labeled and unlabeled data, we use the sparsity inducing penalty (Das and Smith, 2012) label propagation algorithm to induce trigram level label distributions from the constructed graph, which is based on the Junto toolkit (Talukdar and Pereira, 2010).

3.2 CRF Training

In the CRF model, assume a graph $G = (V, E)$ comprising a set V of vertices or nodes together with a set E of edges or lines and $Y = \{Y_v | v \in V\}$ so Y is indexed by the vertices of G. The joint distribution over the label sequence Y given X is presented as the form:

$$P_\theta(y|x) \propto exp\left(\sum_{e\in E,k} \lambda_k f_k(e, y|_e, x) + \sum_{v\in V,k} \mu_k g_k(v, y|_v, x)\right)$$

The f_k and g_k are the feature functions and μ_k and λ_k are the parameters that are trained from specific dataset (Lafferty et al., 2001). The feature set employed in the CRF learning is also the optimized one as shown in Table 1. The training method utilized for the CRF model is a quasi-newton algorithm[2]. The automatically annotated corpus by the graph based label propagation will affect the trained parameters μ_k and λ_k.

4. Experiments

4.1 Data

We employ the SIGHAN bakeoff-3 (Levow, 2006) MSRA (Microsoft research of Asia) training and testing data as standard setting. To testify the effectiveness of the GBSSL method for CRF model in CNER tasks, we utilize some plain (unannotated) text from SIGHAN bakeoff-2 (Emerson, 2005) and bakeoff-4 (Jin and Chen, 2008) as external unlabeled data. The data set is introduced in Table 2 from the aspect of sentence number.

	Bakeoff-3 Corpus		External
Sentence Number	Training	Testing	Unlabeled
	50,425	4,365	31,640

Table 2: Corpus Information.

4.2 Result Analysis

We set two baseline scores for the evaluation. One baseline is the simple left-to-right maximum matching model (MaxMatch) based on the training data, another baseline is the closed CRF model (Closed-CRF) without using unlabeled data. The employment of GBSSL model into semi-supervised CRF learning is denoted as GBSSL-CRF.

The training costs of the CRF learning stage are detailed in Table 3. The comparison shows that the extracted features grow from 8,729,098 to 11,336,486 (29.87%) due to the external dataset, and the corresponding iterations and training hours also grow by 12.86% and 77.04% respectively.

	Training Costs		
	Feature	Iteration	Time (h)
Closed-CRF	8,729,098	350	4.53
GBSSL-CRF	11,336,486	395	8.02

Table 3: Training Cost for CRF Learning.

The evaluation results are shown in Table 4, from the aspects of recall, precision and the harmonic mean of recall and precision (F1-score). The evaluation shows that both the Closed-CRF and GBSSL-CRF models have largely outperformed baseline-1 model (MaxMatch). As compared with the Closed-CRF model, the GBSSL-CRF model yielded a higher performance in precision score, a lower performance in recall score, and finally resulted in a faint improvement in F1 score. Both the GBSSL-CRF and Closed-CRF show higher performance in precision and lower performance in recall value.

	Evaluation Scores		
Total-score	Total-R	Total-P	Total-F
MaxMatch	48.8	59.0	53.4
Closed-CRF	**77.95**	90.27	83.66
GBSSL-CRF	77.84	**90.62**	**83.74**

Table 4: Evaluation Results.

To look inside the GBSSL performance on each kind of entity, we denote the detailed evaluation results from the aspect of F1-score in Table 5. The detailed evaluation from three kinds of entities shows that both the GBSSL-CRF and Closed-CRF show higher performance in LOC entity type, and lower performance in PER and ORG entities.

	Detailed Evaluation		
Sub-F-score	PER-F	LOC-F	ORG-F
MaxMatch	61.4	53.1	46.9
Closed-CRF	77.95	**88.56**	80.88
GBSSL-CRF	**78.17**	88.39	**81.35**

Table 5: Detailed Evaluation Results.

Fortunately, the GBSSL model can enhance the CRF learning on the two kinds of difficult entities PER and ORG with the better performances of 0.28% and 0.58% respectively. However, the GBSSL model decreases the F1 score

2 http://www.nag.com/numeric/fl/nagdoc_fl23/html/E04/e04conts.html

on LOC entity by 0.19%. The lower performance of GBSSL model on LOC entity may be due to that the unlabeled data is only as much as 62.75% of the training corpus, which is not large enough to cover the Out-of-Vocabulary (OOV) testing words of LOC entity; on the other hand, the unlabeled data also bring some noise into the model.

5. Related Work

Nadeau (2007) employs the semi-supervised learning method to recognize 100 entity types on English documents with little supervision. Similarly, Liao and Veeramachaneni (2009) propose a simple semi-supervised algorithm for English entity recognition. Liu et al. (2011) design an interesting application of the semi-supervised learning model for online tweets document for English NER.

Pham et al. (2012) use semi-supervised learning method of CRFs into the Vietnamese NER task with generalized expectation criteria. Similarly, Vo and Ock (2012) utilize a hybrid approach semi-supervised learning approach into the NER task for Vietnamese document.

Wang et al. (2013) and Che et al. (2013) recently propose the usage of bilingual constraints to enhance the NER accuracy.

Some advanced technologies of GBSSL methods are introduced in the papers Zhu and Lafferty (2005), Culp and Michailidis (2008), and Zhang and Wang (2011), etc.

6. Conclusion and Future Work

This paper makes an effort to see the effectiveness of the GBSSL model for the traditional CNER task. The experiments verify that the GBSSL can enhance the state-of-the-art CRF learning models. The improvement score is a little weak because the unlabeled data is not large enough. In the future work, we decide to use larger unlabeled dataset to enhance the CRF learning model.

The feature set optimized for CRF learning may be not the best one for the similarity calculation in graph construction stage. So we will make efforts to select the best feature set for the measuring of vertices similarity in graph construction on CNER documents.

In this paper, we utilized the Microsoft research of Asia corpus for experiments. We will use more kinds of Chinese corpora for testing, such as CITYU and LDC corpus, etc.

The GBSSL model generally improves the tagging accuracy of the Out-of-Vocabulary (OOV) words in the test data, which are unseen in the training corpora. In the future work, we plan to give a detailed analysis of the GBSSL model performance on the OOV words for CNER tasks.

Acknowledgements

This work was supported by the Research Committee of the University of Macau (Grant No. MYRG2015-00175-FST and MYRG2015-00188-FST) and the Science and Technology Development Fund of Macau (Grant No. 057/2014/A). The first author was supported by NWO VICI under Grant No. 277-89-002.

References

A. Blum, & Chawla, S. 2001. Learning from labeled and unlabeled data using graph mincuts. In *ICML-2001*.

Asli Celikyilmaz, Marcus Thint, and Zhiheng Huang. 2009. A graph-based semi-supervised learning for question-answering. In *Proceedings of the Joint Conference of the 47th Annual Meeting of the ACL and the 4th International Joint Conference on Natural Language Processing of the AFNLP: Volume 2 - Volume 2 (ACL '09),* Vol. 2. Association for Computational Linguistics, Stroudsburg, PA, USA, 719-727.

Wanxiang Che, Mengqiu Wang and Christopher D. Manning. 2013. Named Entity Recognition with Bilingual Constraints. In *NAACL* 2013.

Mark Culp and George Michailidis. 2008. Graph-Based Semisupervised Learning. *IEEE TRANSACTIONS ON PATTERN ANALYSIS AND MACHINE INTELLIGENCE*, VOL. 30, NO. 1.

Dipanjan Das and Noah A. Smith. 2012. Graph-based lexicon expansion with sparsity-inducing penalties. In *Proceedings of NAACL*, pages 677-687.

Thomas Emerson. 2005. The Second International Chinese Word Segmentation Bakeoff. *Proceedings of the Fourth SIGHAN Workshop on Chinese Language Processing*. Pp. 123-133.

Andrew B. Goldberg and Xiaojin Zhu. 2006. Seeing stars when there aren't many stars: graph-based semi-supervised learning for sentiment categorization. In *Proceedings of the First Workshop on Graph Based Methods for Natural Language Processing (TextGraphs-1).* Association for Computational Linguistics, Stroudsburg, PA, USA, 45-52.

Aaron Li-Feng Han, Derek F. Wong, and Lidia S. Chao. 2013. Chinese Named Entity Recognition with Conditional Random Fields in the Light of Chinese Characteristics. In *Language Processing and Intelligent Information Systems. Lecture Notes in Computer Science*, Volume 7912, pp 57-68.

J. Lafferty, McCallum, A., Pereira, F.C.N. 2001. Conditional random fields: Probabilistic models for segmenting and labeling sequence data. In: *Proceeding of 18th International Conference on Machine Learning*, pp. 282–289. Massachusetts.

Gina-Anne Levow. 2006. The Third International Chinese Language Processing Bakeoff: Word Segmentation and Named Entity Recognition. *Proceedings of the Fifth SIGHAN Workshop on Chinese Language Processing*, pages 108–117, Sydney.

Wenhui Liao and Sriharsha Veeramachaneni. 2009. A Simple Semi-supervised Algorithm For Named Entity Recognition. *Proceedings of the NAACL HLT Workshop on Semi-supervised Learning for Natural Language Processing*, pages 58–65.

Xiaohua Liu , Shaodian Zhang , Furu Wei , Ming Zhou. 2011. Recognizing Named Entities in Tweets. *Proceedings of the 49th Annual Meeting of the Association for Computational Linguistics: Human Language Technologies*.

G. Jin, and X. Chen. 2008. The fourth international CLP bakeoff: Chinese word segmentation, named entity recognition and Chinese pos tagging. In: *Sixth SIGHAN Workshop on CLP*, pp. 83–95.

Elaine Marsh, and Dennis Perzanowski. 1998. MUC-7 Evaluation of IE Technology: Overview of Results. Technical report.

Xinnian Mao; Yuan Dong; Saike He; Sencheng Bao; Haila Wang. 2008. Chinese Word Segmentation and Named Entity Recognition Based on Conditional Random Fields. *Proceedings of the Sixth SIGHAN Workshop on Chinese Language Processing*. pp. 90-93.

David Nadeau. 2007. Semi-Supervised Named Entity Recognition-Learning to Recognize 100 Entity Types with Little Supervision. PHD thesis. University of Ottawa

Thi-Ngan Pham, Le Minh Nguyen, and Quang-Thuy Ha. 2012. Named Entity Recognition for Vietnamese Documents Using Semi-supervised Learning Method of CRFs with Generalized Expectation Criteria. In *Proceedings of the 2012 International Conference on Asian Language Processing*. IEEE Computer Society, Washington, DC, USA, 85-88.

Hyunjung Shin, N. Jeremy Hill, and Gunnar R¨atsch. 2006. Graph Based Semi-Supervised Learning with Sharper Edges. *ECML* 2006, LNAI 4212, pp. 402–413.

Amarnag Subramanya, Slav Petrov, and Fernando Pereira. 2010. Efficient graph-based semi-supervised learning of structured tagging models. In *Proceedings of the 2010 Conference on Empirical Methods in Natural Language Processing (EMNLP '10)*. Association for Computational Linguistics, Stroudsburg, PA, USA, 167-176.

Partha Pratim Talukdar and Fernando Pereira. 2010. Experiments in Graph-based Semi-Supervised Learning Methods for Class-Instance Acquisition. *Proceedings of the 48th Annual Meeting of the Association for Computational Linguistics*, pages 1473–1481.

E. F. Tjong Kim Sang. 2002. Introduction to the CoNLL-2002 Shared Task: Language-Independent Named Entity Recognition. *CONLL*-02.

E. F. Tjong Kim Sang; De Meulder, Fien. 2003. Introduction to the CoNLL-2003 shared task: Language-independent named entity recognition. *CoNLL*-2003.

Duc-Thuan Vo, Cheol-Young Ock. 2012. A Hybrid Approach of Pattern Extraction and Semi-supervised Learning for Vietnamese Named Entity Recognition. *Lecture Notes in Computer Science* Volume 7653, 2012, pp 83-93.

Junhui Wang and Xiaotong Shen. 2007. Large Margin Semi-supervised Learning. *Journal of Machine Learning Research*.

Mengqiu Wang, Wanxiang Che, Christopher D. Manningy. 2013. Effective Bilingual Constraints for Semi-supervised Learning of Named Entity Recognizers. In *AAAI*-2013.

Xiaofeng Yu; Wai Lam; Shing-Kit Chan; Yiu Kei Wu; Bo Chen. 2008. Chinese NER Using CRFs and Logic for the Fourth SIGHAN Bakeoff. *Proceedings of the Sixth SIGHAN Workshop on Chinese Language Processing*. pp. 102-105.

Xiaodong Zeng; Derek F. Wong; Lidia S. Chao; Isabel Trancoso. 2013. Graph-based Semi-Supervised Model for Joint Chinese Word Segmentation and Part-of-Speech Tagging. *ACL* 2013.

Zheng-Jun Zha; Tao Mei; Jingdong Wang; Zengfu Wang; Xian-Sheng Hua. 2008. Graph-based semi-supervised learning with multi-label. *Multimedia and Expo, 2008 IEEE International Conference on*, pp.1321-1324.

Changshui Zhang, Fei Wang. 2011. Graph-based semi-supervised learning. *Frontiers of Electrical and Electronic Engineering in China*. Volume 6, Issue 1, pp 17-26.

Suxiang Zhang; Ying Qin; Juan Wen; Xiaojie Wang. 2006. Word Segmentation and Named Entity Recognition for SIGHAN Bakeoff3. *Proceedings of the Fifth SIGHAN Workshop on Chinese Language Processing*, pages 158–161.

Tongtao Zhang, Rongrong Ji, Wei Liu, Dacheng Tao, and Gang Hua. 2013. Semi-supervised learning with manifold fitted graphs. In *Proceedings of the*

Twenty-Third international joint conference on Artificial Intelligence (IJCAI'13), Francesca Rossi (Ed.). AAAI Press 1896-1902.

Hai Zhao; Chunyu Kit. 2008. Unsupervised Segmentation Helps Supervised Learning of Character Tagging for Word Segmentation and Named Entity Recognition. *Proceedings of the Sixth SIGHAN Workshop on Chinese Language Processing*. pp. 106-111.

Junsheng Zhou; Liang He; Xinyu Dai; Jiajun Chen. 2006. Chinese Named Entity Recognition with a Multi-Phase Model. *Proceedings of the Fifth SIGHAN Workshop on Chinese Language Processing*, pages 213–216.

Xiaojin Zhu. 2005. Semi-Supervised Learning with Graphs. PHD thesis. CMU-LTI-05-192.

X. Zhu, & Lafferty, J. 2005. Harmonic mixtures: combining mixture models and graph-based methods for inductive and scalable semi-supervised learning. In *ICML*-2005.

Xiaojin Zhu. 2008. Semi-Supervised Learning Literature Survey. University of Wisconsin.

Sentence selection for automatic scoring of Mandarin proficiency

Jiahong Yuan[1], Xiaoying Xu[2], Wei Lai[2], Weiping Ye[2], Xinru Zhao[2], Mark Liberman[1]

[1]Linguistic Data Consortium
3600 Market St., Suite 810
Philadelphia, PA 19104, USA

[2]Beijing Normal University
19 Xinjiekou Wai Street
Haidian district, Beijing 100875, China

Jiahong@ldc.upenn.edu, xuxiaoying2000@bnu.edu.cn, laiwei_0508@126.com
yeweiping@bnu.edu.cn, xrzhao@bnu.edu.cn, myl@ldc.upenn.edu

Abstract

A central problem in research on automatic proficiency scoring is to differentiate the variability between and within groups of standard and non-standard speakers. Along with the effort to improve the robustness of techniques and models, we can also select test sentences that are more reliable for measuring the between-group variability. This study demonstrated that the performance of an automatic scoring system could be significantly improved by excluding "bad" sentences from the scoring procedure. The experiments on a dataset of *Putonghua Shuiping Ceshi* (Mandarin proficiency test) showed that, compared to all available sentences, using only best-performed sentences improved the speaker-level correlation between human and automatic scores from r = .640 to r = .824.

1 Introduction

Automatic scoring of spoken language proficiency has been widely applied in language tests and computer assisted language learning (CALL) (Wang et al., 2006; Zechner et al., 2009; Streeter et al., 2011). A central problem in this research area is to differentiate the variability between and within groups of standard and non-standard speakers. One way to tackle the problem is, as done in most previous studies, to improve the robustness and reliability of techniques and models. There is also another way to look at the problem: not every sentence is equally good for revealing a speaker's language proficiency. The purpose of this study is to demonstrate that, given an automatic scoring technique, we can significantly improve the performance of the technique by selecting well-performed sentences (with respect to the given technique) as input for scoring.

Most of the automatic scoring systems rely on automatic speech recognition (ASR). The common practice is to build HMM-based acoustic models using a large amount of "standard" speech data. To assess an utterance, pronunciation scores such as log likelihood scores and posterior probabilities are calculated by performing speech recognition (or forced alignment if the sentence is known) to the utterance based on the pre-trained acoustic models (Franco et al., 1997; Neumeyer et al., 2000; Witt and Young, 2000; Yan and Gong 2011; Hu et al., 2015). Prosody scores, e.g., duration, F_0, and pauses, have also been shown important (Cucchiarini et al., 2000; Nava et al., 2009). These individual scores are combined with statistical models such as linear regression, SVM, and neural network to produce an overall score for the test utterance (Franco et al., 2000; Ge et al., 2009).

The performance of model-based automatic scoring systems much depends on the amount and quality of the training data. For the purpose of this study, we adopted a simple, comparison-based approach. This approach is to measure the goodness of a test utterance by directly comparing it to a standard version of the same sentence and calculating the distance between the two (Yamashita et al., 2005; Lee and Glass, 2013).

2 Data

We used a dataset of *Putonghua Shuiping Ceshi* (PSC) from Beijing Normal University. PSC is the national standard Mandarin proficiency test in China, which is taken by several million people each year. The test consists of four parts: The first two parts are to read 100 monosyllabic and 50 disyllabic words; the third part is to read an article of 300 characters, randomly selected from a pool of 60 articles; and the last part is to speak freely on a given topic. The four parts are graded separately with a numeric score, and the total score (out of 100 points) is converted to a categorical proficiency level.

Proceedings of the Eighth SIGHAN Workshop on Chinese Language Processing (SIGHAN-8), pages 21–25,
Beijing, China, July 30-31, 2015.

Our dataset consists of recordings of ~800 college students at Beijing Normal University who took the PSC test in 2011 and the grades they received on the test. We only used the part of article reading in this study. The students who read an article being selected for less than 9 other students (i.e., the total number of students reading that article is less than 10) were excluded. The final dataset contains 630 speakers reading 42 articles. Each student was graded by two examiners. The distribution of the examiners' scores on this part (out of 30 points, averaged by two examiners' scores) is shown in Figure 1. The correlation between the two examiners' scores on this part is r = 0.819.

As a demonstration, two professional voice talents have recorded the 60 articles in PSC (one male and one female, each read 30 articles). We used their spoken articles as a reference standard to which the students' were compared.

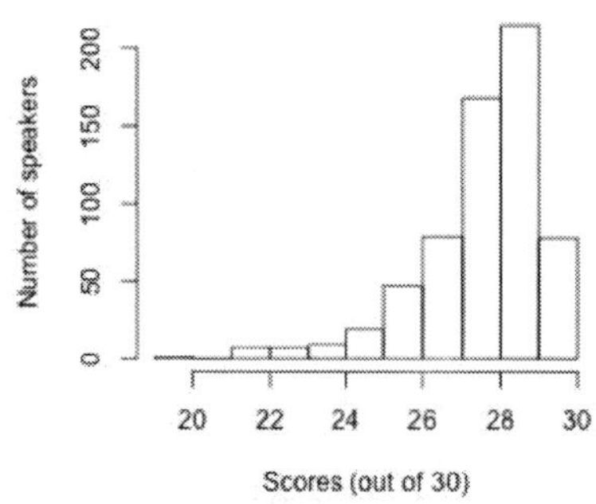

Fig. 1. Distribution of human scores in the dataset.

3 Method

Using a state-of-the-art Mandarin forced aligner (Yuan et al., 2014), we extracted utterances (delimited by a punctuation mark in the text) from the spoken articles and also obtained phonetic boundaries in the utterances. All utterances from a speaker share the same proficiency score, which is the average of the two examiners' scores the speaker received on the test.

In the dataset, every sentence has at least 10 utterance versions, each from a different speaker, plus one standard version. The goodness of a sentence to be used for automatic scoring is measured by the correlation between the distances of the students' utterances from the standard version and the utterances' proficiency scores, as shown in Figure 2. We expect negative correlations for "good" sentences: a greater difference from the standard version should result in a lower proficiency score.

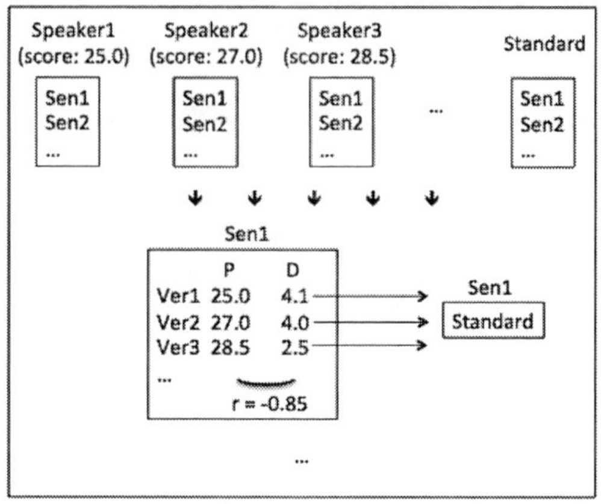

Fig. 2. Paradigm for measuring sentence goodness.

The distance between an utterance and its standard version was calculated, respectively, on three acoustic dimensions: duration, F_0, and spectrum. For each of the distance measures, an experiment was conducted using the top 10%, 20%, ..., 100% sentences to obtain a distance score for every speaker, i.e., the average distance of all utterances of the speaker. The correlation between the speakers' distance scores and their human-graded proficiency scores are reported to show the effect of sentence selection.

Finally, we combined the three distance scores based on duration, F_0, and spectrum, plus a statistic of pauses, to build an automatic scoring system, and compared the performance of the system between using all available sentences and using best-performed sentences only.

4 Experiments and results

4.1 Sentence selection based on duration

The distance on duration between a test utterance and its standard version was calculated from the root mean square difference between paired segments (syllables, phones, or words) in the utterances, as shown in (1). Segment durations were derived from forced aligned boundaries.

$$D_{dur} = \sqrt{\frac{\sum_{i=1}^{n} (d_{test,i} - d_{ref,i})^2}{n}} \quad (1)$$

where $d_{test,i}$ is the duration of the ith segment in the test utterance, $d_{ref,i}$ is the duration of the ith segment in the standard utterance, and n is the total number of segments in an utterance.

To remove the effect of speaking rate on the duration distance, the segment durations in the test utterance were normalized in a way that the total duration of the test utterance (excluding pauses) is the same as that of the standard one, as shown in (Norm 1.1):

$$d_{test,i} = d_{test,i} * \frac{\sum_{k=1}^{n} d_{ref,k}}{\sum_{k=1}^{n} d_{test,k}} \quad \text{(Norm 1.1)}$$

Figure 3 shows the correlation (-1*r) between the speakers' duration distance scores and their proficiency scores when using all sentences, top 90%, top 80%, ..., and top 10% sentences (as described in Section 3). We can see that the correlation increases when excluding more "bad" sentences from being used for calculating the duration distance scores. With respect to the performance of different types of segments, syllables and words are better than phones.

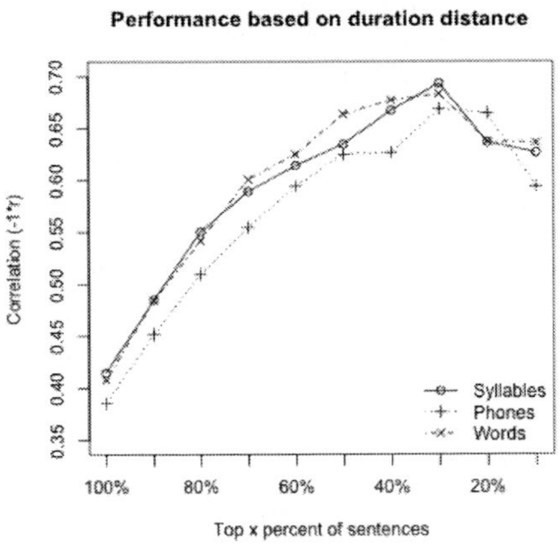

Fig. 3. Duration distance: different types of segments.

Another way to normalize the segment duration is to transform the durations to Z-scores per spoken article, as shown in (Norm 1.2).

$$d_{test,i} = \frac{d_{test,i} - \mu_{test,article}}{\sigma_{test,article}} \qquad d_{ref,i} = \frac{d_{ref,i} - \mu_{ref,article}}{\sigma_{ref,article}} \quad \text{(Norm 1.2)}$$

where μ is the mean of the durations of all segments in the spoken article; σ is the standard deviation of the durations.

Figure 4 compares the performance of the two normalization methods (Norm 1.1 and Norm 1.2), as well as the performance of using unnormalized durations (Raw). Syllable durations were used for the comparison. From Figure 4, we can see that the normalization using z-scores per article (Norm 1.2) outperforms the normalization based on per utterance pair (Norm 1.1). Both normalizations significantly improved the correlation, compared to using unnormalized durations.

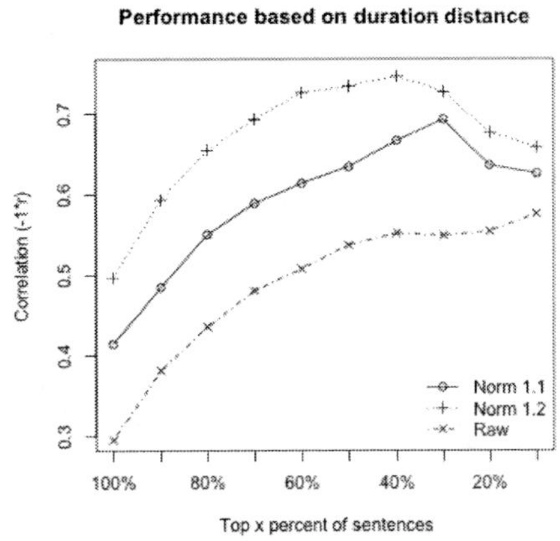

Fig. 4. Duration distance: different normalizations.

4.2 Sentence selection based on F_0

The F_0 contours of the utterances were extracted using *esps/get_f0* with a 10 ms frame rate. The contours were linearly interpolated to be continuous over the unvoiced segments, and smoothed by passing them (both forward and reverse to avoid phase distortion, *filtfilt*) through a Butterworth low-pass filter with normalized cutoff frequency at 0.1.

The distance on F_0 between a test utterance and its standard version was calculated from the root mean square difference between F_0s in paired syllables. Because the number of F_0s in a syllable is determined by the syllable duration, we normalized the number of F_0s in each pair of syllables with Python spline interpolation (*scipy.interpolate.UnivariateSpline, smoothing factor = 0.001)*, for which the number of F_0s in the standard syllable was used as the normalized number. After the normalization, the distance was calculated using all F_0s in an utterance.

The values of F_0s were also normalized to remove the effects of pitch range (e.g., female is higher than male). *Z*-scores were used for the normalization, calculated both per utterance (Norm 2.1) and per article (Norm 2.2).

Figure 5 shows the correlation (-1*r) between the speakers' F_0 distance scores and their proficiency scores for the two normalizations, (Norm 2.1) and (Norm 2.2). We can see that the correlation improves when excluding more "bad" sentences, which is the same as the result on duration. With regard to the two normalization methods, the per-utterance normalization (Norm 2.1) outperforms the per-article normalization (Norm 2.2).

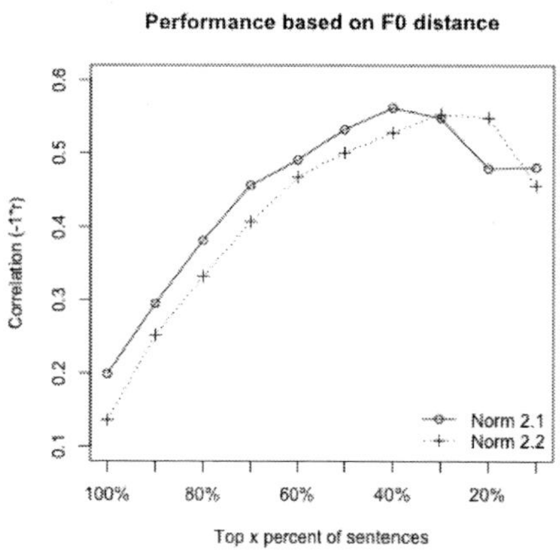

Fig. 5. F_0 distance: different normalizations.

4.3 Sentence selection based on spectrum

Dynamic Time Warping (DTW) was used to calculate the spectral distance between a test utterance and its standard version. The feature vector consists of the standard 39 PLP coefficients, of which the 13 static ones were zero-meaned per utterance. As shown in Figure 6, the correlation increases when excluding more "bad" sentences, which is the same as the results on both duration and F_0.

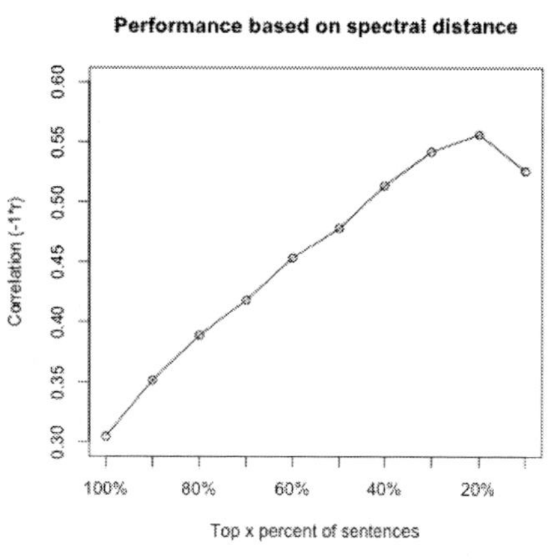

Fig. 6. The performance of spectral distance.

4.4 Combining distance scores

In this section, we investigate the combination of different distance scores. A statistic of pause was also included, which is the average number of pauses per utterance for a speaker. A SVM regression model was trained to predict human graded scores from the calculated distance scores at the speaker level. We employed 5-fold cross validation to separate training and test data. The correlations between model-predicted scores and human scores on the test data are reported in Table 1, for both using all available sentences and using only the best-performed sentences, determined by the experiments above.

Distance scores used	All sentences	Best sentences
D	.495	.747
F_0	.173	.562
S	.296	.514
D + F_0	.526	.786
D + F_0 + S	.566	.804
D + F_0 + S + P	.640	.824

D: syllable duration, normalized per article;
F_0: normalized per utterance; S: spectrum; P: pauses

Table 1: Speaker-level correlations between SVM-predicted and human scores.

From Table 1 we can see that compared to using all available sentences, using only best-performed sentences significantly improved the performance. When all the three distance scores as well as the pause statistic are combined, the correlation increased from .640 to .824, which is comparable to the correlation (r = .819) between the two examiners' scores. We should note that, however, the human scores used in the experiments are the averages of the two examiners' scores, and that although training and test data were separated in building SVM models for score combination, all data have been used to determine best-preformed sentences.

5 Conclusion

We proposed a method to select well-performed sentences for automatic scoring of spoken language proficiency. Our experiments demonstrated that the speaker-level correlation between human and machine scores could be significantly improved when excluding "bad" sentences from automatic scoring. Continuing research is needed to understand the linguistic factors that determine the goodness of a sentence for automatic proficiency scoring, and to understand the speech characteristics that differentiate the variability between and within groups of standard and non-standard speakers.

References

Catia Cucchiarini, Helmer Strik, and Lou Boves. 2000. Quantitative assessment of second language learners' fluency by means of automatic speech recognition technology. *Journal of the Acoustical Society of America*, 107(2):989-99.

Horacio Franco, Leonardo Neumeyer, Vassilios Digalakis, and Orith Ronen. 2000. Combination of Machine Scores for Automatic Grading of Pronunciation Quality. *Speech Communication*, 30(2-3):121-130.

Horacio Franco, Leonardo Neumeyer, Yoon Kim, and Orith Ronen. 1997. Automatic pronunciation scoring for language instruction. *Proceedings of ICASSP 1997*, pp. 1471-1474.

Fengpei Ge, Fuping Pan, Changliang Liu, Bin Dong, Shui-duen Chan, Xinhua Zhu, and Yonghong Yan. 2009. An SVM-Based Mandarin Pronunciation Quality Assessment System. In: *Advances in Intelligent and Soft Computing,* Vol. 56, pp. 255-265.

Wenping Hu, Yao Qian, Frank K. Soong, and Yong Wang. 2015. Improved mispronunciation detection with deep neural network trained acoustic models and transfer learning based logistic regression classifiers. *Speech Communication*, 67:154-166.

Ann Lee and James Glass. 2013. Pronunciation assessment via a comparison-based system. *Proceedings of SLaTE 2013*, pp. 122-126.

Emily Nava, Joseph Tepperman, Louis Goldstein, Maria Luisa Zubizarreta, and Shrikanth S. Narayanan. 2009. Connecting rhythm and prominence in automatic ESL pronunciation scoring. *Proceedings of Interspeech 2009*, pp. 684-687.

Leonardo Neumeyer, Horacio Franco, Vassilios Digalakis, and Mitchel Weintraub. 2000. Automatic scoring of pronunciation quality. *Speech Communication*, 30(2-3):83-93.

Lynn Streeter, Jared Bernstein, Peter Foltz, and Donald DeLand. 2011. *Pearson's automated scoring of writing, speaking, and mathematics* (White Paper). Retrieved from http://researchnetwork.pearson.com

Ren-Hua Wang, Qingfeng Liu, and Si Wei. 2006. Putonghua Proficiency test and evaluation. In: *Advances in Chinese Spoken Language Processing*, pp. 407-429.

Silke Maren Witt and Steve Young. 2000. Phone-level pronunciation scoring and assessment for interactive language learning. *Speech Communication*, 30(2-3):95-108.

Yoichi Yamashita, Keisuke Kato, and Kazunori Nozawa. 2005. Automatic Scoring for Prosodic Proficiency of English Sentences Spoken by Japanese Based on Utterance Comparison. *IEICE Transactions on Information and Systems*, E88-D(3):496-501.

Ke Yan and Shu Gong. 2011. Pronunciation Proficiency Evaluation based on Discriminatively Refined Acoustic Models. *International Journal of Information Technology and Computer Science*, 3(2):17-23.

Jiahong Yuan, Neville Ryant, and Mark Liberman. 2014. Automatic phonetic segmentation in Mandarin Chinese: boundary models, glottal features and tone. *Proceedings of ICASSP 2014*, pp. 2539-2543.

Klaus Zechner, Derrick Higgins, Xiaoming Xi, and David M. Williamson. 2009. Automatic Scoring of Non-Native Spontaneous Speech in Tests of Spoken English. *Speech Communication*, 51(10):883–895.

ACBiMA: Advanced Chinese Bi-Character Word Morphological Analyzer

Ting-Hao (Kenneth) Huang, Yun-Nung Chen, and Lingpeng Kong
Language Technologies Institute, Carnegie Mellon University
5000 Forbes Ave, Pittsburgh, PA 15213, USA
{tinghaoh, yvchen, lingpenk}@cs.cmu.edu

Abstract

While morphological information has been demonstrated to be useful for various Chinese NLP tasks, there is still a lack of complete theories, category schemes, and toolkits for Chinese morphology. This paper focuses on the morphological structures of Chinese bi-character words, where a corpus were collected based on a well-defined morphological type scheme covering both Chinese derived words and compound words. With the corpus, a morphological analyzer is developed to classify Chinese bi-character words into the defined categories, which outperforms strong baselines and achieves about 66% macro F-measure for compound words, and effectively covers derived words.

1 Introduction

Considering that Chinese is an analytic language without inflectional morphemes, Chinese morphology mainly focuses on analyzing morphological word formation. In this paper, we conceive the Chinese word forming process from a syntactic point of view (Packard, 2000). The analysis and prediction of the intra-word syntactic structures, i.e., the "morphological structures", have been shown to be effective in various Chinese NLP tasks, e.g., sentiment analysis (Ku et al., 2009; Huang, 2009), POS tagging (Qiu et al., 2008), word segmentation (Gao et al., 2005), and parsing (Li, 2011; Li and Zhou, 2012; Zhang et al., 2013). Thus, this paper focuses on analyzing the morphological structures of Chinese bi-character content words.

Huang et al. (2010) observed that 52% multi-character Chinese tokens are bi-character[1], which reflects that the core task of Chinese morphological analysis should be aimed at bi-character words. Previous work tended to focus on longer unknown words (Tseng and Chen, 2002; Tseng et al., 2005; Lu et al., 2008; Qiu et al., 2008) or the functionality of morphemic characters (Galmar and Chen, 2010), and none of them effectively covered Chinese bi-character words. To the best of our knowledge, Huang et al. (2010) is the only work focused on Chinese bi-character words, where they analyzed Chinese morphological types and developed a suite of classifiers to predict the types. However, their work covers only a subset of Chinese content words and has limited scalability. Therefore, this paper addresses the issues, which expands their work by developing a more detailed scheme and collecting more words to produce a generalized analyzer.

Our contributions are three-fold:

- Linguistic – we propose a morphological type scheme for full coverage of Chinese bi-character content words, and developed a corpus containing about 11K words.
- Technical – we develop an effective morphological classifier for Chinese bi-character words, achieving 66% macro F-measure for compound words, and and effectively covers derived words.
- Practical – we release the collected data and the analyzer with the trained model to provide additional Chinese morphological features for other NLP tasks. [2]

2 Morphological Type Scheme

Our morphological type category scheme is developed based on the literature (X.-H. Cheng, 1992; Lu et al., 2008; Huang et al., 2010) and the naming conventions of Stanford typed dependency (Chang

[1] The uni-character tokens do not contain any morphological structures.

[2] http://acbima.org/

Proceedings of the Eighth SIGHAN Workshop on Chinese Language Processing (SIGHAN-8), pages 26–31,
Beijing, China, July 30-31, 2015. ©2015 Association for Computational Linguistics and Asian Federation of Natural Language Processing

Table 1: The category description and examples for derived words

Class	Morphological Characteristics	Example
dup	Two *duplicate* characters.	天天/tian-tian/day-day/everyday
pfx	The first character is a *prefix* character, e.g. 阿/a.	阿姨/a-yi/a-aunt/aunt
sfx	The second character is a *suffix* character, e.g. 仔/zi.	牛仔/new-zi/cow-zi/cowboy
neg	The first character is a *negation* character, e.g. 不/bu.	不能/bu-neng/no-capable/unable
ec	The first character is an *existential construction*, e.g. 有/you/have;exists.	有人/you-ren/exists-human/people

Table 2: The category description and examples for compound words

Class	Syntactic Role		Example
	Char 1	Char 2	
a-head	modifier	adjective head	最大/zui-da/most-big/biggest
n-head	modifier	nominal head	平台/ping-tai/flat-platform/(flat)platform
v-head	modifier	verbal head	主辦/zhu-ban/major-handle/host
nsubj	nominal subject	predicate (verb)	身經/shen-jing/body-experience/experience
vobj	predicate (verb)	object	開幕/kai-mu/open-screen/opening of event
vprt	predicate (verb)	particle	投入/tou-ru/throw-in to/throw in
conj	play coordinate roles in a word		男女/nan-nu/male-female/men and women (people)
els	else		transliterations, abbreviations, idiomatic words, etc.

et al., 2009; catherine De Marneffe and Manning, 2008) shown in Figure 1.

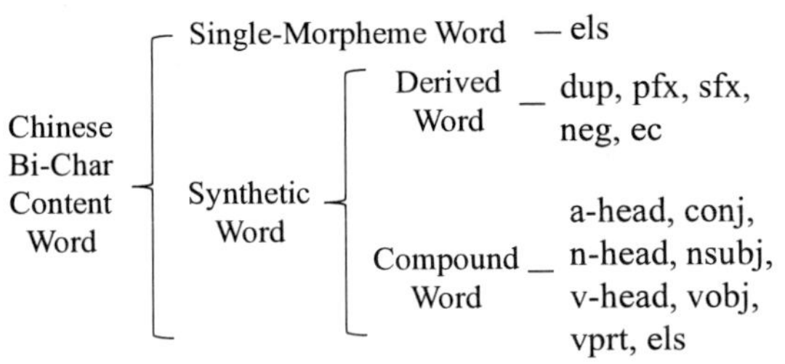

Figure 1: The morphological category scheme of Chinese bi-character content words

The two major categories of Chinese bi-character content words are *derived words* and *compound words*. Derived words are words formed in certain formations (e.g. duplication), while compound words are composed of constituent characters following certain syntactic relations. Table 1 and 2 present detailed category schemes. Note that for derived words, the characters "有/you/have" and "是/shi/be" are of a special type of existential constructions (Tao, 2007), so we isolate them from common prefixes to distinguish their unique characteristics. The "els" type (compound words) consists of exceptional words that cannot be categorized into our compound words scheme.

3 Morphological Type Classification

Due to the difference between derived words and compound words, we respectively adopt rule-based and machine learning approaches to predict their morphological types. Note that all of our approaches and features assume that Chinese morphological structures are independent from word-level contexts (Tseng and Chen, 2002; Li, 2011).

3.1 Derived Word: Rule-Based Approach

By definition, a morphological derived word can be recognized based on its formation. Therefore, we apply the pattern matching rules described in Table 1 to build a rule-based classifier.

To evaluate the coverage of these developed rules, we run the classifier on Chinese Treebank 7.0 (CTB) (Levy and Manning, 2003), where 2.9% of bi-character content words are annotated as derived words (842 unique word types). Our rules are able to capture derived words with a precision of 0.97. The false positives are caused by the ambiguity of Chinese characters "子/zi" and "兒/er".[3] The ambiguity results

[3]These two characters are common Chinese suffixes which mean "son/kid".

Table 3: Features for the Compound Word C1C2 (Dict: Revised Mandarin Chinese Dictionary (Ministry of Education (MoE), 1994); CTB: Chinese Treebank 5.1 (Xue et al., 2005))

Category		Feature	Description
Character Feature (for both C_i)	uni-char word	Tone	All possible tones (0-4) of C_i
		Pronunciation	All possible pronunciations, consonants, and vowels of C_i
		TF in CTB	The POS distribution of C_i in CTB
		Majority POS in CTB	The most frequent POS of C_i in CTB
		Character POS	Two POS tags when parsing the 2-token sentence C_1C_2
	uni-char morpheme	Dist. of Senses in Dict	POS distribution of the senses of C_i in dictionary
		Majority POS in Dict	POS of C_i with the most senses in dictionary
	alphabet symbol	Root	The radical (also referred to as "character root") of C_i
		CTB Prefix/Suffix Dist.	The occurrence distribution of the n-char words with C_i as the prefix/suffix corresponding to each POS in CTB.
		Dict Prefix/Suffix Dist.	The occurrence distribution of the n-char dictionary entry words with C_i as the prefix/suffix
		Example Word Prefix/Suffix Dist.	Same as above, but calculate the distribution in dictionary example words.
Word Feature (for C_1C_2)		Typed dependency	Typed dependency relation between C_1 and C_2
		Stanford Word POS	Single POS tag of a single token (word)

in mis-classifications such as "父子/fu-zi/father-son/father and son" into the "sfx" type instead of the "conj" type. Table 1 defines the patterns we consider as derived words, and the words that do not belong to the defined classes will be considered as compound words.

3.2 Compound Word: Machine Learning Approach

To automatically predict morphological types for compound words, we perform machine learning techniques to capture generalizations from various features. For each bi-character word C_1C_2, we extract *character-level* features for C_1 and C_2 individually, as well as a single *word-level* feature for C_1C_2. Table 3 describes our feature set. For character-level features, a Chinese character may take on 3 different roles: word, morpheme, or alphabet symbol, where the extracted features are organized according to these roles. In addition, we propose word-level features, e.g. POS of C_1C_2, to capture the word information dismissed by the previous work (Huang et al., 2010) with consideration that such clue helps classification.

We experiment with various ML classification models: Naïve Bayes (John and Langley, 1995), Random Forest (Breiman, 2001), and Support Vector Machine (Platt, 1999; Keerthi et al., 2001; Hastie and Tibshirani, 1998) for the classification task. The three types of baselines are compared:

Table 4: Morphological category distribution

Category	Initial Set 3,052 words	Whole Set 11,366 words
nsubj	1.2%	1.6%
v-head	7.7%	8.7%
a-head	1.1%	1.8%
n-head	36.7%	34.0%
vprt	9.4%	9.3%
vobj	14.3%	14.6%
conj	25.5%	26.9%
els	4.1%	3.3%

Majority, Stanford Dependency Map, and Tabular Models. The Tabular Models first assign the POS tags to each known character C based on different heuristics (i.e., the most frequent POS of C in CTB, the POS of C with most senses in Dict, and the POS of C annotated by Stanford Parser), and then assigns the most frequent morphological type obtained from training data to each POS combination, e.g., "(VV, NN) = vobj". The Stanford Dependency Map takes the dependency relation between C_1 and C_2 as predicted by the Stanford Parser (Chang et al., 2009) , and maps it to a corresponding morphological type, which is learned from training data. The Majority baseline always outputs the majority type, i.e., the "n-head" type.

Table 5: 10-fold cross-validation classification performance (MF: Macro F-measure, ACC: Accuracy)

Approach	nsubj	v-head	a-head	n-head	vprt	vobj	conj	els	MF	ACC
Majority	0	0	0	.507	0	0	0	0	.172	.340
Stanford Dep. Map	0	0	0	.525	.351	.438	.213	.010	.332	.388
Tabular (Stanford POS)	0	.296	0	.524	.389	.434	.162	.064	.349	.395
Tabular (CTB POS)	.021	.337	.009	.645	.397	.529	.421	.095	.479	.508
Tabular (Dict POS)	0	.292	.060	.670	.253	.572	.494	.035	.495	.526
Naïve Base	.273	.406	.195	.523	.679	.566	.547	.188	.519	.518
Random Forest	.250	.421	.063	**.760**	**.803**	.643	**.656**	.076	.647	**.674**
SVM	**.413**	**.541**	**.288**	.748	.791	**.657**	.636	**.271**	**.662**	.665
Avg Difficulty Level	1.74	1.55	1.64	1.36	1.38	1.38	1.47	1.95	-	-

4 ACBiMA Corpus 1.0

We develop a Chinese morphological type corpus containing 11,366 bi-character compound words, referred to as "ACBiMA Corpus 1.0." This corpus is incrementally developed in two stages:

The "initial set" is first developed for preliminary study and analysis. We randomly extracted about 3,200 content words from Chinese Treebank 5.1 (Xue et al., 2005), and removed the derived words. After manually checking for and removing errors, the initial set contains 3,052 words, which are further annotated with "morphological types" and "difficulty level of determining" (1, 2, or 3) by trained native speakers and examined again by experts. The inter-annotator agreement on a 50-word held-out set, averaged over all annotator pairs, is 0.726 Kappa.

In the second stage, we expand on the initial set into a larger corpus for practical use. We sampled about 3,000 words from CTB 5.1 and annotated them with their morphological types. Moreover, we obtained the 6,500-word corpus developed by Huang et al. (2010)[4] and manually split its "Substantive-Modifier" words into "a-head", "n-head", or "v-head" types to match our category scheme. In total, the expanded dataset consists of 11,366 unique bi-character compound word types (see Table 4).

5 Experiments

We performed 10-fold cross-validation experiments on the entire dataset to evaluate our approaches for compound words.[5] As mentioned in §3.2, we compared against different baselines. Table 5 presents the results of our experiments, and the average human-judged difficulty level (in initial set) is also listed for comparison.

Random Forest and SVM outperformed all other models and baselines. The best accuracy is 0.674; 65% of words in the initial set are labeled as "easy" by human annotators, suggesting that our classifiers are comparable to human performance on the "easy" instances. Also, we achieved similar level of performance in macro F1-measure when compared to Huang et al. (2010)[6], despite our task being more challenging due to having two extra types.

6 Conclusion and Future Work

In this paper, we developed a set of tools and resources for leveraging morphology of Chinese bi-character words. We propose a category scheme, develop a corpus, and build an effective morphological analyzer. In future work, we intend to explore other NLP tasks where we can take advantage of ACBiMA and our tools to improve performance.

Acknowledgments

We thank anonymous reviewers for their useful comments. We are also grateful to Yanchuan Sim for his helpful feedback and all participants who helped to annotate the data.

[4]The words in Huang et al. (2010) are sampled from the NTCIR CIRB040 news corpus, and the distribution of types is similar to that of our initial set. This suggests that the morphological types distribution between different Chinese corpora are similar.

[5]For the 3 machine learning algorithms, we used the implementations found in the Weka toolkit (Hall et al., 2009).

[6]They reported macro F1-measure of 0.67.

References

Leo Breiman. 2001. Random forests. *Machine Learning*, 45(1):5–32.

Marie catherine De Marneffe and Christopher D. Manning, 2008. *Stanford typed dependencies manual.*

Pi-Chuan Chang, Huihsin Tseng, Dan Jurafsky, and Christopher D. Manning. 2009. Discriminative reordering with chinese grammatical relations features. In *Proceedings of the Third Workshop on Syntax and Structure in Statistical Translation*, SSST '09, pages 51–59, Stroudsburg, PA, USA. Association for Computational Linguistics.

Bruno Galmar and Jenn-Yeu Chen. 2010. Identifying different meanings of a chinese morpheme through semantic pattern matching in augmented minimum spanning trees. *Prague Bull. Math. Linguistics*, 94:15–34.

Jianfeng Gao, Mu Li, Andi Wu, and Chang-Ning Huang. 2005. Chinese word segmentation and named entity recognition: A pragmatic approach. *Comput. Linguist.*, 31(4):531–574, December.

Mark Hall, Eibe Frank, Geoffrey Holmes, Bernhard Pfahringer, Peter Reutemann, and Ian H. Witten. 2009. The weka data mining software: An update. *SIGKDD Explor. Newsl.*, 11(1):10–18, November.

Trevor Hastie and Robert Tibshirani. 1998. Classification by pairwise coupling. *The Annals of Statistics*, 26(2):451–471, 04.

Ting-Hao Huang, Lun-Wei Ku, and Hsin-Hsi Chen. 2010. Predicting morphological types of chinese bi-character words by machine learning approaches. In Nicoletta Calzolari (Conference Chair), Khalid Choukri, Bente Maegaard, Joseph Mariani, Jan Odijk, Stelios Piperidis, Mike Rosner, and Daniel Tapias, editors, *Proceedings of the Seventh International Conference on Language Resources and Evaluation (LREC'10)*, Valletta, Malta, may. European Language Resources Association (ELRA).

Ting-Hao Huang. 2009. Automatic extraction of intra- and inter- word syntactic structures for chinese opinion analysis. Master's thesis, Graduate Institute of Networking and Multimedia, National Taiwan University.

George H. John and Pat Langley. 1995. Estimating continuous distributions in bayesian classifiers. In *Proceedings of the Eleventh Conference on Uncertainty in Artificial Intelligence*, UAI'95, pages 338–345, San Francisco, CA, USA. Morgan Kaufmann Publishers Inc.

S. S. Keerthi, S. K. Shevade, C. Bhattacharyya, and K. R. K. Murthy. 2001. Improvements to platt's smo algorithm for svm classifier design. *Neural Comput.*, 13(3):637–649, March.

Lun-Wei Ku, Ting-Hao Huang, and Hsin-Hsi Chen. 2009. Using morphological and syntactic structures for chinese opinion analysis. In *Proceedings of the 2009 Conference on Empirical Methods in Natural Language Processing: Volume 3 - Volume 3*, EMNLP '09, pages 1260–1269, Stroudsburg, PA, USA. Association for Computational Linguistics.

Roger Levy and Christopher Manning. 2003. Is it harder to parse chinese, or the chinese treebank? In *Proceedings of the 41st Annual Meeting on Association for Computational Linguistics - Volume 1*, ACL '03, pages 439–446, Stroudsburg, PA, USA. Association for Computational Linguistics.

Zhongguo Li and Guodong Zhou. 2012. Unified dependency parsing of chinese morphological and syntactic structures. In *Proceedings of the 2012 Joint Conference on Empirical Methods in Natural Language Processing and Computational Natural Language Learning*, EMNLP-CoNLL '12, pages 1445–1454, Stroudsburg, PA, USA. Association for Computational Linguistics.

Zhongguo Li. 2011. Parsing the internal structure of words: A new paradigm for chinese word segmentation. In *Proceedings of the 49th Annual Meeting of the Association for Computational Linguistics: Human Language Technologies - Volume 1*, HLT '11, pages 1405–1414, Stroudsburg, PA, USA. Association for Computational Linguistics.

Jia Lu, Masayuki Asahara, and Yuji Matsumoto. 2008. Analyzing chinese synthetic words with tree-based information and a survey on chinese morphologically derived words. In *IJCNLP'08*, pages 53–60.

Taiwan Ministry of Education (MoE). 1994. Revised mandarin chinese dictionary. Online Version. Available at http://dict.revised.moe.edu.tw.

Jerome L. Packard, 2000. *The Morphology of Chinese: A Linguistic and Cognitive Approach*, chapter 3.1.1.4. Cambridge University Press, New York.

John C. Platt. 1999. Advances in kernel methods. chapter Fast Training of Support Vector Machines Using Sequential Minimal Optimization, pages 185–208. MIT Press, Cambridge, MA, USA.

Likun Qiu, Changjian Hu, and Kai Zhao. 2008. A method for automatic pos guessing of chinese unknown words. In *Proceedings of the 22Nd International Conference on Computational Linguistics - Volume 1*, COLING '08, pages 705–712, Stroudsburg, PA, USA. Association for Computational Linguistics.

Hongyin Tao. 2007. Subjectification and the development of special-verb existential/presentative constructions. *Language and Linguistics*, 8(2):575–602.

Huihsin Tseng and Keh-Jiann Chen. 2002. Design of chinese morphological analyzer. In *Proceedings of the First SIGHAN Workshop on Chinese Language*

Processing - Volume 18, pages 1–7, Stroudsburg, PA, USA. Association for Computational Linguistics.

Huihsin Tseng, Daniel Jurafsky, and Christopher Manning. 2005. Morphological features help pos tagging of unknown words across language varieties.

X.-L. Tian. X.-H. Cheng. 1992. *Modern Chinese*. Bookman Books Ltd.

Naiwen Xue, Fei Xia, Fu-dong Chiou, and Marta Palmer. 2005. The penn chinese treebank: Phrase structure annotation of a large corpus. *Nat. Lang. Eng.*, 11(2):207–238, June.

Meishan Zhang, Yue Zhang, Wanxiang Che, and Ting Liu. 2013. Chinese parsing exploiting characters. In *ACL (1)*, pages 125–134. The Association for Computer Linguistics.

Introduction to SIGHAN 2015 Bake-off for Chinese Spelling Check

Yuen-Hsien Tseng[1], Lung-Hao Lee[1], Li-Ping Chang[2], Hsin-Hsi Chen[3]
[1]Information Technology Center, National Taiwan Normal University
[2]Mandarin Training Center, National Taiwan Normal University
[3]Dept. of Computer Science and Information Engineering, National Taiwan University
samtseng@ntnu.edu.tw, lhlee@ntnu.edu.tw,
lchang@ntnu.edu.tw, hhchen@ntu.edu.tw

Abstract

This paper introduces the SIGHAN 2015 Bake-off for Chinese Spelling Check, including task description, data preparation, performance metrics, and evaluation results. The competition reveals current state-of-the-art NLP techniques in dealing with Chinese spelling checking. All data sets with gold standards and evaluation tool used in this bake-off are publicly available for future research.

1 Introduction

Chinese spelling checkers are relatively difficult to develop, partly because no word delimiters exist among Chinese words and a Chinese word can contain only a single character or multiple characters. Furthermore, there are more than 13 thousand Chinese characters, instead of only 26 letters in English, and each with its own context to constitute a meaningful Chinese word. All these make Chinese spell checking a challengeable task.

An empirical analysis indicated that Chinese spelling errors frequently arise from confusion among multiple-character words, which are phonologically and visually similar, but semantically distinct (Liu et al., 2011). The automatic spelling checker should have both capabilities of identifying the spelling errors and suggesting the correct characters of erroneous usages. The SIGHAN 2013 Bake-off for Chinese Spelling Check was the first campaign to provide data sets as benchmarks for the performance evaluation of Chinese spelling checkers (Wu et al., 2013). The data in SIGHAN 2013 originated from the essays written by native Chinese speakers. Following the experience of the first evaluation, the second bake-off was held in CIPS-SIGHAN Joint CLP-2014 conference, which focuses on the essays written by learners of Chinese as a Foreign Language (CFL) (Yu et al., 2014).

Due to the greater challenge in detecting and correcting spelling errors in CFL leaners' written essays, SIGHAN 2015 Bake-off, again features a Chinese Spelling Check task, providing an evaluation platform for the development and implementation of automatic Chinese spelling checkers. Given a passage composed of several sentences, the checker is expected to identify all possible spelling errors, highlight their locations, and suggest possible corrections.

The rest of this article is organized as follows. Section 2 provides an overview of the SIGHAN 2015 Bake-off for Chinese Spelling Check. Section 3 introduces the developed data sets. Section 4 proposes the evaluation metrics. Section 5 compares results from the various contestants. Finally, we conclude this paper with findings and offer future research directions in Section 6.

2 Task Description

The goal of this task is to evaluate the capability of a Chinese spelling checker. A passage consisting of several sentences with/without spelling errors is given as the input. The checker should return the locations of incorrect characters and suggest the correct characters. Each character or punctuation mark occupies 1 spot for counting location. The input instance is given a unique passage number *pid*. If the sentence contains no spelling errors, the checker should return "pid, 0". If an input passage contains at least one spelling error, the output format is "pid [, location, correction]+", where the symbol "+" indicates there is one or more instance of the predicted element "[, location, correction]". "Location" and "correction", respectively, denote the location of incorrect character and its correct version. Examples are given as follows.

Proceedings of the Eighth SIGHAN Workshop on Chinese Language Processing (SIGHAN-8), pages 32–37,
Beijing, China, July 30-31, 2015.

- Example 1
  Input: (pid=A2-0047-1) 我真的洸碗我可以去看你
  Output: A2-0047-1, 4, 希, 5, 望
- Example 2
  Input: (pid=B2-1670-2) 在日本，大學生打工的情況是相當普偏的。
  Output: B2-1670-2, 17, 遍
- Example 3
  Input: (pid=B2-1903-7) 我也是你的朋友，我會永遠在你身邊。
  Output: B2-1903-7, 0

There are 2 wrong characters in Ex. 1, and correct characters "希," and "望" should be used in locations 4, and 5, respectively. In Ex. 2, the 17th character "偏" is wrong, and should be "遍". Location "0" denotes that there is no spelling error in Ex. 3

3 Data Preparation

The learner corpus used in our task was collected from the essay section of the computer-based Test of Chinese as a Foreign Language (TOCFL), administered in Taiwan. The spelling errors were manually annotated by trained native Chinese speakers, who also provided corrections corresponding to each error. The essays were then split into three sets as follows

(1) Training Set: this set included 970 selected essays with a total of 3,143 spelling errors. Each essay is represented in SGML format shown in Fig. 1. The title attribute is used to describe the essay topic. Each passage is composed of several sentences, and each passage contains at least one spelling error, and the data indicates both the error's location and corresponding correction. All essays in this set are used to train the developed spelling checker.

(2) Dryrun Set: a total of 39 passages were given to participants to familiarize themselves with the final testing process. Each participant can submit several runs generated using different models with different parameter settings of their checkers. In addition to make sure that the submitted results can be correctly evaluated, participants can fine-tune their developed models in the dryrun phase. The purpose of dryrun is to validate the submitted output format only, and no dryrun outcomes were considered in the official evaluation

(3) Test Set: this set consists of 1,100 testing passages. Half of these passages contained no spelling errors, while the other half included at least one spelling error. The evaluation was conducted as an open test. In addition to the data sets provided, registered participant teams were allowed to employ any linguistic and computational resources to detect and correct spelling errors. Besides, passages written by CFL learners may yield grammatical errors, missing or redundant words, poor word selection, or word ordering problems. The task in question focuses exclusively on spelling error correction.

```
<ESSAY title="學中文的第一天">
<TEXT>
<PASSAGE id="A2-0521-1"> 這位小姐說：你應
該一直走到十只路口，再右磚一直走經過一家銀
行就到了。</PASSAGE>
<PASSAGE id="A2-0521-2">應為今天是第一天，
老師先請學生自己給介紹。</PASSAGE>
</TEXT>
<MISTAKE id="A2-0521-1" location="15">
<WRONG>十只路口</WRONG>
<CORRECTION>十字路口</CORRECTION>
</MISTAKE>
<MISTAKE id="A2-0521-1" location="21">
<WRONG>右磚</WRONG>
<CORRECTION>右轉</CORRECTION>
</MISTAKE>
<MISTAKE id="A2-0521-2" location="1">
<WRONG>應為</WRONG>
<CORRECTION>因為</CORRECTION>
</MISTAKE>
</ESSAY>
```

Figure 1. An essay represented in SGML format

4 Performance Metrics

Table 1 shows the confusion matrix used for performance evaluation. In the matrix, TP (True Positive) is the number of passages with spelling errors that are correctly identified by the spelling checker; FP (False Positive) is the number of passages in which non-existent errors are identified; TN (True Negative) is the number of passages without spelling errors which are correctly identified as such; FN (False Negative) is the number of passages with spelling errors for which no errors are detected.

The criteria for judging correctness are determined at two levels as follows.

(1) Detection level: all locations of incorrect characters in a given passage should be completely identical with the gold standard.

(2) Correction level: all locations and corresponding corrections of incorrect characters should be completely identical with the gold standard.

In addition to achieve satisfactory detection/correction performance, reducing the false positive rate, that is the mistaken identification of errors where none exist, is also important (Wu et al., 2010). The following metrics are measured at both levels with the help of the confusion matrix.

- False Positive Rate (FPR) = FP / (FP+TN)
- Accuracy = (TP+TN) / (TP+FP+TN+FN)
- Precision = TP / (TP+FP)
- Recall = TP / (TP+FN)
- F1= 2 *Precision*Recall/(Precision+Recall)

<table>
<tr><td colspan="2" rowspan="2">Confusion Matrix</td><td colspan="2">System Result</td></tr>
<tr><td>Positive (Erroneous)</td><td>Negative (Correct)</td></tr>
<tr><td rowspan="2">Gold Standard</td><td>Positive</td><td>TP</td><td>FN</td></tr>
<tr><td>Negative</td><td>FP</td><td>TN</td></tr>
</table>

Table 1. Confusion matrix for evaluation.

For example, if 5 testing inputs with gold standards are "A2-0092-2, 0", "A2-0243-1, 3, 健, 4, 康", "B2-1923-2, 8, 誤, 41, 情", "B2-2731-1, 0", and "B2-3754-3, 10, 觀", and the system outputs the result as "A2-0092-2, 5, 玩", "A2-0243-1, 3, 件, 4, 康", "B2-1923-2, 8, 誤, 41, 情", "B2-2731-1, 0", and "B2-3754-3, 11, 觀", the evaluation tool will yield the following performance:

- False Positive Rate (FPR) = 0.5 (=1/2) Notes: {"A2-0092-2, 5"}/{"A2-0092-2, 0", "B2-2731-1, 0"}
- Detection-level
  - Accuracy =0.6 (=3/5)

    Notes: {"A2-0243-1, 3, 4", "B2-1923-2, 8, 41", "B2-2731-1, 0"} / {"A2-0092-2, 5", A2-0243-1, 3, 4", "B2-1923-2, 8, 41", "B2-2731-1, 0", "B2-3754-3, 11"}
  - Precision = 0.5 (=2/4)

    Notes: {"A2-0243-1, 3, 4", "B2-1923-2, 8, 41"} / {"A2-0092-2, 5", A2-0243-1, 3, 4", "B2-1923-2, 8, 41", "B2-3754-3, 11"}
  - Recall = 0.67 (=2/3).

    Notes: {"A2-0243-1, 3, 4", "B2-1923-2, 8, 41"} / {A2-0243-1, 3, 4", "B2-1923-2, 8, 41", "B2-3754-3, 10"}
  - F1=0.57 (=2*0.5*0.67/(0.5+0.67))
- Correction-level
  - Accuracy =0.4 (=2/5)

    Notes: {"B2-1923-2, 8, 誤, 41, 情", "B2-2731-1, 0"} / {"A2-0092-2, 5, 玩", "A2-0243-1, 3, 件, 4, 康", "B2-1923-2, 8, 誤, 41, 情", "B2-2731-1, 0", "B2-3754-3, 11, 觀"}
  - Precision = 0.25 (=1/4)

    Notes: {"B2-1923-2, 8, 誤, 41, 情"} / {"A2-0092-2, 5, 玩", "A2-0243-1, 3, 件, 4, 康", "B2-1923-2, 8, 誤, 41, 情", "B2-3754-3, 11, 觀"}
  - Recall = 0.33 (=1/3)

    Notes: {"B2-1923-2, 8, 誤, 41, 情"} / {, "A2-0243-1, 3, 健, 4, 康", "B2-1923-2, 8, 誤, 41, 情", "B2-3754-3, 10, 觀"}
  - F1=0.28 (=2*0.25*0.33/(0.25+0.33))

5 Evaluation Results

Table 2 summarizes the submission statistics for 9 participant teams including 4 from universities and research institutions in China (CAS, ECNU, SCAU, and WHU), 4 from Taiwan (KUAS, NCTU & NTUT, NCYU, and NTOU), and one private firm (Lingage). Among 9 registered teams, 6 teams submitted their testing results. In formal testing phase, each participant can submit at most three runs that adopt different models or parameter settings. In total, we received 15 runs.

Table 3 shows the task testing results. The research team NCTU&NTUT achieved the lowest false positive rate at 0.0509. For the detection-level evaluations, according to the test data distribution, a baseline system can achieve an accuracy level of 0.5 by always reporting all testing cases as correct without errors. The system result submitted by CAS achieved promising performance exceeding 0.7. We used the F1 score to reflect the tradeoff between precision and recall. As shown in the testing results, CAS provided the best error detection results, achieving a high F1 score of 0.6404. For correction-level evaluations, the correction accuracy provided by the CAS system (0.6918) significantly outperformed the other teams. Besides, in terms of correction precision and recall, the spelling checker developed by CAS also outperforms the others, which in turn has the highest F1 score of 0.6254. Note that it is difficult to correct all spelling errors found in the input passages, since some sentences contain multiple errors and only correcting some of them are regarded as a wrong case in our evaluation.

Table 4 summarizes the participants' developed approaches and the usages of linguistic resources. Among 6 teams that submitted the official testing results, NCYU did not submit the report of its developed method. None of the submitted systems provided superior performance in all metrics, though those submitted by CAS and NCTU&NTUT provided relatively best overall performance when different metric is considered. The CAS team proposes a unified framework for Chinese spelling correction. They used HMM-based approach to segment sentences and generate correction candidates. Then, a two-stage filter process is applied to re-ranking the candidates for choosing the most promising candidates. The NCTU&NTUT team proposes a word vector/conditional random field based spelling error detector. They utilize the error detection results to guide and speed up the time-consuming language model rescoring procedure. By this way, potential Chinese spelling errors could be detected and corrected in a modified sentence with the maximum language model score.

Participant (Ordered by abbreviations of names)	**#Runs**
Chinese Academy of Sciences (**CAS**)	3
East China Normal University (**ECNU**)	0
National Kaohsiung University of Applied Sciences (**KUAS**)	3
Lingage Inc. (**Lingage**)	0
National Chiao Tung University & National Taipei University of Technology (**NCTU & NTUT**)	3
National Chiayi University (**NCYU**)	1
National Taiwan Ocean University (**NTOU**)	2
South China Agriculture University (**SCAU**)	3
Wuhan University (**WHU**)	0
Total	**15**

Table 2. Submission statistics for all participants

Submission	**FPR**	**Detection-Level**				**Correction-Level**			
		Acc.	**Pre.**	**Rec.**	**F1**	**Acc.**	**Pre.**	**Rec.**	**F1**
CAS-Run1	0.1164	0.6891	0.8095	0.4945	0.614	0.68	**0.8037**	0.4764	0.5982
CAS-Run2	0.1309	**0.7009**	0.8027	0.5327	**0.6404**	**0.6918**	0.7972	**0.5145**	**0.6254**
CAS-Run3	0.2036	0.6655	0.7241	**0.5345**	0.6151	0.6491	0.7113	0.5018	0.5885
KUAS-Run1	0.2327	0.5009	0.5019	0.2345	0.3197	0.4836	0.4622	0.2	0.2792
KUAS-Run2	0.2091	0.5164	0.5363	0.2418	0.3333	0.4982	0.4956	0.2055	0.2905
KUAS-Run3	0.1818	0.5318	0.5745	0.2455	0.3439	0.5145	0.537	0.2109	0.3029
NCTU&NTUT-Run1	**0.0509**	0.6055	**0.8372**	0.2618	0.3989	0.5782	0.8028	0.2073	0.3295
NCTU&NTUT-Run2	0.0655	0.6091	0.8125	0.2836	0.4205	0.5809	0.7764	0.2273	0.3516
NCTU&NTUT-Run3	0.1327	0.6018	0.7171	0.3364	0.4579	0.5645	0.6636	0.2618	0.3755
NCYU-Run1	0.1182	0.5245	0.586	0.1673	0.2603	0.5091	0.5357	0.1364	0.2174
NTOU-Run1	0.0909	0.5445	0.6644	0.18	0.2833	0.5327	0.6324	0.1564	0.2507
NTOU-Run2	0.5727	0.4227	0.422	0.4182	0.4201	0.39	0.3811	0.3527	0.3664
SCAU-Run1	0.5327	0.3409	0.2871	0.2145	0.2456	0.3218	0.2487	0.1764	0.2064
SCAU-Run2	0.1218	0.5464	0.6378	0.2145	0.3211	0.5227	0.5786	0.1673	0.2595
SCAU-Run3	0.6218	0.3282	0.3091	0.2782	0.2928	0.3018	0.2661	0.2255	0.2441

Table 3. Testing results of our Chinese spelling check task.

Participant	Approaches	Linguistic Resources
CAS	• Candidate Generation • Candidate Re-ranking • Global Decision Making	• SIGHAN-2013 CSC Datasets • CLP-2014 CSC Datasets • SIGHAN-2015 CSC Training Data • Taiwan Web Pages as Corpus • Chinese Words and Idioms Dictionary • Pinyin and Cangjie Code Table • Web-based Resources
KUAS	• Rules-based Method • Linear Regression Model	• Chinese Orthographic Database
NCTU & NTUT	• Misspelling Correction Rules • CRF-based Parser • Word Vector/CRF-based Spelling Error Detector • Trigram Language Model	• CLP-2014 CSC Datasets • SIGHAN-2015 CSC Training Data • Sinica Corpus
NTOU	• N-gram Model • Rule-based Classifier	• SIGHAN 2013 CSC Datasets • CLP-2014 CSC Datasets • Showen Jiezi and the Four-Corner Encoding • Sinica Corpus • Google N-gram Corpus
SCAU	• Bi-gram Language Model • Tri-gram Language Model	• SIGHAN-2013 CSC Datasets • CLP-2014 CSC Datasets • CCL • SOGOU

Table 4. A summary of participants' developed systems

6 Conclusions and Future Work

This paper provides an overview of SIGHAN 2015 Bake-off for Chinese spelling check, including task design, data preparation, evaluation metrics, performance evaluation results and the approaches used by the participant teams. Regardless of actual performance, all submissions contribute to the knowledge in search for an effective Chinese spell checker, and the individual reports in the Bake-off proceedings provide useful insight into Chinese language processing.

We hope the data sets collected for this Bake-off can facilitate and expedite future development of effective Chinese spelling checkers. Therefore, all data sets with gold standards and evaluation tool are made publicly available at http://ir.itc.ntnu.edu.tw/lre/sighan8csc.html.

The future direction focuses on the development of Chinese grammatical error correction. We plan to build new language resources to help improve existing techniques for computer-aided Chinese language learning. In addition, new data sets obtained from CFL learners will be investigated for the future enrichment of this research topic.

Acknowledgments

We thank all the participants for taking part in our task. We would like to thank Bo-Shun Liao for developing the evaluation tool.

This research is partially supported by the "Aim for the Top University Project" and "Center of Learning Technology for Chinese" of National Taiwan Normal University (NTNU), sponsored by the Ministry of Education, Taiwan, R.O.C. and is also sponsored in part by the "International Research-Intensive Center of Excellence Program" of NTNU and Ministry of Science and Technology, Taiwan, R.O.C. under the Grant no. MOST 104-2911-I-003-301, MOST 102-2221-E-002-103-MY3, and MOST 103-2221-E-003-013-MY3.

References

Chao-Lin Liu, Min-Hua Lai, Kan-Wen Tien, Yi-Hsuan Chuang, Shih-Hung Wu, and Chia-Ying Lee. 2011. Visually and phonologically similar characters in incorrect Chinese words: Analyses, identification, and applications. *ACM Transaction on Asian Language Information Processing*, 10(2), Article 10, 39 pages.

Shih-Hung Wu, Yong-Zhi Chen, Ping-che Yang, Tsun Ku, and Chao-Lin Liu. 2010. Reducing the false alarm rate of Chinese character error detection and correction. *Processing of the 1st CIPS-SIGHAN Joint Conference on Chinese Language Processing* (*CLP-10*), pages 54-61.

Shih-Hung Wu, Chao-Lin Liu, and Lung-Hao Lee. 2013. Chinese spelling check evaluation at SIGHAN Bake-off 2013. *Proceedings of the 7th SIGHAN Workshop on Chinese Language Processing* (*SIGHAN-13*), pages 35-42.

Lian-Chih Yu, Lung-Hao Lee, Yuen-Hsien Tseng, and Hsin-Hsi Chen. 2014. Overview of SIGHAN 2014 Bake-off for Chinese spelling check. *Processing of the 3rd CIPS-SIGHAN Joint Conference on Chinese Language Processing* (*CLP-14*), pages 126-132.

HANSpeller++: A Unified Framework for Chinese Spelling Correction

Shuiyuan Zhang[123], **Jinhua Xiong**[12], **Jianpeng Hou**[123], **Qiao Zhang**[123], **Xueqi Cheng**[12]
[1] CAS Key Laboratory of Network Data Science and Technology
[2]Institute of Computing Technology, Chinese Academy of Sciences
[3]University of Chinese Academy of Sciences
shuiyuanzhang@gmail.com, xjh@ict.ac.cn

Abstract

Increased interest in China from foreigners has led to a corresponding interest in the study of Chinese. However, the learning of Chinese by non-native speakers will encounter many difficulties, Chinese spelling check techniques for Chinese as a Foreign Language(CFL) learners is highly desirable. This paper presents our work on the SIGHAN-2015 Chinese Spelling Check task. The task focuses on spelling checking on Chinese essays written by CFL learners. We propose a unified framework called HANSpeller++ based on our previous HANSpeller for Chinese spelling correction. The framework consists of candidate generating,candidates re-ranking and final global decision making. Experiments show good performance on the test data of the task.

1 Introduction

The number of people learning Chinese as a Foreign Language (CFL) is booming in recent decades. Chinese is rated as one of the most difficult languages to learn for people whose native language is English, together with Arabic, Japanese and Korean. There are many difficulties when learning Chinese such as confusing four tones, many words that change their meanings based on what other words are around them. When CFL learners write Chinese essays, they are prone to generate more and diversified spelling errors than native language learners. Therefore, spelling correction tools to support such learners become very necessary and valuable.

As for spelling correction on Chinese essays of CFL learners, we are facing more challenges because of the uniqueness of Chinese language:

(1) Chinese characters number in the tens of thousands, many of them have same pronunciation or similar shape, it is easy to confuse these characters.

(2) There are no natural delimiters such as spaces between Chinese words, which may result in the error on word splitting, and accumulate the errors by the splitting.

(3) Chinese corpora for spelling correction, especial for public available ones, are rare, compared with English corpora. Such situation impedes more works on this practical topic.

(4) There are many different versions including simple Chinese and traditional Chinese. It is very difficult to distinguish them for CFL learners.

(5) The number of error types is more than that of other cases, because CFL learners are prone to different kinds of errors which we can not imagine as a native speaker.

To address the above challenges, we present a unified framework for Chinese essays spelling error detecting and correction. Our method combines different methods to improve performance. The main contributions compared with our previous work (Xiong et al., 2014) are:

(1) A HMM-based approach is used to segment sentences and generate candidates for sentences spelling correction. Furthermore, some error types which can be found in CFL learners essays frequently are added to the candidates generating process.

(2) A two stage filter process help to re-rank the candidates efficiently and accurately. The first stage filter enable us to filter out a lot of wrong candidates efficiently, and the second filter process help us to choose the most promising candidates accurately.

Proceedings of the Eighth SIGHAN Workshop on Chinese Language Processing (SIGHAN-8), pages 38–45,
Beijing, China, July 30-31, 2015.

In order to address evolving features of Chinese language, We crawl many web pages from some famous Taiwan websites as corpus, these high quality corpus is used to build the n-gram language model; and the online search resources are also used in the ranking stage, which can also improve the performance significantly.

The rest of the paper is organized as follows. We start with discussing related work in Section 2, followed by introducing our unified framework approach in Section 3, where we focus on the basic processes of our method. In Section 4, we present the detailed setup of the experimental evaluation and the results of the experiments. Finally, in Section 5, we come to conclude the paper and explore future directions.

2 Related work

In recent years, a lot work has been done in the spelling correction field. Chinese essays spelling correction as a special kind of spelling correction research effort has been promoted by efforts such as the SIGHAN bake-offs (Yu et al., 2014) (Wu et al., 2013) (Liu et al., 2011). Spelling correction aims at identifying the misspellings and choosing the optimal words as suggested corrections, and it can be mainly divided into single word spelling correction and context-sensitive spelling correction.

Single word spelling error commonly uses dictionary-based method. (Angell et al., 1983) introduced an automatic correction of misspellings using a trigram similarity measure. This method replace a word by that word in a dictionary which is the nearest neighbour of the misspelling.

For the context-sensitive spelling errors, there are two major kinds of processing methods:Rule-based methods and Statistics-based methods.

(Mangu and Brill, 1997) proposed a transition-based learning method for spelling correction. Their methods generated three types of rules from training data, which constructed a high performance and concise system for English.

(Mays et al., 1991) proposed a context based spelling correction method. This method statistic errors and is able to detect and correct some of these errors when they occur again in sentences.

(Golding and Roth, 1999) introduced an algorithm combining variants of Winnow and weighted-majority voting for context-sensitive spelling correction. When dealing test set which comes from a different corpus, this method can combines supervised learning on the training set with unsupervised learning on the test set.

With the development of Internet, online spelling correction service became available. (Suzuki and Gao, 2012) proposed a transliteration based character method using an approach inspired by the phrase-based statistical machine translation framework and get a good performance on online spelling correction.

Also,there are some online resources can be used for spelling checking. (Microsoft, 2010) provides web n-gram service on real-world web-scale data. (Google, 2013) provides Google books n-gram viewer,it displays how some phrases have occurred in a corpus of books.

As to Chinese Spelling correction, the situation is quite different. Chinese is a character based language, there are many potentially confusing aspects to this language. The nature of Chinese makes the correction much more difficult than that of English.

An early work was by (Chang, 1995), which used a character dictionary of similar shape, pronunciation, meaning, and input-method-code to deal with the spelling correction task. The system replaced each character in the sentence with the similar character in dictionary and calculated the probability of all modified sentences based on language model.

Some Chinese spelling checkers have incorporated word segmentation technique. (Huang et al., 2007) used a word segmentation tool (CKIP) to generate correction candidates, and then to detect Chinese spelling errors.

Some hybrid approach is applied to the Chinese spelling correction. (Jin et al., 2014) integrated three models including n-gram language model, pinyin based language model and tone based language model to improve the performance of Chinese checking spelling error system.

In our system, we need to detect and correct spelling errors on Chinese essays written by CFL learners. It has some different concerns with query text or query spelling correction. Noting that spelling correction methods require lexicons and/or language corpora, we adopt the method based on statistics combined with lexicon and rule-based methods.

3 A Unified Framework for Chinese Spelling Correction

For this Chinese Spelling Check task, we propose a unified framework called HANSpeller++. The main improvement of HANSpeller++ is the candidate re-ranking module. For some features used in the re-ranking process will cost a lot time to generate, we introduce a new two stage filter model to re-rank the candidates efficiently and accurately.

The framework coverts this task to 2 main parts, the first part is to generate possible candidates for a given input sentence, the second part is to choose the most promising candidate to output.Figure 1 shows the architecture of the unified framework.

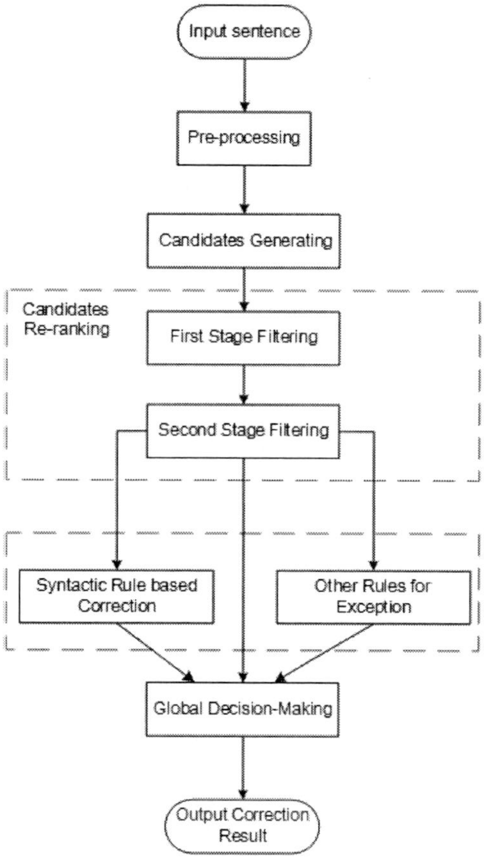

Figure 1: A unified framework for Chinese spelling correction(HANSpeller++).

It separates the Chinese spelling correction system into four major steps. First is to preprocess the input sentence to some sub sentences, then use the extended HMM model to generate top-k candidates for these sub sentences. We then use a two stage filter method to re-rank the correction candidates for later decision. Rule-based correction method is then used to consider some situation such as the usage of three confusable words "的", "地" and "得". Finally, we use global decision method to output the original sentence directly or the most promising candidate based on some constraint and the performance in previous step.

This framework provides a unified approach for spelling correction tasks, which can be regarded as a language independent framework and can be tailored to different scenarios. To move to another scenario, you need to prepare a language related corpus, but you do not need to be an expert of that language.

3.1 Data Preprocessing

Data provided by organizer is in the form of long sentences, and contains some non-Chinese characters.In our framework, sub sentence is the basic unit of the error correction process. We split long sentences into sub sentences by punctuation, and remove non-Chinese characters determined by its unicode code.

The policy of this task is an open test. We also use CLP-2014 CSC Datasets and SIGHAN-2013 CSC Datasets as our training data. The training data include real mistake by CFL learners and its correction, we treat this as confusion pair. Character-based confusion pair and word-based confusion pair are extracted from the whole training data, these 2 confusion pair sets will be used in the candidates generating process.

3.2 Candidates Generating

Generating candidates is the basic part for the whole task, for it determines the upper bound of recall rate of the approach.

Figure 1 shows the flow chart of the candidates generating module.

We first initialize a fixed size priority queue for a certain input sub sentence, this queue is used to store intermediate sub sentences.

For each character of sentences in the priority queue, we try to replace it by its candidate character. The possible candidate character include its homophone, near-homophone, similar shape character and confusion pair. Confusion pair set is extracted from the given training data, we collect the wrong character written by CFL learners and its corresponding correct character as a confusion pair.

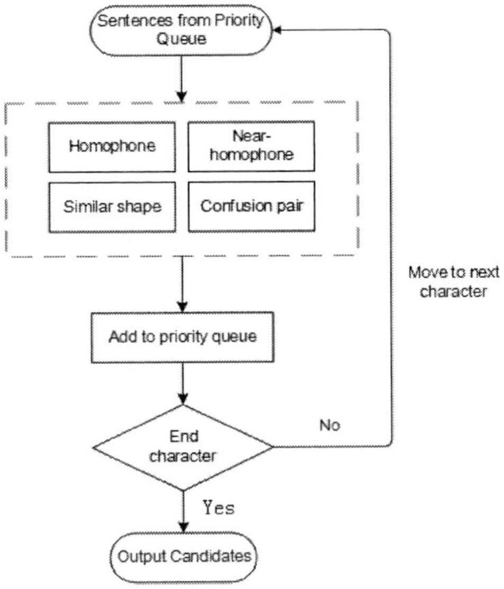

Figure 2: Flow chart of candidates generating module.

Different weight will be set to these different replacement type. Candidates generated by character replacement will be enqueued to the priority queue. When the queue is full candidate with low priority will be discarded, "priority" is defined as Follows.

Let $S = w_1w_2w_3 \ldots w_N$ be a sub sentence needed to be corrected, where each item $\mathrm{w_i}$ is a character.$C = \tilde{w}_1\tilde{w}_2\tilde{w}_3 \ldots \tilde{w}_{|r|} \ldots w_N$ is a candidate generated by replacing the r-th character. The priority of this candidate defined as $P(C|S)$. According to noisy channel model, probability $P(C|S)$ can be expressed as Equation 1.

$$P(C|S) = \frac{P(S|C)P(C)}{P(S))} \quad (1)$$

As $P(S)$ is always same for candidates of the same raw input, Equation 1 can be simplified as Equation 2.

$$log(P(C|S)) \propto log(P(S|C) + log(P(C)) \quad (2)$$

Conceptually, Equation 2 can be calculated approximately by using edit distance and n-gram language model. Priority finally defined as Equation 3.

$$priority = \alpha * log(P(C)) + \beta * edit\_dist \quad (3)$$

3.3 Candidates Re-Ranking

In the candidates generating phase, a lot candidates for a sentence are generated. But at most one candidate for a input sentence is correct,the goal of this re-ranking module is to discard a lot of wrong candidates. We convert this ranking problem to a classification problem, the right candidates are regarded as positive samples while the wrong candidates are regarded as negative samples.

A lot of features can be used in the classifier, but some features are too time-consuming. For a given sub sentence, we may get hundreds of candidates, it will waste a lot time to extract all features for these candidates. In view of this situation, we proposed a two stage filter method. The main purpose of this method is to pre-filter the candidates using a fast model with some simple features, a more accurate model with more features will be used for candidates after filtration.

In the first stage, we train a simple but fast logistic regression classifier with some simple features, generating these features will not be too time-consuming. Then the candidates in the list will be filtered up to 20 at this stage based on the probability score generated by the trained classifier. Features used in this stage list below.

- **Language model features**: which calculates the n-gram text probability of candidate sentences and the original sentence.
- **Dictionary features**: which counts the number and proportion of phrases and idioms in candidates after segmentation according to our dictionaries.
- **Edit distance features**: which compute the edit number and its weight, from the original sentence to candidate sentences. Here different edit operations are given different edit weights.
- **Segmentation features**: which uses the results of the Maximum Matching Algorithm and the CKIP Parser segmentation.

In the second stage, We add some time-consuming features to obtain a more accurate model. For the candidate count decreases a lot after the first filter stage, these time-consuming features are acceptable. We choose top-5 candidates after this stage. Features used in the second stage list below.

- **Web based features**:which use Bing or other search engine's search results, when submitting the spelling correction part and the corresponding part of the original sentence to the search engine.

- **Translation features**: which use Yandex to compare English translation of the original sentence and each candidate sentence. Right candidate sentence tend to have more fluent English translation.

- **Microsoft Web N-Gram Service probability**: which compute the English translation N-gram probability by using Microsoft Web N-Gram Service.Traditional Chinese corpora for spelling correction, especially for public available ones, are rare. Microsoft Web N-Gram Service provide N-gram probability on real-world web-scale data, so we take advantage of this service by using English translation of each candidate.

In this two stage filter method, a wide variety of features are taken into account in order to obtain the candidate sentences accordance with the actual quality of candidates as much as possible. The first stage filter enhances the overall speed, and the second stage filter can help to improve the performance of final spelling correction. After this re-ranking module, top-5 candidates for a sub sentence will be output to the final global decision.

3.4 Rule-based Correction

After candidates re-ranking, some common errors are still difficult to be distinguished, such as the usage of three confusable words "的", "地", "得". In order to correct such errors, syntactic analysis is necessary to develop. The following sentence contains an error of Chinese syntax:

今天/我/穿着/刚/买/地/新/衣服。

Here the character "地" should be corrected to another character "的". To deal with these kinds of errors, sentence parsing must be done before the syntactic rules are applied to check and correct such errors. We have summarized three rules of the usage for "的", "地", "得" according to Chinese grammar as follows:

The Chinese character "的" is the tag of attributes, which generally used in the front of subjects and objects. Words in front of "的" are generally used to modify, restrict things behind "的".

The Chinese character "地" is adverbial marker, usually used in front of predicates (verbs, adjectives). Words in front of "地" are generally used to describe actions behind "地".

The Chinese character "得" makes the complement, generally used behind predicates. The part follows "得" is generally used to supplement the previous action.

Another common error is the usage of "他", "她", "它". In the following sentence the character "他" should be corrected to another character "她", for it refers to the word "媽媽" which is a female.

媽 媽/不 會/說/中 文， 而 且/他/不 要/一 個 人/在/家裡。

We collect some simple rules that map keyword to one of the character "ta",such as "姐姐" maps to "她","父亲" maps to "他". When a gender specific word shows in the previous sub sentence, we use the keyword map as the basis for the character "ta".

There is also another situation that the character "ta" shows exactly in front of a gender specific word, such as "他女朋友","她男朋友".

The usage of "ta" is far more complex, we only deal with some obvious cases using simple rules. More complicated situation can be processed by using syntactic analysis.

In addition, some other specific rules are also needed to improve the final performance, which can be concluded from the training data and corpus.

3.5 Global Decision Making

Through the above processing steps, We get top-5 candidates for each sub-sentence. To make the final decision on spelling correction, some global constrains should be considered.

First, we filter out some candidates ,If the n-gram prob of the raw sentence is close to the most promising candidate, the raw sentence will be output. The closeness is measured relatively.

Then the rest candidates is sorted based on a combination of factors. The probability score in the second filter stage is a key factor, for it consider many useful features. Replacement type in the candidates generating process is another factor that can influence the decision making. We set different weights for different types of spelling errors by experience. For example, the confusion pair replacement need to be paid more weight than others, as these replacement are really happen frequently in the training data, and we assume the test data is consistent with the training data.

Also, we use some global constraints to limit the number of errors. If there are more than 2 errors in a sub sentence, this candidate will be dropped. If there are more than 3 sub sentence errors in a long sentence, this long sentence will not be modified. These rules will increase the precision rate.

Finally, the precision rate and recall rate is balanced by controlling the number of error sentences.

In this task, we regulate some constraints and weights to get our final runs, this step has a great influence on the final performance.

4 Experiments

4.1 Resources

The following corpora are used in our experiment,including Taiwan Web as Corpus, a traditional Chinese dictionary of words and idioms, a pinyin mapping table and a cangjie code table of common words. The details of them are described below.

- **SIGHAN Datasets**

  We extract confusion set from the given training data, but the given training data is not enough, so we also use CLP-2014 CSC Datasets and SIGHAN-2013 CSC Datasets as our training data. Character-based confusion pair and word-based confusion pair are extracted from the whole training data, these 2 confusion pair sets will be used in the candidates generating process.

- **Taiwan Web Pages as Corpus**

  we try to find Taiwan webs whose pages contain high quality traditional Chinese text, to build the corpus. We gathered pages from the artificial selected Webs under .tw domain to build the corpus. And then the content extracted from these pages is used to build traditional n-gram language model, where n is from 2 to 4.

- **Chinese Words and Idioms Dictionary**

  As introduced in (Chiu et al., 2013), we also obtained the Chinese words and Chinese idioms published by Ministry of Education of Taiwan, which are built from the dictionaries and related books. There are 64,326 distinct Chinese words and 48,030 distinct Chinese idioms.

- **Pinyin and Cangjie Code Table**

  We collected more than 10000 pinyins of words commonly used in Taiwan to build the homophone and near-homophone words table, which will be used in candidate generation phase. In addition, cangjie code can be used to measure the form/shape similarity between Chinese characters. Therefore, we collected cangjie codes to build the table of Similar-form characters.

- **Web based Resources**

  We use some web based resources to improve the performance. These resources include CKIP online parser, Bing search service, Yandex translate service and Microsoft Web N-Gram Service. In order to improve efficiency, these resources are only used in the second stage of candidate re-ranking process.

4.2 Evaluation

The criteria for judging correctness is divided into two levels. One is detection level and the other is correction level. For detection level, all locations of incorrect characters in a given passage should be completely identical with the gold standard. For correction level, all locations and corresponding corrections of incorrect characters should be completely identical with the gold standard.

$$FalsePositiveRate = \frac{FP}{FP + TN} \quad (4)$$

$$Accuracy = \frac{TP + TN}{TP + TN + FP + FN} \quad (5)$$

$$Precision = \frac{TP}{TP + FP} \quad (6)$$

$$Recall = \frac{TP}{TP + FN} \quad (7)$$

$$F1 - Score = \frac{2 * Precision * Recall}{Precision + Recall} \quad (8)$$

Team	False Positive Rate	Accuracy	Precision	Recall	F1
CAS*	0.1309	0.7009	0.8027	0.5327	0.6404
NCTU+NTUT	0.1327	0.6018	0.7171	0.3364	0.4579
NTOU	0.5727	0.4227	0.422	0.4182	0.4201

Table 1: Top 3 performance in Detection Level.

Team	False Positive Rate	Accuracy	Precision	Recall	F1
CAS*	0.1309	0.6918	0.7972	0.5145	0.6254
NCTU+NTUT	0.1327	0.5645	0.6636	0.2618	0.3755
NTOU	0.5727	0.39	0.3811	0.3527	0.3664

Table 2: Top 3 performance in Correction Level.

Confusion Matrix		System Results	
		Positive (Error)	Negative (No Error)
Gold Standard	Positive	TP	FN
	Negative	FP	TN

Table 3: Confusion Matrix.

The evaluation metrics, including false positive rate, accuracy rate, precision rate, recall rate and F1-score, are used in this task. Formula of these indicators are listed in Equation 4-8. Table 3 is confusion matrix which help to calculate the related indicators.

There are 1100 sentences with/without spelling errors on the evaluation test. Detection level results illustrated in Table 1, correction level results illustrated in Table 2. Our performance ranks first place among all participating teams, which means that our method is feasible. Meanwhile, since such an open test is an extremely challenging task, there is still much room for further improvement.

5 Conclusion

This paper propose a unified framework called HANSpeller++ based on our previous HANSpeller. Candidate generating, candidates re-ranking and final global decision making are included in this framework, some rule-based strategies are used to improve the performance. Our approach has been evaluated at SIGHAN-2015 Chinese Spelling Check task, and achieved a good result.

Some interesting future works on Chinese spelling correction include: (1) Some more valuable features can be added in the re-ranking process. (2) Using machine learning method to make global decision is worth trying. (3) Implementing an online toolkit and service for Chinese spelling correction is a stimulator of this empirical research topic.

Acknowledgments

This research was supported by the National High Technology Research and Development Program of China (Grant No. 2014AA015204), the National Basic Research Program of China (Grant No. 2014CB340406), the NSFC for the Youth (Grant No. 61402442) and the Technology Innovation and Transformation Program of Shandong (Grant No.2014CGZH1103).

References

Richard C Angell, George E Freund, and Peter Willett. 1983. Automatic spelling correction using a trigram similarity measure. *Information Processing & Management*, 19(4):255–261.

Chao-Huang Chang. 1995. A new approach for automatic chinese spelling correction. In *Proceedings of Natural Language Processing Pacific Rim Symposium*, volume 95, pages 278–283. Citeseer.

Hsun-wen Chiu, Jian-cheng Wu, and Jason S Chang. 2013. Chinese spelling checker based on statistical machine translation. In *Sixth International Joint Conference on Natural Language Processing*, page 49.

Andrew R Golding and Dan Roth. 1999. A winnow-based approach to context-sensitive spelling correction. *Machine learning*, 34(1-3):107–130.

Google. 2013. Ngram viewer. `https://books.google.com/ngrams`.

Chuen-Min Huang, Mei-Chen Wu, and Ching-Che Chang. 2007. Error detection and correction based on chinese phonemic alphabet in chinese text. In *Modeling Decisions for Artificial Intelligence*, pages 463–476. Springer.

Peng Jin, Xingyuan Chen, Zhaoyi Guo, and Pengyuan Liu. 2014. Integrating pinyin to improve spelling errors detection for chinese language. In *Proceedings of the 2014 IEEE/WIC/ACM International Joint Conferences on Web Intelligence (WI) and Intelligent Agent Technologies (IAT)-Volume 01*, pages 455–458. IEEE Computer Society.

C-L Liu, M-H Lai, K-W Tien, Y-H Chuang, S-H Wu, and C-Y Lee. 2011. Visually and phonologically similar characters in incorrect chinese words: Analyses, identification, and applications. *ACM Transactions on Asian Language Information Processing (TALIP)*, 10(2):10.

Lidia Mangu and Eric Brill. 1997. Automatic rule acquisition for spelling correction. In *ICML*, volume 97, pages 187–194. Citeseer.

Eric Mays, Fred J Damerau, and Robert L Mercer. 1991. Context based spelling correction. *Information Processing & Management*, 27(5):517–522.

Microsoft. 2010. Microsoft web n-gram services. `http://research.microsoft.com/web-ngram`.

Hisami Suzuki and Jianfeng Gao. 2012. A unified approach to transliteration-based text input with online spelling correction. In *Proceedings of the 2012 Joint Conference on Empirical Methods in Natural Language Processing and Computational Natural Language Learning*, pages 609–618. Association for Computational Linguistics.

Shih-Hung Wu, Chao-Lin Liu, and Lung-Hao Lee. 2013. Chinese spelling check evaluation at sighan bake-off 2013. In *Proceedings of the 7th SIGHAN Workshop on Chinese Language Processing*, pages 35–42. Citeseer.

Jinhua Xiong, Qiao Zhao, Jianpeng Hou, Qianbo Wang, Yuanzhuo Wang, and Xueqi Cheng. 2014. Extended hmm and ranking models for chinese spelling correction. *CLP 2014*, page 133.

Liang-Chih Yu, Lung-Hao Lee, Yuen-Hsien Tseng, and Hsin-Hsi Chen. 2014. Overview of sighan 2014 bake-off for chinese spelling check. *CLP 2014*, page 126.

Word Vector/Conditional Random Field-based Chinese Spelling Error Detection for SIGHAN-2015 Evaluation

Yih-Ru Wang
National Chiao Tung University
HsinChu, Taiwan
yrwang@mail.nctu.edu.tw

Yuan-Fu Liao
National Taipei University of Technology, Taipei, Taiwan
yfliao@ntut.edu.tw

Abstract

In order to detect Chinese spelling errors, especially for essays written by foreign learners, a word vector/conditional random field (CRF)-based detector is proposed in this paper. The main idea is to project each word in a test sentence into a high dimensional vector space in order to reveal and examine their relationships by using a CRF. The results are then utilized to constrain the time-consuming language model rescoring procedure. Official SIGHAN-2015 evaluation results show that our system did achieve reasonable performance with about 0.601/0.564 ac-curacies and 0.457/0.375 F1 scores in the detection/correction levels.

1 Introduction

Chinese spelling check could be treated as an abnormal word sequence detection and correction problem. Convention approaches to do this job often heavenly rely on a language models (LM) trained from a large text corpus (for example Chinese Gigaword[1]) to find potential errors and provide suitable candidate words (Bengio 2003, Wang 2013) to replace them. These approaches usually could be successfully applied to examine essays written by Chinese element or junior school students.

However, for essays written by foreign learners, conventional LM methods may not be so helpful. Because, the writing behaviors of foreign learners are usually different with native Chinese writers. They may embedded spelling errors into rarely used word sequences (low LM scores, but are somehow grammar or syntactic corrected). For example:

- 然後你們工廠應該要蓋起來比較高高厚厚的床比。("床比" should be "牆壁")
- 小孩不過不知道那個好那個不好，也不知道那作法是適合，難怪常常看到他們用部是對的。("部" should be "不")
- 王大明今天六點半起來就洗澡穿上就去廚房吃早飯他等公車十分就坐上，他坐著坐著到學校來了。("穿上" should be "穿衣")

They may also produce some semantic errors (but are all grammar and syntactic corrected and therefore with high LM scores). This type of errors are difficult, if not impossible, to detect using only LM models trained from conventional Chinese text corpora. For example:

- 吃了碗飯以後，我們兩個人馬上去看電影。("碗" should be "晚")
- 他戴著眼鏡跟襪子入睡了。("襪子" should be "穿著襪子")
- 我跟我的同學學數學。我們對號碼有興趣。("號碼" should be "數字")

In order to properly deal with those errors, it is necessary to understand foreign learners' writing behaviors. Therefore, this paper focus on how to automatically learn the behaviors of foreign learners. Our major idea is to transform the problem into a machine learning task. To this end, the vector representations of the words were first constructed and then CRF-based approach was adopted to detect the errors.

2 Overview of the proposed system

The block diagram of our system is shown in Fig. 1. There are four main components including (1) a misspelling correction rules frontend, (2) a CRF-based parser, (3) a word vector/CRF-based spelling error detector and (4) a 120k tri-gram LM.

Basically, our approach is to utilize the error detection results to guide and speed up the time-consuming LM rescoring procedure. It iteratively exchanges potential error words with their confusable ones and examine the modified sentence using the tri-gram LM. The final goal is to produce a modified sentence with maximum LM

[1] http://www.aclclp.org.tw/use_asbc_c.php

Proceedings of the Eighth SIGHAN Workshop on Chinese Language Processing (SIGHAN-8), pages 46–49,
Beijing, China, July 30-31, 2015. ©2015 Association for Computational Linguistics and Asian Federation of Natural Language Processing

score. By this way, potential Chinese spelling errors could be detected and corrected.

Since, the details of our parser, LM modules and character replacement procedure could be found in (Wang 2013), only the newly added word vector/CRF-based error detection module will be further described in the following subsections.

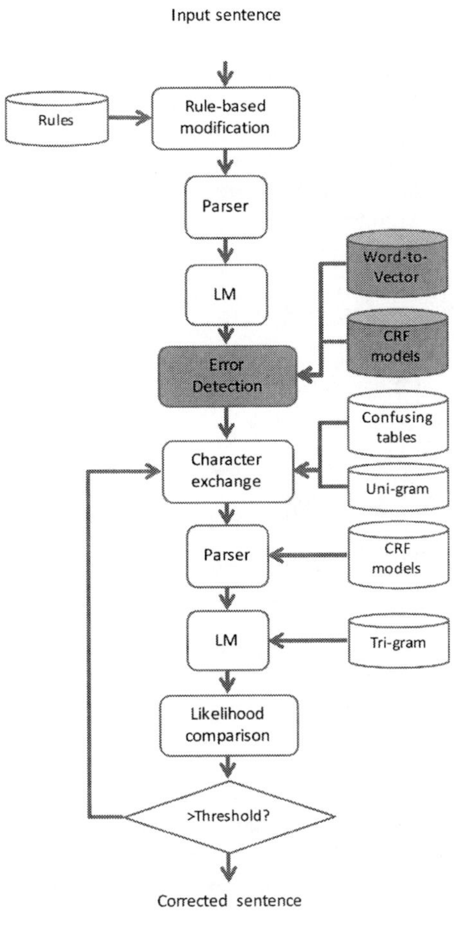

Fig. 1: The schematic diagram of the proposed Chinese spelling checker. The are four modules including a rule-based frontend, a CRF-based parser, a tri-gram LM and a word vector/CRF-based spelling error detector. Among them, the spelling error detector is newly added for SIGHAN-2015 evaluation.

3 Word Vector/CRF-based Spelling Error Detector

Fig. 2 shows the block diagram of the word vector/CRF-based Chinese spelling error detection module. Its two main modules, i.e., word2vec and CRF will be discussed in the following subsections.

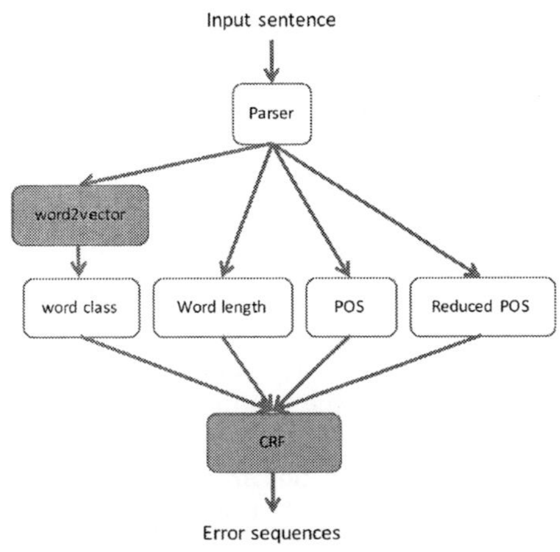

Fig. 2: The schematic diagram of the proposed Chinese spelling error detector. The input features of the CRF includes word classes tagged by word2vec, length, POS and reduced POS provided by parser module.

3.1 Word vector representation

The word to vector algorithm proposed by Tomas Mikolov (Mikolov 2013a, 2013b) is adopted in this paper to encode words. It uses the CBOW (continuous bag of words, as shown in Fig. 3) representations to project each word into a high dimensional vector space.

These representations have been shown to be capable to capture deep linguistic information beyond surface words (Mikolov 2013). Therefore, CBOW is used here to reveal the prosperities and relationship between normal and abnormal word sequences.

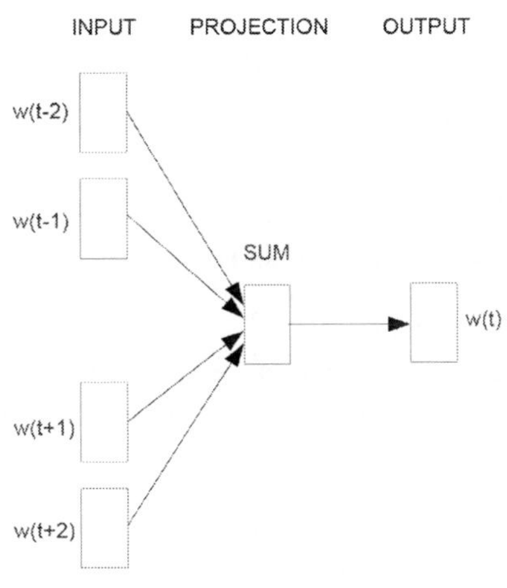

Fig. 3: The CBOW word to vector encoding architecture that predicts the current word based on the context.

3.2 CRF Chinese spelling error detector

To detect potential spelling errors, the word vectors and parser outputs are further combined into a feature sequences for CRF error detector. CRF then learns from a set of labels samples (ground-truth) to tell between correct and incorrect word spellings instances.

Fig. 4 shows a typical example of the extracted feature sequences of a training sample. Here each word is transformed into a 5 dimensional vector including (1) the length of the word, its (2) POS and (3) reduced POS tags, (4) the word class index and the ground-truth (correct or error spelling) labels.

聽起來	3	D	ADV	436	c
是	1	SHI	Vt	441	c
一	1	Neu	DET	136	c
份	1	Nf	M	162	c
很	1	Dfa	ADV	441	c
好	1	VH	Vi	398	c
的	1	DE1	T	390	c
公司	2	Nc	N	609	c
。	1	PM	M	-2	c
又	1	Caa	C	551	w
意思	2	Na	N	77	c
又	1	Caa	C	551	c
很多	2	Neqa	DET	441	c
錢	1	Na	N	270	c
。	1	PM	PM	-2	c

Fig. 4: A typical example of a training sample (from left to right) the word segmentation results and the corresponding input features (word length, POS, reduced POS and word class index) and ground-truth labels.

4 Evaluation Results

4.1 System setting

Basically, the parser, 120K tri-gram LM and word vector representation were all trained using Sinica Balanced Corpus version 4.0[2]. There is in total about 4.4 billion words in the corpus.

For the parser, its F-measure of the word segmentation is 96.72% and 97.67% for the original and manually corrected corpus. The accuracy of the 47-type POS tagging is about 94.24%. To build the word vector representation, a window of 17 (8+1+8) words was used. Each word was first projected into a 200 dimensional CBOW vector and then further clustered into one of 1024 classes.

On the other hand, to build the CRF-based spelling error detector, Bake-off 2014 and SIGHAN-2015 development corpora were utilized. There are in total 106,815 words in the training set. Among them, only 4,537 words are incorrect. For the test set, there are 11,808 words including 498 errors.

4.2 Error detection frontend results

First of all, Fig. 5 shows a typical output of the word vector/CRF-based spelling error detector. It is worth to note that the last column in Fig. 5 shows the correct scores reported by the CRF. If the scores are less than 0.5, the corresponding words will be treated as good ones, otherwise spelling errors will be reported. For example, the last word "阿" has a very low score 0.0048 and is therefore will be labelled as an error.

但是	2	Cbb	C	441	0.9999
我	1	Nh	N	738	0.9998
不能	2	D	ADV	441	0.9833
去	1	D	ADV	738	0.9945
參加	2	VC	Vt	723	0.9985
，	1	PM	PM	-2	0.9998
因為	2	Cbb	C	441	0.9999
我	1	Nh	N	738	0.9999
有一點	3	Dfa	ADV	738	0.9997
事情	2	Na	N	441	0.9687
阿	1	T	T	820	0.0048
！	1	PM	PM	-2	0.9999

Fig. 5: A typical example of the CRF outputs. The last column shows the scores given by the CRF's correct spelling nodes.

Moreover, Table 1 show the evaluation results of the error detection frontend on Bake-off 2014 and SIGHAN-2015 development corpora. From the table, it can be found that the detection results for the training set is quite good. But for test set, there is serious bias issue. This may due to the over-fitting problem since there are unbalanced numbers of correct and incorrect spelling word samples in the training set. To alleviate the difficulties, we will try to lower detector's decision threshold for the following LM rescoring procedure to cover more hypotheses.

4.3 Overall detection and correction results

Finally, three system configurations (Run1~3) were tested to explore different LM rescoring space. i.e., using three different CRF score thresholds including 0.999, 0.98 and 0.95.

[2] http://www.aclclp.org.tw/use_asbc_c.php

Among them, the search space of Run1 is very restricted and Run3 is much larger than others.

Table 2 show the official evaluation results given by the SIGHAN-2015 evaluation organizer. From Table 2, it can be found that Run1 had lowest false positive and recalls rates in both measures. On the other hand, Run3 had highest recall rates and F1 scores but produced many more false alarms.

In summary, these results show that our approach had achieved reasonable performance. But the settings of our systems (even Run3) were still too conservative. Therefore, there are still some rooms to further lower the threshold in order to improve the F1 scores.

		Acc.	Pre.	Rec.	F1
Training	C		99.92	99.98	99.95
	W		99.21	97.47	98.33
	All	99.90	99.90	99.90	99.90
Test	C		98.23	99.03	98.63
	W		54.10	38.98	45.31
	All	97.32	97.32	97.32	97.32

Table 1: Detection results of the proposed word vector/CRF-based error detector on Bake-off 2014 and SIGHAN-2015 corpora. The table shows the accuracy (Acc.), precision (Pre.), recall (Rec.) and F1 score for both the training and test sets (C: correct, W: wrong words).

Run	F/P	Detection Level			
		Acc.	Pre.	Rec.	F1
1	0.050	0.605	0.837	0.261	0.398
2	0.065	0.609	0.812	0.283	0.420
3	0.132	0.601	0.717	0.336	0.457
Run	F/P	Correction Level			
		Acc.	Pre.	Rec.	F1
1	0.050	0.578	0.802	0.207	0.329
2	0.065	0.580	0.776	0.227	0.351
3	0.132	0.564	0.663	0.261	0.375

Table 2: Official evaluation results of the proposed systems for SIGHAN-2015 Chinese spelling check task. The table shows the false positive (F/P) rate, accuracy (Acc.), precision (Pre.), recall (Rec.), and F1 score for both the detection and correction levels.

5 Conclusions

In this paper, a word vector/CRF-based Chinese spelling error detector have been newly added to improve our spelling check system. Evaluation results show that our systems had achieved reasonable performance. Especially, configuration Run3 achieves about 0.601/0.564 accuracies and 0.457/0.375 F1 scores in the detection/correction level, respectively.

Experimental results also showed that our error detector frontend suffered serious overfitting problem. Beside, the time consuming LM scoring procedure should be replaced with a candidate word predictor (for example the CBOW structure shown in Fig. 3). These two issues will be further studied in the future. Finally, our latest traditional Chinese parser is available on-line at http://parser.speech.cm.nctu.edu.tw.

Acknowledgments

This work was supported by the Ministry of Science and Technology, Taiwan, under the projects with contract MOST 103-2221-E-027-079 and MOST 103-2221-E-009-125-MY2.

References

Y. Bengio, R. Ducharme, P. Vincent, and C. Jauvin (2003), "A neural probabilistic language model, Journal of Machine Learning Research", 2003, No. 3(2), pp. 1137–1155.

Chao-Lin Liu, Min-Hua Lai, Kan-Wen Tien, Yi-Hsuan Chuang, Shih-Hung Wu, and Chia-Ying Lee (2011). Visually and phonologically similar characters in incorrect Chinese words: Analyses, identification, and applications, ACM Trans. Asian Lang. Inform. Process. 10, 2, Article 10 (June 2011).

Tomas Mikolov, Kai Chen, Greg Corrado, and Jeffrey Dean (2013a). Efficient Estimation of Word Representations in Vector Space. In Proceedings of Workshop at ICLR, 2013.

Tomas Mikolov, Ilya Sutskever, Kai Chen, Greg Corrado, and Jeffrey Dean (2013b). Distributed Representations of Words and Phrases and their Compositionality. In Proceedings of NIPS, 2013.

Yih-Ru Wang, Yuan-Fu Liao, Yeh-Kuang Wu and Liang-Chun Chang (2013). Traditional Chinese Parser and Language Model-Based Chinese Spelling Checker. Proceedings of the 7th SIGHAN Workshop on Chinese Language Processing (SIGHAN'13), Nagoya, Japan, 14 October, 2013, pp. 69-73.

Shih-Hung Wu, Chao-Lin Liu, and Lung-Hao Lee (2013). Chinese Spelling Check Evaluation at SIGHAN Bake-off 2013. Proceedings of the 7th SIGHAN Workshop on Chinese Language Processing (SIGHAN'13), Nagoya, Japan, 14 October, 2013, pp. 35-42.

H. Zhao, C. N. Huang and M. Li (2006), "An Improved Chinese Word Segmentation System with Conditional Random Field", the Fifth SIGHAN Workshop on Chinese Language Processing 2006, pp. 108-117.

Introduction to a Proofreading Tool for Chinese Spelling Check Task of SIGHAN-8

Tao-Hsing Chang
Department of Computer Science and Information Engineering
National Kaohsiung University of Applied Sciences
changth@gm.kuas.edu.tw

Hsueh-Chih Chen
Department of Educational Psychology and Counseling
National Taiwan Normal University
chcjyh@ntnu.edu.tw

Cheng-Han Yang
Department of Computer Science and Information Engineering
National Kaohsiung University of Applied Sciences
1101108129@kuas.edu.tw

Abstract

The detection and correction of erroneous Chinese characters is an important problem in many applications. This paper proposed an automatic method for correcting erroneous Chinese characters. The method is divided into two parts, which separately handle two types of erroneous character: the occurrence of an erroneous character in a word length of one, and the occurrence in a word length of two or more. The first primarily makes use of a rules-based method, while the second integrates parameters of similarity and syntax rationality using a linear regression model to predict erroneous characters. Experimental results shown that the F1 and FPR of the proposed method are 0.34 and 0.18 respectively.

1 Introduction

The detection and correction of erroneous characters is a key problem in many applications. For example, approaches for information retrieval need to analyze a document's lexicon, syntax, and semantics, but the analysis of documents containing erroneous characters is likely to result in errors in the results of such analysis. Furthermore, with regard to language teaching, tools that can automatically correct erroneous characters can be of considerable assistance to a student's independent learning. To detect misspelled words within an alphabetic writing system, a dictionary method can generally be employed: if a word is not found in the dictionary and is not a newly created word, then it is incorrect. Moreover, proofreading for misspelled words can use a similarity comparison with currently available vocabulary to seek words that can correct the misspelled words.

There are great differences between the problems encountered in the automatic correction of erroneous characters in Chinese and the problems in alphabetic writing systems. Because there are no spaces between Chinese words, which would allow for their identification, it is quite difficult to use the dictionary method. Furthermore, Chinese words are composed of at least one character, so that an erroneous character may make up an existing word in combination with its adjacent characters. This results in difficulties in terms of identification. Additionally, a Chinese character may constitute a word in itself, and thus it is difficult to distinguish between a single-character word and an erroneous character. These characteristics of pictographs mean that different methods must be developed to resolve problems related to the correction of Chinese script from those used with alphabetic writing systems.

Since Chang (1995) proposed research into the automatic detection and correction of erroneous Chinese words, many methods have been advanced successively to do this. In the early stages, the most method used was that of correcting commonly confused character sets. There are three ways to establish commonly confused character sets: the first is using manually established confused character sets; the second is based on the

Proceedings of the Eighth SIGHAN Workshop on Chinese Language Processing (SIGHAN-8), pages 50–55,
Beijing, China, July 30-31, 2015.

statistical occurrence of biased error text corpus words composed of erroneous characters and their frequency; and the third is the method of calculating the degree of similarity so as to enter characters with similar phonetic values and forms in a list of confused character sets. The main problem with the confused character set method lies in the presence of erroneous characters that are not in confused character sets and are therefore undetectable.

The objective of this paper is to propose an automatic method for correcting erroneous Chinese characters. The method is divided into two parts, which separately handle two types of erroneous character: the occurrence of an erroneous character in a word length of one, and the occurrence in a word length of two or more. The first primarily makes use of a rules-based method, while the second integrates parameters of similarity and syntax rationality using a linear regression model to predict erroneous characters. The other sections of this paper are organized as follows: Section 2 introduces the progress made and methods used in related research in recent years. Section 3 gives a detailed explanation of the method proposed by this paper. Section 4 shows the experimental results achieved by this method in a test text corpus. Section 5 discusses the characteristics, limitations, and future research directions of this method.

2 Related Works

Proposed automated detection and correction methods for Chinese erroneous characters can be traced back to the detection and correction method put forward by Chang (1995). This method used the four commonly occurring forms of erroneous characters–"characters with similar pronunciation," "characters with similar form," "characters with similar connotation," and "characters with similar input code value"–to establish relationships of confusion between the characters. Using such databases of computer characters that may produce erroneous character relationships, it is possible to provide a list of corrections for use in attempting to detect erroneous characters and correct sentences. The input sentences use confused character sets one by one as substitutes for the Chinese computer characters in the sentence, producing a variety of possible combination sentences as candidate sentences. By calculating sentence probability based on a bi-gram model, the system seeks to obtain the optimum solution in relation to the candidate sentences that have been produced. If the optimum solution differs from the original sentence, it then compares the differing computer character and serves as the corrected result. In recent years, since some competitions have been held to correct Chinese erroneous characters, many studies have proposed a wide variety of methods to resolve this problem.

These methods can be divided essentially into three categories. The first consists of initially processing the sentence using a Chinese word segmentation tool, then detecting whether erroneous characters occur among serial single Chinese character sequences (abbreviated to SSCS below). Chang, Chen, Tseng, & Zheng (2013) searched for possible correct words among each character in an SSCS, and using the three parameters of "similarity of phonetic value," "similarity of form," and "probability of co-occurrence of adjacent characters" established a linear regression prediction model. Wang and Liao (2014) used the Chinese word segmentation system to analyze a sentence's word segments, and then, if there was a suspected occurrence of an erroneous character in a two-character word or single-character word, used a character with a high degree of similarity of phonetic value and form to replace the possible erroneous character. Finally, they used a tri-gram model to assess whether to conduct a replacement.

The second category is the direct utilization of a probability model to detect an erroneous character. Han and Chang (2013) proposed using maximum entropy in relation to 5311 characters and the seven-grams trained model to correct erroneous characters. The fundamental hypothesis of this study was: if there was a possible erroneous character in the sentence, then the matched pairs that the character and the characters preceding and following it produced may not exist in the text corpus. Conversely, if the matched pair made by the character and the character preceding it or following it is commonly seen in the text corpus, then that character's degree of erroneousness is very low here. Xiong et al. (2014) proposed using the Hidden Markov Model (HMM) as the basis for a model to detect and correct erroneous characters. This method presupposes that unknown erroneous characters exist in the sentence, and seeks out each character's substitute character by means of phonetic writing (pinyin) and the Cangjie input code using Bayes' rule as its basis. Because there are many substitute characters, this method then uses methods such as n-gram and statistics from internet search results to determine substitute words. Gu, Wang, & Liang (2014) use SSCS as their target in the same way but use character blocks within SSCS. Exploiting the statistical method of serial computer characters forming character blocks, it is possible to detect and correct erroneous characters while not utilizing a word segmentation system.

The third method uses multiple prediction models to predict different categories of erroneous character. For example, Xin, Zhao, Wang, & Jia (2014) converted the problem of erroneous characters into the problem of seeking the shortest pathway in a graph. Because the graph model can only identify erroneous characters in long words, for erroneous single-character words it additionally uses rule-based methods and a CRF model to make corrections.

3 Methods

There are two patterns for the formation of Chinese words. One pattern is that of a character itself as a word, such as "我" (meaning 'I'), which is termed a single-character word; the other is a long word of two or more characters combined, such as "工作" (meaning 'work.') If we suppose that an erroneous character appears in a certain long word, word segmentation will break up the word into a series of single characters. Therefore, detecting whether an SSCS appears in a sentence after it has been segmented is an effective method for detecting an erroneous character. Section 3.1 of this paper is based on research by Chang et al. (2013), which proposed a method for correcting erroneous characters in long words. In section 3.2, this paper also uses the characteristics of erroneous single-character words to put forward a rules-based correction method based on syntactic structure.

3.1 Correcting erroneous characters in long words

With regard to each character of an SCSS, we hypothesize that it is not an erroneous character, and also that it may be a character in a long word. Hence, we use the dictionary method to seek out all long words containing this character. Using as an example the Chinese sentence "因_偽_他_必須_工作" (because he must work,) long words that contain the character include "因為" (because) and '因素" (factor,) etc. If we determine that "因素" is the correct word in this sentence, then "偽" is an erroneous character for "素". This paper refers to these long words as "candidate words," and refers to the candidate words' corresponding original sentence character sequence as "suspected word blocks." For example, the candidate words for the suspected word block "因_偽" include "因素".

Because there are numerous candidates for each suspected word block, it is necessary to go through a filtering process to verify whether there are words among the candidate words suitable for substituting for the suspect word block. Chang et al. (2013) noted that the majority of erroneous characters were caused by a similarity of character form or phonetic value, and thus only gave consideration to suspected word blocks where candidate words were similar in character form or phonetic value. In addition, some suspected word blocks are commonly encountered SSCSs and are not erroneous characters. Furthermore, in terms of syntactical structure, the sequence of parts of speech in some suspected word blocks sometimes makes more sense than candidate words' parts of speech within the structure of the entire sentence. Hence, the method proposed by this paper envisages four parameters: similarity of phonetic value, similarity of character form, frequency ratio, and probability ratio for parts of speech, to determine whether candidate words should be used in the correction of suspected word blocks. If a suspected word block has no candidate word within the parameters for deciding that it qualifies for correcting the word group, then it is determined that the suspected word block does not contain an erroneous character.

The first parameter is similarity of phonetic value, and the method proposed by this paper is to seek out pronunciations from all of the 37 phonetic notation symbols that are both similar and easily confused, and then to state in advance a defined degree of similarity, for example, the initial consonants "ㄅ" and "ㄆ," "ㄕ" and "ㄙ" and the vowels "ㄣ" and "ㄥ", etc. By separately calculating the difference between two characters' initial consonants, medials, vowels, and tones, it is possible to derive the degree of similarity of phonetic value between two characters. For example, the medials, vowels, and tones of the characters "讀" (to read) and "圖" (picture) are identical, but the degree of similarity of their initial consonants is 0.5; thus, the degree of phonetic similarity between the two characters is

$$(0.5+1.0+1.0+1.0)/4=0.875.$$

The second parameter is degree of similarity in terms of form. This paper proposes using the 439 basic Chinese script components and 11 types of structural relation put forward by Chen et al. (2011) and disassembling Chinese characters into a composite stroke structure. Taking the character "大" (big) as an example, its composite stroke structure is

[{一},{月 1}+(1:5@3),{[尺 /]}~(1:5@0)~(2:3@0)].

Subsequently, the LCS-based calculation algorithm put forward by Chang et al. (2014) is utilized to calculate the degree of similarity of form between the two characters.

If the suspected word block is indeed a correct serial single-character word combination and does not contain an erroneous character, then these words should have appeared together in the broad scale text corpus. On the other hand, if there is an erroneous character within the word block, then other single-character words should appear together very rarely between the erroneous character and word block in the broad scale text corpus. Thus, if it is assumed that the suspected word block frequency of co-occurrence is FS, and the corresponding candidate word's frequency of occurrence is FT, we can use the frequency ratio of the two FT/FS to assess whether the frequency of the suspected word block is sufficiently greater than the candidate word's frequency of occurrence. If so, then the suspected word block may not contain any erroneous characters. Hence, this ratio can act as a third parameter for determining the possibility of erroneous characters occurring.

Furthermore, after a sentence undergoes a process of tagging parts of speech, the parts of speech of each word will be tagged. Generally speaking, the most common method of tagging parts of speech is that of using such probability model as HMM to seek out the various possible parts of speech sequences with the highest probability within an entire sentence. When comparing a sentence containing an erroneous character with a corrected sentence, the latter should have a higher probability value. Since sentences containing an erroneous character and corrected sentences may differ in terms of the number of words, the probability values of the two must undergo standardization before they can be compared. If we suppose that, following the probability standardization of the original sentence's parts of speech tagging, its value is PS, and the sentence following the use of candidate word correction is PT, we can use the parts of speech sequence probability ratio of the two, PT/PS, to evaluate whether the original sentence's parts of speech sequence probability is sufficiently greater than the probability for the corrected sentence. If it is, then the original sentence may not contain an erroneous character. Hence, this ratio can act as a fourth parameter for determining the possibility of occurrence of an erroneous character.

Using the above four parameter values as regression coefficients for each sentence within training materials, this paper established a linear regression model to act as a prediction model to detect and correct erroneous characters occurring in long words. If an original sentence containing a suspected word block and a corresponding candidate word's corrected sentence undergoes predictive model calculation, and the predicted value exceeds the threshold value, then it is determined that the suspected word block should be corrected using the candidate word. If the same suspected word block's multiple candidates' prediction values all exceed the threshold value, then the word with the highest predicted value is used as the corrective word.

3.2 Correction of single-character erroneous words

Unlike erroneous characters in long words, two single-character words frequently stand as a correct word and erroneous word in relation to each other, and we term this a single-character word confusion set. Words in a single-character confusion set frequently must be examined in the context of the whole sentence or even the preceding and following sentences, before it is possible to determine whether an erroneous character has occurred. Hence, it is very difficult to use a partial statistical model to correct an erroneous character. Furthermore, single-character erroneous characters may occur in any word, but erroneous characters are particularly likely to appear in some words. Thus, in light of these characteristics, this paper has adopted a rules-based method to differentiate between six types of erroneous words common in single-character word confusion sets. The six confusion sets are respectively {的、地、得, *de*}, {再、在, *zai*}, {子、字, *zi*}, {阿、啊, *a*}, {者、著, *zhe*}, {座、坐, *zuo*}, and {他、她, *ta*}.

The establishment of rules is mainly based on knowledge of grammar. For example, the character "的" should be used between adjectives and nouns, as in for instance, "快樂的小孩" (happy child), while "地" should be used between adverbs and verbs, as in "飛快地奔跑" (run like lightning). Based on the characteristic usage of these single-character words, this paper has established rules for identification of syntax in these confusion sets. The generation of these rules was summarized as possibilities following manual observation of training materials, followed by the correctness of its rules, and the state of the exceptions was verified from an extensive text corpus, before the rules were further amended. This process was repeated until the correctness of the rules reached an acceptable level. This paper established a total of 33 rules of this kind.

In addition, with regard to confusion sets {"她" (she) and "他" (he)}, we employed semantic identification rules. The basic concept that gave rise to the rules was first to seek an object referred to by a pronoun, and then decide on the correct single-character word based on the object's gender. For example, in the text "媽媽工作很辛苦、但是他從來不抱怨" (Mother works very hard but he never complains), the character "他" (he) is the pronoun used for Mother, but because Mother is female it is determined that "她" (she) should be used in order for the usage to be correct. This paper listed manually the gender of every personal noun in the dictionary as the basis for corrections.

4 Experimental Results

This method employs test data released by the Chinese Spelling Check competition held by SIGHAN-8 as its basis for evaluation. The data set is made up of 1100 sentences, of which half are completely correct sentences, and the other half are incorrect sentences containing erroneous characters. In some of the incorrect sentences, there is more than one erroneous character. Evaluation items are divided into items for detection and correction, and each item uses Accuracy, Recall, Precision, and F1-measure to evaluate the method's effectiveness. In addition, False Positive Rate was used to calculate the proportion of correct sentences and misjudged incorrect sentences. Since the proportion of erroneous characters is not high in ordinary documents, a low false positive rate would not puzzle users. Table 1 shows the test results of this method.

	Accuracy	Precision	Recall	F1	False Positive Rate
Detection Level	0.5318	0.5745	0.2455	0.3439	0.1818
Correction Level	0.5145	0.537	0.2109	0.3029	

Table 1 Effectiveness evaluation of the method proposed in this paper

5 Discussion And Future Work

After analysis of the reasons for this method's misjudgments, it is possible to summarize three factors.

1) This method employs rules-based handling of erroneous single-character words and it is unable to detect non-rule based erroneous characters. However, for many erroneous single-character words, it is also very difficult to use only syntactic rules detection. For example, in the wrong sentence "我每天六天起床" (every day I get up at six days," the character "六天" (six days) should corrected by "六點" (six o'clock). In terms of syntax, the erroneous word does not cause a problem, and it is necessary to rely on semantic rules to handle this type of problem. However, given the results of the experiment, the formulation of semantic rules is far more difficult than that of syntactic rules.

2) Erroneous characters do not exist in an SSCS form, but rather have become constituent characters in another vocabulary. For example, in the sentence "我聽說這個禮拜六你要開一個誤會" (I hear that you will hold a misunderstanding on Saturday,) the two-character word "誤會" (misunderstanding) should be "舞會" (dance party). However, "舞會" and "誤會" are both vocabulary words and this method cannot handle such erroneous characters that are not in SSCS.

3) Serially-occurring erroneous characters. For example, in the sentence "可是福物生對我們很客氣" (but the *fuwusheng* [untranslateable] is very polite to us), the word "福物生" (*fuwusheng*) is an erroneous version of "服務生" (waiter). However, because this method's way of defining candidate words is based on an assumption that an erroneous character is paired with a correct character, it will not classify the word "服務" as a candidate word.

It follows that there will be two major directions for primary work to follow in the future. The first is aimed at further improving the limitations of the aforementioned three methods, and increasing the accuracy of identification. The second is exploring a single prediction model that can integrate different categories, long words, and single-character erroneous characters. Such a model would bring effective training and prediction even closer and be more stable in terms of its application.

Acknowledgements

This work is supported in part by the Ministry of Science and Technology, Taiwan, R.O.C. under the Grants MOST 103-2511-S-151-001. It is also partially supported by the "Aim for the Top University Project" and "Center of Learning Technology for Chinese" of National Taiwan Normal University (NTNU), sponsored by the Ministry of Education, Taiwan, R.O.C. and the "International Research-Intensive Center of Excellence Program" of NTNU and Ministry of Science and Technology, Taiwan, R.O.C. under Grant MOST 104-2911-I-003-301.

References

Chang, C. H. 1995. A new approach for automatic Chinese spelling correction. *Proceedings of Natural Language Processing Pacific Rim Symposium*, 95:278-283.

Chang, T. H., Chen, H. C., Tseng, Y. H., & Zheng, J. L. 2013. Automatic detection and correction for Chinese misspelled words using phonological and orthographic similarities. *Proceedings of the Seventh SIGHAN Workshop on Chinese Language Processing* (SIGHAN-7), 97-101.

Chen, H. C., Chang, L. Y., Chiou, Y. S., Sung, Y. T., & Chang, K. E. 2011. Construction of Chinese Orthographic Database for Chinese Character Instruction. *Bulletin of Educational Psychology,* 43:269-290.

Gu, L., Wang, Y., & Liang, X. 2014. Introduction to NJUPT Chinese Spelling Check Systems in CLP-2014 Bakeoff. *Proceedings of the 3rd CIPS-SIGHAN Joint Conference on Chinese Language Processing* (CLP-2014), 167-172.

Han, D., & Chang, B. 2013. A Maximum Entropy Approach to Chinese Spelling Check. *Proceedings of the Seventh SIGHAN Workshop on Chinese Language Processing* (SIGHAN-7), 74-78.

Wang, Y. R., & Liao, Y. F. 2014. NCTU and NTUT's Entry to CLP-2014 Chinese Spelling Check Evaluation. *Proceedings of the 3rd CIPS-SIGHAN Joint Conference on Chinese Language Processing* (CLP-2014), 216-219.

Xin, Y., Zhao, H., Wang, Y., & Jia, Z. 2014. An Improved Graph Model for Chinese Spell Checking. *Proceedings of the 3rd CIPS-SIGHAN Joint Conference on Chinese Language Processing* (CLP-2014), 157-166.

Xiong, J., Zhao, Q., Hou, J., Wang, Q., Wang, Y., & Cheng, X. (2014). Extended HMM and Ranking models for Chinese Spelling Correction. *In Proceedings of the 3rd CIPS-SIGHAN Joint Conference on Chinese Language Processing* (CLP-2014), 133-138.

Overview of Topic-based Chinese Message Polarity Classification in SIGHAN 2015

Xiangwen Liao
College of Mathematics and Computer Science, Fuzhou University, China
liaoxw@fzu.edu.cn

Binyang Li
School of Information Science and Technology, University of International Relations,
byli@uir.cn

Liheng Xu
National Laboratory of Pattern Recognition, Institute of Automation Chinese Academy of Sciences,
lhxu@nlpr.ia.ac.cn

Abstract

This paper presents the overview of Topic-based Chinese Message Polarity Classification in SIGHAN 2015 bake-off. Topic-based message polarity classification plays an important role in sentiment analysis, information extraction, event tracking, and other related research areas. This task is designed to evaluate the techniques for Chinese message polarity classification towards a given topic. The task organizers manually constructed 25 topics together with 24,374 corresponding messages which were annotated to construct the training and testing datasets. The evaluation results achieved by the participators provide good suggestion for the future research.

1 Introduction

Recently, with the popularity of social media, such as microblogs, weblogs, and discussion forums, interests in analyzing sentiment and mining opinions in user-generated contents has grown rapidly. There are much work focusing on the overall polarity identification of a sentence, paragraph, or the document (Wiebe et al., 2005; Hu and Liu, 2004; Pang et al., 2002), without the consideration of the message polarity classification towards a specific topic. To this end, SIGHAN 2015 proposes a Topic-based Chinese Message Polarity Classification (TCMPC) task, which targets on classifying the polarity to the given topic in Chinese messages.

The task of Topic-based Chinese Message Polarity Classification is motivated by the need of microblog search where users attempt to discover popular sentiments on a topic. Similar pilot task has been proposed in the Chinese Opinion Analysis Evaluation (COAE) since 2008 (Zhao et al., 2008; Xu et al., 2009), which aimed at the document level based on blog corpus. Generally speaking, the mainstream techniques for COAE 2008 followed the thoughts of information retrieval, and adopted two-step approaches that first retrieved the documents relevant to the query, i.e. topic, and then identify the polarity for those retrieved documents. (Xu et al., 2009)

Currently, as the social media become popular, much research turned towards on short texts, e.g. messages. The task of Topic-based Chinese Message Polarity Classification in SIGHAN 8 bake-off is designed on the basis of task of Sentiment Analysis in Twitter in SemEval 2015 workshop. (Rosenthal et al., 2015) In this task, the organizers provide a collection of messages corresponding to a given topic and restricted sentiment resources which contain partial list of sentiment words. Participants are required to classify the topical messages into positive, negative, or neutral. This task is similar to COAE 2008 and 2009, but it focuses on sentiment polarity classification in short texts.

In the remainder of this paper, we first describe the task of topic-based message polarity classification. We then describe the process of data collection and annotation. We list and briefly describe the participating systems, and the results in our evaluation. Finally, we conclude and review the evaluation for future research.

2 Task Description

Topic-Based Chinese Message Polarity Classification is motivated by the function of microblog search where users attempt to discover popular sentiments towards on a topic.

Proceedings of the Eighth SIGHAN Workshop on Chinese Language Processing (SIGHAN-8), pages 56–60,
Beijing, China, July 30-31, 2015.

Organizers collect messages from Chinese microblog platforms[1] according to the predefined topics. Example 1 gives the sample of a topic together with the messages.

<Topic> "iphone6" (TopicID 0) **</Topic>**
<M15113801> 苹果公司已经发布了新产品 iphone6。 **</M15113801>**
<M15113803> iphone6 运行速度快，还是不错的。**</M15113803>**
<M15113805> 但是，iphone6 好像太薄了，容易折断，另外摄像头怎么是凸出的啊？？ **</M15113805>**

Example 1: Sample of input.

The participants are required to classify whether the message is of positive, negative, or neutral sentiment towards the given topic. For messages expressing both a positive and negative sentiment towards the topic, whichever is the stronger sentiment should be chosen. The analysis results are defined in the following format: <*runID; topicID*; *evalID*; *mesID*; *Polarity*>.

- *runID* is the team name of each participant;
- *topicID* is the name of each topic;
- *evalID* denotes different runs for the team;
- *mesID* is message *ID*;
- *Polarity* can be predicted sentiment polarity of topic (1 for positive, -1 for negative and 0 for neutral).

The first run by *team 1* of sample 1 is expected to be returned as follows:

<1; 0; 1; *M15113801*; 0>
<1; 0; 1; *M15113803*; 1>
<1; 0; 1; *M15113805*; -1>

In this task, the participants are required to submit two kinds of results based on: (1) restricted resource for fair comparison, e.g. sentiment lexicon, corpus; and (2) unrestricted resource. We believe that a freely available, annotated corpus that can be used as a common testbed is needed in order to promote research that will lead to a better understanding of how opinions are expressed in microblogs.

3 Datasets

In this section, we will describe our data collection and annotation.

3.1 Data Collection

We first identify the popular topics that widely arouse people's comments and sentiments from the newspapers. For this purpose, we utilized conventional topic detection techniques for detecting hot topics over a three months spanning from January 2015 to March 2015. Then, we also did some manual selection for the topics. First, we excluded topics that were incomprehensible, ambiguous, or were too general. Second, we removed microblogs that were just mentioning the topic, but not really about the topic, e.g. advertisements.

Given the set of identified topics, we further crawled the microblogs from the Chinese microblog platforms during the same time period that involved the topics. There were 24,374 messages among 25 topics in total, and the topics of test data were different from training data. In practice, most of the collected microblogs were likely to concentrate in the neutral class. To avoid class imbalance, we removed messages without sentiment-bearing words using NTUSD[2] as the repository of sentiment words.

3.2 Annotation

Three annotators were trained to annotate the dataset independently. Given a collection of messages, the annotation task is to label each message as positive, negative, or neutral with respect to the given topic. To avoid conflict, we pruned the messages which were classified into three categories by different annotators.

The Kappa coefficient indicating agreement was 0.8832 for the positive/negative classification and was 0.7829 for fine-grained annotation, where the annotator should annotate the stronger sentiment when both positive and negative sentiments towards the topic. Some statistics of the annotation results are displayed in Table 1 and Table 2. 538 out of 4,905 messages are labeled as negative accounting for 10.97%, while 394 messages are labeled as positive accounting for 8.03% in the training set. 3639 out of 19,469 messages are labeled as negative accounting for 18.69%, while 1152 messages are labeled as positive accounting for 5.91% in the testing set.

Table 1: Training dataset statistics.

Topics	Neg.	Neu.	Pos.	Total
三星 S6	95	646	246	987
疯抢日本马桶	168	776	29	973
央行降息	42	848	94	984
油价	108	880	9	997
雾霾	125	823	16	964
Total	538	3973	394	4905

[1] http://weibo.com
[2] http://www.datatang.com/data/44317/

Table 2: Testing dataset statistics.

Topics	Neg.	Neu.	Pos.	Total
12306 验证码	614	330	47	991
也门撤侨	4	951	42	997
何以笙箫默	33	852	115	1000
刘翔退役	28	817	137	982
跨省买墓	226	690	1	917
天使的城	5	951	39	995
孙楠退赛	142	828	13	983
少年四大名捕	17	940	40	997
就业季	392	540	4	936
延迟退休	438	522	27	987
换头手术	245	640	84	969
日修改教科书	333	630	4	967
日现大量中国游客	387	544	41	972
沪指 4000 点	29	844	103	976
漳州 PX 项目	48	945	2	995
美图手机	28	773	191	992
陶华碧	37	684	193	914
隆平超级稻	44	949	5	998
香港反水客	564	352	7	923
黄冈辉煌不再	25	896	57	978
Total	3639	14678	1152	19469

4 Evaluation Metrics

In the evaluation, both the resource-restricted and resource-unrestricted runs were adopted the same metrics. The messages were categorized into three classes, i.e., to assign one of the following three labels: positive, negative or objective/neutral. We evaluated the systems in terms of precision, recall, and F1 score for predicting positive and negative messages, respectively, Then we used macro-averaged F1 score for system comparison in the evaluation.

$$precision = \frac{System.Correct}{System.Proposed} \quad (1)$$

$$recall = \frac{System.Correct}{Golden} \quad (2)$$

$$F - measure = \frac{2 \times precision \times recall}{precision + recall} \quad (3)$$

$$Macro - F = \frac{F^{+} + F^{-}}{2} \quad (4)$$

5 Evaluation

Table 3 summarizes the submission statistics for 13 participant teams. Among 17 registered teams, 13 teams submitted their testing results of the Topic-based Chinese Message Polarity Classification. For this task, each participant is required to submit two kinds of results based on: restricted resource and unrestricted resource. Finally, we received 12 results based on restricted resource and 12 results based on unrestricted resource as shown in Table 3.

Table 4 showed the testing results based on restricted resource of the TCMPC task, and Table 5 showed the testing results based on unrestricted resource of the TCMPC task. In addition to *precision*, *recall* and *F1*, there are other fine-grained performance criteria, i.e., *precision+* reflects the percentage of correct positive messages among the positive messages submitted by each team; and *recall-* reflects the percentage of correct negative messages submitted by each team among the negative messages in dataset.

For general evaluations, the team TICS-dm achieved promising results in both restricted and unrestricted resources. Their results were about 10% higher than the second ranked team. Team ZWK, NEUDM1 and NEUDM2 also achieved nearly 75% performances. In general, most of teams perform better on unrestricted resource than restricted resource.

For fine-grained evaluations, the team TICSdm performed even more outstanding than other teams, i.e., their positive results were about 30% higher than the second ranked team on unrestricted resource. The team HLT HITSZ also performed well, i.e., their positive results were about 10% higher than the third ranked team on unrestricted resource. Overall, each team performed better on negative messages than positive messages.

6 Conclusion

This paper provides an overview of SIGHAN 2015 Bake-off Task 2: Topic-Based Chinese Message Polarity Classification, including task design, data preparation, evaluation metrics, and performance evaluation results. The task requires each participant to submit two kinds of result based on restricted resource for fair comparison and unrestricted resource. Regardless of actual performance, all submissions contribute to the common effort to produce an effective Chinese message polarity classifier, and the individual report in the bake-off proceedings provide useful insight into Chinese language processing. We believe that a freely available, annotated corpus that can be used as a common testbed is needed in order to promote research that will lead to a better understanding of how sentiment is conveyed in microblogs. All datasets with gold standards are publicly available for research purposes.

Table 3: Submission statistics for all participants.

Participant (Ordered by name of institution)		Restricted	Unrestricted
Team Name	Institution		
LCYS TEAM	Beijing Institute of Technology	1	1
yhz	East China Normal University	1	0
MSIIP THU0	Multimedia Signal and Intelligent Information Processing Laboratory, Tsinghua University	1	1
NUSTM	Nanjing University of Science and Technology	1	1
CUCSas	National Broadcast Media Language Resources Monitoring & Research Center, Communication University of China	1	1
KUASISLAB	National Kaohsiung University of Applied Sciences	0	1
NEUDM1	Northeastern University, China	1	1
NEUDM2	Northeastern University, China	1	1
neu sighan	Northeastern University, China	1	1
SIGSDS SCAU	South China Agricultural University	1	1
HLT HITSZ	Shenzhen Graduate School, Harbin Institute of Technology	1	1
TICS-dm	Tecent Intelligent Computing and Search Lab	1	1
ZWK	University of Montreal	1	1
Total		12	12

Table 4: Testing results based on restricted resource of the TCMPC task.

	Restricted						
	Pre.+	**Rec.+**	**F1+**	**Pre.-**	**Rec.-**	**F1-**	**Macro-F**
LCYS TEAM	0.2615	0.0590	0.0963	0.4023	0.1041	0.1655	0.1309
yhz	0.0364	0.0017	0.0033	0.2593	0.0879	0.1313	0.0673
MSIIP THU0	0.0988	0.0946	0.0967	0.3320	0.3768	0.3530	0.2249
NUSTM	0.1368	0.4922	0.2141	0.4052	0.5040	0.4492	0.3317
CUCSas	0.1202	0.2613	0.1647	0.3345	0.2336	0.2751	0.2199
NEUDM1	0.1418	0.1710	0.1551	0.3689	0.3528	0.3607	0.2579
NEUDM2	0.3188	0.0825	0.1310	0.4446	0.0827	0.1395	0.1353
neu sighan	0.0921	0.2977	0.1407	0.2700	0.1234	0.1694	0.1551
SIGSDS SCAU	0.1631	0.2813	0.2065	0.3607	0.3174	0.3377	0.2721
HLT HITSZ	0.2154	0.4045	0.2811	0.4584	0.6048	0.5216	0.4014
TICS-dm	0.6258	0.5139	0.5643	0.8232	0.4672	0.5961	**0.5802**
ZWK	0.2335	0.0920	0.1320	0.3047	0.1852	0.2304	0.1812

Table 5: Testing results based on unrestricted resource of the TCMPC task.

	Unrestricted						
	Pre.+	**Rec.+**	**F1+**	**Pre.-**	**Rec.-**	**F1-**	**Macro-F**
LCYS TEAM	0.1415	0.1128	0.1255	0.3635	0.1979	0.2562	0.1909
MSIIP THU0	0.1212	0.1788	0.1445	0.3412	0.3954	0.3663	0.2554
NUSTM	0.1767	0.5104	0.2626	0.4829	0.5191	0.5003	0.3815
CUCSas	0.1840	0.3602	0.2435	0.5011	0.3877	0.4372	0.3404
KUASISLAB	0.0886	0.0764	0.0821	0.2944	0.4089	0.3423	0.2122
NEUDM1	0.2696	0.1163	0.1625	0.4664	0.3333	0.3888	0.2757
NEUDM2	0.1763	0.0451	0.0719	0.4079	0.0566	0.0994	0.0857
neu sighan	0.0476	0.0564	0.0516	0.3296	0.3056	0.3171	0.1844
SIGSDS SCAU	0.1626	0.2899	0.2084	0.3784	0.3237	0.3489	0.2787
HLT HITSZ	0.2414	0.4167	0.3057	0.5159	0.5485	0.5317	0.4187
TICS-dm	0.5880	0.6207	0.6039	0.7918	0.6175	0.6938	**0.6489**
ZWK	0.1983	0.0200	0.0363	0.4072	0.0525	0.0930	0.0647

Acknowledgements

This work is partially supported by the National Natural Science Foundation of China (No. 61300105), the Research Fund for Doctoral Program of Higher Education of China (No. 2012351410010), Fundamental Research Funds for the Central Universities (3262014T75, 3262015T20), the Key Project of Science and Technology of Fujian (No. 2013H6012), Shenzhen Fundamental Research Program (JCYJ20130401172046450) and the Project of Science and Technology of Fuzhou (No. 2012-G-113, 2013-PT-45). Special thanks to Hongfei Lin for providing the Chnese sentiment resources. We also thank Chen Chang, Yang Dingda, Ma Feixiang, Zhang liyao, Chen Xingjun for their annotation.

Reference

Minqing Hu and Bing Liu. 2004. Mining and summarizing customer reviews. In Proceedings of the 10th ACM SIGKDD International Conference on Knowledge Discovery and Data Mining, KDD '04, pages 168-177, New York, NY, USA.

Bo Pang, Lillian Lee, and Shivakumar Vaithyanathan. 2002. Thumbs up?: Sentiment classification using machine learning techniques. In Proceedings of the Conference on Empirical Methods in Natural Language Processing - Volume 10, EMNLP '02, pages 79-86, Philadephia, Pennsylvania, USA.

Sara Rosenthal, Preslav, Nakov, Svetlana Kiritchenko, Sif M Mohammad, Alan Ritter, Veselin Stoyanov. 2015. In Proceedings of the Seventh International Workshop on Semantic Evaluation, SemEval 2015.

Janyce Wiebe, Theresa Wilson, and Claire Cardie. 2005. Annotating expressions of opinions and emotions in language. Language Resources and Evaluation, 39(2- 3):165-210.

Hongbo Xu, Tianfang Yao, Xuanjing Huang, Huifeng Tang, Feng Guan, and Jin Zhang. 2009. Overview of Chinese Opinion Analysis Evaluation 2009. In Proceedings of the Second Chinese Opinion Analysis Evaluation.

Jun Zhao, Hongbo Xu, Xuanjing Huang, Songbo Tan, Kang Liu, and Qi Zhang. 2008. Overview of Chinese Opinion Analysis Evaluation 2008. In Proceedings of the First Chinese Opinion Analysis Evaluation.

A Joint Model for Chinese Microblog Sentiment Analysis

Yuhui Cao, Zhao Chen, Ruifeng Xu*, **Tao Chen and Lin Gui**
Shenzhen Engineering Laboratory of Performance Robots at Digital Stage,
Harbin Institute of Technology Shenzhen Graduate School, Shenzhen, China
caoyuhuiszu@gmail.com xuruifeng@hitsz.edu.cn

Abstract

Topic-based sentiment analysis for Chinese microblog aims to identify the user attitude on specified topics. In this paper, we propose a joint model by incorporating Support Vector Machines (SVM) and deep neural network to improve the performance of sentiment analysis. Firstly, a SVM Classifier is constructed using N-gram, N-POS and sentiment lexicons features. Meanwhile, a convolutional neural network is applied to learn paragraph representation features as the input of another SVM classifier. The classification results outputted by these two classifiers are merged as the final classification results. The evaluations on the SIGHAN-8 Topic-based Chinese microblog sentiment analysis task show that our proposed approach achieves the second rank on micro average F1 and the fourth rank on macro average F1 among a total of 13 submitted systems.

1 Introduction

With the development of the Internet, microblog has become a popular user-generated content platform where users share the newest events or their personal feelings with each other. Topic-based microblogs are the most common interactive way for users to share their opinions towards a specified topic. To identify the opinions of users, sentiment analysis techniques are investigated to classify texts into different categorizations according to their sentiment polarities.

Most existing sentiment classification techniques are based on machine learning algorithms, such as Support Vector Machine, Naïve Bayes and Maximum Entropy. The machine learning based approach uses feature vectors as the input of classification to predict the classification results. Thus, feature engineering, a method for extracting effective features from texts, plays an important role. Some commonly used features in sentiment classification are unigram, bigram and sentiment words. However, these features cannot work well for cross-domain sentiment classification because of the lack of domain knowledge.

Danushka Bollegala et al. (2011) used multiple sources to construct a sentiment sensitive thesaurus to overcome the lack of domain knowledge. New sentiment words expansion is another kind of approach to improve the performance of sentiment analysis. Strfano Baccianella et al. (2010) constructed SentiWordNet by extending WordNet with sentiment information. It is now widely used in sentiment classification for English. As for Chinese sentiment analysis, Minlie Huang et al. (2014) proposed a new word detection method by mining the frequent sentiment word patterns. This method may discover new sentiment words from a large scale of unlabeled texts.

With the rapid development of pre-trained word embedding and deep neural networks, a new way to represent texts and features is devloped. Mikolov et al. (2013) showed that word embedding represents words with meaningful syntactic and semantic information effectively. Recursive neural network proposed by Socher et al. (2011a; 2011b; 2013) is shown efficient to construct sentence representations based on the word embedding. Convolutional neural networks (CNN), another deep learn model which achieved success in image recognition field, was applied to nature language processing with word embed-

Proceedings of the Eighth SIGHAN Workshop on Chinese Language Processing (SIGHAN-8), pages 61–67,
Beijing, China, July 30-31, 2015.

dings. Yoon Kim (2014) used CNN with pre-trained word embedding to achieve state-of-the-art performances on some sentence classification tasks, including sentiment classification. Siwei Lai et al. (2015) incorporated global information in a recurrent convolutional neural network. It obtained further improvements comparing to other deep learning models.

In this paper, we propose a joint model which incorporates traditional machine learning based method (SVM) and deep learning model. Two different classifiers are developed. One is a word feature based SVM classifier which uses word unigram, bigram and sentiment words as features. Another one is a CNN-based SVM classifier which takes paragraph representations features learned by CNN as input features. The classification results of these two classifiers are integrated to generate the final classification results. The evaluations on the SIGHAN-8 Topic-based Chinese microblog sentiment analysis task show that our proposed approach achieves the second rank on micro average F1 and the fourth rank on macro average F1 among a total of 13 submitted systems. Furthermore, the joint classifier strategy brings further performance improvement on individual classifiers.

The rest of this paper is organized as follows. Section 2 presents the design and implementation of our proposed joint model. Section 3 gives the evaluation results and discussions. Finally, Section 4 gives the conclusion and future research directions.

2 Our Approach

The SIGHAN8 topic-based Chinese polarity classification task aims to is to classify Chinese microblog into three topic-related sentiment classes, namely neutral, positive and negative. This task may be generally regarded as a three-category classification problem. The SVM classifier which has been shown effective to document classification is adopted as the core classifier. Here, two different feature representation models, namely word-based vector space model and CNN-based composition representation, are adopted to generate the classification features for two classifiers, respectively. The classification outputs of two classifiers are integrated to generate the final output.

2.1 Data preprocessing

Chinese microblog text is obviously different from formal text. Many microblogs have noises, including nickname, hashtag, repost or reply symbols, and URL. Therefore, before the feature representation and extraction, preprocessing is performed to filter out noise text in the microblogs. Meanwhile, the advertising text and topic-irrelevant microblog are identified as neutral text. Especially, this task is designed to identify the topic-relevant sentiments. Therefore, the information coming from the reply, repost and sharing parts should be filtered out to avoid their influences to the sentiment analysis of the microblog author. Generally speaking, such filtering is based on rules. The table 1 shows the example data preprocessing rules with illustrations.

Table 2 shows the rules for identifying the advertisement and topic-irrelevant microblogs. The identified microblogs are labeled as neutral for topic-based sentiment classification.

2.2 Word feature based classifier

The word feature based classifier is designed based on the vector model. Firstly, the new sentiment words from unlabeled sentences data are recognized to expand the sentiment lexicon. The classification features are extracted from the labeled training data and sentiment lexicon resources. In order to alleviate the influences of unbalanced training data, SMOTE, which is an oversampling algorithm, is applied to training data before classifier training. Finally, a SVM classifier is trained on the balanced data. The framework of word feature based classifier is shown in Figure 1.

2.2.1 Feature selection

Unigram, Bigram, Uni-Part-of-Speech and Bi-Part-of-Speech features are selected as the basic features. CHI-test based feature selection is applied to obtain the top 20000 features. To improve the performance of sentiment classification, additional features based on lexicons including sentiment word lexicons, negation word lexicons, and adverb word lexicons, are incorporated.

Rules	Raw Text	Processed Text
Sharing news with personal comments	好看？吗？//【Galaxy S6：三星证明自己能做出好看的手机】http://t.cn/RwHRsIb(分享自 @ 今日头条)	好看？吗？
Removing HashTag	# 三星 Galaxy S6# 三星 GALAXY S6，挺中意 [酷][酷] [位置] 芒砀路	三星 GALAXY S6，挺中意 [酷][酷]
Removing URL	699 欧元起传三星 Galaxy S6/S6 Edge 售价获证实（分享自 @ 新浪科技）http://t.cn/RwTo3on	699 欧元起传三星 Galaxy S6/S6 Edge 售价获证实（分享自 @ 新浪科技）
Removing nickname	玻璃取代塑料，更美 Galaxy S6 的 5 大妥协 http://t.cn/RwHY6Az 罗永浩我去小米和三星这是要闹哪样，，，老罗。。不能忍啊，，，，，@ 锤子科技营销帐号 @ 罗永浩	http://t.cn/RwHY6Az 罗永浩我去小米和三星这是要闹哪样，，，老罗。。不能忍啊，，，，，
Removing information sources	【视频：三星 S6 对比苹果 iPhone6 MWC2015 @youtube 科技 】http://t.cn/RwHQzJ8（来自于优酷安卓客户端）	【视频：三星 S6 对比苹果 iPhone6 MWC2015 @youtube 科技 】http://t.cn/RwHQzJ8

Table 1: Data preprocessing rules with illustrations.

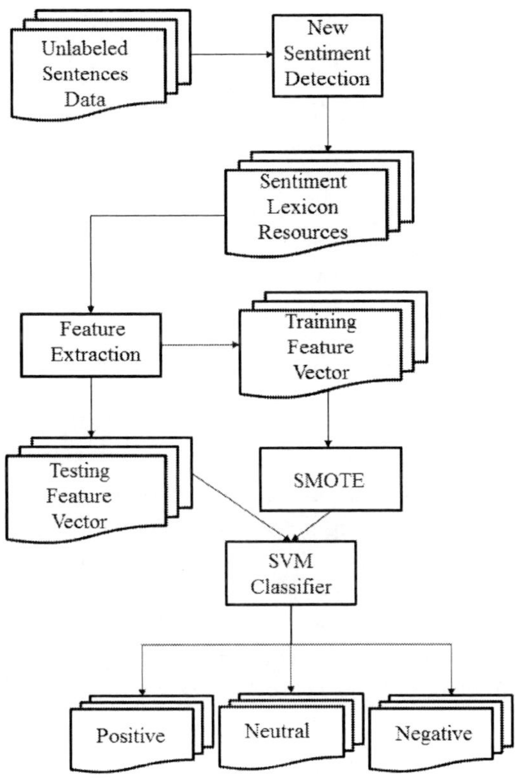

Figure 1: Framework of word feature based classifier

Rules	Type
Including many different topic ("#...#") tag.	Advertisement
Including many words like "微商", "商机", "想赚钱", "面膜".	Advertisement
No actual content	Topic-irrelevant

Table 2: Microblog text matching rules.

By analyzing the expressions of the microblog text in training data, some special expression features in microblog text are identified. For example, the continuous punctuations are always used to express a strong feeling and thus, the microblog with continuous punctuations tends to be subjective. Another adopted feature for microblog text is the use of emoticons.

2.2.2 Sentiment lexicon expansion

In microblogs, abundant new or informal sentiment words are widely used. Normally, these new sentiment words are short but meaningful for expressing a strong feeling. These new sentiment words play an important role in Chinese microblog sentiment classification. Therefore, sentiment word identification is performed to recognize new sentiment words as the supplement of sentiment lexicon.

Twenty million microblog text collected from Sina Weibo Platform are used in new sentiment word detection. Considering that new words normally cannot be correctly segmented by the existing segmentor, identifying new words from preliminary segmentation results together with their POS tags is a feasible method. Here, potential components for new words are limited to the segmentation tokens shorter than three. Using word frequency, mutual information and context entropy as the evaluation indicators for words, the most possible new word candidates are obtained. With the help of word embedding construction model, each word in the corpus can be represented as a low dimension vector together with its context information. Hence, the distances between the new words and the existed sentiment words corresponding to difference sentiment polarity are estimated. The new words are then classified into one of the three polarity classes by following voting mechanism.

2.2.3 Classification

Two steps are performed to determine the topic-relevant sentiment for input microblogs. The first step is to distinguish topic relevant messages from topic irrelevant messages. Sentiment classification is then applied to topic relevant messages in the second step.

Topic relevant words generated by clustering analysis are employed as distinguishable features to filter out topic irrelevant microblogs because normally the topic irrelevant microblogs have few intersections with topic relevant words. Some advertisement posts consisting of several hot topic hash tags are also filtered out by considering the number of hash tag types in the microblog.

The provided labeled dataset is used to train the SVM classifier with linear kernel. A new challenge is that the provided training set is imbalanced. There are about 3973 neutral microblogs, while the numbers of positive and negative microblogs are 394 and 538, respectively. In order to reduce the influences of imbalanced training dataset, the SMOTE algorithm (Chawla et al., 2002) is applied to oversampling the samples on minority class. Oversampling ratio is set to 10 and 7.4 for positive class and negative class, respectively. In this way, the training dataset becomes balanced.

2.3 CNN-based SVM classifier

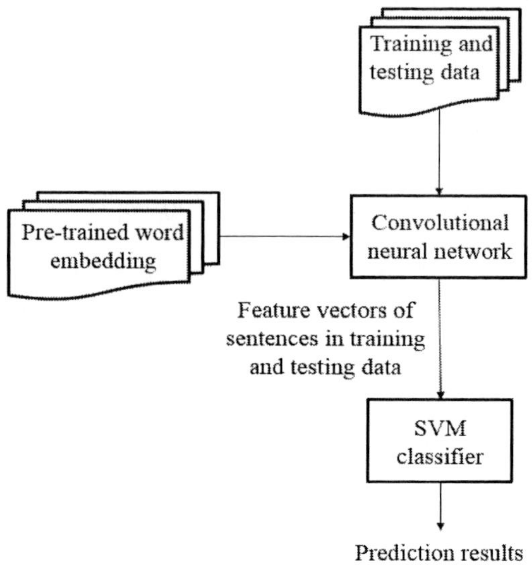

Figure 2: CNN and SVM joint classifier.

Another classifier is CNN-based SVM classifier. The classifier framework is shown in Figure 2. Firstly, continuous bog of word (CBOW) model (Mikolov et al., 2013) is used to learn word embeddings from Chinese microblog text. A deep convolutional neural networks (CNN) model is applied to learn distributed paragraph representation features for Chinese microblog training and testing data. Finally, the distributed paragraph representation features are used in SVM classifier to learn the probability distribution over sentiment labels.

2.3.1 Word embedding construction

Word embedding, wherein words are projected from a sparse, 1-of-V encoding (here V is the vocabulary size) onto a lower dimensional vector space via a hidden layer, are essentially feature extractors that encode semantic features of words in their dimensions. Mikolov et al. (2013) introduced CBOW model to learn vector representations which captures a large number of syntactic and semantic word relationships from unstructured text data. The main idea of this model is to find word representations which use the surrounding words in a sentence or a document to predict current word.

In this study, we train the CBOW model by using 16GB Chinese microblog text. Finally, we obtain 200-dimension word embeddings for Chinese microblog text.

2.3.2 CNN-based SVM classifier

In the CNN-based SVM classifier, the input is a matrix which is composed of the word embeddings of microblogs. There are windows with the lengths of three, four and five words, respectively. A convolution operation involves three filters which are applied to these windows to produce new features. After convolution operation, a max-over-time pooling operation is applied over these features. The maximum value is taken as the feature corresponding to this particular filter. The idea is to capture the most important feature which has the largest value. Since one feature is extracted from one filter, the model uses multiple filters (with varying window sizes) to obtain multiple features. These features constitute the distributed paragraph feature representation. In the last step, a SVM classifier is applied on these distributed paragraph representation features to obtain the probability distributions over labels (positive, negative, and neutral).

2.4 Outputs Merging

Classifier 1	Classifier 2	Final result
positive	neutral	neutral
negative	neutral	neutral
neutral	positive	neutral
neutral	negative	neutral
positive	negative	negative
negative	positive	positive

Table 3: Merging rules for two classifiers.

A set of merging rules is designed to incorporate the individual classification results of the two classifiers for generating the final result. If the two classification outputs are the same, naturally, the final output is the same. If the two classification outputs are different, the final result is determined from the merge rules shown in Table 3. Simply speaking, if any of two classifiers output neutral category, the final output is neutral. If two classifiers outputs positive and negative, respectively, the final output is the result of CNN-based classifier. Such a classification outputs merging strategy is based on the statistical analysis on the individual classifier performances on training dataset.

3 Experimental results and analysis

3.1 Data set

In the SIGHAN-8 Chinese sentiment analysis bakeoff dataset, 4905 topic-based Chinese microblog are provided as training data which consists of 394 positive, 538 negative and 3973 neutral microblogs corresponding to 5 topics, namely “央行降息”, “油价”, “日本马桶”, “三星 S6” and “雾霾”. In the testing data, there are 19,469 microblogs corresponding to 20 topic, such as “12306 验证码”, “中国政府也门撤侨”, “何以笙箫默”, “刘翔退役”.

3.2 Metrics

Precision, recall and F1-value are used as the evaluation metrics, as shown below:

$$Precision = \frac{SystemCorrect}{SystemOutput} \quad (1)$$

$$Recall = \frac{SystemCorrect}{HumanLabeled} \quad (2)$$

$$F1 = \frac{2 \times Precision \times Recall}{Precision + Recall} \quad (3)$$

Where $System.Output$ refers to the total number of the submitted results, $System.Correct$ refers to the number of correctly classified results in the submitted results, $Human.Labeled$ refers to the total number of manually labeled results in the Gold Standard.

The evaluation metrics corresponding to positive, negative and overall are estimated, respectively. The corresponding micro-average and macro-average performances are then estimated. The micro-average estimates the average performance of the three evaluation metrics over the entire dataset. The macro-average estimates the average performances of the evaluation metrics on positive, negative and neutral, respectively.

3.3 Experimental results and analysis

There are two subtasks in SIGHAN-8 topic-based Chinese microblog polarity classification

	All			Positive			Negative		
Team Name	Precision	Recall	F1	Precision	Recall	F1	Precision	Recall	F1
TICS-dm	0.83	0.83	0.83	0.62	0.51	0.56	0.82	0.46	0.59
NEUDM2	0.74	0.74	0.74	0.31	0.08	0.13	0.44	0.08	0.13
LCYS_TEAM	0.72	0.64	0.68	0.26	0.05	0.09	0.40	0.10	0.16
HLT_HITSZ	0.68	0.68	0.68	0.21	0.40	0.28	0.45	0.60	0.52

Table 4: Performances in restricted resource subtask.

	All			Positive			Negative		
Team Name	Precision	Recall	F1	Precision	Recall	F1	Precision	Recall	F1
TICS-dm	0.85	0.85	0.85	0.58	0.62	0.60	0.79	0.61	0.69
xk0	0.74	0.74	0.74	0.19	0.01	0.03	0.40	0.05	0.09
NEUDM1	0.74	0.74	0.74	0.26	0.11	0.16	0.46	0.33	0.38
HLT_HITSZ	0.71	0.71	0.71	0.24	0.41	0.30	0.51	0.54	0.53

Table 5: Performances in unrestricted resource subtask.

	All			Positive			Negative		
Approach	Precision	Recall	F1	Precision	Recall	F1	Precision	Recall	F1
Classifier 1	0.67	0.67	0.67	0.20	0.42	0.27	0.44	0.49	0.46
Classifier 2	0.60	0.60	0.60	0.18	0.61	0.28	0.42	0.67	0.52
Merging	0.71	0.71	0.71	0.24	0.41	0.30	0.51	0.54	0.53

Table 6: Performances by different classifiers in unrestricted resource subtask.

task: restricted resource and unrestricted resource subtasks.

Table 4 gives the performances in restricted resource subtask. The first column lists the name of participants who achieves higher macro average F1 values while out system is named as HLT_HITSZ. It is observed that our proposed approach achieves better performance on negative and positive categories, but obviously lower performance on neutral category. The good performance on the recall of minority classes showed the effectiveness of our consideration on imbalanced dataset training.

The achieved performances in the unrestricted resource subtask are listed in Table 5. Our system achieves about 3% of performance improvement on each category, respectively. It shows the contributions of extra training corpus and merging rules.

In order to validate the effectiveness of merging rules, the performances of Classifier 1 and Classifier 2 are evaluated, individually. The achieved performances are given in Table 6. It is observed that generally speaking, Classifier 1 achieves a higher classification precision because many features are coming from manually compiled sentiment-related lexicons. However, these features are limited to training data so that Classifier 1 achieved a lower recall. On the contrary, Classifier 2 may learn the representation features automatically from training data which is better for generalization. Thus, a good recall is achieved. Meanwhile, the achieved performances show that our joint model obtains better performances compared to two individual classifiers which indicate the effectiveness of our proposed joint classification strategy.

4 Conclusion

In this work, we propose a joint model for sentiment topic analysis on Chinese microblog messages. A word feature based SVM classifier and a SVM classifier using CNN-based paragraph representation features are developed, respectively. To overcome the limitation of each classifier, their classification outputs are merged to generate the final output while the merging rules are based on statistical analysis on the performances on training dataset. Experimental results show that our proposed joint method achieves better sentiment classification performance over individual classifiers which show the effectiveness of the joint classifier strategy. In future, we intend to study the way to distinguish the subjective messages from objective messages for further improving the sentiment classification performance.

Acknowledgements

This work is supported by the National Natural Science Foundation of China (No.61370165,61203378), National 863 Program of China 2015AA015405, the Natural Science Foundation of Guangdong Province (No.S2013010014475), Shenzhen Development and Reform Commission Grant No.[2014]1507, Shenzhen Peacock Plan Research Grant KQCX20140521144507925 and Baidu Collaborate Research Funding.

References

Stefano Baccianella, Andrea Esuli, and Fabrizio Sebastiani. 2010. Sentiwordnet 3.0: An enhanced lexical resource for sentiment analysis and opinion mining. In *Proceedings of the International Conference on Language Resources and Evaluation (LREC)*.

Danushka Bollegala, David Weir, and John Carroll. 2011. Using multiple sources to construct a sentiment sensitive thesaurus for cross-domain sentiment classification. In *Proceedings of the 49th Annual Meeting of the Association for Computational Linguistics (ACL)*, pages 132–141. Association for Computational Linguistics.

Nitesh V. Chawla, Kevin W. Bowyer, Lawrence O. Hall, and W. Philip Kegelmeyer. 2002. Smote: synthetic minority over-sampling technique. *Journal of Artificial Intelligence Research*, 16:321–357.

Minlie Huang, Borui Ye, Yichen Wang, Haiqiang Chen, Junjun Cheng, and Xiaoyan Zhu. 2014. New word detection for sentiment analysis. In *Proceedings of the 52nd Annual Meeting of the Association for Computational Linguistics (ACL)*, pages 531–541, Baltimore, Maryland, June. Association for Computational Linguistics.

Yoon Kim. 2014. Convolutional neural networks for sentence classification. In *Proceedings of the 2014 Conference on Empirical Methods in Natural Language Processing (EMNLP)*, pages 1746–1751, October.

Siwei Lai, Liheng Xu, Kang Liu, and Jun Zhao. 2015. Recurrent convolutional neural networks for text classification. In *Proceedings of the Twenty-Ninth AAAI Conference on Artificial Intelligence, January 25-30, 2015, Austin, Texas, USA.*, pages 2267–2273.

Tomas Mikolov, Kai Chen, Greg Corrado, and Jeffrey Dean. 2013. Efficient estimation of word representations in vector space. In *Proceedings of Workshop at the International Conference on Learning Representations (ICLR)*.

Richard Socher, Eric H. Huang, Jeffrey Pennington, Andrew Y. Ng, and Christopher D. Manning. 2011a. Dynamic pooling and unfolding recursive autoencoders for paraphrase detection. In *Advances in Neural Information Processing Systems 24: 25th Annual Conference on Neural Information Processing Systems (NIPS)*, pages 801–809.

Richard Socher, Jeffrey Pennington, Eric H Huang, Andrew Y Ng, and Christopher D Manning. 2011b. Semi-supervised recursive autoencoders for predicting sentiment distributions. In *Proceedings of the Conference on Empirical Methods in Natural Language Processing (EMNLP)*, pages 151–161. Association for Computational Linguistics.

Richard Socher, Alex Perelygin, Jean Y Wu, Jason Chuang, Christopher D Manning, Andrew Y Ng, and Christopher Potts. 2013. Recursive deep models for semantic compositionality over a sentiment treebank. In *Proceedings of the Conference on Empirical Methods in Natural Language Processing (EMNLP)*, pages 1631–1642. Association for Computational Linguistics.

Learning Salient Samples and Distributed Representations for Topic-Based Chinese Message Polarity Classification

Xin Kang[1,2]* **Yunong Wu**[3]* **Zhifei Zhang**[4]*
[1]Department of Electronics and Information, Tongji University
[2]Faculty of Engineering, Tokushima University
[3]Department of Research and Development, Business Big Data Co., Ltd.
[4]Department of Computer Science and Operations Research, University of Montreal
[1]xkang@tongji.edu.cn, [2]kang-xin@tokushima-u.ac.jp
[3]wuyunong@brandbigdata.com, [4]zhanzhif@iro.umontreal.ca

Abstract

We describe our participation in the Topic-Based Chinese Message Polarity Classification Task, based on the restricted and unrestricted resources respectively. In the restricted resource based classification, we focus on the selection of parameters in a multi-class classification model with highly-biased training data. In the unrestricted resource based classification, we explore the distributed representation of Chinese words through unsupervised feature learning and the annotation of salient samples through active learning, with a raw corpus of over 90 million messages extracted from Chinese Weibo Platform. For two classification subtasks, our submitted results ranked the 4th and the 2nd respectively.

1 Introduction

The ZWK team participates in the Topic-Based Chinese Message Polarity Classification Task, the purpose of which is to predict the message polarities in the Positive, Negative, and Neutral classes towards particular topics. Learning classification models on the training corpus with bag-of-words features is very challenging, given the fact that the class labels are highly-biased in the corpus and that the number of training samples is an order of magnitude lower than the number of observed word features. Therefore, our work focuses on the active learning and unsupervised feature learning algorithms, to avoid over-fitting the parameters of a linear classification model. To predict polarities with respect to specific topics, we re-evaluate the features with respect to their distances to topical words in a message.

Because the class labels are highly-biased in the training corpus, most of which are Neutral, we explore an active learning algorithm to incrementally obtain the knowledge of different polarities from a large raw corpus. In the iterative procedure of active learning, salient samples are firstly selected from a large raw corpus, based on the amount of information in their polarity predictions, their representativeness within the raw corpus, and their distinctiveness in the selection. The selection procedure ensures that samples of the minor classes are more probably selected than samples of the major class(es) and that the extension of training data with these samples has the most potential to improve the current classification model. Then, class labels are annotated to the salient samples by querying oracles, and all labeled samples are appended to the training corpus to update the classification model before the next iteration in active learning. We select and append the salient samples in a batch-mode, to efficiently re-balance the training corpus and incrementally improve the polarity classification model.

And because the number of training messages (around 5K) turns much smaller than the number of unique words (17.5K), a linear classification model can be easily over-fitted with bag-of-word features. To avoid over-fitting, we project the 17.5K-dimensional word space to a 200-dimensional vector space through an unsupervised feature learning. We employ word2vec (Mikolov et al., 2013a; Mikolov et al., 2013b; Mikolov et al., 2013c) as the unsupervised feature learning algorithm, based on a raw corpus of over 90 million messages extracted from Chinese Weibo Platform. One of the most significant advantage of learning with word2vec is that the vector representations are additively composable, which means we can represent the semantic composition of multiple words by adding the respective vector representations. For the topic-based polarity classifica-

*These authors contributed equally to this work.

Proceedings of the Eighth SIGHAN Workshop on Chinese Language Processing (SIGHAN-8), pages 68–73,
Beijing, China, July 30-31, 2015. ©2015 Association for Computational Linguistics and Asian Federation of Natural Language Processing

tion problem, we only compose words around the specific topics as features, with an exponentially decreasing weight along the word sequence.

The rest of this paper is arranged as follows: section 2 reviews the related work of polarity classification, section 3 describes our active learning algorithm for retrieving salient samples, section 4 illustrates the unsupervised learning algorithm for reducing feature dimensions, section 5 shows our experiment results on polarity classification and discusses the over-fitting problem, and section 6 concludes our work.

2 Related Work

Polarity classification has been a popular field in natural language processing. In polarity classification, the main difficulty is to find effective language features for distinguishing positive, negative, and neutral sentiments (Kiritchenko et al., 2014). Because overwhelming ambiguities exist in word polarity expressions, polarity prediction results based on lexicons (Taboada et al., 2011) could be unreliable.

To incorporate such ambiguity in sentiment modeling, a few studies resort to the hierarchical Bayesian models, in which the ambiguity of sentiments in words has been transformed into the joint probability of words, word clusters (topics), and sentiments (Ren and Kang, 2013; Wu et al., 2014; Rao et al., 2014). Another solution of resolving such ambiguity in sentiment classification is to directly represent words in sentimental vectors (Maas et al., 2011; Socher et al., 2013; Tang et al., 2014; Kalchbrenner et al., 2014; Kim, 2014). Compared to the Bayesian models, vectorized representation relates the semantic information directly to each entry of the word vector, and the results can be easily transformed in a simple classifier. We employ an unsupervised algorithm word2vec (Mikolov et al., 2013a; Mikolov et al., 2013b; Mikolov et al., 2013c) to learn such vectorized word representation from a large raw corpus.

In most of these sentiment classification researches, the class labels are not as skewed as the polarity labels in this task. To rebalance the training data, we develop an novel active learning (Settles, 2010) algorithm which automatically selects the salient samples from a large raw corpus and costs the minimum labor for annotation. TwitterHawk (Boag et al., 2015) notably places 1st in topic-based sentiment classification subtask of the SemEval-2015 shared task on Sentiment Analysis in Twitter, which uses many hand-crafted features and a classic classifier. The overall solution of our work is basically consist with it.

3 Active Learning of Salient Samples

Active learning (Settles, 2010) is a subfield of machine learning. An active learning algorithm will automatically select salient samples from the unlabeled data set, and will incrementally improve machine learning by obtaining knowledge from these samples and merge them to the training data.

In the polarity classification problem, we developed an active learning algorithm for obtaining the knowledge of different polarities from a large raw corpus of over 90 million messages. The algorithm begins with a restricted corpus L, in which the polarity labels are highly-biased i.e., 394 positive labels, 538 negative labels, and 3,973 neutral labels. By iterating through three sample selection steps, the algorithm incrementally adds salient messages to L after querying labels from oracles, and generates a less-biased corpus finally with 1,003 positive labels, 1,060 negative labels, and 4,242 neutral labels.

Before the first step of sample selection, a multi-label Logistic Regression classifier is trained on L, and a batch of 1,000,000 messages is extracted from the raw corpus as an unlabeled pool U. We get probabilistic prediction y for each message x in U, and evaluate the amount of information in its probabilistic prediction by entropy

$$E(x) = -\sum_{y} p(y|x) \log p(y|x). \quad (1)$$

The largest entropy $E(x)$ is approached by those x with the most evenly distributed predictions in y. Because the classifier is trained on a biased corpus, its prediction would favor the major label of neutral. Therefore, the true labels for messages in U with larger entropies are more probably positive and negative than neutral, since a truly neutral x will get odd probabilistic predictions and locates far from the large entropies. Our algorithm selects the top 10,000 messages for S_1 as the first step.

For the second step, the algorithm calculates Euclidean distances between every pair of messages x_i and x_j in S_1 by

$$d(x_i, x_j) = \sqrt{x_i \cdot x_i - 2x_i \cdot x_j + x_j \cdot x_j}, \quad (2)$$

where $\cdot$ is the dot product of two message vectors. We evaluate the representativeness of a message x

by its average distance between all other messages in S_1 as

$$R(x) = \frac{1}{|S_1| - 1} \sum_{x_i \in S_1} d(x, x_i), \quad (3)$$

and select the smallest 1,000 messages for S_2. This is because a representative x must be surrounded by many similar x_i's in the Euclidean space, and $R(x)$ is usually smaller than $R(x')$ for x' in a very sparse region[1]. We select the representative messages for S_2 because they are potentially more general samples.

In the third step, the algorithm iteratively select the most distinctive messages from S_2 and move them to an empty set S_3. For x in S_2, its distinctiveness is evaluated by the minimum Euclidean distance between x and every x_i in $L \cup S_3$

$$D(x) = \min_{x_i \in L \cup S_3} d(x, x_i). \quad (4)$$

Then the message with the largest distinctiveness

$$x^* = \arg\max_{x \in S_2} D(x) \quad (5)$$

is moved from S_2 to S_3. This procedure selects 100 most distinctive x^* for S_3, by ensuring the diversity in selected samples. The active learning algorithm then queries oracles (i.e., human experts) for polarity labels in S_3, and merges the labeled S_3 to L at the end of this step.

4 Unsupervised Learning of Word Features

The bag-of-word feature is simple for usage in learning a polarity classification model. However, the feature dimension is an order of magnitude higher than the size of training data. In such case, the trained classifier is only sensible to messages in the training corpus, but not generalizable to new messages, which is an over-fitting problem. And a further problem in bag-of-word feature is that the semantic information in words is not fully represented by single feature indexes.

We employ a dimension reduction method to solve this problem, which projects the large word space to a small vector space through unsupervised learning of distributed word representations. The algorithm for unsupervised learning is word2vec[2], and we employ its python implementation[3] to learn a 200-dimensional vector representation for words with a 90-million-message corpus. The algorithm learns word representations by constructing a recurrent neural network with each word and its context associated with as a layer (vector) of neurons respectively and fitting a 3-layer neural network to recurrently predict the next word given the current word and its context. More detailed implementations are described in (Mikolov et al., 2013a; Mikolov et al., 2013b; Mikolov et al., 2013c). The algorithm learned vector representations for 1 million words.

An important property of the word2vec algorithm is that both the vector representation and the addition (subtraction) on vector representations are semantically meaningful. This can be examined by the word pair relationships (Mikolov et al., 2013a) as follows. We calculate the semantic relation between words w_1("China") and w_2("Beijing") by subtracting their vector representations, and use this to examine if a same relationship exists between w_3("American") and w_4("Washington, D.C."), by searching through the learned words in V

$$w^* = \arg\max_{w \in V} \cos(w_1 - w_2 + w_4, w). \quad (6)$$

w^* equals w_3 with the cosine similarity 0.6433, which ensures the additive compositionality exists in our learned model.

We assume words around the topical word have greater impact to the message polarity than the distant words. To compose the semantic information in feature vector x for polarity prediction, we attach exponentially decreasing weights around the topical word

$$x = \sum_{i \neq t} \exp(-|i - t|/l) w_i, \quad (7)$$

where i and t are the word and topic locations in a message. l controls the decreasing speed in weights, which is set to 5 in our work.

5 Experiment and Discussion

The Topic-Based Chinese Message Polarity Classification task provides 4,095 topic-message pairs from Chinese Weibo Platform for developing a basic polarity classifier over positive, negative,

[1] This is not always true in Euclidean space, but has been employed in many active learning algorithms.

[2] https://code.google.com/p/word2vec/

[3] https://radimrehurek.com/gensim/models/word2vec.html

	RUN0			RUN1			RUN2			RUN3		
	Prec.	Recall	F1	Prec.	Recall	F1	Prec.	Recall	F1	Prec.	Recall	F1
Neg	30.47	18.52	23.04	40.65	**24.54**	**30.60**	**43.07**	16.74	24.10	40.72	5.25	9.30
Neu	77.25	88.43	82.46	**78.98**	87.08	82.83	78.01	91.98	84.42	76.08	**97.88**	**85.61**
Pos	23.35	9.20	13.20	19.08	**18.06**	18.55	**24.73**	16.06	**19.47**	19.93	2.00	3.63
Mac	43.69	38.72	39.57	46.24	**43.22**	**44.00**	**48.60**	41.49	42.67	45.54	35.04	32.85
Acc		70.68			71.30			73.42			**74.89**	

Table 1: Polarity classification results.

and neutral sentiments, and 19,469 topic-message pairs for evaluating the classification results. In this task, further resources are required to improve the classifier.

We employ a raw corpus of 90 million messages from Chinese Weibo Platform, for developing salient samples with active learning and for learning distributed representation of words with unsupervised feature learning. All these messages are randomly collected from April to September in 2013.

Based on the One-vs-All Logistic Regression algorithm from scikit-learn[4], we construct several polarity classifiers $\mathrm{clf_i}$ with different features. For the basic classifier $\mathrm{clf_0}$, we explore the bag-of-word feature by collecting words which occur more than "min_occur" times in the training corpus and by removing the most frequent "stop_num" words in the collection. We select model parameters "C", "penalty", "class_weight" and feature parameters "min_occur", "stop_num" through grid search with 5-fold cross validation on the training corpus.

We employ an active learning algorithm to generate a less-biased training corpus as shown in Figure 2. Class labels have been significantly balanced after 14 loops of sample selection. Classifier $\mathrm{clf_1}$ is trained on this corpus, with a similar parameter selection procedure as $\mathrm{clf_0}$.

We employ the word2vec algorithm to project the large word space to a small vector space. The algorithm has learned a 200-dimensional distributed representation for 1 million different words in the raw corpus. Classifier $\mathrm{clf_2}$ is trained on the basic corpus with composed word2vec features as in Eq. 7.

To evaluate the classification results, we calculate precision, recall, and F1 scores for each polarity, the macro average of these scores, and the overall accuracy. Table 1 shows the evaluation of

[4]http://scikit-learn.org/dev/index.html

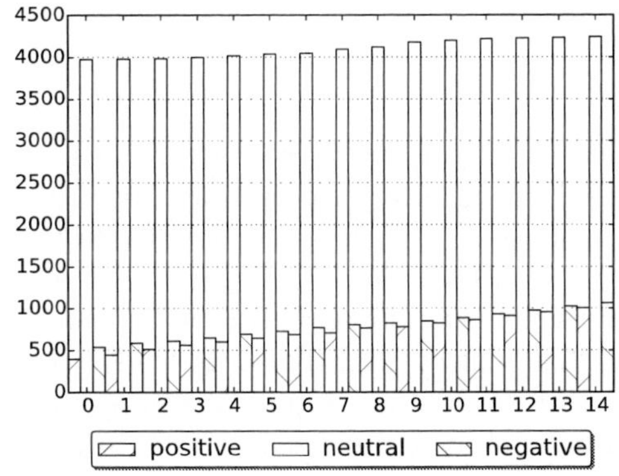

Figure 1: Label counts in active learning.

4 RUNs on the test corpus, with each RUN described below.

- RUN0 generates predictions from $\mathrm{clf_0}$.
- RUN1 generates predictions from $\mathrm{clf_1}$.
- RUN2 summarizes probabilistic predictions by

$$Y = \arg\max \sum_{i\in\{0,1,2\}} \mathrm{pclf_i}(X)$$

where $\mathrm{pclf_i}$ generates the probabilistic predictions over (negative, neutral, positive) for $\mathrm{clf_i}$, and $\arg\max$ generates the class label with the largest accumulated probabilistic prediction.

- RUN3 combines probabilistic predictions by

$$Y = \mathrm{clf_3}\left([\mathrm{pclf_0}(X); \mathrm{pclf_1}(X); \mathrm{pclf_2}(X)]\right)$$

where $\mathrm{clf_3}$ takes three probabilistic predictions as features and generates polarity predictions in Y. $\mathrm{clf_3}$ has been trained on the labeled corpus, with parameters optimized over classification accuracy.

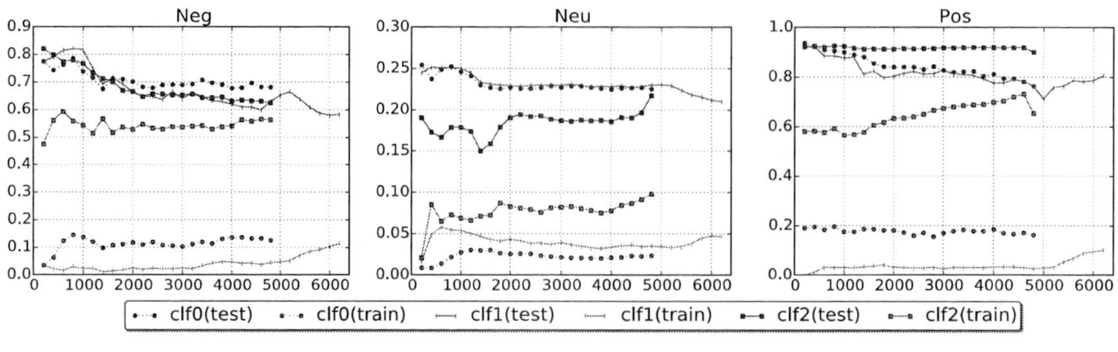

Figure 2: Learning curves.

RUN3 achieves the highest accuracy since its classifier is optimized over classification accuracy on training data. RUN1 yields the highest macro recall and F1 scores, which suggests that our active learning has effectively selected salient samples for training the polarity classifier. RUN2 yields the highest macro precision by summarizing the probabilistic predictions from three classifiers. Among the results from all participants for the restricted and unrestricted source based classifications, our submitted results in RUN0 and RUN3 have been ranked the 4th and the 2nd, respectively.

To further examine the problems in learning procedure we plot learning curves for each class label. A learning curve represents the error rates of a classifier, trained with different sizes of data. Learning curves of clf_0 and clf_1 suggest an over-fitting problem since the models fit well on the training data but generalize poorly on the test data. Compard to clf_0, clf_1 is more generalizable with extra samples selected by active learning. The learning curves of clf_2 on negative and positive labels suggest an under-fitting problem, which implies that the composed word2vec features have lost some important information for predicting these labels. Improvement is possible to be achieved by increasing the dimension of word vectors in the word2vec algorithm.

6 Conclusion

We report our approach for solving the Topic-Based Chinese Message Polarity Classification problem. The basic polarity classifier is over-fitted with highly-biased labels in the training data. We employ an active learning algorithm to select salient samples from a large raw corpus, and improve the learning procedure with less-biased labels in a larger training data. We then resort to a dimension reduction technique, by reducing the feature dimension from 17.5K to 200 with the word2vec algorithm, to further relief the over-fitting problem. However, because the feature reduction loses some important information, the model suffers an under-fitting problem. We believe developing the topic-based features in a properly low dimension and incrementally selecting salient samples would help improving the classification results. Moreover, we want to analyze the function of sentence syntactics for topic-based polarity classification in the future, since the syntactic structures can better interpret the significance of a feature relevant to a specified topic. Last but not least, we hope to further improve the classification algorithm based on the distributed representations of words as features.

Acknowledgments

This work has been partially supported by the China Postdoctoral Science Foundation funded project, under Grant No. 2014M560351, and the Quebec-China Postdoctoral Scholarship (File No. 188040).

References

William Boag, Peter Potash, and Anna Rumshisky. 2015. TwitterHawk: A feature bucket based approach to sentiment analysis. In *Proceedings of the 9th International Workshop on Semantic Evaluation*, pages 640–646. ACL.

Nal Kalchbrenner, Edward Grefenstette, and Phil Blunsom. 2014. A convolutional neural network for modelling sentences. In *Proceedings of the 52nd Annual Meeting of the Association for Computational Linguistics*, pages 655–665. ACL.

Yoon Kim. 2014. Convolutional neural networks for sentence classification. In *Proceedings of the 2014 Conference on Empirical Methods in Natural Language Processing*, pages 1746–1751. ACL.

Svetlana Kiritchenko, Xiaodan Zhu, and Saif M Mohammad. 2014. Sentiment analysis of short informal texts. *Journal of Artificial Intelligence Research*, 50:723–762.

Andrew L Maas, Raymond E Daly, Peter T Pham, Dan Huang, Andrew Y Ng, and Christopher Potts. 2011. Learning word vectors for sentiment analysis. In *Proceedings of the 49th Annual Meeting of the Association for Computational Linguistics: Human Language Technologies*, pages 142–150. ACL.

Tomas Mikolov, Kai Chen, Greg Corrado, and Jeffrey Dean. 2013a. Efficient estimation of word representations in vector space. *arXiv preprint arXiv:1301.3781*.

Tomas Mikolov, Ilya Sutskever, Kai Chen, Greg S Corrado, and Jeff Dean. 2013b. Distributed representations of words and phrases and their compositionality. In *Advances in Neural Information Processing Systems*, pages 3111–3119.

Tomas Mikolov, Wen-tau Yih, and Geoffrey Zweig. 2013c. Linguistic regularities in continuous space word representations. In *Proceedings of the 2013 Conference of the North American Chapter of the Association for Computational Linguistics: Human Language Technologies*, pages 746–751. ACL.

Yanghui Rao, Qing Li, Xudong Mao, and Wenyin Liu. 2014. Sentiment topic models for social emotion mining. *Information Sciences*, 266:90–100.

Fuji Ren and Xin Kang. 2013. Employing hierarchical Bayesian networks in simple and complex emotion topic analysis. *Computer Speech & Language*, 27(4):943–968.

Burr Settles. 2010. Active learning literature survey. *University of Wisconsin, Madison*, 52(55-66):11.

Richard Socher, Alex Perelygin, Jean Y Wu, Jason Chuang, Christopher D Manning, Andrew Y Ng, and Christopher Potts. 2013. Recursive deep models for semantic compositionality over a sentiment treebank. In *Proceedings of the 2013 Conference on Empirical Methods in Natural Language Processing*, pages 1631–1642. ACL.

Maite Taboada, Julian Brooke, Milan Tofiloski, Kimberly Voll, and Manfred Stede. 2011. Lexicon-based methods for sentiment analysis. *Computational Linguistics*, 37(2):267–307.

Duyu Tang, Furu Wei, Nan Yang, Ming Zhou, Ting Liu, and Bing Qin. 2014. Learning sentiment-specific word embedding for Twitter sentiment classification. In *Proceedings of the 52nd Annual Meeting of the Association for Computational Linguistics*, pages 1555–1565. ACL.

Yunong Wu, Kenji Kita, and Kazuyuki Matsumoto. 2014. Three predictions are better than one: Sentence multi-emotion analysis from different perspectives. *IEEJ Transactions on Electrical and Electronic Engineering*, 9(6):642–649.

An combined sentiment classification system for SIGHAN-8

Qiuchi Li[1], Qiyu Zhi[2] and Miao Li[1]
[1]Multimedia Signal and Intelligent Information Processing Lab,
Department of Electronic Engineering, Tsinghua University, Beijing, P.R.China
[2]School of Information and Communication Engineering,
Beijing University of Posts and Telecommunications, Beijing, P.R.China
liqc@126.com, zhiqiyubupt@gmail.com, miao-li10@mails.tsinghua.edu.cn

Abstract

This paper describes our system (MSIIP_THU) used for Topic-Based Chinese Message Polarity Classification Task in SIGHAN-8. In our system, a lexicon-based classifier and a statistical machine learning-based classifier are built up, followed by a linear combination of these two models. The overall performance of the proposed framework ranks in the middle of all terms participating in the task.

1 Introduction

Sentiment analysis is becoming an alluring task in natural language processing(NLP). Since an increasing amount of data is available on the World Wide Web, sentiment analysis is playing an important role in lots of real-world applications. In particular, sentiment analysis on microblogs is especially essential as microblog becomes one of the most fashionable ways for people to communicate with each other, express opinions and acquire newest information. However, with limited length, sentiment analysis on microblog remains a challenging task.

In this paper, we focus on sentiment classification for Chinese microblog, i.e. Weibo. The research on Weibo sentiment starts later and produces higher challenges due to the complexity in Chinese language. On one hand, different from alphabetic languages such as English, word segmentation is needed and is more difficult for Chinese sentences. On the other hand, polysemy in Chinese is abundant.

As for existing works in the area of Weibo sentiment analysis, some methods are proposed on the lexicon basis. (Taboada et al., 2011) proposed Semantic Orientation CALculator (SO-CAL) using dictionaries of words annotated with their semantic orientation, (Baccianella et al., 2010) presented SENTIWORDNET 3.0, a lexical resource explicitly devised for supporting sentiment classification and opinion mining applications. Other researchers focus on machine learning approaches. (Mullen and Collier, 2004) introduced an approach to sentiment analysis which used support vector machines (SVMs) to bring together diverse sources of potentially pertinent information. The same framework is adopted in (Mohammd et al., 2013), where systematic experiments on a great variety of features were conducted, leading to the best-performed results in SEMEVAL-2013 Twitter Sentiment Classification competition. In this task, we combine these two typical methods to build our system.

The rest of this paper is organized as follows. Section 2 describes the topic-based sentiment classification task and its dataset. Section 3 introduces our preprocess procedure for Weibo. Section 4 and Section 5 respectively shows the lexicon-based model and the statistical model used in this task. Section 6 describes the combination method and the experimental results. Finally we conclude this paper in Section 7.

2 Task Description

The paper is targeted on the Topic-Based Chinese Message Polarity Classification. Given a message from Chinese Weibo Platform and a topic, one needs to classify whether the message is of positive, negative, or neutral sentiment towards the given topic. Each participant is required to submit two results based on the restricted resource and unrestricted resource respectively. The restricted resource includes restricted lexicon and corpus, which have been released together with the test data.

The given training corpus has around 5,000 Chinese Weibos from 5 different topics. After duplicate removal we obtain 4619 Weibos. The 3-class annotation of all Weibos are given in another file. Moreover, we collected 43789 Weibos from

Proceedings of the Eighth SIGHAN Workshop on Chinese Language Processing (SIGHAN-8), pages 74–78,
Beijing, China, July 30-31, 2015. ©2015 Association for Computational Linguistics and Asian Federation of Natural Language Processing

NLPCC 2012,2013 and 2014 evaluation. These Weibos have no topic labels, but are annotated with 3-class labels. We use the collection as extra resource for the unrestricted resource task. The test data involves 19489 Weibos from 20 topics. These topics are different from the ones in the training corpus. The task is to annotate each Weibo in the test data.

The key measures for evaluation are overall accuracies and F-parameters for positive label and negative label. The mathematical formulations for these measures are omitted here because they are the most commonly used ones in sentiment analysis evaluations.

3 Preprocess Procedure

Although having a 140-character limitation, most Weibo has some unexpected characters, which poses an obstacle for us to extract features from the corpus and segment the sentence. Hence, preprocessing the Weibo data is a necessary step in sentiment analysis.

With regard to the corpus of this task, we first eliminate all the rare characters, then we extract all the punctuation, URLs and Weibo functional symbols such as "@" and "#". Finally we use NLPIR (Zhang et al., 2003) to segment the Weibo sentence.

4 Lexicon-based Approaches

Here we present our Lexicon-Based sentiment analysis approach. Sentiment lexicon is a simple, direct and efficient method to analyze sentiment by statistical method. In this section, the lexicon is firstly introduced, and then the algorithms for restricted and unrestricted lexicon are presented.

4.1 Basic Sentiment Lexicon

There are lots of lexicons that can be used for our task, such as Hownet Sentiment Dictionary (Dong, 2000), National Taiwan University Sentiment Dictionary (NTUSD) (Ku and Chen, 2007) and Chinese Emotion Word Ontology (CEWO) (Yan et al., 2008). Since Hownet labels every word with different emotion intensity, such as 3,5,7,9, and CEWO covers words with too many different categories, We choose NTUSD as our base sentiment lexicon. The composition of this sentiment lexicon is shown in Table 1.

Table 1: NTUSD Sentiment Lexicon

Polarity	Number
1	2810
-1	8276

4.2 Weibo Emoticon Lexicon

Emoticon is proved to be important for Weibo sentiment classification task. Since sarcasm is common in Weibo expressions, a sentiment word may express the opposite emotion in sarcasm case, while the emoticons often reflect the real sentiment of the writer. We build a Weibo emoticon lexicon for unrestricted resources task. We first extract all of the emoticons in training corpus, and then incorporate common emoticons from Weibo platform, including all emoticons in the first three emoticon pages. We manually label every emoticon in our lexicon with $10, -10, 1, -1, 0$. ± 10 represents the sentiment intensity for an emoticon strong enough to affect the sentiment of the whole sentence, while ± 1 refers to an emoticon with clear sentiment but not enough to decide the sentence sentiment. 0 represent emoticon without any emotional tendency. The composition of this emoticon lexicon is shown in Table 2.

Table 2: Emoticon Sentiment Lexicon

Polarity	Number
-10	12
10	22
-1	89
1	85
0	85

4.3 The Lexicon-based classifier

Like many Lexicon-based methods, we simply calculate the score of a Weibo sentence by adding up the scores of each sentiment words appeared in the sentence. For restricted resource task, only NTUSD Lexicon is used. Our Emoticon Lexicon is added to the Lexicon in unrestricted resource task.

5 Machine Learning-Based Approaches

Support Vector Machine (SVM)(Cortes and Vapnik, 1995) is used as the statistical classifier. We use a rich feature set to build the model.

5.1 Features

5.1.1 Linguistic Features

In this part, different linguistic features are considered. For the choice of n-gram, we only consider n=1 (refer to as unigram) and n=2 (refer to as bigram) due to the limited size of training corpus. For other linguistic features, we also extract character-bigram and TFIDF features from the training dataset. In section 5.2 we will discuss ways to select these features.

5.1.2 Weibo-Based Features

Apart from linguistic features, we also extract a series of Weibo-based features shown as follows:

- **Textlength**. It is believed that long Weibos tend to contain more sentiment terms, and thus are more likely to be non-neutral in sentiment.

- **Hashtag**. We consider Hashtags ("#") because they usually include topic information for a Weibo. The number of Hashtags are extracted in our experiment.

- **Punctuation**. We assume that punctuation is relevant to Weibo sentiment. We extract the number of four commonly used punctuation as features: period("。"), comma("，"), exclamation ("！") and question ("？").

- **Emoticon**. Based on the pre-constructed dictionary, we extract the number of positive and negative emoticons respectively for a Weibo, forming a 2-dimension feature vector.

- **POS**. It is spontaneous that a Weibo's sentiment can be reflected in the Part-Of-Speech (POS) features. In this paper the number of nouns, adjectives, verbs and adverbs are extracted, forming a 4-dimension feature vector.

- **URL**. The contents in the url link may be relevant to the content of the Weibo and the sentiment polarity. The number of URLs is extracted in our model.

- **ATSign**. ATSigns ("@") associate a Weibo with other people, and prior knowledge of those people may affect the Weibo sentiment. The number of ATSigns is extracted in our model.

Table 3: results for feature selection

features	neuF	posF	negF
all	0.6096	0.1975	0.3194
-Unigram	0.6091	0.1941	0.3258
-Bigram	0.6444	0.2083	0.3296
-Character-Bigram	0.7099	0.2210	0.3410
-TFIDF	0.6313	0.2105	0.3358
-textLength	0.5969	0.1905	0.3459
-#	0.6096	0.1979	0.3182
-punctuation	0.6159	0.1949	0.3282
-Emoticon	0.6134	0.1987	0.3194
-POS	0.5482	0.178	0.3346
-URL	0.5987	0.1934	0.3194
-@	0.5995	0.1837	0.3580

5.2 Feature Selection

The feature selection method is inspired by (Mohammd et al., 2013). For a detailed description, we first experiment on all aforementioned features, and then in turn kick out every feature and repeat the experiment. To make a fair comparison, in each experiment a five-fold cross validation method is proposed on the training set, and we average the F-parameters for negative, neutral and positive labels over the five sub-experiments to measure the performance of the feature combination. For the SVM training setup, we use linear kernel and default parameter. The results for the feature selection experiments are shown in Table 3.

From Table 3, the elimination of Bigram, Character-Bigram and TFIDF bring about increased performance, the elimination of POS leads to decreased performance, while the elimination of other features does not influence much of the performance. Therefore, we choose Unigram as the only linguistic feature, and remain all the Weibo-based features.

6 Model-Fusion Framework

Our final system is set up by merging the two models discussed in Chapter 4 and 5 respectively. The merging method is shown as follows. For a Weibo w, we have

$$decisionValue(w) = \lambda C_{dic}(w) + (1-\lambda)C_{svm}(w) \quad (1)$$

where $C_{dic}(w)$ and $C_{svm}(w)$ are the classification results for the lexicon-based system and the machine learning-based system, and $\lambda \in [0, 1]$ is the linear combination parameter. The computed decision value $decisionValue(w)$ is a real-valued number in [-1,1], based on which we obtain the final sentiment polarity as the output of our model-fusion framework:

$$sentiment(w) = \begin{cases} 1 & decisionValue(w)\text{>=0.5} \\ 0 & |decisionValue(w)|\text{<0.5} \\ -1 & decisionValue(w)\text{<=-0.5} \end{cases}$$

7 Experiments

7.1 Experimental Setup

The model-fusion framework is adopted on both restricted and unrestricted requirements, but the parameter choices are slightly different for these two cases.

For restricted results, the parameter λ is set to be 1, which means only lexicon-based system is adopted. Since only two different results can be submitted, we submit the results by considering I) main body of the Weibo only and II)main body and forward chains.

For unrestricted results, we combine the provided training corpus with extra training dataset to train the SVM classifier for machine learning-based system. For lexicon-based system, the main body only is considered, but the emoticon lexicon is incorporated. The two results were generated by setting the fusion parameter λ as 1(lexicon-based only) and 0.5 respectively.

7.2 Results and Discussions

For each subtask (restricted and unrestricted), the better performed system is automatically chosen from the two submitted results, and performance and rank are returned. The results for our system is shown in table 4.

The results show that our system generally ranks in the middle of the 13 teams who participated in the evaluation, which proves the effectiveness of our system. Since our system is targeted on improving F-values, and most Weibos are of neutral sentiment for both training and testing corpus, more non-neutral labels will be generated but with low accuracy. Therefore, our system is unsatisfactory in overall accuracy and precision, but rather competitive in terms of recall and F-values.

It is further revealed that the other system has consistently higher F-values than the accepted system for both tasks. This means that the abandoned system generates more non-neutral polarities, resulting in higher F-values for both positive and negative class, but the overall accuracy is also lower than the recorded system, so it is neglected automatically by the evaluation system.

Table 4: Performance and ranks of our system in evaluation.

	value	best	rank
U-ACC	**0.6351**	**0.8535**	**11**
U-pre+	0.1212	0.5880	10
U-rec+	0.1788	0.6203	6
U-F1+	**0.1445**	**0.6039**	**7**
U-2-F1+	**0.2108**	**0.6039**	**5**
U-pre-	0.3412	0.7917	9
U-rec-	0.3954	0.6175	5
U-F1-	**0.3663**	**0.6938**	**6**
U-2-F1-	**0.4096**	**0.6938**	**5**
ACC	**0.6489**	**0.8357**	**9**
pre+	0.0988	0.6258	10
rec+	0.0946	0.5139	9
F1+	**0.0967**	**0.5643**	**10**
2-F1+	**0.1480**	**0.5643**	**7**
pre-	0.3320	0.8232	9
rec-	0.3767	0.4671	4
F1-	**0.3530**	**0.5960**	**5**
2-F1-	**0.3805**	**0.5960**	**4**

Note: Words that start with '"U-" stand for unrestricted situation. Words that end with "+" and "-" stand for results on positive and negative polarities. Words that contains "2" refer to the other submitted system. The highlighted values correspond to key measures in the evaluation.

Nevertheless, the system still needs further improvements. The topic information is not considered, which is a major drawback for our system. The author believes that it will probably be an improvement to discover the topic-specific knowledge using some unsupervised methods prior to the whole system. These knowledge can not only be somehow incorporated into the lexicon-based approach, but be treated as extra features for the machine learning-based system.

8 Conclusion

In this paper, a combined system is proposed on the task of topic-based Chinese Weibo sentiment analysis. It conducts a linear combination between a lexicon-based sentiment classification system and an SVM sentiment classifier. The evaluation results prove the feasibility of the system, and further highlight the advantageous performance in measures of recall and F-values for non-neutral sentences.

References

Stefano Baccianella, Andrea Esuli, and Fabrizio Sebastiani. 2010. Sentiwordnet 3.0: An enhanced lexical resource for sentiment analysis and opinion mining. In *LREC*, volume 10, pages 2200–2204.

Corinna Cortes and Vladimir Vapnik. 1995. Support-vector networks. *Machine Learning*, 20:273–297.

Zhengdong Dong. 2000. Introduction to hownet. `http://www.keenage.com`.

Lun-Wei Ku and Hsin-Hsi Chen. 2007. Mining opinions from the web: Beyond relevance retrieval. *Journal of the American Society for Information Science and Technology*, 58(12):1838–1850.

Saif M Mohammd, Svetlana Kirichenko, and Xiaodan Zhu. 2013. NRC-Canada: Building the State-of-the-Art in Sentiment Analysis of Tweets. *Second Joint Conference on Lexical and Computational Semantics*, 2:321–327.

Tony Mullen and Nigel Collier. 2004. Sentiment analysis using support vector machines with diverse information sources. In *EMNLP*, volume 4, pages 412–418.

Maite Taboada, Julian Brooke, Milan Tofiloski, Kimberly Voll, and Manfred Stede. 2011. Lexicon-based methods for sentiment analysis. *Computational linguistics*, 37(2):267–307.

Jiajun Yan, David B Bracewell, Fuji Ren, and Shingo Kuroiwa. 2008. The creation of a chinese emotion ontology based on hownet. *Engineering Letters*, 16(1):166–171.

Hua-Ping Zhang, Hong-Kui Yu, De-Yi Xiong, and Qun Liu. 2003. Hhmm-based chinese lexical analyzer ictclas. In *Proceedings of the second SIGHAN workshop on Chinese language processing-Volume 17*, pages 184–187. Association for Computational Linguistics.

Linguistic Knowledge-driven Approach to Chinese Comparative Elements Extraction

Minjun Park
Dept. of Chinese Language and Literature
Peking University
Beijing, 100871, China
karmalet@163.com

Yulin Yuan
Dept. of Chinese Language and Literature
Peking University
Beijing, 100871, China
yuanyl@pku.edu.cn

Abstract

The BI (比)-structure, which highlights a contrasting characteristic between two items, is the key comparative sentence structure in Chinese. In this paper, we explore the methods of extracting the 6 constituents of the BI-structure. Previous studies are often restricted to probabilistic classification methods, where the feature used hardly embodies linguistic knowledge, therefore unintuitive. As an alternative, we propose the use of two linguistic knowledge-driven approaches, namely the POS chunking-based and TBL-based methods. The first model effectively captures grammatical restrictions over POS sequential patterns. The second model set up on new and lesser templates performs better than Brill's (1995). Experimental results show that the proposed models are simple and effective methods for Chinese comparative element extraction task.

1 Introduction

Comparison is the most representative figure of evaluation. Much of evaluative information is now available in the web, and comparative sentences prevail in Chinese web texts in increasing numbers. A significant amount of research has been conducted on automatic identification of Chinese comparative sentence and its semantic elements. However, the techniques proposed in earlier works are mostly based on statistical classification method. Due to the opaque nature of stochastic features, it is often difficult to comprehend what linguistic aspects are applied to the model.

In this paper, we present a detailed analysis on linguistic behavior of the BI (比)-structure, which is the key comparative structure in Chinese. The application of the two rule-based approaches suggested in this paper are different from previous models in that they fully use syntactic and lexical features which are intrinsic to the structure.

This paper first presents a brief literature review on the subject. The target of extraction task, i.e. Comparative Elements (CE) is then defined before demonstration of the two proposed approaches, i.e. POS chunking-based and TBL-based extraction models. Finally, we discuss the experiment's results and present our conclusion.

2 Related Work

The research on comparative sentence has been a main concern from the beginning of modern Chinese linguistics research. The different types of Chinese comparative sentences were first mentioned in *Mashi Wentong* (1898) and their classification was elaborated later by Chinese grammarians such as Lü (1942), Ding (1961) and Liu (1983). Following by their preliminary work, a series of research focused on defining syntactic and semantic structure of the Chinese comparative sentence was conducted. Li (1986) demonstrates the Chinese BI-structure simplifying rules. Shao (1990) investigates the rule of replacing and omitting elements in Chinese comparative structure.

On the other hand, Studies in Natural Language Processing mainly dealt with the identification of comparative sentence and its elements. Based on Jindal and Liu's research (2006) on comparative sentences in English, Huang(2008) and Song(2009) made a stochastic classifier based on SVMs and CRFs to tackle the Chinese comparative sentence identification and element extraction task. Besides, many models were also suggested in the fifth Chinese Opinion Analysis Evaluation (COAE2013) track. Zhou(2014) and Li(2013) made use of pattern matching technique, and Wei(2013) proposed a rule-based decision making approach based on CRF sequential tag-

Proceedings of the Eighth SIGHAN Workshop on Chinese Language Processing (SIGHAN-8), pages 79–85,
Beijing, China, July 30-31, 2015.

ging. Despite all these models, their performance has not shown satisfying results[1]. The identification of Chinese comparative elements especially still remains as a big challenge. A TBL-based approach, which showed good performance in Korean (Yang and Ko, 2011), would be an alternative to usual methods.

3 Task Description

3.1 Comparative Elements (CE)

We refer to Comparative Elements (CE) as entities and attributes which directly occur within comparative sentences. We defined 6 CEs as below.

e.g. 新飞度车身结构的刚度比前代提高了 164%。
The solidity of XinFeiDu's body structure has increased 164% than the previous design.

新飞度	刚度	比	前代	提高	164%
XinFeiDu	solidity	BI	previous design	increased	164%
SUB	DIM	BI	OBJ	RES	EXT

CE (label)	Definition
Subject Entity (SUB)	An element of comparison, i.e. topic of the sentence.
Comparative Marker (BI)	Comparative sentence marker, which is BI(比) in Chinese Bi-structure[2].
Object Entity(OBJ)	An entity that is being compared to. It is often the complement of Bi-prepositional phrase.
Dimension (DIM)	Shared property of entities being compared.
Comparative Result (RES)	The relation between entities being compared. It is often the syntactic head of comparative predicate.
Comparative Extent (EXT)	Relative difference in degree or quantity between entities in terms of DIM.

Table 1: Comparative Elements (CE) in BI-structure

Our task is to automatically extract these 6 CEs from the sentences. Note that these elements cannot simply be determined by syntactic criteria. They are involved with semantic category to some extent, but we do not use additional semantic features such as semantic role labels or lexical taxonomies in this paper.

[1] In COAE 2013 Task 2 (Chinese Comparative Element Identification), the best performance F1-score was 0.35 (Tan et al. 2013:25).

[2] There are other comparative markers such as 比不过, 不如, 优于 which are sometimes combined with RES morphologically. However, BI(比) is the only comparative marker in the scope of this paper.

3.2 Corpus

The corpus used in this experiment consists of 1,036 Chinese BI-structure sentences, coming from the open dataset of COAE 2013 Task 2 (Tan et al. 2013). The sentences are a collection of customer reviews and opinions from different Chinese websites pertaining to cars and electronics.

1) Preprocessing: We first conduct word segmentation and POS tagging by using ICTCLAS[3]. Second, we had to manually revise to avoid any errors because of the informal language used on the web. Three annotators were appointed to revise typos. In addition, 3,000 word-size domain-specific lexicons[4] are also utilized to guarantee the quality of word segmentation and POS tagging.

2) CE labeling: The 6 types of Comparative Elements (CE) in the 1,036 sentences were manually annotated with the corresponding CE labels of Table 1. This task was done by three trained annotators of Chinese linguistics major. Their work was double-checked by one another, and any inconsistencies between annotators were discussed before reaching an agreement. The annotated corpus was then transformed to IOB format.

4 Two methods of Comparative Elements Extraction

We now present two different proposed techniques. Model 1 uses basic part-of-speech chunking-based method and Model 2 employs Transformation-Based Error-Driven Learning (TBL) (Brill, 1995) for identifying CEs.

4.1 POS chunking-based CE extraction

4 elements of CEs, i.e. BI, OBJ, RES and EXT, form a regular sequential pattern across the sentences. First, OBJ generally occurs as complements of BI-prepositional phrase, which is mostly a noun phrase. Second, RES and EXT usually form predicates, modified by the BI-prepositional phrase, i.e. [[比 OBJ]$_{prep}$ [RES EXT]$_{pred}$]. Noticing this pattern, we can define chunk patterns with regular expressions as below.

Punctuation as delimiter, the sentence is divided into small clauses

If the clause contains“比/p”, the following chunk rules are applied to create chunks.

[3] http://ictclas.nlpir.org/downloads

[4] Acquired from Sougou's open database. http://pinyin.sogou.com/dict/

```
Rule1. BI: {<P><.*>*}
Rule2. RES: <.*>}{<V>|<A[DN]*>|<D>
Rule3. RES: <D>|<V>|<VSHI>|<VYOU>|
       <A[DN]*>{}<V>|<A[DN]*>|<D>
Rule4. RES: <.*>{}<.*>*?<UDE1>[^<W
       J>][^$]
```

Label the items in the first chunk as BI and OBJ, and label the second chunk as RES.

For RES chunks, Rule 5 is applied to chunk EXT.

```
Rule 5. EXT:<A>|<V[N]*>|<Y>{(<MQ>|<
        M>|<Q>|<RY>|<X>|<D>)<.*>*}
```

Table 2: chunking-based CE extraction process[5]

We now give a step-by-step illustration of the actual extraction process of Table 2.

Step 1 Detecting BI (比)-Chunk
For clauses containing the comparative marker BI (比), we create a chunk that begins with it (Rule 1). We call it BI (比)-Chunk.

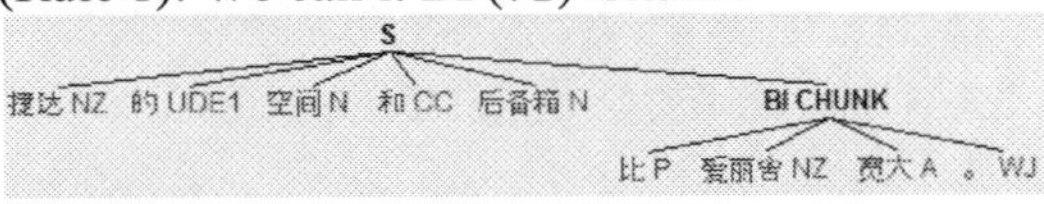

Step 2 Splitting into Two Phrases
BI (比)-Chunk can be divided into two chunks, i.e. BI-prepositional phrase and predicate because they belong to very distinctive syntactic categories. The former cannot appear independently, usually taking a noun as its object. The latter functions as the predicate, and is mostly an adjective or a verb[6]. Therefore, we designed Rule 2 to split them.

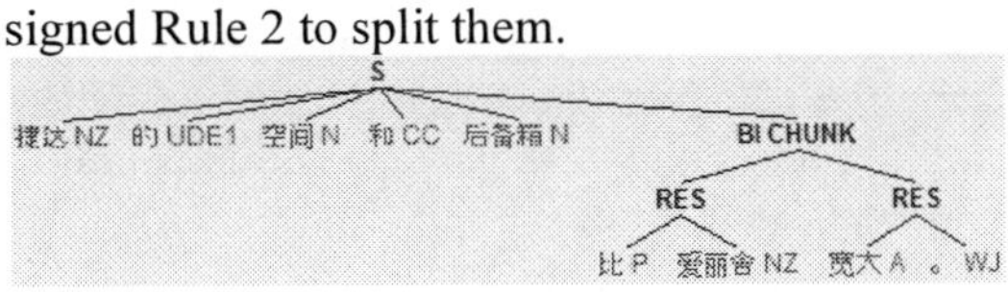

Step 3 Merging Incorrectly Separated Predicates
In most cases, however, the predicate is a complex phrasal structure. Therefore, Rule 2 incorrectly splits chunk that should have not been separated. To solve this, we employ Rule 3 to merge incorrectly divided elements of the predicate group.

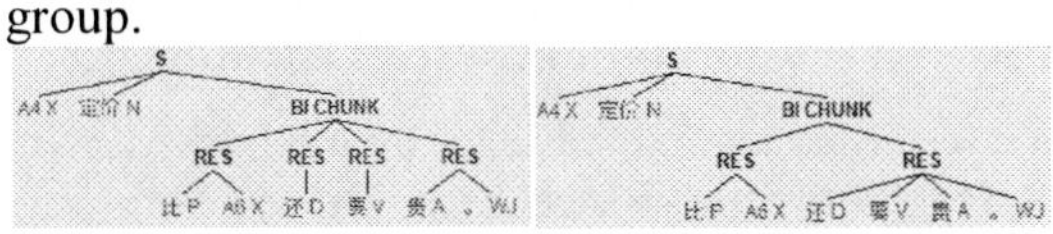

Step 4 Dealing with DE (的)-Structure
In Chinese, DE (的) is often used to mark modification[7]. It can be attached to various types of syntactic categories and modify the following word. DE (的)-structure can be simplified as [[XP 的] NP]. When a verb or adjective phrase takes the position of XP, the same error as in Step 3 occurs. To tackle this problem, we use Rule 4 that enunciates the unity of modifying elements occurring at the position of XP.

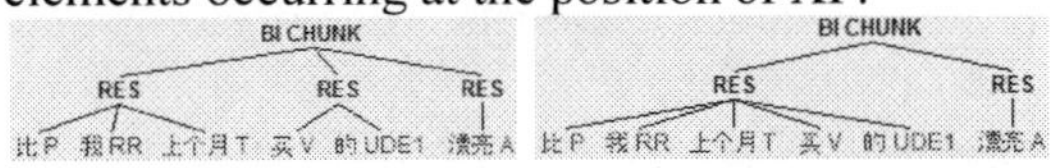

Note that DE (的) is not necessarily restricted to modification marker. When occurring at the end of the sentence, it simply marks a subjective tone. Rule 4 makes use of punctuation tag (WJ) to discern this modal particle of DE (的) from modification marker.

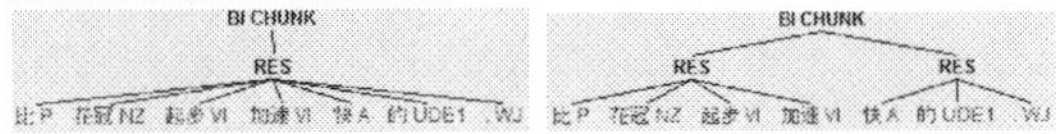

Step 5 CE Labeling
After successfully extracting the two chunks (BI-prepositional phrase and predicate) following the above mentioned 4 steps, we label each item in these chunks with BI, OBJ and RES tags.

Step 6 (optional) EXT Identification
Comparative Extent (EXT) usually begins with numerals, following the head of the predicate. Rule 5 detects possible EXTs in RES chunk.

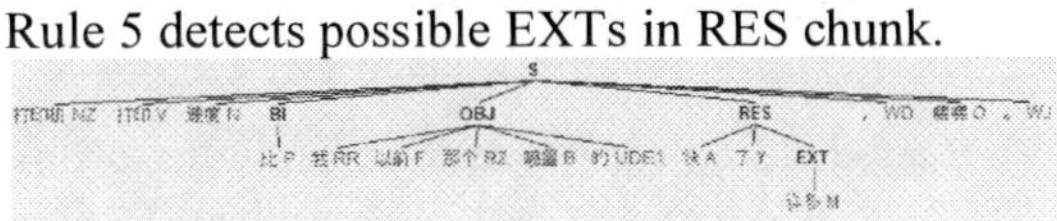

4.2 TBL-based CE extraction

The advantage of using the POS chunking-based method is that it allows direct capture of linguistic information. However, (a) it requires painstaking process of manual rule construction; (b)

[5] For specifying chunk rules intuitively, we directly quote NLTK's description of chunking operator (Bird et al. 2009).
(1) <T> represents for any token tagged with T.
(2) {<pattern >} represents for Chunk Rule, which means creating a chunk with the given regex pattern within curly braces.
(3) <pattern1>}{<pattern2> represents for Split Rule, which means splitting a chunk into two chunks based on the specified pattern.
(4) <pattern1>{}<pattern2> represents for Merge Rule, which means merging two chunks together based on the specified pattern.

[6] Strictly speaking, verb and adjective are also able to occur in BI- prepositional phrase. Such a case will be handled in Step 4.

[7] It may be an inadequate way of defining DE (的) because of its flexible and diverse nature. Exceptional cases will be discussed in 5.1. See Zhu(1961) for further details.

and an error in any step could damage the performance of the whole CE extraction process.

4.2.1 Transformation-Based Learning

We tested an automated learning method, known as Transformation-Based Error-Driven Learning (TBL) (Brill, 1995). The basic idea of TBL is "learning from mistakes". First, the researcher may apply an initial-state annotator to the training corpus. Second, the set of user-defined templates are then used to form candidate rules. Third, each of the rules is in turn applied to the training corpus. At the same time, the net improvement of the rule is calculated and recorded for evaluation of candidate rules. Throughout the training, the process of deriving rules, scoring and selecting rules and applying them is iterated, creating an ordered sequence of transformation rules.

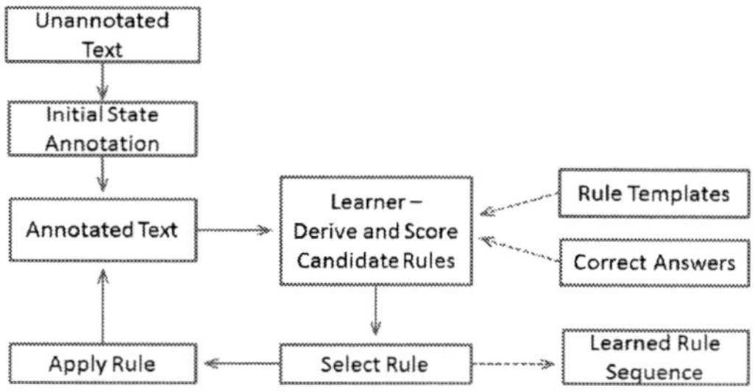

Figure 1: Learning Procedure of TBL
Modified from Brill(1995), Ramshaw and Marcus(1999)

TBL has a well-known advantage, i.e. perspicuity of linguistically meaningful rules. Different from the POS chunking-based model, the TBL-based model is more robust and possibly captures useful information that may not be noticed by the human engineer (Brill, 1995:552). Therefore, the use of TBL allows us to capture some otherwise ignored CE patterns.

4.2.2 Preliminary TBL-based CE Tagger

We treated CE extraction task as a tagging problem. Each token in training data is given an initial tag by ICTCLAS tagger. The TBL learner with user-defined templates is then trained on the training data. Consequently, we obtain the TBL-based CE tagger as a CE extraction model.

The templates play a key role in this model because the TBL-learner uses these templates to generate possible rules, which directly affect the overall performance. In order to see which type of feature contributes more to the TBL-based model accuracy rate, we divide the original template proposed in Brill (1995:553, 556) into three template subsets: (a) tag features template; (b) lexical features template; (c) both features template.

Type of features	# of templates	# of candidate rules	Accuracy (%)
(a) Tag	11	21,815	83.15
(b) Lexicon	15	59,442	85.39
(c) Tag & Lexicon	26	81,257	88.38

Table 3: CE Extraction Accuracy based on different feature templates

Since the result of (c) is the best, we take it as a standard template. Table 4 shows evaluation results using TBL-based model with 26 templates (c). We regard this score as our baseline performance.

	SUB	DIM	BI	OBJ	RES	EXT
Pre.	53.48	60.90	97.08	77.24	88.02	82.04
Rec.	19.31	38.07	97.22	80.82	69.86	69.57
F.	28.24	46.37	97.14	78.97	77.86	75.16

Table 4: The result of baseline system (%)

4.2.3 Search for Optimal Template

We now present how we obtained our proposed TBL-based CE extraction model. The baseline system is based on a relatively large amount of rules and templates. Therefore, the reduction of rules is preferable for efficient application of TBL. According to Brill (1995: 560), although the accuracy of TBL-based tagger increases with the number of transformation rules, its marginal effect dramatically decreases, and leads to computational cost. We found that 200~300 rules are desirable for our CE detecting task. As for templates, we achieved the best performance when using tag and lexicon sequences within a radius of 3 tokens as features.

For every token in BI-structure, change tag a to tag b when:	
1. The current word is ***w***.	W_0
2. One of the three preceding words is tagged *z*.	$T_{-3,-2,-1}$
3. One of the three following words is tagged *z*.	$T_{1,2,3}$
4. The word two after is tagged *z*.	T_2
5. The word two before is tagged *z*.	T_{-2}
6. The following word is tagged *z*.	T_1
7. The preceding word is tagged *z*.	T_{-1}
8. The preceding word is ***w***.	W_{-1}
9. The current word is ***w***, and the preceding tag is ***t***.	W_0 & T_{-1}
10. The preceding tag is ***t***, the current tag is t_2 and the following word is ***w***.	T_{-1} &T_0&W_1

Table 5: 10 proposed templates

Based on the above-mentioned templates, the TBL-based model generates a set of possible candidate rules. Table 6 lists 10 transformation rules of highest score.

Pass	Old tag	Context	New tag
1	P	W_0 = 比	BI
2	A	$T_{-3,-2,-1}$ = BI	RES
3	NZ	$T_{-3,-2,-1}$ = BI	OBJ
4	N	$T_{-3,-2,-1}$ = BI	OBJ
5	M	$T_{-3,-2,-1}$ = RES	EXT
6	A	$T_{-3,-2,-1}$ = OBJ	RES
7	N	$T_{1,2,3}$ = BI	DIM
8	NZ	$T_{1,2,3}$ = BI	SUB
9	UDE1	$T_{-3,-2,-1}$ = BI	OBJ
10	X	$T_{-3,-2,-1}$ = BI	OBJ

Table 6: 10 Rules of highest score

With the rules given above, the model takes example (1a) as an input, and applies the rules in order of 1 → 2 → 3 → 5 → 7 → 8 → 9, producing the CE-tagged result of example (1b).

(1a) E1-471/nz ,/wd 声音/n 比/p AS4752/nz 的/ude1 好/a 多/m 了/y 哦/e

(1b) E1-471/sub ,/wd 声音/dim 比/bi AS4752/obj 的/obj 好/res 多/ext 了/y 哦/e

In addition, Examples (2-5) below illustrate some of the linguistically meaningful transformation rules that the TBL model based on 10 templates (Table 5) has captured.

(2) `VYOU->RES if Word:更@[-1]`
比/bi 同价位/obj 机型/obj 更/d 有/res 分量/res 。/wj
BI same-price model more have amount
(This product) has more amounts for the same price.

(3) `EXT->RES if Word:要@[-1]`
比/bi 捷达/obj 的/obj 要/v 多/res 得/ude3 多/ext 。/wj
BI Jetta DE should more DE much
(A car model's something) should be much more than a Jetta's.

In (2-3), "更" is equivalent to "more" in English, and "要" conveys subjective meaning of difference in degree. The proposed model makes use of them as an RES marker because they frequently occur before RES.

(4) `RZ->OBJ if Word:比@[-1]`
诺基亚/sub 5230/sub 同等/b 价位/n 下/f 比/bi 其它/obj 手机/obj 都/d 好/res
Nokia 5230 is even better than the equivalent class of other cellphones.

(5) `RES->EXT if Word:好@[0]& Pos:RES@[-1]`
比/bi 老/obj 天籁/obj 的/ude1 油漆/dim 硬/res 好/ext 多/ext 。/wj
(A car model's coating) is much stronger than the coatings of Teana.

In (4), the pronoun following BI "其它" is likely to be a constituent of OBJ. "好" is very likely to be a degree complement, i.e. EXT, if RES precedes it. Instead of functioning as RES, it stresses the degree of RES as shown in example (5).

5 Results

5.1 Result of POS Chunking-based Model

The overall performance of the chunking-based CE extraction model (Section 4.1) is as follow.

	BI	OBJ	RES	EXT
Precision	96.94	75.96	42.03	63.33
Recall	96.94	82.63	86.65	60.03
F-score	96.94	79.15	56.60	61.63

Table 7: The results of chunking-based CE extraction (%)

The CE mining process of chunking-based model is based on simplistic grammatical assumptions: (a) Only nominal elements serve as the complement of BI-prepositional phrase; (b) Predicates can be a word or a group of words (phrase) that are adjectives or verbs; (c) Within the BI (比)-Chunk, the elements occurring before the modifier marker DE (的) are all regarded as modifier. These assumptions, of course, are somewhat over-generalized, and do not fit in many real cases[8]. However, the 5 Rules applied based on these assumptions show a fair performance in Table 7 when applied to a limited scope of BI-Chunk.

5.2 Result of TBL-based Model

All evaluations of TBL-based model in this paper are based on a 5-fold cross validation. The proposed TBL-based model with 10 templates shows the results below.

	SUB	DIM	BI	OBJ	RES	EXT
Pre.	53.35	62.13	97.41	77.16	87.94	79.78
Rec.	23.04	40.70	97.04	83.15	69.50	72.31
F.	31.88	48.46	97.22	80.01	77.58	75.79

Table 8: The results of TBL-based CE extraction (%)

Guided by our new templates (Table 5), the model first locates comparative marker BI (比), then searches the surroundings for the tag/lexical features while gradually narrowing its scope. As a result, the 10 templates enable an effective detection of elusive CE instances such as those in example (2-7).

[8] Under many circumstances in Chinese, a noun (or noun phrase) can also serve as predicate; Transferred-designation(转指) "XP 的" construction can also act as subject other than as a modifier.

Model	SUB	DIM	BI	OBJ	RES	EXT
POS chunking-based	-	-	96.94	79.15	56.60	61.63
TBL-based (baseline, 26 Templates)	28.24	46.37	97.14	78.97	77.86	75.16
TBL-based (proposed, 10 Templates)	31.88	48.46	97.22	80.01	77.58	75.79

Table 9: Comparison between models (f-score, %)

Table 9 compares the scores of two CE mining methods, the POS chunking-based and the TBL-based approach. Compared to the TBL-based model, the POS chunking-based model is unable to extract SUB and DIM. Because these two elements frequently occur outside a BI-prepositional phrase, it is hard to capture their irregular occurrence positions in the sentence. In contrast, the TBL-based model is able to detect SUB and DIM. However, their identification rate is relatively low.

Nevertheless, our proposed TBL-based model outperforms the baseline system by using much smaller templates. It shows we found a simple and more expressive set of rule templates.

Moreover, the proposed TBL-based model achieved an increase of 21% for RES and 14% for EXT f-score in comparison with the POS chunking-based model. This improvement mainly benefits from the proper use of both tag and lexical information.

(6) 市场/nz 中/f 比/p 它/rr 靓/a 的/ude1 产品/n 很/d 少/a 。/wj

There are very few products prettier than that one in the market.

(a) 市场/n 中/f 比/bi 它/obj 靓/obj 的/ude1 产品/obj 很/res 少/res 。/WJ

(b) `RES->A if Word:很@[-1]`
市场/n 中/f 比/bi 它/obj 靓/res 的/ude1 产品/n 很/d 少/a 。/WJ

(7) 花冠/nz 比/p 伊兰特/nz 贵/a 近/a 3 万/m

Corollas are more expensive than Elantras by nearly 30 thousand RMB.

(a) 花冠/nz 比/bi 伊兰特/obj 贵/res 近/res 3 万/ext

(b) `RES->EXT if Word:近@[0]`
花冠/nz 比/bi 伊兰特/obj 贵/res 近/ext 3 万/ext

As for examples (6-7), the POS chunking-based model (Section 4.1) incorrectly identifies “少, 近” as RES. As we can see in example (6a), the POS chunking-based model wrongly identifies “很少” as RES because the BI-chunk “比它靓” occurs in front of the modification marker “的”. In (7a), the model mistook “近” for RES because it cannot discern “近” from “贵” only with the tag information. In contrast, TBL-based model makes a correct decision of (6b) and (7b) based on lexical information.

6 Conclusion

In order to make the best use of meaningful features in linguistic context, we have proposed the use of two rule-based methods for Chinese comparative element (CE) extraction. The POS chunking-based model performs well with basic Chinese grammatical rules. We then use the TBL-based method to extract other linguistic patterns that the first model can hardly detect. Results showed that our TBL-based model achieved higher score than Brill’s (1995), demonstrating that our new 10 templates can effectively extract the distinct features of Chinese BI-structure as shown in examples (1-7).

Chinese comparative element mining involves techniques of various domains including coreference resolution, named entity recognition and parsing. However, the linguistic features used in this paper are limited to instances of regular (type-3) grammars. In our future work, we plan to investigate some feasible Chinese linguistic features on the level of context-free grammars.

References

Bird, Steven, Edward Loper and Ewan Klein. 2009. Natural Language Processing with Python. O’Reilly Media Inc.

Brill, Eric. 1992. A Simple Rule-Based Part of Speech Tagger. In *Proceedings of the workshop on Speech and Natural Language*, pp.112-116.

Brill, Eric. 1995. Transformation-Based Error-Driven Learning and Natural Language Processing: A Case Study in Part-of-Speech Tagging. *Computational Linguistics*, 21(4): 543-565.

Ding, Shengshu. 1961. Xiandai Hanyu Yufa Jianghua. *Beijing: Commercial Press.*

Huang, Xiaojiang et al. 2008. Learning to Identify Chinese Comparative Sentences. *Journal of Chinese Information Processing*, 22(5): 30-37.

Jindal, Nitin and Bing Liu. 2006. Identifying Comparative Sentences in Text Documents. In *Proceedings of SIGIR’06*, pp.244-251.

Jindal, Nitin and Bing Liu. 2006. Mining Comparative Sentences and Relations. In *AAAI* (22): 1331-1336.

Li, Linding. 1986. Hanyu Jufa Juxing. *Beijing: Commercial Press*, pp.285-301.

Li, Yan et al. 2013. PRIS_COAE at COAE 2013 Track. In *Proceedings of the fifth Chinese Opinion Analysis Evaluation*, pp. 53-69.

Liu, Yuehua. 1983. Shiyong Xiandai Hanyu Yufa. *Beijing: Foreign Language Teaching and Research Press*, pp.833-854.

Lü, Shuxiang. 1942. Zhongguo Wenfa Yaolüe. *Beijing: Commercial Press*, pp.352-370.

Ma, JianZhong. 1989. Mashi Wentong. *Beijing: Commercial Press*, pp. 134-142.

Ramshaw, Lance. A. and Mitchell P. Marcus. 1999. Text Chunking Using Transformation-based Learning. In *Natural language processing using very large corpora*, pp. 157-176. Springer Netherlands.

Shao, Jingmin. 1990. Biziju Tihuan Guilü Chuyi. *Zhongguo yuwen, vol.6.*

Song, Rui et al. 2009. Chinese Comparative Sentences Identification and Comparative Relations Extraction. *Journal of Chinese Information Processing*, 23(2): 102-122.

Tan, Songbo et al. 2013. Overview of Chinese Opinion Analysis Evaluation 2013. In *Proceedings of the fifth Chinese Opinion Analysis Evaluation*, pp. 5-33.

Wei, Xianhui et al. 2013. DUTIR: Method Research of Sentiment Analysis and Elements Extraction of Chinese Short Text. In *Proceedings of the fifth Chinese Opinion Analysis Evaluation*, pp. 116-128.

Yang, Seon and Youngjoong Ko. 2011. Extracting Comparative Entities and Predicates from Text Using Comparative Type Classification. In *Proceedings of the 49th Annual Meeting of the Association for Computational Linguistics: Human Language Technologies*, pp. 1636-1644.

Zhou, Hongzhao et al. 2014. Chinese Comparative Sentences Identification and Comparative Elements Extraction Based on Semantic Classification. *Journal of Chinese Information Processing*, 28(3): 136-141.

Zhu, Dexi. 1961. Shuo De. *Zhongguo yuwen*, 12:1-15.

Appendix

ICTCLAS Part-of-Speech Tags

Tag	Part-of-speech	
A	Adjective	形容词
AD	Adverbial adjective	副形词
AN	Nominal adjective	名形词
D	Adverb	副词
E	Exclamative particle	叹词
M	Numeral	数词
N	Noun	名词
NZ	Proper noun	专有名词
P	Preposition	介词
Q	Classifier	量词
RY	Wh-pronoun	疑问代词
UDE1	"De"	的
VSHI	"Shi"	是
VN	Gerund	名动词
VYOU	"You"	有
WJ	Period	句号
X	Character	字符
Y	Modal particle	语气词

A CRF Method of Identifying Prepositional Phrases in Chinese Patent Texts

Hongzheng Li and Yaohong Jin
Institute of Chinese Information Processing, Beijing Normal University, Beijing, 100875, China
CPIC-BNU Joint Laboratory of Machine Translation, Beijing Normal University, Beijing, 100875, China
lihongzheng@mail.bnu.edu.cn, jinyaohong@bnu.edu.cn

Abstract

This paper presents a Conditional Random Field (CRF) method of identifying prepositional phrases (PP) in Chinese patent documents. By using the CRF model, the identification process can be recognized as sequence labelling issue. After analyzing the characteristics of PP chunks in large scale corpus, we design several essential and helpful features and feature templates for recognizing PP chunks, and then use a CRF toolkit to train the model to identify PPs. At last, some experiments are conducted to justify the effects of the model, both the precision and recall rates are over 92%, higher than the baseline, indicating the method is reasonable and effective.

1 Introduction

Prepositional phrases (PP), as a traditional important phrase type, are widely distributed in Chinese patent documents. According to (Li, et al., 2014), in 500 randomly extracted sample patent sentences, 226 sentences contained PP chunks, accounting for 45.2% of the sample. Compared with other Chinese domain texts, PP chunks in patent documents tend to have following more specific features.

To begin with, they usually have more complex and longer structures with more words, they can be composed of prepositions (prep.) and noun phrases (NP), verb phrases (VP) or even clauses. Second, some preposition in PP are multi-category words, the preposition may also serve as a noun, verb, conjunction etc. in various contexts. Last but not least, there also exists many parallel and nested PPs. While coordinate PPs means several PPs appear together in a sentence, nested refer to those PPs composed of another PP and other ingredients. Following is an example in patent texts:

该真空工具[PP1 通过[PP3 在控制器中]连接这些网络环片段][PP2 为实验装置]提供一个低温泵。(The vacuum tool can provide a pump for the experiment instrument by connecting the network ring parts in the controller.)

As shown, the example contains three PPs, in which PP1 and PP2 are parallel, and in the long nested PP1 chunk "通过……片段", there exists another PP3 "在控制器中"(in the controller).

All these features result in more difficulties in identifying PPs. However, it is worth noting that, recognizing the PPs properly plays positive roles in various application fields of Natural Language Processing (NLP).

Assuming in the Chinese sentence S=W_1, W_2, W_3……W_n, string W_i, W_{i+1}……W_j is the supposed PP, the main task of PP identification is actually to identify W_i as left boundary word(LBW)and W_j as right boundary word(RBW) of the PP and then recognize the whole string as PP chunk. More specifically, since the LBW is the preposition itself, how to identify the RWB correctly is a key issue in the whole identification process.

Considering the wide distribution of PPs in patent documents and its important impacts on processing modules such as chunking and parsing in NLP, in this paper, we tried to apply the Conditional Random Field (CRF) model to PP identification in patent texts. By designing some features and labelling the PP sequences in corpus first and then training the features with the CRF toolkit, PP chunks can be identified. We also conducted experiments to justify the effects of the method, and the experimental results showed the proposed approaches can improve the performance of identifying Chinese PPs significantly.

The rest of this paper are organized as follow. Section 2 discusses some related work, section 3 presents the CRF-based identification method, section 4 conducts some experiments and gives

Proceedings of the Eighth SIGHAN Workshop on Chinese Language Processing (SIGHAN-8), pages 86–90,
Beijing, China, July 30-31, 2015.

related analysis, and the last section discusses the conclusion and future work.

2 Related Work

As a powerful statistical sequence modeling framework that combines the advantages of both the generative model and the classification model, CRF was first introduced into language processing in (Lafferty, et al., 2001). Since then, the model has been applied to various NLP tasks such as word segmentation (Tseng, et al., 2005), Semantic Role Labelling (Cohn and Blunsom, 2005) and parsing (Finkel, et al., 2008; Yoshimasa, et al., 2009), gaining great achievement. And CRF has become increasingly popular in recent years.

PP structures in sentences has been studied for long decades. However, differences in syntactic structures between Chinese and English have resulted in various research strategies: for English PP, researchers mainly focus on PP attachment disambiguation based on statistic and corpus methods (Brill, et al., 1994; Pantel and Lin, 1998; Briscoe and Carroll, 1995; Schwartz, et al., 2003; McLauchlan, 2004).

On the other hand, for Chinese PP, mainly focus on identifying and parsing the PP chunks by using rule-based method (Liang, et al. 2013, Hu, 2015) and popular statistical models, including HMM (Xi and Luo, 2007; Zhang, et al., 2011), SVM (Wen and Wu, 2009), Maximum Entropy (ME) Model (Lu, et al., 2010), and CRF models (Tan et al., 2005; Hu, 2008; Zhang, 2013). (Chen, et al.)(2005) proposed four models (SVMs, CRFs, TBL and MBL) to describe an empirical study of Chinese chunking on a corpus extracted from UPENN Chinese Treebank-4 (CTB4). Some others (Fu and Li, 2010; Zan, et al., 2013) also presented hybrid methods to recognize PPs by combining rules with statistic methods. Generally, recognizing Chinese PPs belongs to the category of shallow parsing in NLP.

While the CRF method has been usually applied to identifying Chinese PPs in common newswire texts, there exists few research on other specific domains. Thus, we decide to apply the method in patent documents.

3 CRF Identification Model

In this paper, we use the CRF++ toolkit (V0.53)[1] to train the model for identifying the PP chunks and test the trained sequences.

3.1 Sequential Labelling

Chunking based on CRF method is usually recognized as sequential labelling issue. Input *X* is a data sequence to be labelled, and Output *Y* is a corresponding labelled sequence, which is taken from a specific tag set. The probability assigned to a labelled sequence for a particular sequence of characters by a CRF model can be defined as follow:

$$P(Y|X) = \frac{1}{Z(X)} exp(\sum_k \lambda_k f_k) \qquad (1)$$

Where *Z(X)* is the normalization factor, f_k is a set of features, and λ_k is the corresponding weight.

We adopt the B-I-E-O scheme as tag sets to label PP chunks in the sentence. B-I-E refers to the Beginning, Intermediate and End elements of PP structure, and O for Outsides of the chunk.

Here is an example in patent text:

本发明*通过采用先进技术*而提高生产力。

(The invention improves the productivity by adopting advanced technology.)

The italic string "通过……技术"is the PP chunk. After word segmentation processing, the sentence can be labelled as:

本发明 O 通过 B 采用 I 先进 I 技术 E 而 O 提高 O 生产力 O 。O

Thus, Input *X* = {本发明 通过 采用 先进 技术 而 提高 生产力 。}

Correspondingly, Output *Y* = {O B I I E O O O O}

3.2 Features

Features play a very important role in the CRF model. Although CRF can define features indefinitely, the more features don't always means the better training result. After analyzing the structural and linguistic features of patent sentences in large scale corpus, we defined following five effective and representative features for the model. Each feature is composed of feature name and its value.

Feature	Value
Word	Each word itself in the sentence.
POS	POS of each word and punctuations (marked as "punc") in the sentence.
Candidate left boundary (LB)	From the current word, find forward to find the prep. If the preposition exists, the value is the preposition itself; otherwise "N".

[1] http://crfpp.googlecode.com/

Candidate right boundary (RB)	If current word can be RBW of PP, mark “Y”; otherwise “N”.
Candidate LW	The word behind the RB, which is also helpful in the identification, is defined as last word (LW). If current word is LW, then mark “Y”; otherwise “N”.

Table 1. Feature Sets of the Model

After word segmentation, we manually label each patent sentence that includes PP chunks with above features.

Table 2 shows a tagged sequence example in part 3.1.

Words	POS	Candidate LBW	Candidate RBW	Candidate LW	Tag Set
本发明	n	N	N	N	O
通过	prep	通过	N	N	B
采用	v	通过	N	N	I
先进	a	通过	N	N	I
技术	n	通过	Y	N	E
而	conj	通过	N	Y	O
提高	v	通过	N	N	O
生产力	n	通过	N	N	O
。	punc	通过	N	N	O

Table 2. A Tagged example

The first five columns are designed features, and the last column represents tag set of the sequences. According to the format of the CRF toolkit, each column is separated by a separator, and each sentence sequence is separated by a line break.

3.3 Feature Templates

We also design essential feature templates for the model according to the defined feature sets. The model generates numerous feature functions, which will directly affect the performance of the model in turn.

CRF models generally include atomic and composite feature templates. Since alone atomic feature templates only show feature information of single locations, which is likely to cause greater deviations between expectations and actual results, leading to inaccurate estimation parameters. Therefore, in our paper, the atomic features are combined to form composite feature templates to describe dependencies between the characteristics of labelled units and contexts by defining window of each feature.

The size of window in the sequences is defined as two. That means, we consider the features of current word (W_0), next word (W_1), second character back W_0 (W_2), previous character (W_{-1}) and second character before W_0 (W_{-2}). All the templates are in the form of Unigram in the toolkit to train the data, and no Bigram templates are used.

3.4 Architecture

Here’s the basic architecture of the CRF model for identifying the PP chunks.

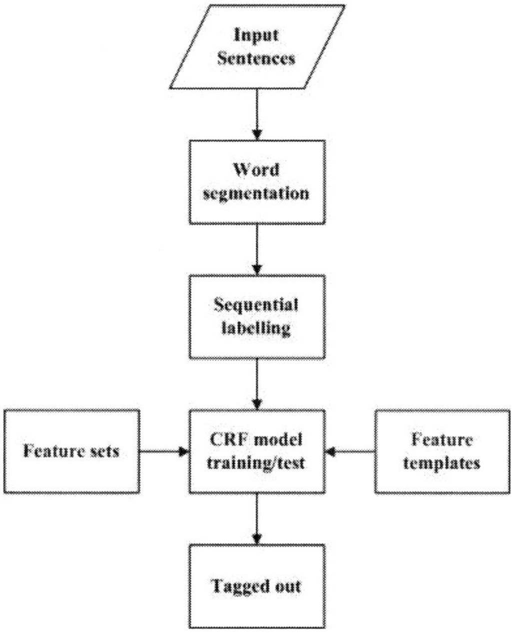

Figure 1. CRF Model Architecture

4 Experiment

After training the model, in this part, we continue use the toolkit to test the identification effects. Precision rate (P), Recall rate (R) and F1, defined as follows, are three evaluation metrics of the experiment.

$$P = \frac{N2}{N1} \times 100\% \quad (2)$$

$$R = \frac{N2}{N} \times 100\% \quad (3)$$

$$F1 = \frac{2 \times P \times R}{P+R} \times 100\% \quad (4)$$

Where *N* refers to the total number of PP chunks in the test set, *N1* refers to the identified number of PP by the model, and *N2* refers to the correctly identified number of PP.

4.1 Test Results

We manually extracted 1017 sentences containing PP chunks as the final test set from the developing set of patent MT subtask in the NTCIR-9 workshop[2], which is composed of 2000 parallel Chinese-English sentences.

The experiment adopted the 5-fold cross validation method: the whole set was divided into five equal parts, in which four parts were used as training sets, and the other one as test set. Thus, we totally conducted five experiments, and the average data of the five experiments were considered as final results. Then, we compared the results with the baseline (Hu, 2015), which used the same test set and tested with a rule-based system (Zhu and Jin, 2012).

Performances of the five experiments and comparison are shown in the following tables.

Test	P (%)	R (%)	F1 (%)
Test1	94.36	91.09	92.70
Test2	92.41	91.77	92.97
Test3	93.10	95.30	94.19
Test4	93.83	92.12	93.51
Test5	91.68	93.22	92.44
Average	**93.08**	**92.71**	**93.16**

Table 3. Performances of the experiments

	P (%)	R (%)
Baseline	90.81	86.64
CRF	93.08	92.71
Gain	**+2.27**	**+6.07**

Table 4. Comparison of Baseline and CRF

4.2 Discussion

In the experiments, the final metrics were all over 92%, and were higher than baseline, clearly indicating that the method performed well in identifying the PP chunks. Different from other three tests, the reason why the recall rates in test 3 and test 5 were higher than the precision rates lied in that the identified numbers of PP were more than the total numbers of PP in the two tests.

Since most experiments in previous related works employed newswire corpus as test set, totally different from the patent texts, thus we suppose that there may exist no necessary comparisons between our results with previous works.

After analyzing the results, we also concluded several following reasons accounting for error identifications:

First, some prepositions almost did not appear in the training test, as a result, the model could not obtain their features, and consequently, while they appeared in the test set, they were more difficult to be correctly identified.

Second, some PP chunks were ambiguous. Under this condition, it was not easy to determine the right boundaries of the chunks. For example, in the sentence "通过本发明的*墨水着色剂*可以有效地使实验产品沉淀。", the italic noun "墨水(ink)" is followed by another noun "着色剂(colorants)", it is not really clear which noun should actually be the proper boundary of the PP chunk. If the two nouns represent a compound noun, then the boundary should be the second noun; on the contrary, if they are independent of each other, then the boundary should be the first noun, and the second noun will serve as subject of the sentence.

Last, the model is quite sensitive to features in the sequences, during the label process, error and improper manually tagged information is inevitable, which can also result in error identifications.

5 Conclusion and Future Work

In this paper, we presented a CRF-based method for identifying the Chinese PP chunks in patent texts. Based on analysis of large scale patent texts, we designed several essential features for the model according to various characteristics of Chinese PPs, after labelling the sequences and training the model by using a CRF toolkit, we conducted some experiments to justify the performance of the method. Both final precision and recall rates were over 92%, and higher than the baseline, indicating the CRF-based method is effective and performs well in identifying PPs, although there still existed some error identifications.

In the future, we will pay more attention to the ambiguous PP chunks, consider more useful and effective features into the model, and continue to expand the size of patent corpus to be labelled, hoping to further improve the identification effects of PP chunks.

Acknowledgements

This work was supported by the National Hi-Tech Research and Development Program of China (2012AA011104).

[2] http://research.nii.ac.jp/ntcir/ntcir-9/data.html

Reference

Brill E. and Resnik P. 1994. A Rule-Based Approach to Prepositional Phrase Attachment Disambiguation. In *Proceedings of the 15th Conference on Computational Linguistics*, 1198-1204.

Chaohua Lu, Guangjun Huang and Zhibing Guo. 2010. Identification of Chinese Prepositional Phrase Based on Maximum Entropy. *Communications Technology*, 43(5):181-183,186.

Edward Briscoe and John Carroll. 1995. Developing and Evaluating a Probabilistic lr Parser of Part-of-Speech and Punctuation Labels. In *Proceedings of the IWPT*, 48–58.

Goto, I., Lu, B., Chow, K. P., Sumita, E., and Tsou, B. K. 2011. Overview of the Patent Machine Translation Task at the NTCIR-9 Workshop. In *Proceedings of NTCIR9*, 559-578.

Hefang Fu and Zhaoxia Li. 2010. Discussion on the Integration of Statistical Learning Method and Artificial Rule Method for Prepositional Phrase Recognition. *Modern Computers*, 11:17-20.

Hongzheng Li, Yun Zhu, Yang Yang and Yaohong Jin. 2014. Reordering Adverbial Chunks in Chinese-English Patent Machine Translation. In *Proceeding of IEEE International Conference on Cloud Computing and Intelligence Systems*, 375-379.

Hongying Zan, Tengfei Zhang and Kunli Zhang. 2013. Automatic Recognition Research on Preposition's Usages Based on Combination of Rules and Statistics. *Computer Engineering and Design*, 34(6):2152-2157.

Jianqing Xi and Qiang Luo. 2009. Research on Automatic Identification for Chinese Prepositional Phrase Based on HMM. *Computer Engineering*, 33(3):172-173,182.

Jie Zhang. 2013. Research on Chinese Prepositional Phrase Identification based on Multi-Layer Conditional Random Fields.

Jenny Rose Finkel, Alex Kleeman and Christopher D. Manning. 2008. Efficient, Feature-based, Conditional Random Field Parsing. In *Proceedings of ACL*, 959-967.

Kunli Zhang, Yingjie Han, Hongying Zan and Yingcheng Yuan. 2011. Prepositional Phrase Boundary Identification Based on Statistical Models. *Journal of Henan Normal University (Natural Science Edition)*, 41(6): 636-640.

Lafferty, John, A. McCallum, and F. Pereira. 2001. Conditional Random Field: Probabilistic Models for Segmenting and Labeling Sequence Data. In *Proceedings of the 18th International Conference on Machine Learning 2001*, 282-289.

Mark McLauchlan. 2004. Thesauruses for Prepositional Phrase Attachment. In *Proceedings of CoNLL*, 73-80.

Mengjie Liang, Yu Song, Yingjie Han and Hongying Zan. 2013. Automatic Annotation Research on Preposition Usage Based on Sorting Rules. *Journal of Henan Normal University (Natural Science Edition)*, 41(3):152-155.

Miaomiao Wen and Yunfang Wu. 2009. Feature-rich Prepositional Phrase Boundary Identification Based on SVM. *Journal of Chinese Information Processing*, 23(5):19-24.

Pantel P, Lin D. 1998. An Unsupervised Approach to Prepositional Phrase Attachment Using Contextually Similar Words. In *Proceedings of Association for Computational Linguistics*, 101-108.

Renfen Hu. 2015. on the Methods of Auto-Identifying Prepositional Phrases in Chinese-English Patent Machine Translation. *Applied Linguistics*, 136-144.

Schwartz L, Aikawa T, Quirk C. 2003. Disambiguation of English PP Attachment Using Multilingual Aligned Data. In *Proceedings of MT Summit IX.*

Silei Hu. 2008. Automatic Identification of Chinese Prepositional Phrase Based on CRF.

Trevor Cohn and Philip Blunsom. 2005. Semantic Role Labelling with Tree Conditional Random Fields. In *Proceedings of the 9th Conference on Computational Natural Language Learning (CoNLL)*, 169–172.

Tseng, H., Chang, P., Andrew, G., Jurafsky, D., and Manning, C. 2005. A Conditional Random Field Word Segmenter for SIGHAN Bakeoff 2005. In *Proceedings of the fourth SIGHAN workshop on Chinese language Processing.*

Wenliang Chen, Yujie Zhang and Hitoshi Isahara. 2006. An Empirical Study of Chinese Chunking. In Proceedings of the COLING/ACL 2006 Main Conference Poster Sessions, 97–104.

Yongmei Tan, Tianshun Yao, Qing Chen, and Jingbo Zhu. 2005. Applying Conditional Random Fields to Chinese Shallow Parsing. In *Proceedings of CICLing-2005*, 167–176.

Yoshimasa Tsuruoka, Jun'ichi Tsujii and Sophia Ananiadou. 2009. Fast Full Parsing by Linear-Chain Conditional Random Fields. In *Proceedings of the 12th Conference of the European Chapter of the ACL*, 790–798.

Yun Zhu and Yaohong Jin. 2012. A Chinese-English Patent Machine Translation System based on the Theory of Hierarchical Network of Concepts. *The Journal of China Universities of Posts and Telecommunications*, 140-146.

Emotion in Code-switching Texts: Corpus Construction and Analysis

Sophia Yat Mei Lee[†], **and Zhongqing Wang**[†,‡]
[†] Department of Chinese and Bilingual Studies, The Hong Kong Polytechnic University
[‡] Natural Language Processing Lab, Soochow University, China
{sophiaym, wangzq.antony}@gmail.com

Abstract

Previous researches have focused on analyzing emotion through monolingual text, when in fact bilingual or code-switching posts are also common in social media. Despite the important implications of code-switching for emotion analysis, existing automatic emotion extraction methods fail to accommodate for the code-switching content. In this paper, we propose a general framework to construct and analyze the code-switching emotional posts in social media. We first propose an annotation scheme to identify the emotions associated with the languages expressing them in a Chinese-English code-switching corpus. We then make some observations and generate statistics from the corpus to analyze the linguistic phenomena of code-switching texts in social media. Finally, we propose a multiple-classifier-based automatic detection approach to detect emotion in the code-switching corpus for evaluating the effectiveness of both Chinese and English texts.

1 Introduction

Due to the popularity of opinion-rich resources (e.g., online review sites, forums, and the micro-blog websites), emotion analysis in text is of great significance in obtaining useful information for studies on social media (Pang et al., 2002; Liu et al., 2013; Lee et al., 2014). Previous researches have mainly focused on analyzing emotion through monolingual text (Chen et al., 2010; Lee et al., 2013a). However, code-switching posts are also common in social media. Emotions can be expressed by either monolingual text or bilingual text in the code-switching posts. Code-switching text is defined as text that contains more than one language ('code') (Adel et al., 2013; Auer, 1999). [E1-E3] are three examples of code-switching emotional posts on *Weibo.com* that contain both Chinese and English texts. [E1] expresses the *happiness* emotion through English, and the *sadness* emotion in [E2] is expressed through both Chinese and English, while the *sadness* emotion in [E3] is expressed through a mixed Chinese-English phrase (hold 不住 '*cannot take it*').

[E1] 玩了一下午轮滑 **so happy**！
(*I went rollerblading the whole afternoon,* ***so happy!***)

[E2] 开学以来，浮躁的情绪。不安稳的心态。确实该自己检讨一下了。。。**sigh~~~**
(*I have been grumpy and emotional since the first day of school, unstable mindset too. It's really time to self-evaluate...**sigh~~~***)

[E3] 上了一天的课，嗓子 **hold 不住**了啊
(*I have been teaching the whole day, my throat* ***can't take it anymore***.)

Despite the important implications of code-switching for emotion analysis, existing emotion analysis approaches fail to accommodate for the code-switching content. Thus, there is a crucial need for analyzing emotions in code-switching texts.

In this paper, we provide a well-defined and efficient method for constructing and analyzing a large-scale code-switching corpus from social media. We believe the annotated corpus provides a valuable resource for both linguistic analysis as well as natural language processing of emotion and code-switching texts. We construct and analyze the corpus using the below steps: First, we extract and filter the code-switching posts from the large-scale dataset by removing monolingual

Proceedings of the Eighth SIGHAN Workshop on Chinese Language Processing (SIGHAN-8), pages 91–99,
Beijing, China, July 30-31, 2015.

and noise posts. Second, we propose an annotation scheme to annotate both emotions and the language(s) expressing the emotions (hereafter caused language(s)) in the data set. Third, we analyze the agreement of the corpus to verify the quality of the annotation and effectiveness of the scheme. We also show some observations and statistics on the corpus to analyze the linguistic phenomena of code-switching texts on social media. Finally, we propose a multiple-classifier-based automatic detection approach to detect emotion in the annotated code-switching corpus for indicating the effectiveness of both Chinese text and English text in code-switching posts in detecting emotions.

The rest of the paper is organized as follows. In Section 2, we give an overview on the related work. In Section 3, we introduce our data collection method and the annotation scheme. In Section 4, we report the analysis of the corpus including the inter-annotator agreement as well as other relevant statistics. In Section 5, we propose an automatic emotion detection framework on code-switching text. Finally, we conclude our work in Section 6.

2 Related Work

In this section, we discuss related works on emotion analysis and code-switching text analysis.

2.1 Emotion Analysis

The earliest research on emotion has focused on the representation and processing of emotion in facial expressions and body language (Andrew, 1963; Ekman and Friesen, 1978). More recently, there has been mounting research on the neurobiological basis of emotion (Olson et al., 2007; Hervé et al., 2012) and how emotion is linked with other aspects of human cognition (Smith and Lazarus, 1993; Smith and Kirby, 2001; Bridge et al., 2010).

Emotion has been well studied in natural language processing, while most previous researches focused on analyzing emotions in monolingual text. Some of these studies focus on lexicon building, for example, Rao et al. (2012) automatically building the word-emotion mapping dictionary for social emotion detection, and Yang et al., (2014) propose a novel emotion-aware topic model to build a domain specific lexicon. Moreover, emotion classification is one of the important tasks in emotion analysis. For example, Liu et al., (2013) used co-training framework to infer the news reader's and comment writer's emotion collectively; Wen and Wan (2014) used class sequential rules for emotion classification of micro-blog texts by regarding each post as a data sequence.

The research of emotion has also been linked to the field of bilingualism. Previous studies have demonstrated that emotion is closely related to second language learning and use (Arnold, 1999; Schumann, 1999), as well as bilingual performance and language choice (Schrauf, 2000; Pavlenko, 2008). For example, there are a number of factors that may impact the use of emotion vocabulary, such as sociocultural competence, gender, and topic (Dewaele and Palvenko, 2002).

Despite a growing body of research on emotion, little has been done on the analysis of emotion in code-switching contexts due to the complications in processing two languages at the same time.

2.2 Analysis of Code-switching Texts

Research on code-switching can be traced back to the 1970s. Several theories have been proposed to account for the motivation behind code-switching such as diglossia (Blom and Gumperz, 1972), communication accommodation theory (Giles and Clair, 1979), the markedness model (Myers-Scotton, 1993), and the conversational analysis model (Auer, 1984).

Code-switched documents have also received considerable attention in the NLP community. Several studies have focused on identification and analysis, including mining translations in code-switched documents (Ling et al., 2013), predicting code-switched points (Solorio and Liu, 2008), identifying code-switched tokens (Lignos and Marcus, 2013), adding code-switched support to language models (Li and Fung, 2012), and learning poly-lingual topic models from code-switching text (Peng et al., 2014).

Another related research topic, multilingual natural language processing, has begun to attract attention in the computational linguistic community due to its broad real-world applications. Relevant studies have been reported in different natural language processing tasks, such as parsing (Burkett et al., 2010), information retrieval (Gao et al., 2009), text classification (Amini et al., 2010), and sentiment analysis (Lu et al., 2011).

However, none have studied the multilingual code-switching issues in the task of emotion detection and classification. This area of research is especially crucial when public emotions are mostly expressed on the Internet. Additionally, the important implications of code-switching in emotion analysis serve as a first step towards an automatic multilingual classification system.

3 Data Collection and Annotation

In this section, we describe how to collect and filter code-switching posts on *Weibo.com*. We also discuss the annotation scheme and the annotation tool.

3.1 Data Collection

We sourced our data set from *Weibo.com*, one of the famous SNS websites in China. We identified a post as code-switched if at least two predicted languages, i.e. Chinese and English, appeared in the text. As the encoding of Chinese and English characters is different (the maximum number of encoded English characters is less than 128), we thus utilized each character code to identify the language in a simple manner. We also remove the noise, and advertisement posts ([E4] and [E5] are the examples of noise and advertisement posts).

[E4]分享 **Carpenters** 的歌曲《**Close To You**》
(*Share* ***Carpenters'*** *music <**Close To You**>*)

[E5]**the face shop** 提供新款化妆品
(***the face shop*** *provides new make-up*)

3.2 Annotation Scheme

Five basic emotions were annotated, namely *happiness*, *sadness*, *fear*, *anger* and *surprise* (Lee et al., 2013b). Two languages, Chinese and English, were annotated as caused languages. Since emotion can be expressed through the two languages separately or collectively, and also could be expressed through mixed phrases e.g. "笑 cry" (*very happy*), we thus need to annotate four kinds of causal situations, i.e. *English*, *Chinese*, *Both*, and *Mixed*. Following are descriptions of these situations:

➢ **Chinese (CN)** means the emotion of the post is individually expressed through the Chinese text. As *Weibo.com* is a Chinese SNS Website, Chinese is the dominant language on this website. Most of the posts express emotions through the Chinese text. [E6] is an example. The emotion of *surprise* is expressed through the Chinese text.

[E6] 静静坐下来看别人 **show** 啦。刚刚在节目里看到妈咪和弟的视频真的很意外！
(*I set down quietly to watch someone else's* ***show****. To my surprise, both my mother and brother appeared on the programme.*)

➢ **English (EN)** means the emotion of the post is individually expressed through the English text. As English is the minority language, there are fewer English words in the posts to express emotions. [E1] is an examples expressing *happiness* emotion and expressed through English text.

➢ **Both (BOTH)** means the emotions of the post are expressed through both Chinese and English text. Note that the emotions expressed through the two languages would either be the same or different. [E2] and [E7] are two examples. The *anger* emotion of [E2] is expressed through both the Chinese and English text. However, the *happiness* emotion of [E7] is expressed through the Chinese text, while the *surprise* emotion is expressed through English.

[E7] 太感动这真是一个大 **surprise** 看的时候就鸡冻屎了
(*I was so touched and excited to see this great* ***surprise****.*)

➢ **Mixed (MIXED)** means the emotion of the post is expressed through a Chinese-English mixed phrase, such as the emotion being expressed through the mixed phrase "hold不住" in [E3]. Note that there are limited mixed patterns, and Table 1 illustrates the examples of mixed phrases in our dataset.

Moreover, the emotions of some posts are expressed implicitly, and do not contain explicit keywords to express emotions. [E8] and [E9] are examples of this, while these two posts both express a *sadness* emotion, [E8] is expressed through Chinese text, and [E9] is expressed through both Chinese and English text.

[E8] 英语的魅力在于，好不容易看懂每个word 却看不懂组成的 **sentence.**
(*The charm of English is that you can't always understand the meaning of the* ***sentence****, even though you understand the meaning of each word in the sentence.*)

[E9] **stream flow, slowly away a few leaf, also taking the memory**.溪水缓慢地流动着，带走了几片落叶，也带走了记忆。

(The Chinese text is translated from English text)

Pattern	Examples
有 feel (*sense*)	-
hold 住	hold 住 *(can take it)* hold 不住 (*cannot take it*)
XX cry	笑 cry (*smile, very happy*) 感动 cry (*touched*) 帅 cry (*awesome*)
太 man 了 (*handsome*)	-

Table 1: Examples of mixed phrases

3.3 Annotation Tool and Format

An annotation tool is designed to facilitate the annotation process which allows better consistency.

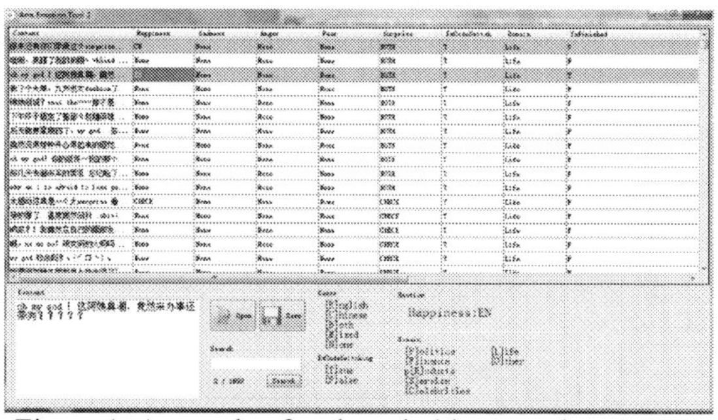

Figure 1: A sample of code-switching emotion annotation using the annotation tool

Figure 1 shows an example instance annotated with both emotion and caused languages using our annotation tool. For each emotion, annotators marked whether the post expresses emotion, together with the caused languages toward the emotion.

Figure 2 is a sample of an annotated instance. Each instance contains the caused language with the emotion tag, e.g., "<Happiness>CN </Happiness>", while the example tag means the post expresses the *happiness* emotion through Chinese text.

<Post id="1">
<Happiness>
CN
</Happiness>
<Sadness>
None
</Sadness>
<Anger>
None
</Anger>
<Fear>
None
</Fear>
<Surprise>
None
</Surprise>
<Content>
baby 生日快乐！附加征婚：此女贤良淑德 拥有现代女性智慧和古典女性的温婉 诚征凹凸曼 非诚勿扰
</Content>
</Post>

Figure 2: A sample of an annotated instance

4 Statistics and Analysis

In this section, we analyze the agreement of the corpus, and present some observations and statistics.

4.1 Agreement Analysis

To verify the quality of the annotation, two human annotators were asked to annotate 1,000 posts. We then calculated the inter-annotator agreement between them using Cohen's Kappa coefficient. Table 2 shows the results of agreement analysis. We find that the agreement is high, indicating that the quality of the annotation and scheme is effective. In addition, the agreement of emotion annotation is lower than that of caused language, which probably due to the fact that some posts express more than one emotion, and some emotions are expressed implicitly.

	Kappa score
Emotion	0.692
Caused Language	0.767

Table 2: Results of agreement analysis

4.2 Statistics and Observations

In this subsection, we discuss some statistics from the dataset.

General Distribution of Data

Out of 4,195 annotated posts, 2,312 posts are found to express emotions. Moreover, 81.4% of emotional posts are expressed through Chinese. Although English contains relatively fewer words in each post, there are still 43.5% of emotional posts are expressed through English. This indicates that English is of vital importance to emotion expression even in code-switching contexts dominated by Chinese. Note that, there are overlaps between Chinese and English emotional posts, since some emotional posts are conducted in both Chinese and English. Besides, although some posts express the same emotion through both Chinese and English text ([E2]), there are still some posts expressed different emotions through different languages. For example, the *happiness* emotion in [E7] is expressed through Chinese, while the *surprise* emotion is expressed through English.

Moreover, as shown in Figure 3, we find that most posts describe people's daily lives, since people like to discuss their life on their microblogs, and posts from financial and political domains were limited.

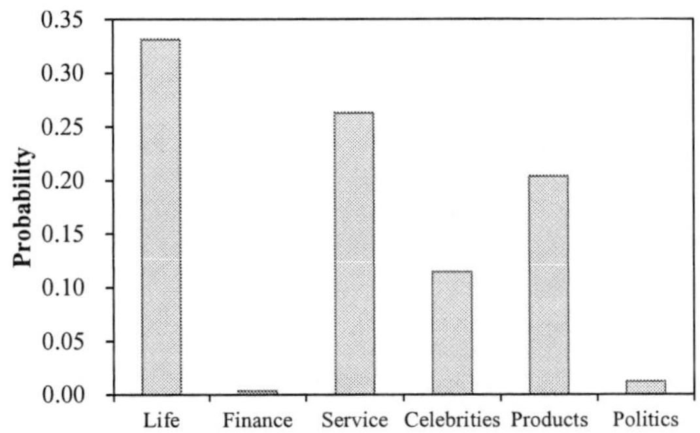

Figure 3: Domain statistics from the data set

Joint Distribution of Emotions and Caused Languages

For the purpose of analyzing the distribution of emotions and the caused languages, we first calculate the joint distribution between emotions and caused languages as in Figure 4. The Y-axis of the figure presents the conditional probability of a post expressing the emotion e_i given that l_j is the caused language, $p(e_i \mid l_j)$.

It is suggested in Figure 4 that: 1) *happiness* occurs more frequently than other emotions; 2) people prefer to use English text to express *happiness* more than *sadness*; 3) the distribution of emotions expressed through Chinese and English text are similar; and 4) *fear* and *surprise* occur less frequently in English text.

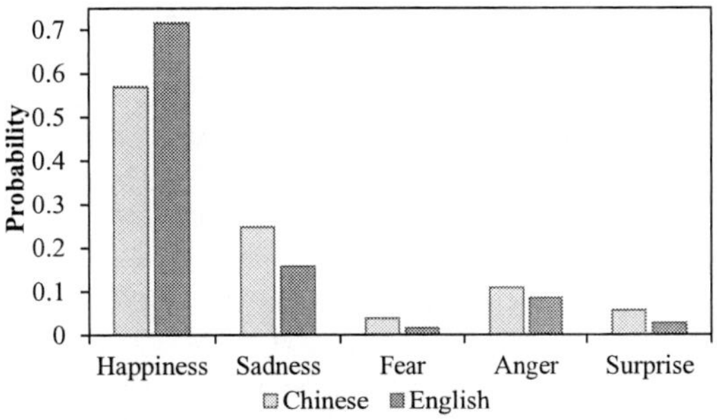

Figure 4: Joint Distribution of Emotions and Caused Languages

Transfer Probability between Emotions

We then examine the conditional probabilities of a post expressing emotion e_i given that the post contains emotion e_j. The conditional probabilities are shown as in Table 3.

From the table, we find that the probability that a post contains more than one emotion is small. Moreover, the probability of polarity shifting between emotions (*happiness* vs. *sadness*, *fear*, *anger*) is limited.

	Happiness	Sadness	Fear	Anger	Surprise
Happiness	-	0.060	0.016	0.025	0.019
Sadness	0.088	-	0.023	0.033	0.023
Fear	0.114	0.114	-	0.068	0.023
Anger	0.090	0.079	0.034	-	0.011
Surprise	0.086	0.071	0.014	0.043	-

Table 3: The transfer probability between emotions

Transfer Probability between Caused Languages

We also examine the conditional probabilities of the emotion(s) expressed in one language l_i given that the emotion is expressed in another language l_j simultaneously in a post. The conditional probabilities are shown as in Table 4.

	Chinese	English
Chinese	-	0.236
English	0.614	-

Table 4: Transfer probability between caused languages

From the table, we find that there is a high probability that the two languages both express emotions, especially when given that the emotion is expressed in English. It is also highly likely that the emotion would be expressed in Chinese.

Sentence Length Distribution of Each Language

Table 5 shows the statistics on the average sentence length of each language. We notice, as our data are always written by Chinese individuals, the length of Chinese words is longer than English words. Besides, the emotions expressed through English text are mostly single words, e.g., *happy*, *high*, and *surprise*. Note that, as mentioned above, although the length of Chinese words is longer than English words, English is of vital importance to emotion expressions even in code-switching context dominated by Chinese.

	#avg. word
Chinese	19.8
English	2.9

Table 5: Statistics on average word length

Distribution of Cue Words

In addition, we count the top-10 frequency emotion cue words of both English and Chinese text as given in Table 6. We find that the most frequent cue words express *happiness* emotions, for example, *happy*, *nice*, and *喜欢* (*like*). What is more, there are several negative expressions in the top-10 English cue words, e.g. *sorry* and *shit*, while the top-10 Chinese cue words are all positive. This may be due to the fact that expressing the negative emotion through native language (Chinese) would be too explicit for Chinese individuals, while most of them tend to express their negative emotions implicitly.

English	**Chinese**
Happy	喜欢 (*like*)
Love	快乐 (*happy*)
Good	希望 (*hope*)
Nice	开心 (*joyful*)
Sorry	哈哈 (*haha*)
Shit	幸福 (*happiness*)
Luck	真心 (*heartfelt*)
Thank	可爱 (*cute*)
Perfect	感谢 (*thank*)
Sweet	成功 (*success*)

Table 6: Statistics of emotional cue words

5 Automatic Emotion Detection in Code-switching Texts

Based on the annotated corpus data, we attempt to detect emotion in code-switching text automatically. Results show both Chinese and English texts are effective, and the classifier combination approach which incorporates both Chinese and English text achieves the best performance.

5.1 Overview of Detection Approach

A straightforward approach to detect emotion in code-switching text is using a supervised learning approach to classify the mixed text without any processing. Besides, we extract unigrams as a feature for each post. As emotions could be expressed in either Chinese or English text, we also adopt two classification approaches which consider Chinese or English texts individually.

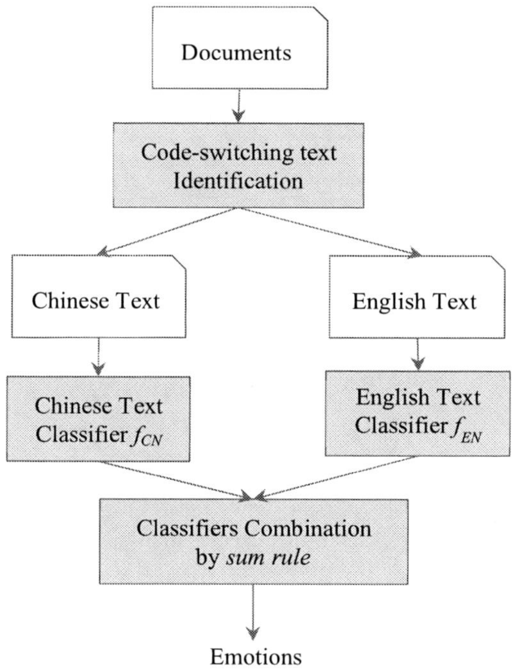

Figure 5: Overview of the multiple-classifiers-based detection framework

However, a more effective way to detect emotion in code-switching posts is incorporating both Chinese and English text through a Multiple Classifier System (MCS). The key issue in constructing a multiple classifier system is to find a suitable way to combine the outputs of the base classifiers. In MCS literature, various methods are available for combining the outputs, such as fixed rules including the voting rule, the product rule and the sum rule (Kittler et al., 1998; Li et al., 2010). In this study, we adopt the sum rule, a popular fixed rule to combining the outputs of both Chinese and English text classifiers.

For utilizing MCS to detect emotion in code-switching texts, we first define the base classifiers. In this paper, we use the Chinese text classifier f_{CN} and English text classifier f_{EN} which only considers Chinese text or English text individually as two base classifiers. Each base classifier provides a kind of confidence measurement, e.g., posterior probabilities of the test sample belonging to each class. Formally, each base classifier f_i assigns a test sample (denoted as x_i) a posterior probability vector $\vec{P}(x_i)$:

$$\vec{P}(x_i) = \left(p(c_1 \mid x_i), ..., p(c_j \mid x_i), ..., p(c_n \mid x_i) \right)^t \quad (1)$$

Where $p(c_j \mid x_i)$ denotes the probability that the i-th base classifier considers the sample belonging c_j .

After we define the two base classifiers, we can use a sum rule to combine the base classifiers by summing the posterior possibilities and using the sum possibility for decision, i.e.

$$\text{assign } y \rightarrow c_j \text{ where } k = \underset{j}{\operatorname{argmax}} \sum_i p(c_j \mid x_i)$$

Figure 5 illustrates the process of the multiple classifier system for emotion detection in code-switching texts.

5.2 Experiments

As described in Section 3, the data are collected from *Weibo.com*. We randomly select half of the posts as the training data and another half as the test data. We use *FudanNLP*[1] for Chinese word segmentation and Maximum Entropy (ME) as the basic supervised classification model, while the ME algorithm is implemented with the *MALLET Toolkit*[2]. Note that, as the number of posts which express *fear* and *surprise* are limited, we only detect the other three kinds of emotions, i.e. *happiness*, *sadness*, and *anger*.

As discussed in the above subsection, we use the following approaches for automatic emotion detection in code-switching text:

- f_{ALL}: which uses all the words of each post as a feature to train a Maximum Entropy (ME) classification model.
- f_{CN}: which only uses the Chinese text of each post as a feature to train a Maximum Entropy (ME) classification model.
- f_{EN}: which only uses the English text of each post as a feature to train a Maximum Entropy (ME) classification model.
- f_{comb}: which combines the results of the Chinese text classifier f_{CN} and English text classifier f_{EN} using the sum rule.

The results of emotion detection are shown in Table 7. The performance indicates the accuracy of detecting emotions in code-switching text.

	Acc.
f_{ALL}	0.509
f_{CN}	0.521
f_{EN}	0.409
f_{comb}	0.539

Table 7: Results of emotion detection in code-switching text

From the table, we find that:

1) The performance of basic approach f_{ALL} which uses mixed text directly is inferior.
2) As Chinese is the dominant language, and the English text is loosely distributed, using Chinese text (f_{CN}) outperforms both using all text (f_{ALL}) and English text (f_{EN}). Besides, as the English texts in the posts are always composed of single words, f_{EN} is much lower than the other two approaches.
3) As incorporating both Chinese classifiers and English classifiers to a multiple classifier system, f_{comb} achieves a better performance than the other approaches. It also indicates that both Chinese text and English text in code-switching posts are effective for detecting emotions.

6 Conclusion

This paper presents the development of a code-switching emotion corpus in which the emotion is expressed through either Chinese or English. We first collect and filter the data from *Weibo.com*, which is annotated with both emotion and caused language; we then analyze the inter-annotator agreement on the dataset, and present our findings and analysis. Finally, we propose a multiple-classifiers-based approach to detect emotion in the annotated code-switching corpus. Results show that both Chinese text and English text in code-switching posts are effective

[1] https://code.google.com/p/fudannlp/
[2] http://mallet.cs.umass.edu

in detecting emotions. We believe that emotions analysis in code-switching text underlies an innovative approach towards a linguistic model of emotion as well as automatic emotion detection and classification.

Acknowledgments

The work is funded by an Early Career Scheme (ECS) sponsored by the Research Grants Council of Hong Kong (No. PolyU 5593/13H), and supported by the National Natural Science Foundation of China (No. 61273320, and No. 61375073) and the Key Project of the National Natural Science Foundation of China (No. 61331011).

Firstly, we need to thank the hard works of the annotators. We thank Prof. Shoushan Li for his useful discussion. We acknowledge Helena Yan Ping Lau for corpus analysis and insightful comments. We also thank anonymous reviewers for their valuable suggestions and comments.

References

Adel H., N. Vu, and T. Schultz. 2013. Combination of Recurrent Neural Networks and Factored Language Models for Code-Switching Language Modeling. In *Proceedings of ACL-13.*

Andrew R. 1963. Evolution of Facial Expressions. *Science*, 142, 1034-1041.

Amini, M., C. Goutte, and N. Usunier. 2010. Combining Coregularization and Consensusbased Self-training for Multilingual Text Categorization. In *Proceeding of SIGIR-10.*

Auer P. 1999. *Code-Switching in Conversation.* Routledge.

Arnold J. 1999. *Affect in Language Learning*. Cambridge, MA: CUP.

Auer P. 1984. *Bilingual Conversation.* Amsterdam: John Benjamins.

Blom J., and J. Gumperz. 1972. Social Meaning in Linguistic Structures: Code Switching in Northern Norway. *Directions in Sociolinguistics*. New York: Winston.

Bridge D., J. Chiao, and K. Paller. 2010. Emotional Context at Learning Systematically Biases Memory for Facial Information. *Memory & Cognition*, 38, 125-133.

Burkett, D., and D. Klein. 2008. Two Languages are Better than One (for Syntactic Parsing). In *Proceedings of EMNLP-08.*

Chen Y., S. Lee, S. Li, and C. Huang. 2010. Emotion Cause Detection with Linguistic Constructions. In *Proceeding of COLING-10.*

Dasgupta S., and V. Ng. 2009. Mine the Easy, Classify the Hard: A Semi-Supervised Approach to Automatic Sentiment Classification. In *Proceedings of ACL-IJCNLP-09.*

Dewaele J., and A. Pavlenko. 2002. Emotion Vocabulary in Interlanguage. *Language Learning*, 52 (2), 265-324.

Ekman, P., and W.V. Friesen. 1978. *Facial Action Coding System.* California: Consulting Psychology Press.

Gao W., J. Blitzer, M. Zhou, and K. Wong. 2009. Exploiting Bilingual Information to Improve Web Search. In *Proceedings of ACL/IJCNLP-09.*

Giles, H., and R. Clair. 1979. *Language and Social Psychology*. London: Basil Blackwell.

Hervé, P., A. Razafimandimby, M. Vigneau, B. Mazoyer, and N. Tzourio-Mazoyer. 2012. Disentangling the Brain Networks Supporting Affective Speech Comprehension. *NeuroImage*, 61(4), 1255-1267.

Kittler J., M. Hatef, R. Duin, and J. Matas. 1998. On Combining Classifiers. *IEEE Trans. PAMI*. 20.226-239.

Lee S., H. Zhang, and C. Huang. 2013a. An Event-Based Emotion Corpus. In *Proceedings of CLSW 2013.*

Lee S., Y. Chen, C. Huang, and S. Li. 2013b. Detecting Emotion Causes with a Linguistic Rule-Based Approach. *Computational Intelligence,* 29(3), 390-416.

Lee S., S. Li, and C. Huang. 2014. Annotating Events in an Emotion Corpus. In *Proceedings of LREC-14.*

Li S., S. Lee, Y. Chen, C. Huang, and G. Zhou. 2010. Sentiment Classification and Polarity Shifting. In *Proceeding of COLING-10.*

Li Y., and P. Fung. 2012. Code-switch Language Model with Inversion Constraints for Mixed Language Speech Recognition. In *Proceedings of COLING-12.*

Ling W., G. Xiang, C. Dyer, A. Black, and I. Trancoso. 2013. Microblogs as Parallel Corpora. In *Proceedings of ACL-13.*

Liu H., S. Li, G. Zhou, C. Huang, and P. Li. 2013. Joint Modeling of News Reader's and Comment Writer's Emotions. In *Proceedings of ACL-13, shorter.*

Lignos C., and M. Marcus. 2013. Toward Web-scale Analysis of Codeswitching. In *Proceedings of Annual Meeting of the Linguistic Society of America.*

Lu B., C. Tan, C. Cardie, and B. Tsou. 2011. Joint Bilingual Sentiment Classification with Unlabeled Parallel Corpora. In *Proceedings of ACL-11.*

Myers-Scotton C. 1997. *Duelling Language: Grammatical Structure in Code-switching*. Oxford: Clarendon.

Olson I., A. Plotzker, and Y. Ezzyat. 2007. The Enigmatic Temporal Poles: A Review of Findings on Social and Emotional Processing. *Brain*.

Pavlenko A. 2008. Structural and Conceptual Equivalence in Acquisition and Use of Emotion Words in a Second Language. *Mental Lexicon*, 3(1): 91-120.

Peng N., Y. Wang, and M. Dredze. 2014. Learning Polylingual Topic Models from Code-Switched Social Media Documents. In *Proceedings of ACL-14*.

Quan C., and F. Ren. 2009. Construction of a Blog Emotion Corpus for Chinese Emotional Expression Analysis. In P*roceedings of EMNLP-09*.

Rao Y., X. Quan, W. Liu, Q. Li, and M. Chen. 2012. Building Word-emotion Mapping Dictionary for Online News. In *Proceedings of SDAD 2012 The 1st International Workshop on Sentiment Discovery from Affective Data*.

Schrauf R. 2000. Bilingual Autobiographical Memory: Experimental Studies and Clinical Cases. *Culture and Psychology*. 6 (4), 387-417.

Schumann J. 1999. A Neurobiological Perspective on Affect and Methodology in Second Language Learning. *Affect in Language Learning*. Cambridge: CUP, 28-42.

Smith C., and L. Kirby. 2001. Toward Delivering on the Promise of Appraisal Theory. *Appraisal processes in emotion: Theory, methods, research*. Oxford, UK: Oxford University Press.

Smith C., and R. Lazarus. 1993. Appraisal Components, Core Relational Themes, and the Emotions. *Cognition and Emotion,* 7, 233–269.

Solorio T., and Y. Liu. 2008. Learning to Predict Code-Switching Points. In *Proceedings of EMNLP-08*.

Volkova S., W. Dolan, and T. Wilson. 2012. CLex: A Lexicon for Exploring Color, Concept and Emotion Associations in Language. In *Proceedings of EACL-12*.

Wen S. and X. Wan. 2014. Emotion Classification in Microblog Texts Using Class Sequential Rules. In *Proceedings of AAAI-14*.

Xu G., X. Meng, and H. Wang. 2010. Build Chinese Emotion Lexicons Using A Graph-based Algorithm and Multiple Resources. In *Proceeding of COLING-10*.

Yang M., B. Peng, Z. Chen, D. Zhu, and K. Chow. 2014. A Topic Model for Building Fine-grained Domain-specific Emotion Lexicon. In *Proceedings of ACL-14*.

Chinese in the Grammatical Framework: Grammar, Translation, and Other Applications

Aarne Ranta
University of Gothenburg
aarne@chalmers.se

Yan Tian
Shanghai Jiao Tong University
tianyan@sjtu.edu.cn

Qiao Haiyan
Sun Yat-sen University
qiaohy@mail.sysu.edu.cn

Abstract

Grammatical Framework (GF) is a grammar formalism based on type theory and functional programming. It is also a platform for multilingual applications such as translation, localization, and information retrieval. To enable non-linguist programmers to build linguistically precise applications, GF provides a Resource Grammar Library (RGL), which defines the basic syntax, morphology, and lexicon of languages in the form of easily usable software libraries. The RGL is an open-source collaborative project, which currently covers 30 languages with a shared tree structure. Chinese, in addition to basic RGL, has a translation lexicon of over 30,000 lemmas and a mobile translation app. This paper gives an overview of GF, emphasizing applications where Chinese is related to other languages. We also address the theoretical question how Chinese fits into the framework with a shared tree structure.

1 Introduction

Computer implementations of grammars used to be an important part of computational linguistics (e.g. TAG (Joshi, 1985), LFG (Bresnan, 1982), CCG (Steedman, 2000), and HPSG (Pollard and Sag, 1994)). But in the last couple of decades, they have been largely overshadowed by statistical methods and machine learning. However, hand-written grammars can still give valuable contributions to natural language processing. For instance, in machine translation (MT), grammars written with guidance from linguistic knowledge have the following advantages:

- Grammars **don't need so much data**, which is useful for language pairs with a lack of parallel texts.
- Systems using grammars are **predictable and programmable**, which is useful in mission-critical applications.
- Grammars are **compact representations** compared with e.g. phrase tables, which is useful in mobile applications.

In Information Retrieval (IR),

- Grammars enable a **precise logical analysis of content**, supporting detailed queries and powerful reasoning.

In Computer-Aided Language Learning (CALL),

- Grammars support **detailed error analysis and explanations**.

The main problems associated with grammars are their **limited coverage** and the **high cost** of building them. However, techniques of shallow parsing such as parsing by chunks (Abney, 1991) make it possible to overcome the limited coverage and, among other things, create robust MT systems based on grammars rather than statistics (Forcada et al., 2011).

The cost of grammar engineering can be reduced by modern software engineering techniques, which have made programming in the 2010's more productive than it used to be in the "golden age" of computational grammars, 1970's and 1980's. Such techniques form the basis of GF (Grammatical Framework, (Ranta, 2004; Ranta, 2011)), which is a programming language designed for multilingual grammar engineering:

- **Functional programming**, enabling powerful abstractions and generalizations;
- **Static type systems**, guaranteeing the consistency of the highly complex programs that grammars are;
- **Advanced module systems**, supporting collaborative work and maximal code reuse;
- **Libraries**, supporting division of labour and encapsulation of expert knowledge.

GF enables building a comprehensive grammar in a few months, e.g. as a Masters thesis project

Proceedings of the Eighth SIGHAN Workshop on Chinese Language Processing (SIGHAN-8), pages 100–109,
Beijing, China, July 30-31, 2015.

(Zimina, 2012). Adapting a GF grammar to a new setting, such as a dialogue system or a domain-specific translator, can be accomplished in a few days (Perera and Ranta, 2007; Ranta et al., 2012).

GF started at Xerox Research Centre Europe in 1998 as a part of a project on **multilingual document authoring** (Dymetman et al., 2000). Released open-source later, GF today is a collaborative project with over 150 developers around the world. In China, GF courses have been organized at Shanghai Jiao Tong University and at Sun Yat-Sen University in Guangzhou. The standard textbook on GF, (Ranta, 2011) has recently been translated to Chinese (Ranta, 2014b).

The GF software and grammar resources, including Chinese, are available from the GF homepage[1]. The licenses of the grammar reaources (LGPL and BSD) permit all kinds of uses, including commercial applications.

This paper gives an overview of the GF resources and applications available for Chinese. Section 2 introduces the idea of multilingual grammars. Section 3 describes the GF tool set and applications enabled by them. Section 4 summarizes the main issues encountered when adding Chinese to GF. Section 5 describes some controlled language applications. Section 6 shows how GF can scale up to wide-coverage translation. Section 7 discusses evaluation and Section 8 related work. Section 9 concludes.

2 Multilingual grammars

A grammar defines a language: a set of strings and the analyses assigned to them, typically trees. In the usual view, every language has its own grammar, and trees in different grammars are distinct objects. Grammar-based translation systems such as (Rayner et al., 2000) typically map the trees of one language into trees of another language.

Monolingual grammars can also be written in GF. But its real power comes with **multilingual grammars**, where several languages use the same trees, called **abstract syntax trees** (ASTs). An AST expresses **pure constituency**, for instance, that a sentence has a certain subject, verb, and object. But it does not specify the actual words, their inflection forms, or the order in which they appear.

To give a simple example, consider the sentence *I love you*. A possible AST is

[1] www.grammaticalframework.org

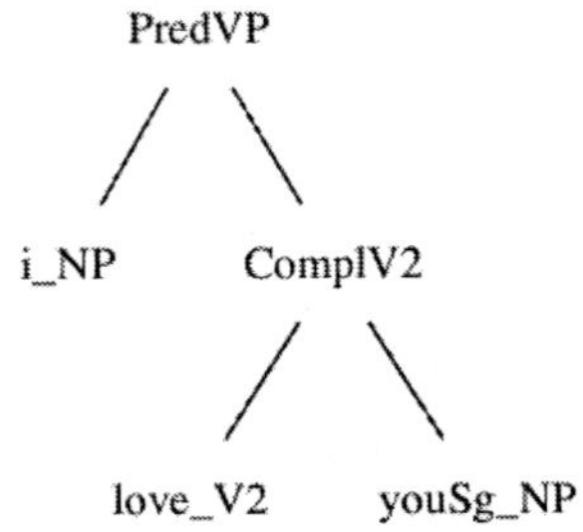

more conveniently represented as a LISP-like term

```
(PredVP i_NP
  (ComplV2 love_V2 youSg_NP))
```

An AST has a function F and 0 or more argument ASTs. In the example, the function is `PredVP`, marking predication. Its arguments are `i_NP`, marking the noun phrase *I* and `(ComplV2 love_V2 youSg_NP)`, which is a verb phrase built from the two-place verb *love* and the pronoun *you* in the singular sense.

The 0-place functions `i_NP`, `love_V2`, and `youSg_NP` have names formed from English words, but they stand for interlingual word senses, so that for instance the plural and singular *you* have distinct functions. A more accurate analysis might also distinguish genders and politeness levels of pronouns.

The AST above corresponds to different strings in different languages. For example:

- English: *I love you*
- Chinese: *wo ai ni* ("I love you", just changing the words)
- Dutch: *ik houd van je* ("I hold of you", adding a preposition)
- French: *je t'aime* ("I you-love", the object pronoun before the verb)
- Italian: *ti amo* ("you love(1st person singular)", dropping the subject pronoun)

(We use Pinyin for most Chinese examples in this paper, but the actual GF implementation uses simplified Chinese characters in UTF-8 encoding.)

Even more variation is shown when question formation is applied to the clause:

```
(QuestCl (PredVP i_NP
  (ComplV2 love_V2 youSg_NP)))
```

Languages use widely different mechanisms to express this:

- English: *do I love you* (auxiliary verb)
- Chinese: *wo ai ni ma* (particle) or *wo ai bu ai ni* (reduplication)

- Dutch: *houd ik van je* (inversion)
- French: *t'aime-je* (inversion)
- Italian: *ti amo* (intonation in spoken question)

Nonetheless, the AST can be shared.

The ASTs have types and are thus terms in type theory. Each function has a type that indicates the types of its arguments and its value. Basic types (**categories**) are introduced by rules such as

```
cat NP
```

Functions are introduced by rules such as

```
fun PredVP : NP -> VP -> Cl
```

stating that PredNP takes two arguments, of types NP and VP, and returns a Cl (clause).

Each function has, for each language in the grammar, a **linearization rule**, which specifies how trees are converted to strings. Thus the rule

```
lin PredVP np vp = np ++ vp
```

says that the first argument (i.e. the linearization of the first subtree) is concatenated (++) to the second argument.

The fun and lin rules together correspond to the context-free rule

```
Cl ::= NP VP
```

and decompose it to a tree-building rule and a string-producing rule. The decomposition makes it possible to build multilingual grammars with shared trees and different strings.

However, to deal with the differences of languages, we need linearization rules that don't just operate on strings but also on **tables** that encode the inflectional forms of words and phrases, and on **records** that store different kinds of grammatical information. We don't want this kind of information enter the abstract syntax, because it is language-specific.

Thus in Chinese, it is enough to linearize noun phrases to strings,

```
lin i_NP = "wo"
```

But in English, noun phrases are linearized to records that have two fields: one labelled s ("string"), which contains an inflection table with nominative and accusative cases, and one labelled a ("agreement"), which contains a record that in turn contains a number n and a person p):

```
lin i_NP = {
  s = table {Nom => "I" ; Acc => "me"} ;
  a = {n = Sg ; p = Per1}
  }
```

The linearization rule of PredVP uses the information in the record to select the nominative case for the subject and guarantee that the verb phase agrees to the subject:

```
lin PredVP np vp =
  np.s ! Nom ++ vp ! np.a
```

(The notation np.s computes the s part from the record np, and vp ! np.a computes the value for np.a from the table vp.)

Just like ASTs, linearizations thus have types, but these types are dependent on language. The linearization type of the category NP in Chinese is defined by the rule

```
lincat NP = Str
```

whereas in English a more complex type is needed,

```
lincat NP = {
  s : Case => Str ;
  a : {n : Number ; p : Person}
  }
```

marking a record that holds a table and the agreement features.

Linearization types vary greatly from one language to another, partly because of morphology; for instance, Finnish noun phrases have 15 cases. But even Chinese, which has no morphological variation, is not entirely context-free (string-based). If we want to keep the common abstract syntax, we need to use records to encode **discontinuous constituents**, that is, phrases in which later functions insert new words. An example is question formation by verb reduplication. The linearization types involved are

```
lincat
  QCl = Str
  Cl = {subj : Str ; vp : VP}
  VP = {verb : Str ;
        neg : Str ; obj : Str}
```

The neg part of the VP is *bu* or *mei*, depending on verb. The question forming function is linearized as follows with reduplication:

```
lin QuestCl cl =
  cl.subj ++ cl.vp.verb ++ cl.vp.neg ++
  cl.vp.verb ++ cl.obj
```

(Questions with particle *ma* could be given as an alternative linearization.)

Multilingual grammars are a generalization of **synchronous grammars** (Aho and Ullman,

1969), originally defined for context-free grammars but later generalized to tree-adjoining grammars (TAG) (Shieber and Schabes, 1990). GF adds to synchronous grammars the explicit notion of abstract syntax, which has replaced the direct transfer of synchronic grammars in modern compiler construction (Appel, 1998). Tables and records are related to unification grammars (Shieber, 1986), but the expressive power of GF is lower: it is equivalent to PMCFG (parallel multiple context-free grammars) (Seki et al., 1991), which enjoys polynomial parsing. The word "parallel" in PMCFG means that an expression may be duplicated in linearization. This is not needed in all languages, but Chinese reduplication questions are an example of it.

3 The GF toolset

The GF set of tools has several components:

- The **GF programming language** and its compiler (Ranta, 2010).
- **PGF, Portable Grammar Format**, the "machine language of GF" generated by the GF compiler (Angelov et al., 2009).
- **Runtime interpreters** for PGF, enabling mobile and web applications (Ranta et al., 2010; Angelov et al., 2014).
- The **Resource Grammar Library** (RGL), currently comprising 30 languages (Ranta, 2009).
- A **wide-coverage translation system** (Hallgren, 2014 2015).
- **Controlled language applications** (Angelov and Ranta, 2009).
- **Conversions** of GF grammars and trees to other formats, such as speech recognition grammars (Bringert, 2007), finite state automata in the Xerox format (Beesley and Karttunen, 2003), dependency trees in the CoNLL format (Eisner, 2007), and phrase tables in the Giza++ format (Och and Ney, 2003).

The last item, conversions, guarantees that GF is not a closed world, but that GF grammars can be reused in other ecosystems. The advantage of GF is that it enables programming on a higher level than e.g. hand-written speech recognition grammars (Perera and Ranta, 2007). This is essential in order for grammar writing to be competitive with machine learning and statistics. Even in statistical systems, writing grammars can be a way to compensate for the lack of data (Jonson, 2006).

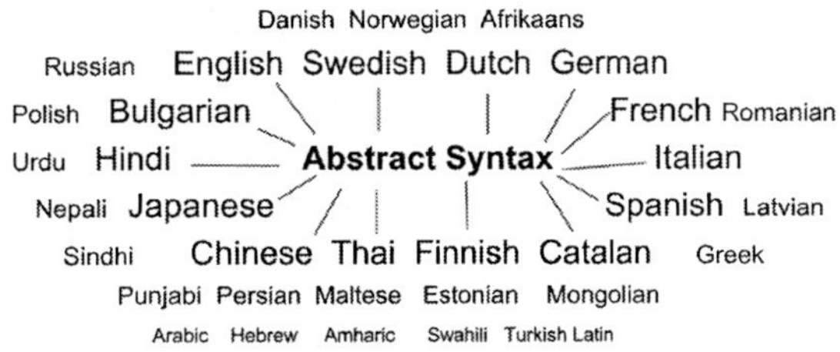

Figure 1: Languages in GF RGL.

The key for a language to enter the GF ecosystem is an RGL implementation. The RGL has a **core abstract syntax** consisting of 86 categories and 216 functions. In addition to this, it a test lexicon of 524 word senses. A language implementation with linearizations for all these functions is accessible in all parts of the "GF ecosystem", via the common abstract syntax.

Figure 1 shows the languages currently available in the RGL. The 14 innermost languages, connected with lines with the abstract syntax, have a large lexicon enabling wide-coverage translation (see Section 6). The layer around them contains 16 languages, which also have complete RGL implementations. The outermost 6 languages have partial RGL implementations and could be completed in weeks or a couple of months.

4 The Chinese grammar

The Chinese resource grammar was started in 2012, as the third East-Asian language of the RGL, after Thai and Japanese, and as the 25th language altogether. (Peng, 2013) gives some details of the first version of the grammar.

Since the abstract syntax of the RGL was originally designed for European languages (English, French, Russian, German, Swedish, Finnish), the question was how well this structure fits on an East-Asian language. Due to the expressive power of GF's linearization rules, it is usually possible to tweak the grammar to work. But if the abstract syntax does not fit well, the grammar needs lots of artificial parameters that make the code more complex than with a more native tree structure. In this respect, Japanese has turned out to be one of the most difficult languages (Zimina, 2012).

language	LoC	CF rules	CF/GF
Chinese	1200	317	7
English	1800	18998	432
Finnish	3000	137558	3126
French	3600	152632	3469
Japanese	3700	4521	103

Table 1: The complexity of some RGL implementations. LoC = lines of GF source code in core RGL (216 functions). CF rules = number of context-free rules generated from a set of 44 functions from the resource grammar.

4.1 How complex is Chinese grammar?

In the case of Chinese, the fear of complexity turned out to be unnecessary. The total core RGL implementation for Chinese has 1,200 lines of code, which is less than for most other languages; see Table 1 for some examples. The amount of code reflects both the inherent complexity of the language (in particular morphology) and the fit of the abstract syntax.

The common abstract syntax of the RGL hides the morphological variation completely, but linearization rules have to address it with tables and records. But even on this level, the abstractions provided by functional programming keep the code sizes similar for different languages, as shown in Table 1.

To get another view on the complexity, one can look at the size of the context-free expansions of the languages. Table 1 gives the number of rules in context-free expansions for the core 44 rules of the resource grammar, together with the context-free/GF rule ratio. As the table also shows the source code size for each language, it gives an idea of the compression that GF grammars achieve in comparison to actual language data. The expansion algorithm is defined in (Bringert, 2007); the result is still only approximative because GF is not context-free. The figures say that every Chinese GF rule can be approximated by just 7 context-free rules, whereas French needs over 3000 context-free rules on the average! The explosion is a multiplicative effect of the parameters involved in the argument and value types of syntactic combination functions. Nevertheless, the source code for French is just 3 times the source code for Chinese.

4.2 Linguistic phenomena

We have already mentioned reduplication as a feature of Chinese that needs attention. Another characteristic feature are **classifiers** attached to common nouns (`CN`) and used in combinations with determiners (`Det`). They can be controlled by a linearization type that has a field for the classifier,

```
lincat CN = {s : Str ; c : Str}
```

The determination rule,

```
fun DetCN : Det -> CN -> NP
```

places the classifier between the determiner and the noun,

```
lin DetCN det cn = det ++ cn.c ++ cn.s
```

Since adjectives and even relative clauses are prefixed to the noun, the classifier can end up arbitrarily far from the noun that it depends on. This is a problem in chunk-based approaches to translation (see Section 5), but not in a proper grammar.

Another feature of Chinese that needed attention in the RGL is the position of adverbials, which need a parameter classifying them to time, place, and manner. Each of the classes has a different place in a sentence.

4.3 Segmentation

Since Chinese sentences are written without spaces between words, word segmentation is an important task in Chinese NLP (see e.g. (Wong et al., 2009)), needed as a preprocessor for almost any application. The Chinese RGL grammar solves this in the simplest possible way: with no preprocessing at all. Thus the GF parser reads Chinese input character by character, treating each character as a token, and tries to build the AST from this input. When the AST is constructed, word boundaries can be read out from it as a by-product.

One advantage of the method is that only grammatically possible word segmentations are returned. Another advantage is that all grammatically possible segmentations are accessible to the parser, while pre-processing segmentation, typically based on less information, might throw away grammatically correct segmentations.

Random testing with grammar-generated data suggests that the method does not slow down the parser significantly, and that different segmentation are not very frequent if they are required to be grammatically possible. However, this by-product of the Chinese GF grammar remains to be evaluated with real data.

5 Controlled language applications

GF was originally designed as a tool for CNL (Controlled Natural Language). In our sense of the word, a CNL is any fragment of natural language that has a precise grammar and can therefore be processed mechanically. The abstract syntax of a CNL is typically built on semantic grounds, so that the ASTs are more like logical formulas than linguistic syntax trees. In this way the grammars can be made more precise and also more idiomatic, because logical meanings are often expressed by different syntactic means in different languages.

Since the RGL takes care of linguistic details such as inflection and word order, GF is a productive way to implement CNLs: linearization rules are written in terms of RGL trees instead of records and tables. A typical CNL can in this way be implemented in a few days (Hallgren et al., 2012). Porting it to new languages is even quicker, because the same RGL functions can be reused most of the time. A new language can often be added to a CNL system in a few hours, which makes it easy to build multilingual systems.

Two major CNLs in GF have been ported to Chinese:

- Attempto Controlled English, a CNL for knowledge representation and reasoning, also available as a multilingual semantic wiki system, (Kaljurand and Kuhn, 2013).
- The MOLTO Phrasebook, a CNL supporting idiomatic translation of tourist phrases, also available as a mobile app (Ranta et al., 2012).

Many other CNLs have been created in the European MOLTO project (Caprotti, 2010 2013) and in other academic and commercial projects. This line of work might be the commercially most promising use of GF, since it can satisfy the needs of companies having to produce multilingual information rapidly and accurately, for instance for e-commerce purposes. For this purpose, the vocabulary and syntax may be restricted enough to support a CNL, and GF can easily make them multilingual. The grammar that is used for translation can also be easily converted to a query interpreter, and the abstract syntax is easy to link with other semantic information, e.g. web ontologies (Damova et al., 2014).

A formalized multilingual grammar can also help learners of foreign languages. For learning a language with a different word order and morphology (or the lack of morphology, as in Chinese), a multilingual grammar can be just the right thing. The grammar need not cover the whole language, but just the key structures in an accurate way. The grammar can support learning by translation, which has been proved an efficient way to learn and to teach foreign languages (Cook, 2010). The teacher can use the grammar to produce an infinite variation of sentence pairs as examples or exercises and show their correspondences and contrasts accurately by using alignments produced from the common AST. Figure 2 shows the word alignments between two different PP attachments: one with the bread, the other with the act of eating; Chinese places the PP to front the element that it modifies. Alignment illustrations like this are automatically generated by GF.

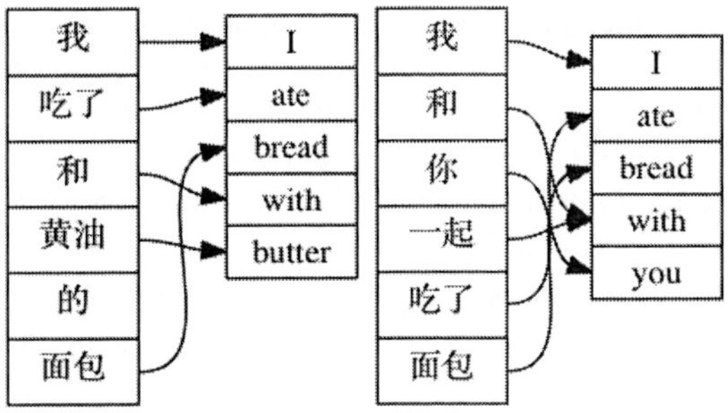

Figure 2: Word alignments for two PP attachments, automatically generated in GF.

6 Wide-coverage lexicon and translation

Unlike a typical CNL, the RGL is not domain-specific but tries to cover the whole language. Thus it is interesting to check if it can be used for "translating anything", like main-streams translation tools do. The GF Wide Coverage Translator, WCT (Hallgren, 2014 2015), is based on the RGL and the following additions:

- **Large lexicon**, with 66,000 word senses.
- **Syntax extensions**, structures not covered by the core RGL.
- **Back-up strategy for parsing**, to guarantee that the system always yields a result.
- **Disambiguation strategy**, to select from a potentially large number of syntax trees.

The current WCT covers 14 languages (Hallgren, 2014 2015). As it uses the ASTs as an interlingua, it enables the translation for $13 \times 14 = 182$

language pairs, 26 of which include Chinese; the languages are shown in Figure 1. Each languages implements at least 20,000 of the word senses.

Extending an RGL implementation to a baseline wide-coverage translator is a small task compared to building the RGL itself: a working system can be built in a few days, if a suitable word list is available. Only the lexicon needs to be implemented separately for each language: the rest is done on the level of the common abstract syntax.

The first version of the Chinese dictionary in WCT was built manually by a class of Chinese undergraduate students, covering 15,000 word senses. It was later completed by 20,000 more words from the Wiktionary. The quality of the automatically added words is lower than the manual words, and continuous checking and revision is a part of the workflow of improving the translator.

In addition to a dictionary, wide coverage translation needs syntax extensions in order to cover structures that are not in the core RGL. This could be done through precise linguistically analysis, like the RGL itself. But a cheaper way to increase coverage is to introduce a **chunking grammar**: a set of rules that enable chunk-by-chunk translation in cases where the entire sentence cannot be covered by a syntax tree.

The quality of chunk-based translation is generally lower than fully syntactic translation. Since there are by definition no grammatical dependencies between chunks, two kinds of errors arise:

- **Agreement**: a chunks cannot determine the features of another chunk.
- **Word order**: the syntactic roles of the chunks are not defined.

The agreement problem is not so visible in Chinese as in European languages, because of the lack of morphology. But a related problem is the choice of classifiers: if *five* and *cats* end up in different chunks when translating

I have five black cats

the result is likely to be

wo you wu ge hei mao

using the most frequent classifier *ge*, rather than

wo you wu zhi hei mao

using the proper cat classifier *zhi*. These effects are familiar from phrase-based statistical translation, where sentences are also built from chunks. The former translation is actually the result from Google translate on the date of writing this, whereas GF produces the latter one due to complete syntactic analysis.

As for word order, a typical problem is the placement of adverbs. In many European languages, adverbs such as the place are at the end of the sentence, but in Chinese, before the verb. A full syntactic analysis is able to "move" the adverb to the right place, but mere chunking cannot do this.

Since Chinese places prepositional phrases in front of they modify (Figure 2), English PP attachment is an ambiguity that cannot be solved by syntax alone: parsing provides both analyses and their linearizations, but it cannot select the correct one, even in clear cases like those in Figure 2. For the final disambiguation, either deeper semantic analysis or an accurate statistical model is needed.

Semantic analysis is easy to implement in a CNL but hard to scale up. Thus the WCT uses statistical disambiguation based on probabilities estimated from the Penn treebank (Marcus et al., 1993). The Penn trees are converted to abstract syntax trees of the RGL, and the frequencies of functions are computed (Angelov, 2011). As the trees are common to all the 30 languages of the RGL, the same model can be used for all of them. But a more adequate model would of course be expected from native treebanks, such as the Chinese Penn treebank (Xue et al., 2005), which remains as future work.

The WCT can be optimized for a special domain by combining it with an **Embedded CNL** (Ranta, 2014a). This means that CNL analyses are given priority over syntactic and chunk-based analyses, whenever available. The translator then generates high quality whenever the input matches the CNL; when not, the other analyses work as a back up that makes the translation robust. The mobile app (Angelov et al., 2014) and the web application (Hallgren, 2014 2015) mark the translations with colours, using green for CNL translations, yellow for syntactic translations, and red for chunk translations. Figure 3 shows the differences between them in the current system: the uppermost, green translation is perfect and idiomatic (using the MOLTO Phrasebook); the middle, yellow translation is syntactically correct but does not capture the meaning of the idiom; the third, red translation results from grammatically incor-

How far is the airport from the hotel?
从旅馆到机场有多远?
The vice dean kicked the bucket.
副院长踢了桶.
Little boy eat big snake.
小男孩吃大蛇.

Figure 3: Embedded CNL translation with syntactic and chunk-based back-ups.

rect input manages to render it chunks of intelligible Chinese.

The clearest advantage of grammars in translation is perhaps their compact size. The whole mobile app for 14 languages and 182 language pairs fits in a 35-megabyte binary file, which runs off-line in a mobile phone. Statistical translators, such as Google, are usually run over the internet; downloading stripped-down versions on Android phones is possible, but requires 200 megabytes per language pair.

7 Evaluation

The wide range of applications of GF creates several things to evaluate. Let us address what is perhaps the most frequent question: translation quality with the usual metrics BLEU and TER. Table 2 shows the first results from an evaluation campaign for English to Chinese translation on two different levels: semantic CNL (the MOLTO phrasebook) and wide-coverage GF translation (WCT). In these evaluations, we have machine-translated a set of sentences and created the reference translations by human post-editing. The CNL sentences come from a MOLTO test suite, whereas the WCT sentences are from news (50%), Europarl (25%), and fiction (25%). The table shows comparisons with systems (in WCT, Moses trained with United Nations data). For the CNL, is also shows Swedish and English comparisons.

As expected, GF outperforms the general-purpose Google translate in the CNL, even though Google can be quite good at idiomatic tourist phrases. The Finnish and Swedish CNLs get better scores because more work has been put to them. In the WCT, Moses is better than GF. It is too early to say how competitive GF can be made in this scenario, but an interesting case would be the translation between Chinese and some other language than English, with less parallel data available to build statistical systems from. GF translation is

task	BLEU	TER
CNL en-zh, GF	**84**	**9.5**
CNL en-zh, Google	50	35
CNL en-sv, GF	**96**	**1.7**
CNL en-sv, Google	61	19
CNL en-fi, GF	**89**	**5.3**
CNL en-fi, Google	44	33
WCT en-zh, GF	21	62
WCT en-zh, Moses	**36**	**43**

Table 2: First evaluation results for CNL (MOLTO Phrasebook) and WCT (the GF wide-coverage translator).

not affected by this problem.

It can be objected that the comparison between GF and Google translate is not fair in the CNL case, because the GF grammar was specifically tailored for the domain. But this is in fact the very point: since GF grammars are easy to adapt to specific domains, they are a useful technique when high quality is expected and the coverage can be limited. This way of using grammars has also shown commercial potential (Ranta et al., 2015).

8 Related work

The Chinese Penn Treebank (Xue et al., 2005) has been used for building grammars. In particular, (Yu et al., 2010) measures the accuracy and coverage of a generated HPSG grammar, and also lists smaller HPSG projects on Chinese. (Zhang et al., 2012) reports on a more comprehensive HPSG grammar and treebank. As for translation, several systems exist between English and Chinese, but for some of the languages in the GF WCT, e.g. Bulgarian and Finnish, only partially documented commercial systems (such as Google translate) are available. As for CNL, (Cardey et al., 2004) makes a suggestion for medical English-Chinese translation, but we haven't found complete CNL systems for Chinese other than those in GF.

9 Conclusion

We have shown the main ideas of GF and how they can be applied in NLP. The most mature applications are controlled-language tasks such as dissemination translation, language teaching, and natural language queries. Such task have commercial potential, and grammars gives full control on quality. GF makes the use of grammars feasible with its engineering tools and its library of 30 languages. The abstract structures originally created for European languages have proven to work for Chinese as well. GF also scales up to wide-coverage translation, but is not yet competitive with statistical methods. The main advantage in this task is the compact size of the system, making it possible to use 182 language pairs off-line in a mobile device.

References

Steven P. Abney. 1991. Parsing by chunks. In *Principle-Based Parsing*, pages 257–278. Kluwer Academic Publishers.

Alfred V. Aho and Jeffrey D. Ullman. 1969. Syntax directed translations and the pushdown assembler. *Journal of Computer and System Sciences*, 3(1):37 – 56.

Krasimir Angelov and Aarne Ranta. 2009. Implementing Controlled Languages in GF. In Norbert Fuchs, editor, *Workshop on Controlled Natural Language, CNL 2009*, volume 5972 of *LNCS/LNAI*.

Krasimir Angelov, Björn Bringert, and Aarne Ranta. 2009. PGF: A Portable Run-Time Format for Type-Theoretical Grammars. *Journal of Logic, Language and Information*.

Krasimir Angelov, Björn Bringert, and Aarne Ranta. 2014. Speech-enabled hybrid multilingual translation for mobile devices. *EACL'14*, pages 41–44.

Krasimir Angelov. 2011. *The Mechanics of the Grammatical Framework*. Ph.D. thesis, Chalmers University of Technology.

Andrew Appel. 1998. *Modern Compiler Implementation in ML*. Cambridge University Press.

Ken Beesley and Lauri Karttunen. 2003. *Finite State Morphology*. CSLI Publications.

Joan Bresnan, editor. 1982. *The Mental Representation of Grammatical Relations*. MIT Press.

Björn Bringert. 2007. Speech Recognition Grammar Compilation in Grammatical Framework. In *SPEECHGRAM 2007: ACL Workshop on Grammar-Based Approaches to Spoken Language Processing, June 29, 2007, Prague*.

Olga Caprotti. 2010–2013. MOLTO: Multilingual Online Translation. `http://www.molto-project.eu`

Sylviane Cardey, Peter Greenfield, and Xiaohong Wu. 2004. Designing a controlled language for the machine translation of medical protocols: The case of english to chinese. In *Machine Translation: From Real Users to Research, 6th Conference of the Association for Machine Translation in the Americas, AMTA 2004, Washington, DC, USA, September 28-October 2, 2004, Proceedings*, pages 37–47.

Guy Cook. 2010. *Translation in Language Teaching*. Oxford University Press.

Mariana Damova, Dana Dannélls, Ramona Enache, Maria Mateva, and Aarne Ranta. 2014. Multilingual natural language interaction with semantic web knowledge bases and linked open data. In *Towards the Multilingual Semantic Web*, pages 211–226. Springer Berlin Heidelberg.

Marc Dymetman, Veronika Lux, and Aarne Ranta. 2000. XML and multilingual document authoring: Convergent trends. In *Proc. Computational Linguistics COLING, Saarbrücken, Germany*, pages 243–249. International Committee on Computational Linguistics.

Jason Eisner, editor. 2007. *Proceedings of the 2007 Joint Conference on Empirical Methods in Natural Language Processing and Computational Natural Language Learning (EMNLP-CoNLL)*. Association for Computational Linguistics, Prague, Czech Republic, June.

Mikel L Forcada, Mireia Ginestí-Rosell, Jacob Nordfalk, Jim O'Regan, Sergio Ortiz-Rojas, Juan Antonio Pérez-Ortiz, Felipe Sánchez-Martínez, Gema Ramírez-Sánchez, and Francis M Tyers. 2011. Apertium: a free/open-source platform for rule-based machine translation. *Machine Translation*, 25(2):127–144.

Thomas Hallgren, Aarne Ranta, John Camilleri, Grégoire Détrez, and Ramona Enache. 2012. Grammar Tools and Best Practices. MOLTO Deliverable D2.3, June.

Thomas Hallgren. 2014–2015. GF Wide Coverage Translation Demo. `cloud.grammaticalframework.org/wc.html`

Rebecca Jonson. 2006. Generating statistical language models from interpretation grammars in dialogue system. In *Proceedings of EACL06, Trento, Italy*.

Aravind Joshi. 1985. Tree-adjoining grammars: How much context-sensitivity is required to provide reasonable structural descriptions. In D. Dowty, L. Karttunen, and A. Zwicky, editors, *Natural Language Parsing*, pages 206–250. Cambridge University Press.

Kaarel Kaljurand and Tobias Kuhn. 2013. A Multilingual Semantic Wiki Based on Attempto Controlled English and Grammatical Framework. In Philipp Cimiano, Oscar Corcho, Valentina Presutti, Laura Hollink, and Sebastian Rudolph, editors, *The Semantic Web: Semantics and Big Data. 10th International Conference, ESWC 2013, Montpellier, France, May 26-30, 2013. Proceedings*, volume

7882 of *Lecture Notes in Computer Science*, pages 427–441. Springer Berlin Heidelberg.

Mitchell P Marcus, Mary Ann Marcinkiewicz, and Beatrice Santorini. 1993. Building a large annotated corpus of English: The Penn Treebank. *Computational linguistics*, 19(2):313–330.

Franz Josef Och and Hermann Ney. 2003. A systematic comparison of various statistical alignment models. *Computational Linguistics*, 29(1):19–51.

Chen Peng. 2013. Implementation of a chinese resource grammar in grammatical framework. *International Journal of Knowledge and Language Processing*, 4(1):26–34.

Nadine Perera and Aarne Ranta. 2007. Dialogue System Localization with the GF Resource Grammar Library. In *SPEECHGRAM 2007: ACL Workshop on Grammar-Based Approaches to Spoken Language Processing, June 29, 2007, Prague*.

Carl Pollard and Ivan Sag. 1994. *Head-Driven Phrase Structure Grammar*. University of Chicago Press.

Aarne Ranta, Krasimir Angelov, and Thomas Hallgren. 2010. Tools for multilingual grammar-based translation on the web. In *Proceedings of the ACL 2010 System Demonstrations*, pages 66–71. Association for Computational Linguistics.

Aarne Ranta, Ramona Enache, and Grégoire Détrez. 2012. Controlled Language for Everyday Use: the MOLTO Phrasebook. In Tobias Kuhn and Norbert Fuchs, editors, *Controlled Natural Language*, volume 7427 of *LNCS/LNAI*. Springer.

Aarne Ranta, Christina Unger, and Daniel Vidal Hussey. 2015. Grammar engineering for a customer: a case study with five languages. In *GEAF-2015: ACL 2015 workshop on Grammar Engineering across Frameworks*. Association for Computational Linguistics.

Aarne Ranta. 2004. Grammatical Framework: A Type-Theoretical Grammar Formalism. *The Journal of Functional Programming*, 14(2):145–189.

Aarne Ranta. 2009. The GF Resource Grammar Library. *Linguistics in Language Technology*, 2:1–65.

Aarne Ranta. 2010. *Grammatical Framework: Programming with Multilingual Grammars*. CSLI Publications. to appear.

Aarne Ranta. 2011. *Grammatical Framework: Programming with Multilingual Grammars*. CSLI Publications, Stanford.

Aarne Ranta. 2014a. Embedded controlled languages. In *Controlled Natural Language - 4th International Workshop, CNL 2014, Galway, Ireland, August 20-22, 2014. Proceedings*, volume 8625 of *LNCS*.

Aarne Ranta. 2014b. *Yufa kuangjia wei duo zhong ziran yuyan yufa biancheng (Grammatical Framework: Programming with Multilingual Grammars). Chinese translation by Yan Tian*. Shanghai Jiao Tong University Press.

Manny Rayner, David Carter, Pierrette Bouillon, Vassilis Digalakis, and Mats Wirén. 2000. *The Spoken Language Translator*. Cambridge University Press, Cambridge.

Hiroyuki Seki, Takashi Matsumura, Mamoru Fujii, and Tadao Kasami. 1991. On multiple context-free grammars. *Theoretical Computer Science*, 88:191–229.

Stuart M. Shieber and Yves Schabes. 1990. Synchronous tree-adjoining grammars. In *COLING*, pages 253–258.

Stuart Shieber. 1986. *An Introduction to Unification-Based Approaches to Grammars*. University of Chicago Press.

Mark Steedman. 2000. *The Syntactic Process*. The MIT Press.

Kam-Fai Wong, Wenjie Li, Ruifeng Xu, and Zhengsheng Zhang. 2009. *Introduction to Chinese natural language processing*, volume 2 of *Synthesis Lectures on Human Language Technologies*. Morgan & Claypool Publishers.

Naiwen Xue, Fei Xia, Fu-dong Chiou, and Marta Palmer. 2005. The penn chinese treebank: Phrase structure annotation of a large corpus. *Natural Language Engineering*, 11(2):207–238.

Kun Yu, Yusuke Miyao, Xiangli Wang, Takuya Matsuzaki, and Jun ichi Tsujii. 2010. Semi-automatically Developing Chinese HPSG Grammar from the Penn Chinese Treebank for Deep Parsing. In Chu-Ren Huang and Dan Jurafsky, editors, *COLING 2010*, pages 1417–1425.

Yi Zhang, Rui Wang, and Yu Chen. 2012. Joint grammar and treebank development for mandarin chinese with hpsg. In *Proceedings of the Eight International Conference on Language Resources and Evaluation (LREC'12). International Conference on Language Resources and Evaluation (LREC-2012), May 23-25, Istanbul, Turkey*. European Language Resources Association (ELRA), 5.

Elizaveta Zimina. 2012. Fitting a round peg in a square hole: Japanese resource grammar in gf. In Hitoshi Isahara and Kyoko Kanzaki, editors, *Advances in Natural Language Processing*, volume 7614 of *Lecture Notes in Computer Science*, pages 156–167. Springer Berlin Heidelberg.

KWB: An Automated Quick News System for Chinese Readers *

Yiqi Bai[1], Wenjing Yang[1], Hao Zhang[1], Jingwen Wang[1], Ming Jia[1], Roland Tong[2], Jie Wang[1]
1. University of Massachusetts Lowell
2. Wantology

Abstract

We present an automated quick news system called KWB. KWB crawls and collects around the clock news items from over 120 news websites in mainland China, eliminates duplicates, and retrieves a summary of up to 600 characters for each news article using a proprietary summary engine. It then uses a Labeled-LDA classifier to classify the remaining news items into 19 categories, computes popularity ranks called PopuRank of the newly collected news items in each category, and displays the summaries of news items in each category sorted according to PopuRank together with a picture, if there is any, on http://www.kuaiwenbao.com and mobile apps. We will describe in this paper the system architecture of KWB, the data crawler structure, the functionalities of the central database, and the definition of PopuRank. We will show, through experiments, the running time of obtaining PopuRank. We will also demonstrate the use of KWB.

1 Introduction

We are living in the era of information explosion. To help people obtain information quickly, we would want to construct an automated system that collects information and provides accurate summarization to the user in a timely fashion. This would be a system that integrates advanced technologies and current research results on text automation, including data collection, storage, classification, ranking, summarization, web displaying, and app development. KWB is such a system that collects news items from the Internet and provides to the reader summarization and PopuRank of each news item, making it easier for people to obtain critical information quickly.

In this paper we will describe the data collection, data storage, and popular ranking of news items for KWB. Descriptions of the other components will be reported in separate papers, including Labeled-LDA classifier and content extractions. KWB uses a proprietary summary engine to retrieve a summary of up to 600 characters for each news item.

This paper is organized as follows. In Section 2 we will describe related work. We will describe the architecture of KWB in Section 3, the KWB Crawler Framework for collecting news items in Section 4, and the KWB central database in Section 5. We will present the PopuRank formula in Section 6. In Section 7 we will describe KWB and we will conclude the paper in Section 8.

2 Related Work

2.1 Web crawling

Web-crawling technologies are important mechanisms for collecting data from the Internet (see, e.g., (Emamdadi et al., 2014; Lin and Bilmes, 2011; Li et al., 2011; Li et al., 2009; Li et al., 2009; Li and Teng, 2010; Zheng et al., 2008)). The general framework of a crawling is given below:

1. Provide the crawler a seed URL.
2. The crawler grabs and stores the target page's content.
3. Enter the URLs contained in the target page in a waiting queue.
4. Process one URL at a time in the queue.
5. Repeat Steps 2 to 4.

A crawler is responsible for the following tasks:

1. **URL fetching.** There are three approaches to grabbing URLs at the target site (initially the

*This work was supported in part by a grant from Wantology. Correspondence: wang@cs.uml.edu.

Proceedings of the Eighth SIGHAN Workshop on Chinese Language Processing (SIGHAN-8), pages 110–119,
Beijing, China, July 30-31, 2015. ©2015 Association for Computational Linguistics and Asian Federation of Natural Language Processing

target site is the seed URL): (1) Grab all the URLs in the target site. This approach may waste computing resources of the crawler machines on materials that are not useful for the applications at hand. (2) Grab a portion of the URLs and ignore certain URLs. (3) Grab only what is needed for the current application.

2. **Content extraction.** Parse the webpage to get the content for the given application. There are two ways to parse a page. One way is to write specific rules for each website, then use a web parsing tool such as Jsoup to extract content. The other way is to write common rules for all websites, such as Google's content extractor.

3. **Visit frequency.** If a crawler visits a target website very frequently in a short period of time, then the website may consider it hostile and block the crawler's IP to stop it. Thus, it is important to not to visit the target website too often in a short period of time to avoid being blocked.

4. **Crawler monitoring.** We should monitor if the target website blocks a crawler's request and if the website changes the structures of the webpages.

2.2 Ranking of importance and popularity

There are a number of methods to measure the importance and popularity of an object or a person in a network. For example, the Pagerank mechanism measures the influence and popularity of a webpage (Page et al., 1999) and the Erdős' collaboration network (Erdős Number Project, 2010) may be used to measure the impact of collaborators (direct and indirect) of Erdős. These measures, however, do not explicitly consider the effect of time in their ranking. To measure the importance and popularity of news items, we need to consider time explicitly. This calls for a new measure and we will present PopuRank to fill this gap.

3 KWB Architecture

KWB consists of five components (see Fig. 1): (1) crawlers, (2) central DB, (3) summary engine, (4) core processing unit, and (5) web display.

Given below are brief descriptions of each of these components:

1. The crawler component is responsible for collecting news items around the clock from over 120 news websites in mainland China.

2. The central DB is responsible for processing the raw data collected from the crawlers, including removing duplicated news items and fetching summaries for each news article.

3. The summary engine is responsible for returning summaries for each new article with different lengths required by applications. This is preparatory technology.

4. The core processing unit consists of three parts: (1) Chinese text fragmentation. (2) News article classifications. (3) Ranking each document according to PopuRank.

5. The web display component is responsible for displaying on a website the news items in each category according to their PopuRanks in each day, their summaries, pictures (if there is any), and links to the original news items.

Fig. 2 describes the data flow in KWB system in which each module will operate data and save new attributes.

4 KWB Crawler Framework

The KWB crawler in our system follows the framework of vertical crawling. It can be reused and customized according to the specific layout of a webpage. We observe that news websites tend to have the same structure: an index page and a number of content pages for news items. When grabbing the index page, we may want to set the crawling depth to 1 to stop the crawler from grabbing the URLs contained in the content page. Meantime, we also want to remove repeating URLs in the URL queue. The KWB crawler framework uses both specific rules and common rules, depending on the individual crawler for a given website.

The KWB crawler framework consists of the following modules (see Fig. 3):

1. **Visual input module**: This module allows the user to specify the patten of the target webpage's layout. The user may specify two kinds of patterns. The first kind is a regular expression representing what the content the user wants to extract. For example, the regular expression matches the opening and

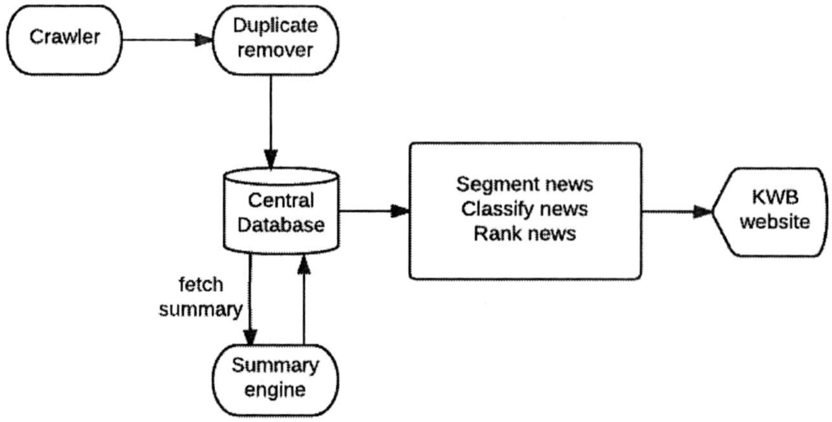

Figure 1: The architecture of KWB

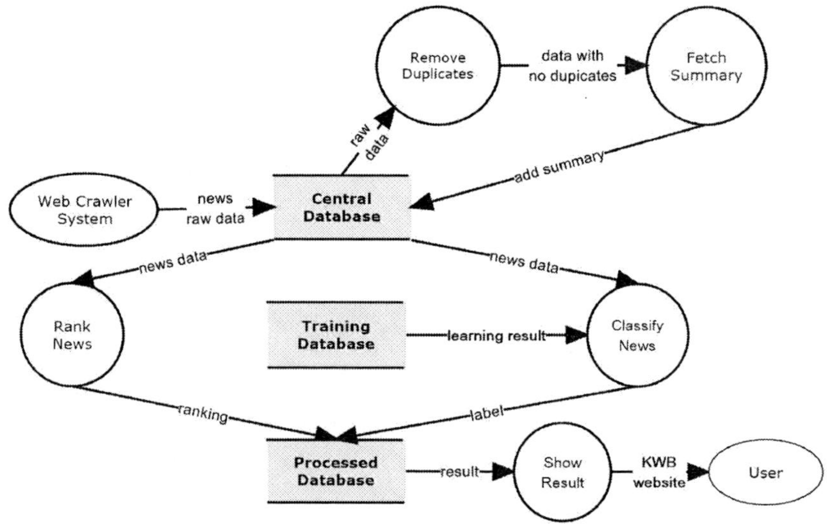

Figure 2: The data flow diagram of KWB

closing pair of a specific HTML tag , within which is content the user wants to extract. The second kind is an XPath structure of the content that the user wants to extract. For example, Suppose that the user wants to select the content enclosed in all the tags. Then the user can specify an XPath query as .

2. **Webpage rule management**. It manages the webpage rules entered by users, including the following operations: deleting, checking, and updating.

3. **The core crawler cluster**. This cluster consists of the following components:

   (1) Thread pool. It is the set of threads in a multitask system.

   (2) URL pool. It is the database with all the pending URL information when a URL was grabbed. We use Bloom filter to detect duplicate URLs and remove them. The crawler will visit and remove a URL one at a time from the remaining URLs in this pool.

   (a) Pattern pool. It is the database of all the webpage rules entered by users.

   (b) DAO module. DAO (data access object) contains the interface for further operations, including data export and data interface.

   (c) Duplicate removal. It removes duplicate URLs in the URL pool and the patterns in the pattern pool.

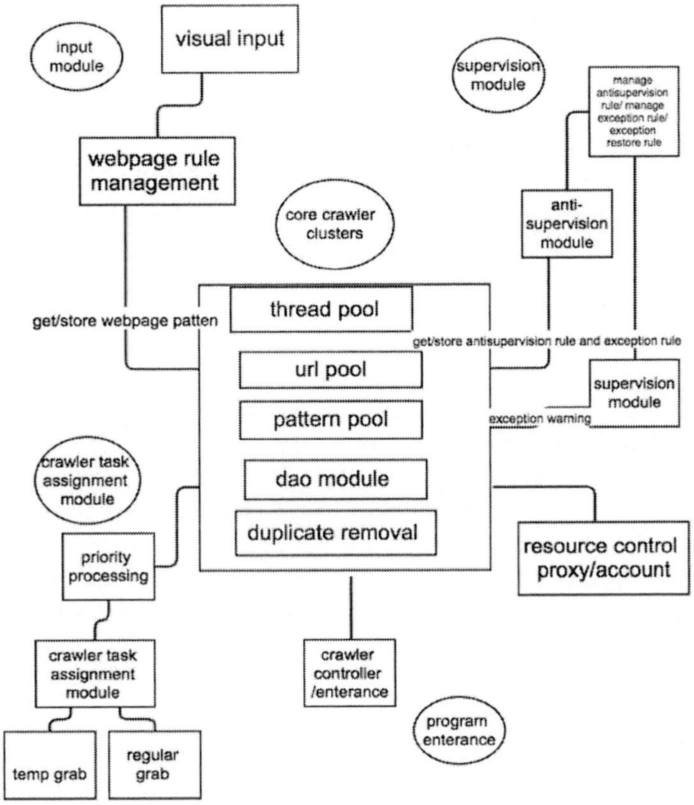

Figure 3: Architecture of the KWB crawler framework

4. **The crawler task module**. This module consists of the following submodules:
   (1) Priority processing. Some websites are updated more frequency than the others. This module determines which sites need more frequent visits.
   (2) Temp grab. Sometimes the user just wants to fetch a website once without paying a return visit. This component handles this type of crawling.
   (3) Regular grab. For most websites, the user sets up a schedule to grab them periodically. This component handles this type of crawling.

5. **The supervision module**. This module consists of the following submodules:
   (1) Resource control (proxy/account). It is a pool containing all the proxy information and account information. The proxy is used to avoid IP blocking problems, and the account is used to log on certain websites that require signing in, such as twitter and facebook.
   (2) Monitoring. It monitors if the crawler functions normally. For example, it monitors whether the target website has blocked the crawler.
   (3) Anti-blocking. When the monitoring submodule detects that a crawler is blocked, it decides whether to restart the crawler, change the pattern, or change proxy to avoid blocking.
   (4) Managing anti-blocking, exception, and restore rules. This submodule allows the user to manage and change patterns of a website rules. It also determines how often to test if a crawler is still functioning normally.

6. **The program entrance**. This component consists of a crawler controller/entrance submodule, which is responsible for starting the entire system.

We implemented the KWB crawler framework using Java. We use httpclient to connect to a website and get the DOM tree of the page. We use

CSS and Jsoup to parse and extract content. We implemented DAO using mysql and JDBC.

5 Central Database

Data collected from the KWB crawler are raw data. Although duplicate URLs are eliminated by the crawler, the same news article may be collected from different URLs because the it may be reposted on different websites. For each news article we need to retrieve its summary of different length (depending on applications) using a proprietary Chinese text summary engine. These two processes are time consuming. To reduce computations, we create a new database called central DB (see Fig. 4) to remove duplicates and retrieve summaries for raw data collected in every hour.

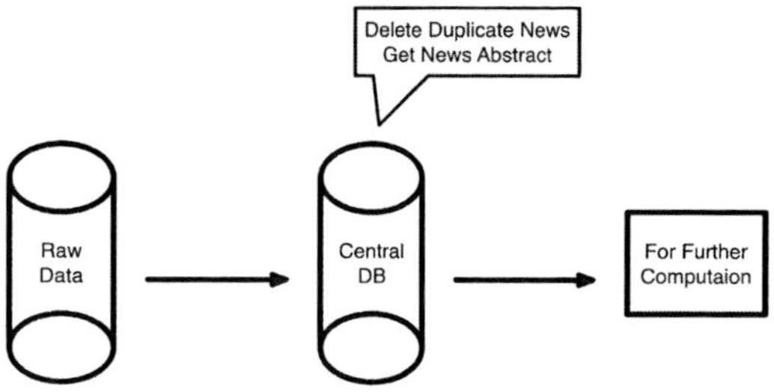

Figure 4: Central DB

There are two different types of duplicates in the raw data: (1) exactly the same news items due to reposting; (2) different news items reporting the same news. We will keep the second type of news items, for they report the same event from different angles, which are useful. To identify the first type of duplicates we may compute cosine similarities for all the raw data collected by the KWB crawlers, but this approach is time consuming. Instead, we take a greedy approach to reducing the number of news items that we need to retrieve summaries by eliminating duplicates posted in a small time window. We will further remove duplicates later before computing news classifications.

The central DB retrieves article summaries and detects duplicates in a parallel fashion. In particular, it sorts all the unprocessed raw data in increasing order according to their IDs. These are incremental IDs given to the news items based on the time they are fetched by the KWB crawler framework. Starting from the first news article, repeat the following:

1. Send a request to the summary engine to retrieve summaries of required lengths.
2. Compute the cosine similarities of the article with the news items whose IDs fall in a small fixed time window after this article. If a duplicate is found, remove the one whose ID is in the time window (i.e., with a larger ID), for it is likely a reposting and the news article with a smaller ID may have already had the summaries generated from the summary engine running on a different server.
3. Move to the next news article in the shorted list

The index of the news items stored in the central DB contains, among other things, the following four fields: news title, news URL, image URL, first and last sentence of the news content. We further remove news items that match any of these fields for all pairs of news items. In other words, for each pair of news items, if there is a match on any of these four fields, then remove the article with a larger ID.

6 PopuRank

KWB implements a Labeled-LDA classifier to classify all the news items stored in the central DB. To do so, it needs to segment each news article into a sequence of words, where a word is a sequence of Chinese characters. We show that using Labeled-LDA achieves higher classification accuracy than SVM (Support Vector Machines) for Chinese news items, and we will report this work in a separate paper.

KWB then determines the popularity ranking, called PopuRank, of news items. We observe that the news items that are popular during crawling are indeed the true popular news. In particular, in a given time period, breaking news will be fast reported and reposted online everywhere. In this case, the term frequency (TF) of certain words describing this news will increase sharply. Meanwhile, the document frequency (DF) of certain words describing the breaking news will also increase. We monitor each word (except stop words) in each time frame every day. By monitoring the TF and DF fluctuations of words, KWB calculates PopuRank of the news items collected in each time unit u. The news item with higher PopuRank is more popular. The time unit u may be changed according to the actual needs and user interests. For example, if we want to determine popular news items in each hour, then we may set u to be the unit of hour. The PopuRank of each article remains valid for a fixed number ℓ of time frames. For example, we may let $\ell = 24$ or 48, when u is hour. The value of ℓ may also be changed.

Let t_v denote the current time frame. Let

$$\mathcal{D}_v = \{D_1, D_2, \cdots, D_N\}$$

denote the corpus of all news items collected in this time frame with duplicates removed, where D_i is a news article and D_i contains N_i words in the model of bag of words, denoted by

$$D_i = (w_1, w_2, ..., w_{N_i}),$$

where each word is a segment of two or more Chinese characters after segmentation.

We define the following terms:

1. **Term frequency (TF)**. The term frequency of word w_j in D_i in time frame t_v, denoted by $tf(w_j, D_i, t_v)$, is the number of times it appears in D_i, denoted by N_{ij}, divided by N_i. That is,

$$tf(w_j, D_i, t_v) = \frac{N_{ij}}{N_i}.$$

   Note that if $w_j \notin D_i$, then $tf(w_j, D_i, t_v) = 0$.

2. **Document frequency (DF)**. The document frequency of word w_j in the corpus $\mathcal{D}_v$, denoted by $df(w_j, \mathcal{D}_v)$, is defined as the total number of documents in $\mathcal{D}_v$ that contain w_j, denoted by N_j, divided by the total number of words in $\mathcal{D}_v$, denoted by N. That is,

$$df(w_j, t_v) = \frac{N_j}{N}.$$

3. **Average term frequency (ATF)**. Let $atf(w_j, \mathcal{D}_v)$ denote the average term frequency of word w_j in corpus $\mathcal{D}_v$. That is,

$$atf(w_j, t_v) = \frac{\sum_{i=1}^{N} tf(w_j, D_i, t_v)}{N}.$$

4. **Term rank (TR)**. We define the term rank of word w_j in document D_i in time frame t_v, denoted by $tr(w_j, D_i, t_v)$, as follows:

$$tr(w_j, D_i, t_v) = \alpha \cdot tf(w_j, D_i, t_v) + \beta \cdot df(w_j, \mathcal{D}_v),$$

   where $\alpha \geq 0$, $\beta \geq 0$, and $\alpha + \beta = 1$. For example, we may let $\alpha = 0.6$ and $\beta = 0.4$ to indicate that we place more weight on term frequency over document frequency.

For each word w_j appearing in $\mathcal{D}_v$, compute $df(w_j, \mathcal{D}_v)$ and $atf(w_j, \mathcal{D}_v)$, and keep them for ℓ number of time frames.

We now define PopuRank of a document. Assume that word w_j appears in the current time frame t_v. Let T denote the following sequence of consecutive time frames, called a window:

$$T = (t_{\ell-v+1}, t_{\ell-v+2}, \cdots, t_v).$$

At each time frame in this window, we monitor the DF and ATF values for each word. Let t_v be the current time frame. For each word w_j in $\mathcal{D}_v$, we have the following two cases:

Case 1: w_j is a new word, that is, it did not appear in the previous time frames in the window T, then we compute the TF-IDF values of all the new words in this time frame and mark the top d percent of the new words as popular words.

Case 2: w_j is not a new word. Compute $atf(w_j, t_v)$ and $df(w_j, t_v)$. If the ATF and DF values of word w_j at time t_v suddenly increase k_1 and k_2 times over the previous average ATF and DF values, respectively, for word w_j, denoted by $avgATF(w_j, t_v)$ and $avgDF(w_j, t_v)$, then we will consider the word w_j a popular word, where

$$\begin{aligned} avgATF(w_j, t_v) &= \frac{ATF(w_j, t_v)}{\ell - 1}, \\ avgDF(w_j, t_v) &= \frac{DF(t_v)}{\ell - 1}, \\ ATF(w_j, t_v) &= \sum_{t_i \in T - \{t_v\}} atf(w_j, t_i), \\ DF(w_j, t_v) &= \sum_{t_i \in T - \{t_v\}} df(w_j, t_i). \end{aligned}$$

To specify the values of k_1 and k_2, let

$$\begin{aligned} ratATF(w_j, t_v) &= \frac{atf(w_j, t_v)}{avgATF(w_j, t_v)}, \\ ratDF(w_j, t_v) &= \frac{df(w_j, t_v)}{avgDF(w_j, t_v)}. \end{aligned}$$

If

$$\begin{aligned} ratATF(w_j, t_v) &> \delta, \\ ratDF(w_j, t_v) &> \sigma, \end{aligned}$$

where δ and σ are threshold values, then we say that word w_j is popular in time frame t_v.

Let H_v denote the set of all popular words in time frame t_v. We define the PopuRank of news article $D_i \in \mathcal{D}_v$ to be the sum of term rank of the popular words in D_i in time frame t_v. Namely,

$$\text{PopuRank}(D_i, t_v) = \sum_{w \in H_v \cup D_i} tr(w, D_i, t_v). \quad (1)$$

	A	B	C
1	Title	Hot Time (timestamp)	PopuRank
2	南宁哪里交通堵刷手机就懂	1430445600	579
3	广西今年投520.7亿为民办实事	1430445600	546
4	春晚福娃邓鸣贺因白血病去世	1430445600	519
5	五月起个人禁乱发布天气预报	1430445600	483
6	巡视追回中粮2.4亿流失国资没见过这么乱的企业	1430445600	478
7	京津冀协同发展2020年北京人口不超2300万	1430445600	475
8	稿购房留意政策新变化 买家迎购房"窗口期	1430445600	465
9	南宁市区小学地段划分将公布	1430917200	458
10	甘肃省人民政府关于进一步加强新时期爱国卫生工作的实施意见	1430445600	457
11	美国炒作蒋介石"婚外情"内幕	1430445600	443
12	成都企业启动"蛛网"计划 民资投	1430445600	440
13	市贸促会副会长李焕亭网谈	1430445600	434
14	抗战期间蒋介石为何布重兵却守不住南京?	1430445600	424
15	海口养生胜地大盘点	1430445600	424
16	互联网+引领白领跨界流动	1430445600	421
17	让万隆精神绽放新的光彩	1430445600	421
18	习近平总书记向全国劳动群众致节日祝贺	1430445600	418
19	武长顺曾遇威胁接电话称某中央领导送书	1430445600	415
20	重磅！ 中央政治局会议释放9大信号	1430445600	413
21	揭秘贪官为何偏爱现金	1430445600	411

Figure 5: The top 20 news items in all categories in a time frame

	A	B	C
1	Title	Hot Time (timestamp)	PopuRank
2	成都将申办世预赛 长远目标已瞄准2026年世界杯	1430917200	265
3	成都某体育校大学生练后空翻 头部着地身亡	1430445600	256
4	青岛与5城市争办国足首个主场 硬件条件不落下风	1430917200	244
5	谈球衣退役纪念和规定 奇葩的故事	1430445600	241
6	浙江马拉松推出积分赛规范赛事 办出特色	1430917200	230
7	四川草根足球缺啥? 缺教练缺裁判缺规范	1430917200	217
8	丁俊晖腹背受敌	1430917200	214
9	一代球王与中国足球的"黄金时代"	1430445600	211
10	CBA解析下赛季新政 续约外援细则限制薪资疯涨	1430445600	204
11	一周体坛论语福原爱自曝单身 卡卡主动请战	1430744400	190
12	LOL季中赛战队AHQ禁选解析	1430445600	187
13	中超前瞻:申花叫板恒大望抢分 京鲁争胜有难度	1430445600	184
14	国象男队夺冠凯旋 余泱漪爆料末轮遭"午夜惊铃"	1430445600	182
15	拳王争霸，赛前已收4亿	1430445600	176
16	刘国梁波尔入乡随俗能力强 他喝啤酒要兑雪碧	1430917200	173
17	互联网巨头开价10亿绿城足球要改门庭?宋卫平暂未回应	1430917200	173
18	成都申办世预赛中卡之战承办权 综合实力有优势	1430917200	171
19	梅西和瓜迪奥拉没联系 伤病不能成拜仁借口	1430917200	169
20	前有上海上港后有多路追兵 恒大为何不再独大	1430445600	164
21	美媒曝世纪大战计分表弄错 帕奎奥被陷害了?	1430917200	160

Figure 6: The top 20 news items in the sports categories in a time frame

Fig. 5 depicts the top 20 news items in all categories within one time frame together with a timestamp when a news article becomes popular, while Fig. 6 depicts the top 20 news items in the category of sports in the time frame. The values of parameters for our PopuRank calculation are $u =$ hour, $\ell = 24$, $d = 20\%$, $\alpha = 0.6$, $\beta = 0.4$, $\delta = 1.5$, and $\sigma = 1.5$. The time stamp 1430445600 is the Unix epoch time, which is equal to the total number of seconds since 00:00:00, January 1, 1970 Greenwich time, corresponding to 22:00:00, April 30, 2015 Eastern Time.

Parameters α and β is related to TR and PopuRank. The value of α and β are decided by which character, TF or DF, is regarded more important.

word	Alpha	TermRank
事故	0.9	0.107
	0.8	0.104
	0.7	0.101
	0.6	0.098
	0.5	0.095
	0.4	0.092
	0.3	0.089
	0.2	0.086
	0.1	0.083

Figure 7: Term Rank (TR) of a word with different values of α

Title	Alpha	PopuRank
决不放弃任何一丝生的希望——"东方之星"沉船水下搜救纪实	0.9	8
	0.8	16
	0.7	15
	0.6	63
	0.5	35
	0.4	34
	0.3	35
	0.2	37
	0.1	54

Figure 8: PopuRank of one news item with different values of α

The Fig. 7 shows the TR of a particular word with different α. Meanwhile, since TR varies, PopuRank of the news also varies, the Fig. 8 shows the different PopuRank of one news with different α and β in same time frame.

Threshold δ and σ decide the numbers of popular words, Fig. 9 shows that the numbers of popular words decrease when δ and σ increase, δ and σ have same value in Fig. 9.

The running time of calculating PopuRank on news items in each time frame depends on the numbers of news items waiting to be processed. Table 1 shows the number of news items in each time frame on an average day and the time to compute PopuRank of all news items in each time frame on a server running QEMU Virtual CPU version 1.2.0 with 2.6 GHz and 16 GB RAM.

7 Web Displays of KWB

KWB is an automated quick news system that collects news items real-time from all major Chinese news websites, classifies the news items into 19 categories, and displays on http://www.kuaiwenbao.com news items in each category with summaries and pictures, sorted according to their PopuRank values. We have also implemented KWB in mobile apps (An-

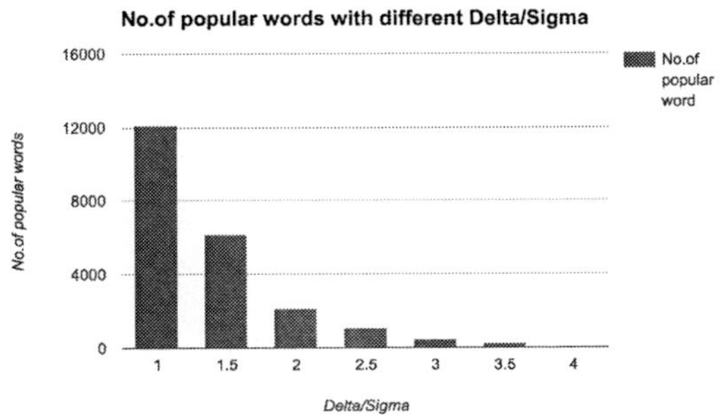

Figure 9: No. of popular words with different values of δ/σ

droid App may be downloaded by entering http://www.kuaiwenbao.com/kuaiwenbao.apk on a web browser of an Android phone). Fig. 10 depicts the web display of KWB, where the left-hand panel is a menu bar of news titles and picture thumbnails. The user simply points their mouse to a particular news title to see the original picture and the summary of of the news items on the right-hand panel. The reader may also click the "read the original" button to the URL of the original news article and read it.

KWB classifiers all news items into 19 categories. Users may click the menu icon on the upper-left corner to display the menu of categories and select a particular category of interests. Fig. 11 depicts the category menu.

8 Conclusion

We described KWB, an automated quick news system for the Chinese reader. In particular, we described the architecture of KWB, the KWB crawler framework, the central DB, the PopuRank, and the use of KWB. Required by blind reviews, we have removed the URL information of KWB in this version.

Table 1: Running time (seconds) for computing PopuRank for news items on an average day

time frame	no. news items	running time
00:00	1238	13.671
01:00	11	0.119
02:00	16	0.116
03:00	5	0.088
04:00	4	0.076
05:00	2	0.070
06:00	3	0.082
07:00	15	0.249
08:00	3	0.196
09:00	7	0.203
10:00	841	6.343
11:00	602	4.735
12:00	6	0.283
13:00	1007	8.848
14:00	2089	38.700
15:00	1444	13.767
16:00	2100	25.918
17:00	2485	40.937
18:00	685	4.437
19:00	5	0.400
20:00	3	0.321
21:00	2	0.320
22:00	4	0.325
23:00	34	0.361

References

Dasgupta, Anirban, Kumar Ravi, and Sujith Ravi. 2013. Summarization Through Submodularity and Dispersion. *IBM Journal of research and development 2.2*, pages 159–165

Emamdadi, Reihaneh, Mohsen Kahani, and Fattane Zarrinkalam. 2014. A focused linked data crawler based on HTML link analysis. *The 4th International eConference onComputer and Knowledge Engineering* (ICCKE), pp. 74–79. IEEE, 2014.

Erdős Number Project (Oakland University). Facts about Erdős numbers and the collaboration graph. 2010. Retrieved from http://wwwp.oakland.edu/enp/trivia/.

Lin, Hui and Jeff Bilmes. 2011. A class of submodular functions for document summarization. *Proc. ACL*, pages 510–520.

Li, Xueming, Minling Xing, and Jiapei Zhang. 2011. A Comprehensive Prediction Method of Visit Priority for Focused Crawler. *The 2nd International Symposium onIntelligence Information Processing and Trusted Computing* (IPTC), pp. 27–30. IEEE, 2011.

Li, Wei-jiang, Ru Hua-suo, Zhao Tie-jun, and Zang Wen-mao. 2009. A New Algorithm of Topical Crawler. *Second International Workshop on Computer Science and Engineering* (WCSE'09), vol. 1, pp. 443–446. IEEE, 2009.

Li, Wei-jiang, Ru Hua-suo, Hong Kun, and Luo Jia. 2009. A New Algorithm of Blog-Oriented Crawler. *International Forum on Computer Science-Technology and Applications* (IFCSTA'09), vol. 1, pp. 428–431. IEEE, 2009.

Li, Peng, and Teng Wen-Da. 2010. A focused web crawler face stock information of financial field.

IEEE International Conference on Intelligent Computing and Intelligent Systems, vol. 2, pp. 512–516. 2010.

Page, Lawrence, Sergey Brin, Rajeev Motwani, and Terry Winograd. 1999. The PageRank citation ranking: Bringing order to the web.

Zheng, Xiaolin, Tao Zhou, Zukun Yu, and Deren Chen. 2008. URL Rule based focused crawler. *IEEE International Conference on e-Business Engineering* (ICEBE'08). pp. 147–154. IEEE, 2008.

Figure 10: Web display of KWB

Figure 11: Web display of KWB with the menu of categories

Chinese Semantic Role Labeling using High-quality Syntactic Knowledge

Gongye Jin **Daisuke Kawahara** **Sadao Kurohashi**
Graduate School of Informatics, Kyoto University
Yoshida-Honmachi, Sakyo-ku, Kyoto, 606-8501, Japan
jin@nlp.ist.i.kyoto-u.ac.jp {dk,kuro}@i.kyoto-u.ac.jp

Abstract

This paper presents an application of Chinese syntactic knowledge for semantic role labeling (SRL). Besides basic morphological information, syntactic structures are crucial in SRL. However, it is difficult to learn such information from limited, small-scale, manually annotated training data. Instead of manually increasing the size of annotated data, we use a large amount of automatically extracted syntactic knowledge to improve the performance of SRL.

1 Introduction

Semantic role labeling (SRL) is regarded as a task that is intermediate between syntactic parsing and semantic analysis in natural language processing (NLP). The main goal of SRL is to extract a proposition from a sentence about *who* does *what* to *whom*, *when*, *where* and *why*. By using semantic roles, the complex expression of a sentence is then interpreted as an *event* and its *participants* (i.e., predicates and arguments such as *agent, patient, locative, temporal* and *manner*). Unlike syntactic level surface cases (i.e., dependency labels such as subject and object), semantic roles can be regarded as a deep case representation for predicates. Because of its ability to abstract the meaning of a sentence, SRL has been applied to many NLP applications, including information extraction (Christensen et al., 2010), question answering (Pizzato and Mollá, 2008) and machine translation (Liu and Gildea, 2010).

Semantically annotated corpora, such as FrameNet (Fillmore et al., 2001) and PropBank (Kingsbury and Palmer, 2002), make this type of automatic semantic structure analysis feasible by using supervised machine learning methods. Automatic SRL processing has two major drawbacks: firstly, the scale of the training data is quite limited and although manually annotated data such as PropBank is available as training data for learning semantic role prediction models, it is still hard to learn lexical preferences due its limited size. Increasing the size and coverage of this resource for improving the quality of learned models is a time consuming task. Secondly, similar to syntactic analysis such as syntactic dependency parsing, whose performance is highly dependent on preceding analysis such as POS tagging, automatic SRL systems are based on syntactic structures along with lower level information including POS tags and lexical information. As a result, SRL suffers from error propagation from the lower levels of the whole framework. Although some studies use automatic analysis of unlabeled data to enrich the training data to solve the first problem (Fürstenau and Lapata, 2009), accumulated errors in such automatic analysis inevitably causes negative effects. Especially, for some hard-to-analyze languages such as Chinese, which is difficult to analyze morphologically, the performance of SRL is always limited due to the above two problems.

In this paper, we focus on Chinese SRL and address the problems mentioned above by using high-quality knowledge automatically extracted from a large-scale corpus. Instead of using high level automatic analyses such as semantic roles, we use lower level syntactic knowledge because lower level analyses are less erroneous compared to higher level analyses. The additional knowledge can provide not only a rich lexicon but also syntactic information, both of which play crucial roles in SRL. In order to show that automatically extracted syntactic knowledge is beneficial, we use predicate-argument structures and case frames (which will be introduced in later sections) in our experiments to validate our claim.

The rest of this paper is organized as follows.

Proceedings of the Eighth SIGHAN Workshop on Chinese Language Processing (SIGHAN-8), pages 120–127,
Beijing, China, July 30-31, 2015. ©2015 Association for Computational Linguistics and Asian Federation of Natural Language Processing

Section 2 contains related work. Section 3 describes the high-quality dependency selection process. Section 4.1 presents a detailed description of our approach, conducted on three languages, along with the results followed by a discussion in Section 4.2. Finally, Section 5 contains our conclusions and future work.

2 Related work

The CoNLL-2009 shared task (Hajič et al., 2009) features a substantial number of studies on SRL that used Propbank as one of the resources. These work can be categorized into two types: joint learning of syntactic parsing and SRL (Tang et al., 2009; Morante et al., 2009), which learns a unique model for syntactic parsing and SRL jointly. This type of framework has the ability to use SRL information in syntactic parsing for improvement, but has a much larger search space during the joint model learning. The other type is called SRL-only task (Zhao et al., 2009; Björkelund et al., 2009), which uses automatic morphological and syntactic information as the input in order to judge which token plays what kind of semantic role. Our work focuses on the second category of SRL. Our framework is based on those used by Björkelund et al. (2009) and Yang and Zong (2014).

There were also several studies using semi-supervised methods for SRL. One basic idea of semi-supervised SRL is to automatically annotate unlabeled data using a simple classifier trained on original training data (Fürstenau and Lapata, 2009). Since there is a substantial amount of error propagation in SRL frameworks, the additional automatic semantic roles are not guaranteed to be of good quality. Contrary to this approach, we only rely on syntactic level knowledge which does not suffer too much from error propagation. Also, some studies assume that sentences that are syntactically and lexically similar are likely to share the same frame-semantic structure (Fürstenau and Lapata, 2009). This allows them to project semantic role information to unlabeled sentences using alignments. However, computation of these alignments requires additional information such as word similarity, whose quality is language dependent. Less sparse features capturing lexical information of words can be also used for semi-supervised learning of SRL. Such lexical representation can be learned from unlabeled data (Bengio et al., 2003). Deschacht and Moens (2009) used word similarity learned from unlabeled data as additional features for SRL. Word embeddings have also been used in several NLP tasks including SRL (Collobert et al., 2011). Instead of using word-level lexical information, our work uses syntactic knowledge as syntactic level lexical information. Zapirain et al. (2009) used selectional preferences to improve SRL. This study is similar to our approaches but the quality of selectional preferences was not concerned at all.

In syntactic level of NLP, rich knowledge such as predicate-argument structures and case frames are strong backups for various kinds of tasks. A case frame, which clarifies relations between a predicate and its arguments, can support tasks ranging from fundamental analysis, such as syntactic dependency parsing and word similarity calculation, to multilingual applications, such as machine translation. Japanese case frames have been successfully compiled (Kawahara and Kurohashi, 2006), where each argument is represented as its case marker in Japanese such as 'ga', 'wo', and 'ni'. For the case frames of other languages such as English and Chinese, because there are no such case markers that can help clarify syntactic structures, instead of using case markers like in Japanese, syntactic surface cases (i.e., subject, object, prepositional phrase, etc.) are used for argument representation (Jin et al., 2014). Case frames can be automatically acquired using a different method such as Chinese Restaurant Process (CRP) (Kawahara et al., 2014) for different languages. In our work, we employ such syntactic level knowledge, which use surface cases as argument representation, to help SRL task. We refer to this kind of knowledge as syntactic knowledge in this paper.

3 Proposed method for SRL

3.1 SRL task description

In previous studies, SRL pipeline[1] can be divided into three main steps: predicate disambiguation (PD), argument identification (AI), and argument classification (AC). In the PD step, the main goal is to identify the "sense id" of each given predicate. Because the sense id for a certain predicate is meaningless for other predicates, classifiers for PD are trained separately for each pred-

[1]Predicate identification (PI) was not concerned in this paper because we use the data from CoNLL-2009 shared task, in which the target predicates are given.

feature	description
PredWord PredPOS PredDeprel PredParentWord PredParentPOS PredParentWord+POS	basic morphologic and syntactic information of the predicate and its parent
ChildWordSet ChildPOSSet ChildDepSet ChildWord+ChildDepSet ChildPOS+ChildDepSet	set feature of the children of predicate
DepSubCat	the concatenation of the dependency labels of predicate's children

Table 1: Features for PD

icate. We used the part of the feature set proposed by Björkelund et al. (2009) and some additional features. Table 1 lists the feature sets used in the PD step. During the prediction, there will be some predicates which have not been seen before in training data. We label the sense of those unseen predicates using the default sense, which is '01' in our work.

Different from syntactic dependency parsing, given a predicate in a sentence, each token has a possibility to hold a semantic relation with the given predicate. Each token is regarded as an argument candidate. The AI step is mainly to recognize these semantic arguments from the argument candidates. In the AC step, which is the last step in the SRL pipeline, each semantic argument is labeled with a semantic role. However, there was some work in which AI and AC step are executed jointly by inducing a new label 'null', which indicates that the token is not a semantic argument of the predicate. As far as we know, there is small amount of debate involving the merging of the AI step and the AC step, especially on whether such merging is beneficial or not. The joint method seems to have an ability to reduce the error propagation from the AI step to the AC step. However, at the same time, since the training samples with label 'null' will consequently outnumber other labels, there is still a drawback during learning. In our work, we apply a separate framework that carries out the AI and AC step in a pipeline since it is much more intuitive. We use features from Björkelund et al. (2009) and Yang and Zong (2014) along with some new features in AI and AC step. Table 2 lists the features used in each step, in which we use the mark † to indicate the proposed features.

3.2 Syntactic knowledge acquisition

We constructed two types of syntactic knowledge namely, predicate-argument structures and case frames.

3.2.1 High-quality predicate-argument structure extraction

Predicate-argument structures (PAS) have been basically acquired from syntactic analyses which varies from phrase chunking to syntactic dependency parsing. For example, English PAS in surface case was acquired in a large scale using a chunking-based system (Kawahara and Kurohashi, 2010). Some phenomena in Chinese, such as omission and complex grammar, make it intractable to automatically extract PAS only using shallow syntactic analysis, such as chunking. Syntactic dependency parsing is applied for Chinese PAS extraction. Arguments are represented by their syntactic dependency labels (i.e., subject, object, etc.)

Due to various factors, Chinese syntactic dependency parsing is relatively worse in performance compared to that of English, Japanese, etc. However, using an existing treebank, it is possible to train a classifier to acquire high-quality PAS by only using highly reliable syntactic dependencies. As a result, we applied syntactic dependency parsing to large-scale raw corpora and adopted the high-quality syntactic dependency selection approach (Jin et al., 2014). Their approach first trains a base parser using a part of the Chinese treebank and then applies syntactic dependency parsing on the raw text of another part of the same treebank. According to the gold-standard annotations, both postive and negative samples are then collected to train a binary classifier, which selects those dependencies more likely to be correct. We also follow their method for the compilation of high-quality PAS, which can provide a massive amount of syntactic knowledge.

3.2.2 High-quality case frame compilation

In NLP, at the level of syntax, case frames, compiled from PAS, were proposed as strong backups

feature	AI	AC	description
PredLemma	•	•	basic morphologic and syntactic information of the predicate
PredPOS	•	•	
PredRel	•	•	
PredLemmaSense	•	•	
Head	•	•	
HeadPOS	•	•	
Pred+HeadWord	•	•	
†PredContextWord-1/-2/+1+2	•		context information of the predicate
†PredContextPOS-1/-2/+1+2	•		
†PredContextRel-1/-2/+1+2	•		
ArgWord	•	•	basic morphologic and syntactic information of the argument
ArgPOS	•	•	
ArgDeprel	•	•	
†ArgContextWord-1/-2/+1+2	•		context information of the argument
†ArgContextPOS-1/-2/+1+2	•		
†ArgContextRel-1/-2/+1+2	•		
DeprelPath	•	•	structural information of the argument in the dependency tree
LeftSiblingWord	•	•	
LeftSiblingPOS	•	•	
RightSiblingWord	•	•	
RightSiblingPOS	•	•	
Position	•	•	
LeftMostDepWord	•	•	
LeftMostDepPOS	•	•	
RightMostDepWord	•	•	
RightMostDepPOS	•	•	
IsThePredNearest	•		binary feature indicating whether the given predicate is the nearest
VerbChainHasSubj	•		binary feature indicating whether there is a dependency label 'SUBJ' between the argument and the predicate

Table 2: Features for AI and AC († marks stand for the features we proposed)

for various kinds of tasks (Kawahara and Kurohashi, 2006). For each predicate, all the PAS are clustered into different case frames to reflect different semantic usages. We show an example of case frames for the verb '谢' in Table 3, which has multiple meanings. '谢(1)' is the case frame used to represent the sense of 'withering of flower'. Similarly, the sense of '谢' which means 'to thank', the applicable case frame is '谢(2)'. '谢(3)' is the case frame for the sense of 'curtain call'. In other words, case frames are knowledge that solves word sense disambiguation (WSD) by clustering the PAS. We applied the CRP method described by Kawahara et al. (2014) for clustering the high-quality PAS to compile high-quality case frames.

3.3 Using syntactic knowledge for SRL

The motivation of using large-scale syntactic knowledge is to complement the syntactic information in the limited size of training data. In SRL, an argument may not contain a direct syntactic relation between a given predicate but still plays a semantic role of the predicate. However, this kind

verb	surface case	instance with frequency in original corpus
谢(1)	nsubj	花儿(flower):14, 花(flower):22
	ad	都(all):16, 也(also):6
谢(2)	nsubj	你们(you):1
	dobj	您(you):8, 我(me):6
	ad	怎么(how):8, 多(very):1
谢(3)	nsubj	大战(battle):1
	dobj	幕(curtain):6
	ad	圆满(successfully):2, 也(also):1, 正式(officially):1
...		

Table 3: Examples of Chinese case frames

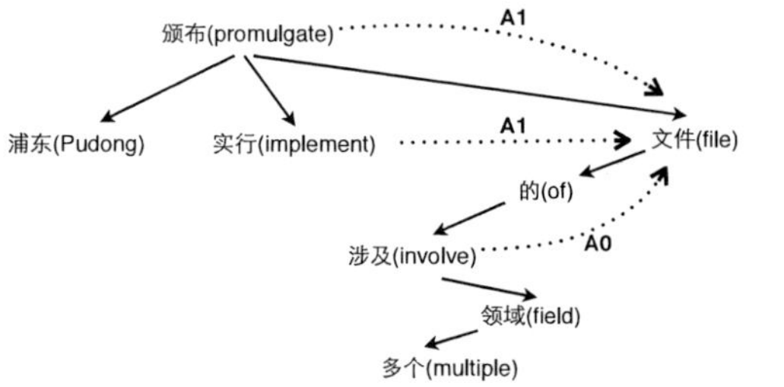

Figure 1: Example of dependency and semantic relations. Solid arrows denote syntactic dependencies and dotted arrows denote semantic dependencies.

of argument can actually form a direct syntactic relation between the predicate when we change the expression of the sentence in other ways. In other words, this kind of argument may hold a direct syntactic relation with the predicate in real world natural languages. This is a frequent phenomenon in multi-verb sentences. Take the sentence in Figure 1 as an example.

This sentence can be translated as "promulgated and implemented files involving multiple fields." "文件(file)" is a child of "颁布(promulgate)" in the dependency tree and labeled as semantic role "A1" of "颁布(promulgate)". Even though "文件(file)" does not have a direct dependency relation with "实行(implement)", it is still regarded as a semantic role "A1" of "实行(implement)". Similarly, "文件(file)" has also a semantic role "A0" of the verb "涉及(involve)" with no direct dependency relation. However, both direct syntactic dependencies "实行(implement) 文件(files)" and "文件(file) 涉及(involve)" appear frequently in real world text. Such patterns in surface cases captured from large-scale corpora would be important clues for SRL.

In addition, some special surface cases such as "BA" and "LB/SB" explicitly indicate accusative case and nominative case, which for most of the time is labeled as "A1" and "A0" respectively in PropBank-style SRL specification. "用/以(use)" is a preposition that strongly indicates the semantic role "MNR" and "在(at)" is a preposition that always stands for the semantic role "LOC" or "TMP". Therefore, it is promising to use large-scale syntactic knowledge as an additional resource.

We created three kinds of additional feature sets extracted from the above mentioned syntactic knowledge for SRL. Firstly, we used large-scale automatically acquired surface case predicate-argument structures. For each predicate-argument pair, we measured their point-wise mutual information (PMI). Secondly, we used the frequency of an argument candidate being a certain syntactic role. Finally, by considering the effect of word sense ambiguity, for each predicate sense, we calculated the frequency of an argument being a certain syntactic role of a predicate from the corresponding case frames. For all of the additional features, we used binned frequency (i.e., high, middle and low).

Note that a case frame id and a PropBank sense id do not correspond to each other. As a result, a mapping process which aligns case frame id(s) to PropBank verb sense is needed. For example, for the sense '谢.01' of the verb '谢', we extracted and grouped all the related predicate-argument structures. Then we calculated the similarity between verb sense '谢.01' and each case frame (i.e., '谢(1)', '谢(2)', etc.) by matching the corresponding predicate-argument structures that they are composed of. To determine the similarity between the two groups of predicate-argument

	w/o selection	select 50%	select 20%
UAS	0.677	0.824	0.920

Table 4: Precision of selected dependencies under different criteria

method	precision	recall	F1
baseline	81.61%	76.40%	78.92
baseline + syntactic knowledge (100%)	81.41%	76.57%	78.92
baseline + syntactic knowledge (50%)	81.57%	76.59%	*79.00
baseline + syntactic knowledge (20%)	81.80%	76.63%	**79.14**

Table 5: Evaluation results of Chinese SRL. The ** mark and * mark mean that the result is regarded as significant (with a p value < 0.01 and a p value < 0.05 respectively) using McNemar's test.

structures, we used the method proposed by Kawahara and Kurohashi (2001). This ensures that each case frame id is aligned to its most similar verb sense in PropBank.

4 Experiments

4.1 Experimental settings

For large-scale syntactic knowledge acquisition, 30 million sentences from Chinese Gigaword 5.0 (LDC2011T13)[2] were used.

For the high-quality dependency selection approach in the knowledge construction pipeline, the Stanford parser was used to apply syntactic dependency parsing on the raw texts from Chinese Gigaword. The training section of Chinese Treebank 7.0 was used to train the dependency parser and the official development section was used to train a classifier for high-quality dependency selection. Judging whether the automatic dependencies are reliable can be regarded as a binary classification problem, for which we utilized support vector machines (SVMs). Specifically, we employed SVM-Light[3] with a linear kernel to select high-quality dependencies from large-scale automatic dependency parses on the Chinese Gigaword for syntactic knowledge construction. Using official evalution section of CTB 7.0, we evaluated the quality of thoses selected dependencies using unlabeled attachment score (UAS), which calculates the percentage of correctly indentified dependency heads.

For SRL, we used the Chinese section of CoNLL-2009 shared task data for experiments. Automatically obtained morphological and syntactic information (the columns begin with "P") was used. PD and AI, AC step are regarded as multi-class classification problems. We employed OPAL[4] to solve this problem. We set the options as follows: polynomial kernel with degree 2; passive aggressive I learner; 20 iterations. The SRL system without using additional syntactic knowledge was used as a baseline. To examine the effect of different quality of syntactic knowledge, we used different set of PAS which was extracted under different dependency selection thresholds (20%, 50%, w/o selection). The official script provided on the CoNLL-2009 shared task website was used for evaluation.

4.2 Experimental results

Tabel 4 shows the quality of selected dependencies using different selection criteria. The precision of automatic syntactic depdencies increases when we lower the recall.

Table 5 shows our experimental results using the syntactic knowledge-based features. Syntactic knowledge (x%) indicates that the top x% (according to the classifier) of the automatically extracted syntactic knowledge was used. '100%' means that dependency selection step was not performed.

Our baseline system outperforms as well as the best system in CoNLL-2009 shared task. As we can see from the result, using large-scale syntactic knowledge can help improve the performance of SRL. Syntactic knowledge extracted from automatic parses without any selection (100%) contains a lot of noise and hence is not beneficial at all. However, filtering noisy syntactic knowledge leads to an significant improvement in Chinese SRL task. This shows that selecting hiqh-quality dependencies is an important aspect of

[2]We only used sentences written in simplified characters in Chinese Gigaword.

[3]`http://svmlight.joachims.org/`

[4]`http://www.tkl.iis.u-tokyo.ac.jp/~ynaga/opal/`

high-quality SRL.

5 Conclusion

In this paper, we have used high-quality syntactic knowledge to improve Chinese SRL. The result showed that this kind of knowledge has a positive effect on the SRL performance. The quality of syntactic knowledge turns out to be an important factor in such a semi-supervised learning approach.

In the future, we plan to make use of other low level knowledge such as word embeddings (Collobert et al., 2011) or word clusters (Koo et al., 2008), which can be complementary to our syntactic level knowledge. Since recent SRL approaches are mostly point-wise, i.e., features are extracted from pairs of the predicate and an argument candidate. We plan to design a higher order system to capture more global features. Also, reranking is widely utilized in many SRL systems and we plan to combine our surface case knowledge with a reranker, in order to further improve Chinese SRL. Finally, we plan to experiment on different languages and compare the effectiveness of syntactic knowledge for different languages.

References

Yoshua Bengio, Réjean Ducharme, Pascal Vincent, and Christian Jauvin. 2003. A neural probabilistic language model. 3:1137–1155, February.

Anders Björkelund, Love Hafdell, and Pierre Nugues. 2009. Multilingual semantic role labeling. In *Proceedings of the Thirteenth Conference on Computational Natural Language Learning (CoNLL 2009): Shared Task*, pages 43–48, Boulder, Colorado, June. Association for Computational Linguistics.

Janara Christensen, Mausam, Stephen Soderland, and Oren Etzioni. 2010. Semantic role labeling for open information extraction. In *Proceedings of the NAACL HLT 2010 First International Workshop on Formalisms and Methodology for Learning by Reading*, pages 52–60, Los Angeles, California, June. Association for Computational Linguistics.

Ronan Collobert, Jason Weston, Léon Bottou, Michael Karlen, Koray Kavukcuoglu, and Pavel Kuksa. 2011. Natural language processing (almost) from scratch. 12:2493–2537, August.

Koen Deschacht and Marie-Francine Moens. 2009. Semi-supervised semantic role labeling using the latent words language model. In *Proceedings of the 2009 Conference on Empirical Methods in Natural Language Processing*, pages 21–29, Singapore, August. Association for Computational Linguistics.

Charles J. Fillmore, Charles Wooters, and Collin F. Baker. 2001. Building a large lexical databank which provides deep semantics. In Benjamin Tsou and Olivia Kwong, editors, *Proceedings of the 15th Pacific Asia Conference on Language, Information and Computation*, Hong Kong.

Hagen Fürstenau and Mirella Lapata. 2009. Semi-supervised semantic role labeling. In *Proceedings of the 12th Conference of the European Chapter of the ACL (EACL 2009)*, pages 220–228, Athens, Greece, March. Association for Computational Linguistics.

Jan Hajič, Massimiliano Ciaramita, Richard Johansson, Daisuke Kawahara, Maria Antònia Martí, Lluís Màrquez, Adam Meyers, Joakim Nivre, Sebastian Padó, Jan Štěpánek, Pavel Straňák, Mihai Surdeanu, Nianwen Xue, and Yi Zhang. 2009. The conll-2009 shared task: Syntactic and semantic dependencies in multiple languages. In *Proceedings of the Thirteenth Conference on Computational Natural Language Learning (CoNLL 2009): Shared Task*, pages 1–18, Boulder, Colorado, June. Association for Computational Linguistics.

Gongye Jin, Daisuke Kawahara, and Sadao Kurohashi. 2014. A framework for compiling high quality knowledge resources from raw corpora. In *Proceedings of the Ninth International Conference on Language Resources and Evaluation (LREC'14)*, pages 109–114.

Daisuke Kawahara and Sadao Kurohashi. 2001. Japanese case frame construction by coupling the verb and its closest case component. In *Proceedings of the Human Language Technology Conference*, pages 204–210.

Daisuke Kawahara and Sadao Kurohashi. 2006. A fully-lexicalized probabilistic model for Japanese syntactic and case structure analysis. In *Proceedings of HLT-NAACL 2006*, pages 176–183.

Daisuke Kawahara and Sadao Kurohashi. 2010. Acquiring reliable predicate-argument structures from raw corpora for case frame compilation. In *Proceedings of LREC 2010*, pages 1389–1393.

Daisuke Kawahara, Daniel Peterson, Octavian Popescu, and Martha Palmer. 2014. Inducing example-based semantic frames from a massive amount of verb uses. In *Proceedings of the 14th Conference of the European Chapter of the Association for Computational Linguistics*, pages 58–67, Gothenburg, Sweden, April. Association for Computational Linguistics.

Paul Kingsbury and Martha Palmer. 2002. From treebank to propbank. In *Language Resources and Evaluation*.

Terry Koo, Xavier Carreras, and Michael Collins. 2008. Simple semi-supervised dependency parsing. In *Proceedings of ACL-08: HLT*, pages 595–603, Columbus, Ohio, June. Association for Computational Linguistics.

Ding Liu and Daniel Gildea. 2010. Semantic role features for machine translation. In *Proceedings of the 23rd International Conference on Computational Linguistics (Coling 2010)*, pages 716–724, Beijing, China, August. Coling 2010 Organizing Committee.

Roser Morante, Vincent Van Asch, and Antal van den Bosch. 2009. Joint memory-based learning of syntactic and semantic dependencies in multiple languages. In *Proceedings of the Thirteenth Conference on Computational Natural Language Learning (CoNLL 2009): Shared Task*, pages 25–30, Boulder, Colorado, June. Association for Computational Linguistics.

Luiz Augusto Pizzato and Diego Mollá. 2008. Indexing on semantic roles for question answering. In *Coling 2008: Proceedings of the 2nd workshop on Information Retrieval for Question Answering*, pages 74–81, Manchester, UK, August. Coling 2008 Organizing Committee.

Buzhou Tang, Lu Li, Xinxin Li, Xuan Wang, and Xiaolong Wang. 2009. A joint syntactic and semantic dependency parsing system based on maximum entropy models. In *Proceedings of the Thirteenth Conference on Computational Natural Language Learning (CoNLL 2009): Shared Task*, pages 109–113, Boulder, Colorado, June. Association for Computational Linguistics.

Haitong Yang and Chengqing Zong. 2014. Multi-predicate semantic role labeling. In *Proceedings of the 2014 Conference on Empirical Methods in Natural Language Processing (EMNLP)*, pages 363–373, Doha, Qatar, October. Association for Computational Linguistics.

Beñat Zapirain, Eneko Agirre, and Lluís Màrquez. 2009. Generalizing over lexical features: Selectional preferences for semantic role classification. In *Proceedings of the ACL-IJCNLP 2009 Conference Short Papers*, pages 73–76, Suntec, Singapore, August. Association for Computational Linguistics.

Hai Zhao, Wenliang Chen, Chunyu Kity, and Guodong Zhou. 2009. Multilingual dependency learning: A huge feature engineering method to semantic dependency parsing. In *Proceedings of the Thirteenth Conference on Computational Natural Language Learning (CoNLL 2009): Shared Task*, pages 55–60, Boulder, Colorado, June. Association for Computational Linguistics.

Chinese Spelling Check System Based on N-gram Model

Weijian Xie, Peijie Huang*, Xinrui Zhang, Kaiduo Hong, Qiang Huang, Bingzhou Chen, Lei Huang
College of Mathematics and Informatics, South China Agricultural University,
Guangzhou 510642, Guangdong, China
tsewkviko@gmail.com, pjhuang@scau.edu.cn,
richardrui@foxmail.com, kd_hong@163.com, kasim0079@qq.com,
cbtpkzm@163.com, hl_mark@163.com

Abstract

This paper presents our system in the Chinese spelling check (CSC) task of SIGHAN-8 Bake-Off. Given a sentence, our systems are designed to detect and correct the spelling error. As we know, CSC is still a hot topic today and it is an open problem yet. N-gram language modeling (LM) is widely used in CSC, since its simplicity and power. We present a model based on joint bi-gram and tri-gram LM and Chinese word segmentation. Besides, we apply dynamic programming to increase efficiency and employ smoothing technique to address the sparseness of the n-gram in training data. The evaluation results show the utility of our CSC system.

1 Introduction

Spelling check is a common task in every written language, which is an automatic mechanism to detect and correct human spelling errors (Wu et al., 2013). Automatic spelling correction began as early as the 1960s (Kukich, 1992). A spelling checker should have both capabilities consisting of error detection and error correction. Spelling error detection is to indicate the various types of spelling errors in the text. Spelling error correction is further to suggest the correct characters of detected errors.

Chinese as a foreign language (CFL) is booming in recent decades. The number of (CFL) learners is expected to become larger for the years to come (Xiong et al., 2014). Automatic Chinese spelling check is becoming a significant task nowadays. For this task, Chinese spelling check (CSC) task are organized at the SIGHAN Bake-offs to provide a platform for comparing and developing automatic Chinese spelling checkers. However, different from English or other alphabetic languages, Chinese is a tonal syllabic and character language, in which each character is pronounced as a tonal syllable (Chen et al., 2013). In Chinese, there is no word delimiters or boundary between words and the length of each Chinese "word" is very short where there may only have two or three characters in most cases. Moreover, types of spelling error are more than other languages, since many Chinese characters resemble in shapes or pronounced the same. Some characters are even similar in both shapes and pronunciations (Wu et al., 2010; Liu et al., 2011).

So much research is under way up to now. For instance, rule-based model (Jiang et al., 2012; Chiu et al., 2013), n-gram model (Wu et al., 2010; Wang et al., 2013; Chen et al., 2013; Huang et al., 2014), graph theory (Bao et al., 2011; Jia et al., 2013; Xin et al., 2014), statistical learning method (Han and Chang, 2013; Xiong et al., 2014), etc, are proposed.

Language modeling (LM) is widely used in CSC, and the most widely-used and well-practiced language model, by far, is the n-gram LM (Jelinek, 1999), because of its simplicity and fair predictive power. Continue to use N-gram LM, this paper proposed a model based on joint bi-gram and tri-gram LM to detect and correct spelling errors. And we try to exploit word segmentation in a pre-processing stage which improves the system performance to a certain extent. In addition, dynamic programming is applied to reduce the running time of our

* Corresponding author

Proceedings of the Eighth SIGHAN Workshop on Chinese Language Processing (SIGHAN-8), pages 128–136,
Beijing, China, July 30-31, 2015. ©2015 Association for Computational Linguistics and Asian Federation of Natural Language Processing

program and additive smoothing is used to solve the data sparseness problem in training set.

The rest of this paper is structured as follows. In Section 2, we briefly present our CSC system, confusion sets and the choice of n-gram order. Section 3 details our Chinese n-gram model. Evaluation results are presented in Section 4. Finally, the last section summarizes this paper and describes our future work.

2 The Proposed System

2.1 System Overview

Figure 1 shows the flowchart of our CSC system. The system is mainly consists of four parts: Chinese Word Segmentation, Confusion sets, Corpus and Language Model. It performs CSC in the following steps:

Step 1. A given sentence was segmented by CSC system with Chinese words segmentation techniques. Result of Chinese words for segmentation will serve as the basis for the next step.

Step 2. According to the judgment conditions our system finds confusion sets of the corresponding word in the sentence.

Step 3. For each character in this sentence which can be replaced (in accordance with corresponding conditions), the system will enumerate every character of its confusion set to replace the original character. We will get a candidate sentence set after this step.

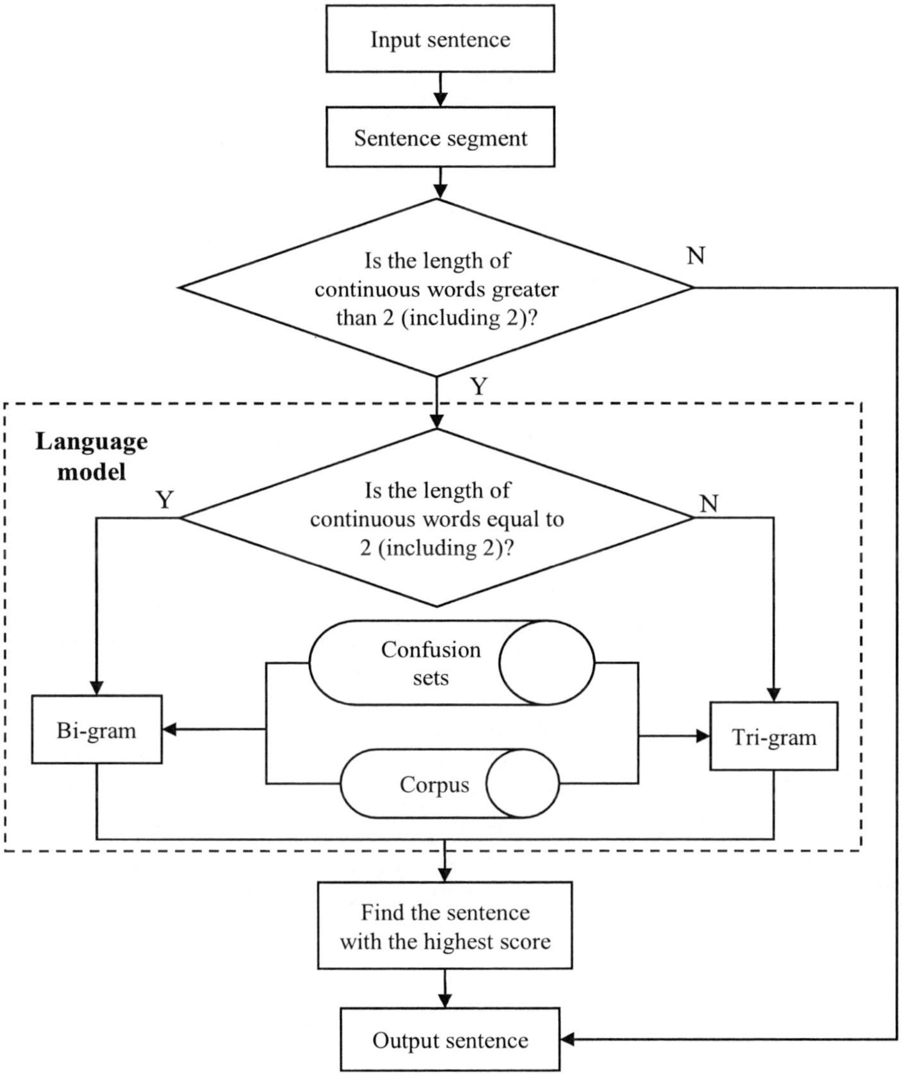

Figure 1. The flowchart of the CSC system.

Step 4. The system will calculate the score of every candidate sentence by using the joint bi-gram and tri-gram LM (using bi-gram and tri-gram based on different conditions). We use the corpus of CCL[1] and SOGOU[2] to generate the frequency of n-gram. Finally, the sentence with the highest score will be chosen as the final output.

In order to decrease the running time in Step 3 and Step 4, we apply dynamic programming to optimize the algorithm.

2.2 Confusion Set

Confusion set, a prepared set which consists of commonly confused characters plays a key role in spelling error detection and correction in texts (Wang et al., 2013). Most Chinese characters have similar characters on shape or pronunciation. Since pinyin input method is currently the most popular Chinese input method, when constructing the confusion sets used in our system, similar pronunciations is predominant. Moreover, characters of similar shapes are not as frequent, but still exist with a significant proportion (Liu et al., 2011). Orthographically similar characters have been also added to the confusion sets of our CSC system. So confusion sets used by the system were created by a number of rules with constraint, including similar pronunciations and similar glyphs.

Some Chinese characters with similar pronunciations, such as the Chinese homonyms ("zi(字)" and "zi(自)"), the nasal ("zang(藏)") and the non-nasal ("zan(赞)"), retroflex ("zhao(找)") and non-retroflex ("zao(早)"), etc.

In addition, it also includes other condition which is easy to confuse (based on statistics) on the pinyin of Chinese character, such as "qi(妻)"-"xi(西)" and "sao(嫂)"-"sou(搜)".

For Chinese characters with similar shape, such as the same radical of Chinese character ("固" and "回") and similar five-stroke input method ("ghnn(丐)" and "ghnv(丏)").

All of these rules are restricted by the strokes of a Chinese character to reduce the size of confusion sets of each character.

2.3 Language Modeling

Lots of previous researchers adopted language modeling to predict which word is correct to replace the possibly erroneous word in sentence, since language modeling can be used to measure the quality of a given word string (Chen et al., 2009; Liu et al., 2011; Wu et al., 2010). The most widely-used and well-practiced language model, by far, is the n-gram language model (Jelinek, 1999), because of its simplicity and fair predictive power.

Choosing an order of the n-gram in n-gram modeling is of a great importance. The higher order n-gram model such as four-gram or five-gram along with larger corpora tends to increase the quality thus will yield lower perplexity for human-generated text. However, the higher order n-gram models usually suffer from sparseness which leads to some zero conditional probabilities (Chen et al., 2013). For this reason, we use bi-gram and tri-gram with different rules for our system to determine which character is the best choice for correction. In our system, based on the result through Chinese Word Segment, we judge if it has any continuous words whose length is greater than or equal to 2. After that, if the length of unbroken words is equal to 2, we use bi-gram, and if it is greater than 2, we use tri-gram.

3 Chinese N-gram Model

3.1 Bi-gram Model

For given a Chinese character string $C = c_1, c_2, \ldots, c_L$, if the sentence has any errors, error words will appear in a continuous single words which will occur after through Chinese Words Segmentation. Generally speaking, the length of consecutive words is no more than 2 after splitting the sentence which has no mistakes. According to this judge, our system will adopt a bi-gram model to detecting and correcting errors when we find the length of continuous words is equal to 2.

For example, like this sentence "李大年的確是一個問提" will be "李大年/的確/是/一個/問/提" after through Chinese Character Segment. And the "題" is the correction of "提". If there are multiple places where the length of consecutive words is equal to 2, which means the sentence maybe has many spots with typo, then we use the bi-gram words in corresponding places. For example, the sentence "李大年的是的確是一個溫題" will be "李大年/的/是/的確/是/一個/溫/題" after through splitting, where the first "是" is a misspelled character of "事" and the "溫" is a misspelled character of "問".

[1] ccl.pku.edu.cn:8080/ccl_corpus/index.jsp?dir=xiandai
[2] www.sogou.com/labs/dl/c.html

The probability of the character string in the bi-gram model is approximated by the product of a series of conditional probabilities as follows (Jelinek, 1999),

$$P(C)=\prod_{l=2}^{L}P(c_l|C^{l-1})\approx\prod_{l=2}^{L}P(c_l|c_{l-1}). \quad (1)$$

In above Bi-gram model, we make the approximation that the probability of a character depends only on the one immediately preceding words.

The easiest way to estimate the conditional probability in Eq. (1) is used by the maximum likelihood (ML) estimation as follows

$$P(c_l|c_{l-1})=\frac{N(c_{l-1},c_l)}{N(c_{l-1})}, \quad (2)$$

where $N(c_{l-1},c_l)$ and $N(c_{l-1})$ denote the number of times the character strings "c_{l-1},c_l" and "c_{l-1}" occur in a given training corpus, respectively.

In our system, bi-gram model used in this way: we utilize the two-tuples word with the maximum score as the correct string to override the old one.

3.2 Tri-gram Model

Based on the above idea of bi-gram, we think it is not suitable to express the sentence's probabilistic model if the length of continuous single words is over 2 after through Chinese splitting. Because there have been three or more consecutive words, we have reason to believe that the sentence appearing in typo may be continuous. So, in this case we use the tri-gram model to detect and correct errors.

Given a Chinese character string $C=c_1,c_2,\dots,c_L$, the probability of the character string in tri-gram model is similar to bi-gram model,

$$P(C)=\prod_{l=3}^{L}P(c_l|C^{l-1})\approx\prod_{l=3}^{L}P(c_l|c_{l-2},c_{l-1}). \quad (3)$$

In the above tri-gram model, we make the approximation that the probability of a character depends only on the two immediately preceding words.

We estimate the conditional probability in Eq. (3) is used by the maximum likelihood (ML) estimation like bi-gram's method as follows,

$$P(c_l|c_{l-2},c_{l-1})=\frac{N(c_{l-2},c_{l-1},c_l)}{N(c_{l-2},c_{l-1})}, \quad (4)$$

where $N(c_{l-2},c_{l-1},c_l)$ and $N(c_{l-2},c_{l-1})$ denote the number of times the character strings "c_{l-2},c_{l-1},c_l" and "c_{l-2},c_{l-1}" occur in a given training corpus, respectively.

3.3 Getscore Function Definition

We define the candidate sentence as $C'=c'_1,c'_2,\dots,c'_L$, which is the character string derived from the original sentence C by replacing some characters using their confusion sets. The *getscore* function is utilized to select the most suitable candidate sentence. Figure 2 (a) and (b) show the pseudo-code of the *getscore* function by using bi-gram and tri-gram model, respectively.

function $getscore1(c'_{i-1},c'_i)$
begin
$\quad ret \leftarrow \frac{N(c'_{i-1},c'_i)}{N(c'_{i-1})}$
$\quad$ *if* $c'_i = c_i$ *then*
$\quad$ *begin*
$\quad\quad ret \leftarrow ret \times \lambda$
$\quad$ *end*
end

(a) Bi-gram model

function $getscore2(c'_{i-2},c'_{i-1},c'_i)$
begin
$\quad ret \leftarrow \frac{N(c'_{i-2},c'_{i-1},c'_i)}{N(c'_{i-2},c'_{i-1})}$
$\quad$ *if* $c'_i = c_i$ *then*
$\quad$ *begin*
$\quad\quad ret \leftarrow ret \times \lambda$
$\quad$ *end*
end

(b) Tri-gram model

Figure 2. Pseudo-code of *getscore* function.

Now we add a rule if $c'_i = c_i$. It will get an extra score λ. In the future work, we will add other rules or algorithms to improve the *getscore* function.

Figure 3 (a) and (b) show the calculating examples of *getscore* function by using bi-gram and tri-gram model, respectively.

For the example of "問{提,題}", in comparing with other string candidates as shown in Figure 3 (a), we found the string of the highest score "問題". So we detect the error spot and select '題' as the corrected character. Analogously, in "十字路{扣,口}", we detect the error spot and select '口' as the corrected character.

$$getscore(\text{"問提"}) = \frac{N(\text{"問提"})}{N(\text{"問"})} \times \lambda = 0.00022$$

$$getscore(\text{"問題"}) = \frac{N(\text{"問題"})}{N(\text{"問"})} = 0.61963$$

(a) Bi-gram model

$$getscore(\text{"十字路"}) = \frac{N(\text{"十字路"})}{N(\text{"十字"})} \times \lambda = 0.37973$$

$$getscore(\text{"字路扣"}) = \frac{N(\text{"字路扣"})}{N(\text{"字路"})} \times \lambda = 0$$

$$getscore(\text{"十字路"}) = \frac{N(\text{"十字路"})}{N(\text{"十字"})} \times \lambda = 0.37973$$

$$getscore(\text{"字路口"}) = \frac{N(\text{"字路口"})}{N(\text{"字路"})} = 0.91304$$

(b) Tri-gram model

Figure 3. *Getscore* function calculating example.

For the example of "問{提,題}", in comparing with other string candidates as shown in Figure 3 (a), we found the string of the highest score "問題". So we detect the error spot and select '題' as the corrected character. Analogously, in "十字路{扣,口}", we detect the error spot and select '口' as the corrected character.

3.4 Dynamic Programming

Due to the high complexity of enumerating candidate sentences, we use the dynamic programming (DP) to optimize the tri-gram model.

The confusion set of c_i is defined as $V[i]$, and each element in the confusion set is label by $0, 1, 2, 3, \ldots$, so the jth element in $V[i]$ will be represented as $V[i][j]$. The score of the candidate sentence with the maximum score is defined as $dp[i][k][l]$, where i is the length. $V[i-1][k]$ is the $i-1^{th}$ character, and $V[i][l]$ is the ith character. Because tri-gram model depends only on the last three characters, we can deduce the state transition equation of the DP algorithm as follows:

$$TupleStr \leftarrow V[i-2][j], V[i-1][k], V[i][l], \quad (5)$$

$$dp[i][k][l] \leftarrow \max(dp[i][k][l], dp[i-1][j][k] * getscore(TupleStr)) \quad (6)$$

The pseudo-code of dynamic programming is shown in Figure 4. The time complexity of the algorithm is reduced to acceptable level as $O(\sum_i^n Len_i N^3)$, where n is the numbers of continuous single words ($C = c_1, c_2, \ldots, c_L$); Len_i, the length of each continuous single words is equivalent to L of c_L; and N is the maximum size of a confusion set.

```
function Trigram_DP(c : string)
begin
  for k ← 0 to V[0].size − 1 do
    for l ← 0 to V[1].size − 1 do
    begin
      if V[0][k] = c_0 then
        dp[1][k][l] ← INIT_Parameter
      else
        dp[1][k][l] ← 1.0
      if V[1][l] = c_1 then
        dp[1][k][l] ← dp[1][k][l] * INIT_Parameter
    end

  for i ← 2 to c.length − 1 do
    for j ← 0 to V[i − 2].size − 1 do
      for k ← 0 to V[i − 1].size − 1 do
        for l ← 0 to V[i].size − 1 do
        begin
          TupleStr ← string(V[i − 2][j], V[i − 1][k], V[i][l])
          dp[i][k][l] ← max(dp[i][k][l], dp[i − 1][j][k] * getscore(TupleStr))
        end
end
```

Figure 4. Pseudo-code of tri-gram dynamic programming.

3.5 Additive Smoothing

In statistics theory, additive smoothing or its alias called Laplace smoothing and Lidstone smoothing, is a technique which is used to smooth categorical data (Chen et al., 1996). For an observation sequence $x = (x_1, x_2, \ldots, x_d)$ from a multinomial distribution with N trials and parameter $\theta = (\theta_1, \theta_2, \ldots, \theta_d)$, a "smoothed" version of the data gives the estimator:

$$\hat{\theta} = \frac{x_i + \alpha}{N + \alpha d} \qquad i = 1,2,\ldots,d , \tag{7}$$

where $\alpha > 0$ is the smoothing parameter ($\alpha = 0$ corresponds to no smoothing). Additive smoothing is a type of shrinkage estimator, as the resulting estimate will be between the empirical estimate x_i / N , and the uniform probability $1/d$.

In our model, the data make up for the number of occurrences of each string in corpus. Because of the sparsity of training data, which means some Chinese characters do not appear in the training data, we use additive smoothing to alleviate this sparsity problem.

We redefine the new *getscore* function as Figure 5.

$function\ getscore(c'_{i-1}, c'_i)$
$begin$
  $ret \leftarrow \frac{N(c'_{i-1}, c'_i) + \alpha}{N(c'_{i-1}) + \alpha d}$
  $if\ c'_i = c_i\ then$
  $begin$
    $ret \leftarrow ret \times \lambda$
  end
end

(a) Bi-gram model

$function\ getscore(c'_{i-2}, c'_{i-1}, c'_i)$
$begin$
  $ret \leftarrow \frac{N(c'_{i-2}, c'_{i-1}, c'_i) + \alpha}{N(c'_{i-2}, c'_{i-1}) + \alpha d}$
  $if\ c'_i = c_i\ then$
  $begin$
    $ret \leftarrow ret \times \lambda$
  end
end

(b) Tri-gram model

Figure 5. Pseudo-code of *getscore* function with additive smoothing.

4 Empirical Evaluation

4.1 Task

Chinese Spelling Check task is organized for the SIGHAN-8 bake-off. The goal of this task is to identify the capability of a Chinese spelling checker and hope to produce more advanced Chinese spelling check techniques. A passage, which is consist of several sentences with/without spelling errors i.e., redundant word, missing word, word disorder, and word selection, will be given as the input. Each character or punctuation occupies one position for counting location. The system to be developed should return the locations of the improper characters and the correct ones, if any typo is in this sentence, otherwise no spelling errors. Two training data (CLP-SIGHAN 2014 CSC Datasets[3] and SIGHAN-7 CSC Datasets[4]) are provided as practice. Passages of CFLs' essays selected from the NTNU learner corpus are also provided.

4.2 Metrics

The criteria for judging correctness are:

(1) Detection level: all locations of incorrect characters in a given passage should be completely identical with the gold standard.

(2) Correction level: all locations and corresponding corrections of incorrect characters should be completely identical with the gold standard.

The following metrics are evaluated in both levels with the help of the confusion matrix.

In CSC task of SIGHAN-8 Bake-Off, nine metrics method are used to evaluate the two aspects and score the performance of a CSC system. They are False Positive Rate (FPR), Detection Accuracy (DA), Detection Precision (DP), Detection Recall (DR), Detection F-score (DF), Correction Accuracy (CA), Correction Precision (CP), Correction Recall (CR) and Correction F-score (CF).

4.3 Evaluation Results

SIGHAN-8 Chinese Spelling Check task attracted 9 research teams to participate. 6 participants of 9 submitted their results. For formal testing, each participant has a right to submit at most three runs that use different models or parameter settings. There are 15 runs submitted in the end.

[3] http://ir.itc.ntnu.edu.tw/lre/clp14csc.html
[4] http://ir.itc.ntnu.edu.tw/lre/sighan7csc.html

Three runs of our system

Three runs of our system submitted to the SIGHAN-8 CSC final test are as follows:

Run1 (Tri-gram + word segmentation): This run replaces each word of a sentence with corresponding confusion sets in turn, and then computes new sentence score using tri-gram model. At the same time, we join the sentence segment to as the one of criterions of score calculation. In other words, we think that the less the total number of segments, the higher the score after sentence splitting, that is the numbers of segmentation is inverse proportion to score.

Run2 (Joint bi-gram and tri-gram + word segmentation): This run is the proposed method using joint bi-gram and tri-gram LMs and word segmentation.

Run3 (Tri-gram): This run is the result using the method of Run1 without the step of Chinese word segmentation. This run is the method that we proposed in the Bake-Off 2014 task last year (Huang et al., 2014). We use it as our baseline.

Validation of Run2

Table 1 indicates the top-3 validation scores of Run2, i.e. the proposed method on validation set that using CLP-SIGHAN 2014 CSC Datasets using different INIT_Parameter and λ that both are 30, 35 and 40 respectively. We utilize Test1's method and parameters as our SIGHAN-8 CSC final test Run2.

SIGHAN CSC15 final test

Table 2 shows the evaluation results of the final test. Run1, Run2 and Run3 are the three runs submitted by our system with different methods. The "Best" indicates the high score of each metric achieved in CSC task. The "Average" represents the average of the 15 runs.

According to the result in Table 2, we can see that the result of our system is close to the average level. The recall rate of our system is the major weakness. The reason might be that we do not apply a separate error detection module.

Although comparing with the baseline of tri-gram model, using joint bi-gram and tri-gram models gets improvement. The potential capability of the N-gram method is far from fully leveraged. Some typical errors of our current system will be presented in the next subsection, and some probably improvements are summarized in the Section 5.

4.4 Error Analysis

Figure 6 shows some typical error examples of our system ("O" original, "M" modified):

Case 1:
O: 生育嬰兒個數在**特**續下滑。
M: 生育嬰兒個數在**特**續下滑。
Case 2:
O: **或**著是人們有了新的想法。
M: **活**著是人們有了新的想法。
Case 3:
O: 一點**鐘**可不可以跟你見面?
M: 一點**中**可不可以跟你見面?

Figure 6. Error examples.

	FPR	DA	DP	DR	DF	CA	CP	CR	CF
Test1	0.2203	0.4680	0.4150	**0.1563**	**0.2271**	0.4576	0.3810	**0.1356**	**0.2000**
Test2	0.1996	**0.4755**	**0.4301**	0.1507	0.2232	0.4652	**0.3943**	0.1299	0.1955
Test3	**0.1940**	0.4746	0.4246	0.1431	0.2141	**0.4661**	0.3941	0.1262	0.1912

Table 1. Validation Scores of Run 2 on CLP-SIGHAN 2014 CSC Datasets.

	FPR	DA	DP	DR	DF	CA	CP	CR	CF
Run1	0.5327	0.3409	0.2871	0.2145	0.2456	0.3218	0.2487	0.1764	0.2064
Run2	**0.1218**	**0.5464**	**0.6378**	**0.2145**	**0.3211**	**0.5227**	**0.5786**	**0.1673**	**0.2595**
Run3	0.6218	0.3282	0.3091	0.2782	0.2928	0.3018	0.2661	0.2255	0.2441
Average	0.2254	0.5419	0.6148	0.3092	0.3978	0.5213	0.5795	0.268	0.3524
Best	0.0509	0.7009	0.8372	0.5345	0.6404	0.6918	0.8037	0.5145	0.6254

Table 2. Evaluation results of SIGHAN-8 CSC final test.

In the first case, because "持" is not in the confusion set of "特", our system can't correct the error of "特績" to "持續".

The second case is an overkill error that belongs to the context problem. Our system didn't recognize the dependencies of "或著" and context, and "活著" get a highest score in the tri-gram model. So our system select "活" to replace "或", and leads to error at the same time.

The third case is also an overkill error which is on account of the out of vocabulary (OOV) problem. In this case, the original sentence is in fact correct but unfortunately, our system modifies it to "一點中" and gave it a high score.

5 Conclusions and Future Work

This paper presents the development and evaluation of the system from team of South China Agricultural University (SCAU) that participated in the SIGHAN-8 Chinese Spelling Check task. The proposed joint bi-gram and tri-gram language model is helpful to determine the better character sequence as the results for detection and correction. Chinese word segmentation is performed on the input sentence. Dynamic programming is used to improve the efficiency of the algorithm to solve the high complexity in the computation process of the tri-gram. Additive smoothing is adopted to solve the data sparseness problem in the training set. In addition, we have optimized the Correction Precision by adding orthographically similar characters to the confusion sets.

It is our second attempt on Chinese spelling check, and the evaluation results of SIGHAN-8 CSC final test shows that comparing to the method we proposed in the CSC task of CLP-SIGHAN Bake-Off 2014 last year, we achieve an improvement of 9.7% in DF and 6.3% in CF. However, we still have a long way from the state-of-arts results. There are many possible and promising research directions for the near future. Language modeling has been extensively used in our CSC. However, the N-gram language models only aim at capturing the local contextual information or the lexical regularity of a language. Future work will explore long-span semantic information for language modeling to further improve the CSC. What's more, we still need to do more research on how to deal with the characters overkill problem to make the CSC more perfect.

Acknowledgments

This work was partially supported by National Natural Science Foundation of China under Grant No. 71472068, Science and Technology Planning Project of Guangdong Province, China under Grant No. 2013B020314013, and the Innovation Training Project for College Students of Guangdong Province under Grant No.201410564294.

References

Zhuowei Bao, Benny Kimelfeld, Yunyao Li. 2011. A Graph Approach to Spelling Correction in Domain-Centric Search. *In Proceedings of the 49th Annual Meeting of the Association for Computational Linguistics (ACL 2011)*, pp. 905–914.

Stanley F. Chen, Joshua Goodman. 1996. An Empirical Study of Smoothing Techniques for Language Modeling. *In Proceedings of the 34th Annual Meeting of the Association for Computational Linguistics (ACL 1996)*, pp. 310-318.

Berlin Chen. 2009. Word Topic Models for Spoken Document Retrieval and Transcription. *ACM Transactions on Asian Language Information Processing*, Vol. 8, No. 1, pp. 2: 1-2: 27.

Kuan-Yu Chen, Hung-Shin Lee, Chung-Han Lee , et al.. 2013. A Study of Language Modeling for Chinese Spelling Check. *In Proceedings of the Seventh 7th Workshop on Chinese Language Processing (SIGHAN-7)*, Nagoya, Japan, 14 Oct., 2013, pp. 79–83.

Hsun-wen Chiu, Jian-cheng Wu and Jason S. Chang. 2013. Chinese Spelling Checker Based on Statistical Machine Translation. *In Proceedings of the 7th SIGHAN Workshop on Chinese Language Processing (SIGHAN-7)*, Nagoya, Japan, 14 Oct., 2013, pp. 49-53.

Dongxu Han, Baobao Chang. 2013. A Maximum Entropy Approach to Chinese Spelling Check. *In Proceedings of the 7th SIGHAN Workshop on Chinese Language Processing (SIGHAN-7)*, Nagoya, Japan, 14 Oct., 2013, pp. 74-78.

Qiang Huang, Peijie Huang, Xinrui Zhang, et al.. 2014. Chinese spelling check system based on tri-gram model. *In Proceedings of the Third CIPS-SIGHAN Joint Conference on Chinese Language Processing (CLP-2014)*, Wuhan, China, 20-21 Oct., 2014. pp.173-178.

Frederick Jelinek. 1999. *Statistical Methods for Speech Recognition*. The MIT Press.

Zhongye Jia, Peilu Wang and Hai Zhao. 2013. Graph Model for Chinese Spell Checking. *In Proceedings of the 7th SIGHAN Workshop on Chinese Language Processing (SIGHAN-7)*, Nagoya, Japan, 14 Oct., 2013, pp. 88-92.

Ying Jiang, Tong Wang, Tao Lin, et al. 2012. A rule based Chinese spelling and grammar detection system utility. *In Proceedings of the 2012 International Conference on System Science and Engineering (ICSSE)*, pp. 437-440.

Karen Kukich. 1992. Techniques for Automatically Correcting Words in Text. *ACM Computing Surveys,* Vol. 24, No.4, pp. 377-439.

Chao-Lin Liu, Min-Hua Lai, Kan-Wen Tien, et al.. 2011. Visually and Phonologically Similar Characters in Incorrect Chinese Words: Analyses, Identification, and Applications. *ACM Transactions on Asian Language Information Processing*, Vol. 10, No. 2, pp. 10: 1-10: 39.

Yih-Ru Wang, Yuan-Fu Liao, Yeh-Kuang Wu, et al.. 2013. Conditional Random Field-based Parser and Language Model for Traditional Chinese Spelling Checker. *In Proceedings of the 7th SIGHAN Workshop on Chinese Language Processing (SIGHAN-7)*, Nagoya, Japan, 14 Oct., 2013, pp. 69-73.

Shih-Hung Wu, Yong-Zhi Chen, Ping-Che Yang, et al.. 2010. Reducing the False Alarm Rate of Chinese Character Error Detection and Correction. *In Proceedings of the First CIPS-SIGHAN Joint Conference on Chinese Language Processing (CLP-2010)*, Beijing, 28-29 Aug., 2010, pp. 54-61.

Yang Xin, Hai Zhao, Yuzhu Wang et al.. 2014. An Improved Graph Model for Chinese Spell Checking. *In Proceedings of the Third CIPS-SIGHAN Joint Conference on Chinese Language Processing (CLP-2014)*, Wuhan, China, 20-21 Oct., 2014. pp.157–166.

Jinhua Xiong, Qiao Zhao, Jianpeng Hou,et al.. 2014. Extended HMM and Ranking Models for Chinese Spelling Correction. *In Proceedings of the Third CIPS-SIGHAN Joint Conference on Chinese Language Processing (CLP 2014)*, Wuhan, China, 20-21 Oct., 2014. pp. 133–138.

NTOU Chinese Spelling Check System in SIGHAN-8 Bake-off

Wei-Cheng Chu and Chuan-Jie Lin
Department of Computer Science and Engineering
National Taiwan Ocean University
No 2, Pei-Ning Road, Keelung 202, Taiwan R.O.C.
{wcchu.cse, cjlin}@ntou.edu.tw

Abstract

This paper describes details of NTOU Chinese spelling check system in SIGHAN-8 Bakeoff. Besides the basic architecture of the previous system participating in last two CSC tasks, three new preference rules were proposed to deal with Simplified Chinese characters, variants, sentence-final particles, and DE-particles. A new sentence likelihood function was proposed based on frequencies of space-removed version of Google *n*-gram datasets. Two formal runs were submitted where the best one was created by the system using Google *n*-gram frequency information.

1 Introduction

Automatic spell checking is a basic and important technique in building NLP systems. It has been studied since 1960s as Blair (1960) and Damerau (1964) made the first attempt to solve the spelling error problem in English. Spelling errors in English can be grouped into two classes: non-word spelling errors and real-word spelling errors.

A non-word spelling error occurs when the written string cannot be found in a dictionary, such as in *fly fron* Paris*. The typical approach is finding a list of candidates from a large dictionary by edit distance or phonetic similarity (Mitten, 1996; Deorowicz and Ciura, 2005; Carlson and Fette, 2007; Chen *et al.*, 2007; Mitten 2008; Whitelaw *et al.*, 2009).

A real-word spelling error occurs when one word is mistakenly used for another word, such as in *fly form* Paris*. Typical approaches include using confusion set (Golding and Roth, 1999; Carlson *et al.*, 2001), contextual information (Verberne, 2002; Islam and Inkpen, 2009), and others (Pirinen and Linden, 2010; Amorim and Zampieri, 2013).

Spelling error problem in Chinese is quite different. Because there is no word delimiter in a Chinese sentence and almost every Chinese character can be considered as a one-character word, most of the errors are real-word errors.

On the other hand, there is also an *illegal-character error* where a hand-written symbol is not a legal Chinese character (thus not collected in a dictionary). Such an error cannot happen in a digital document because all characters in Chinese character sets such as BIG5 or Unicode are legal.

There have been many attempts to solve the spelling error problem in Chinese (Chang, 1994; Zhang *et al.*, 2000; Cucerzan and Brill, 2004; Li *et al.*, 2006; Liu *et al.*, 2008). Among them, lists of visually and phonologically similar characters play an important role in Chinese spelling check (Liu *et al.*, 2011).

This bake-off is the third Chinese spelling check evaluation project. A CSC system will be evaluated in two levels: error detection and error correction. The task is organized based on some research works (Wu *et al.*, 2010; Chen *et al.*, 2011; Liu *et al.*, 2011; Yu *et al.*, 2014).

2 NTOU CSC System Description

This year, the architecture of NTOU CSC system mostly follows the previous version, only that three new preference rules are added. The architecture of previous NTOU CSC system is explained as follows.

Figure 1 shows the architecture of NTOU Chinese spelling checking system. A sentence under consideration is first word-segmented. New sentences are generated by replacing candidates of spelling errors with their similar characters one at a time. New sentences are also word-segmented. Their likelihoods of being

Proceedings of the Eighth SIGHAN Workshop on Chinese Language Processing (SIGHAN-8), pages 137–143,
Beijing, China, July 30-31, 2015.

acceptable Chinese sentences are measured by sorted by *n*-gram linguistic model. If the new sentence with the top-1 likelihood is better than the original sentence, a spelling error is reported.

There are 6 kinds of **confusion sets** used in this system. One of them was generated from the Four-Corner Code system, proposed by us in CSC 2014 (Chu and Lin, 2014). The other 5 were provided by the organizers in CSC 2013 (Wu *et al.*, 2013). They are characters with the same sound in the same tone, characters with the same sound in different tones, characters with similar sound in the same tone, characters with similar sound in different tones, and visually similar characters.

There are three cases of spelling error candidates in our system. Two of them have been described in our CSC 2014 system description paper. Multi-word replacement will be explained in Section 3.1.

One-character word replacement: every one-character word in the original sentence is considered as a spelling error candidate and should be replaced with its similar characters in its confusion set. For example, "座" in Topic A2-0101-2 is a one-character word and its similar characters are 柞坐雁挫..., the replacement is as follows.

A2-0101-2, Original:
所以我們沒位子可以座
Replaced:
所以我們沒位子可以柞
所以我們沒位子可以坐
所以我們沒位子可以雁
所以我們沒位子可以挫
...

Multi-character word replacement: the method to create multi-character word confusion sets has been proposed by Lin and Chu (2015). Given a multi-character word, if one of the characters is replaced with a similar character and becomes another legal word, these two words are considered as collected into each other's multi-character word confusion set. The resource to create our word confusion set is the Revised Mandarin Dictionary by the Ministry of Education[1].

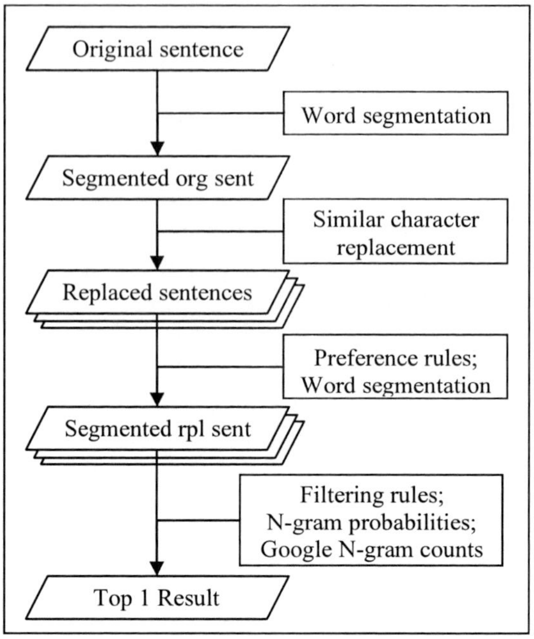

Figure 1. Architecture of NTOU Chinese Spelling Check System

Every multi-character word in the original sentence is considered as a spelling error candidate and should be replaced with its similar words. For example, "不過" and "漢子" in Topic A2-1308-1 are multi-character words. Their similar words are "補過", "不果"..., "蚶子", "漢字"... The replacement is as follows.

A2-1308-1, Original:
不過一個漢子也看不懂
Replaced:
補過一個漢子也看不懂
不果一個漢子也看不懂
不過一個蚶子也看不懂
不過一個漢字也看不懂
...

Two **filtering rules** are again adopted this year.

Rule-1 No error in personal names: discard a replacement if it becomes a personal name; it is unlikely to see errors in personal names. Take C1-1701-2 in the CLP Bakeoff 2014 CSC test set as an example as an example. When the one-character word "位" is replaced by its similar character "魏", "魏產齡" is identified as a personal name, so this replacement is discarded.

[1] http://dict.revised.moe.edu.tw/

C1-1701-2, Original segmented:
每 位 產 齡 婦女
Replaced *and discarded*:
每 [魏]產齡(PERSON) 婦女

Rule-2 Stopword filtering: discard a replacement if the original character is a personal anaphora (你'you', 我'I', 他她它祂牠'he/she/it') or numbers from 1 to 10 (一二三四五六七八九十).

N-gram linguistic models, word-unigram, word-bigram, and POS-bigram models, were trained by using a large Chinese corpus, Academic Sinica Balanced Corpus (Chen *et al.*, 1996).

N-gram preference score is defined as $[P(S_{new}) \ / \ P(S_{org}) - 1]$, where $P(S)$ is the probability of a sentence S in a language model. When sorting, word-bigram preference score has the higher priority, word-unigram preference score has the second priority, and POS-bigram preference score has the lowest priority.

If the top-1 sentence is a newly generated sentence, and all of its preference scores are not lower than predefined thresholds, report it as an error with the location of the replacement. Otherwise, report "no error". The threshold of word-bigram preference score is 0.0571, and 0.0171 for word-unigram, 0 for POS-bigram preference scores.

3 New Features in 2015

3.1 Multi-word replacement

In our observation, a spelling error occurs in at least three different cases. The first case is that the error alone is identified as a one-character word. The second case is that one character in a multi-character word is misused but the wrong word is still a legal word. The third case is that the erroneous character, combining with the character to its left or to its right, is misidentified as a multi-character word. Take Topic 00043 in the SIGHAN7 Bakeoff 2013 CSC Datasets as an example. The error "帶" occurs in a multi-character word "膠帶", but the correct word "塑膠袋" is a longer word.

Topic 00043, Original:
外面也會包塑膠帶啦
Segmented:
外面 也 會 包 塑 膠帶 啦
Correct:
外面 也 會 包 塑膠[袋] 啦

To deal with such an error case, we proposed a new replacement procedure: if a multi-character word is preceded or followed by a one-character word, each character in this multi-character word is substituted with its similar characters one by one. Again, take Topic 00043 as an example. "外面" and "膠帶" are multi-character words and adjacent to one-character words, so they are candidates of spelling errors. By replacing similar characters of "外", "面", "膠", and "帶", newly generated sentences are as follows.

Topic 00043, Segmented:
外面 也 會 包 塑 膠帶 啦
Replaced:
[舀]面也會包塑膠帶啦
外[麵]也會包塑膠帶啦
外面也會包塑[穋]帶啦
外面也會包塑膠[袋]啦
...

3.2 Preference rules

Three kinds of preference rules were proposed this year to deal with special cases: Simplified Chinese characters or variants, sentence-final particles, and DE-particles. If any of the rules are matched, an error is reported immediately.

Rule 1: Simplified and variant Chinese character detection

Because the sentences in the datasets are written in Traditional Chinese, all Simplified Chinese characters or variants of Traditional Chinese characters appearing in the datasets are marked as errors.

A mapping table (Lin *et al.*, 2012) from variants (including Simplified Chinese characters) to their corresponding Traditional Chinese characters is adopted to correct such a kind of errors.

Take B1-0840-2 in the CLP Bakeoff 2014 CSC Datasets as an example of Simplified Chinese character replacement, where "尔" is a Simplified Chinese character and should be replaced with its corresponding Traditional Chinese character "爾" directly.

B1-0840-2, Original:
首尔是韓國的首都
Correct:
首[爾]是韓國的首都

Take B1-3981-1 in the CLP Bakeoff 2014 CSC Datasets as an example of variant replacement, where "偺" is a variant of the more-common Traditional Chinese character "咱", so it should be replaced directly.

B1-3981-1, Original:
然後偺俩就一塊兒出去打球
Correct:
然後咱俩就一塊兒出去打球

Rule 2: Sentence-final particle detection

In our observation, some sentence-final particles were frequently misspelled in the datasets, including "嗎", "吧", and "啊". We collected the errors in the dataset whose corrections were these particles and created the following three replacement rules:

1. If a sentence ends with a one-character word "碼" or "馬", it should be replaced with "嗎".
2. If a sentence ends with a one-character word "把" or "巴", it should be replaced with "吧".
3. If a sentence ends with a one-character word "阿", it should be replaced with "啊".

The following examples show the application of these rules.

B1-0381-2, Original:
你喜歡西式的餐廳馬？
Correct:
你喜歡西式的餐廳嗎？

B1-1125-4, Original:
應該沒有問題把？
Correct:
應該沒有問題吧？

B1-1589-1, Original:
像討論活動啊，遊戲阿，
Correct:
像討論活動啊，遊戲啊，

Rule 3: DE-particle detection

In Chinese, "的", "得", and "地" serve as function words in various different cases. They are grouped together and receive a special POS "DE". However, despite their usages are different, they are easily messed up with one another, even for native speakers.

Patterns	Correction
得/地 Na	的
得/地 PERIODCATEGORY	的
VC 的/地 VC	得
VA 的/地 VH	得
VCL 的/地 VH	得
VH 的/得 VE	地

Table1. Replacement Rules for DE-particles

To deal with such kind of errors, we extracted most frequently-seen POS patterns in the training set. Table 1 lists the 6 patterns learned and used in our system. To demonstrate how to apply these rules, take B1-0184-3 in the CLP Bakeoff 2014 CSC Datasets as an example. The DE-particle "得" is followed by a common noun (whose POS is "Na") and matched the first DE-particle replacement rule in Table 1, so it is replaced with "的".

B1-0184-3, Original:
我 得 英文(Na) 那麼 好
Correct:
我的英文那麼好

3.3 Google N-gram Scoring Functions

As described in Section 2, our previous language models were trained by Academia Sinica Balanced Corpus. We found that the volume and vocabulary of ASBC was not large enough. So we turn to use Chinese Web 5-gram dataset [2] instead. Several *n*-gram scoring functions have been proposed by Lin and Chu (2015). Some examples from the Chinese Web 5-gram dataset are given here:

Unigram:	稀釋劑	17260
Bigram:	蒸發量 超過	69
Trigram:	能量 遠 低於	113
4-gram:	張貼 色情 圖片 或	73
5-gram:	幸好 我們 發現 得 早	155

Moreover, in order to avoid interference of word segmentation errors, we further design some likelihood scoring functions which utilize substring frequencies instead of word *n*-gram frequencies.

By removing space between *n*-grams in the Chinese Web 5-gram dataset, we constructed a new dataset containing identical substrings with

[2] https://catalog.ldc.upenn.edu/LDC2010T06

Run	FPAlarm	Accuracy	Precision	Recall	F1
Formalrun1_NTOU	9.09	**54.45**	**66.44**	18.00	28.33
Formalrun2_NTOU	**57.27**	42.27	42.20	**41.82**	**42.01**

Table 2: Formal Run Performance in Error-Detection Level

Run	FPAlarm	Accuracy	Precision	Recall	F1
Formalrun1_NTOU	9.09	**53.27**	**63.24**	15.64	25.07
Formalrun2_NTOU	**57.27**	39.00	38.11	**35.27**	**36.64**

Table 3: Formal Run Performance in Error-Correction Level

their web frequencies. For instances, n-grams in the previous example will become:

Zhar=3: 稀釋劑	17260
Zhar=5: 蒸發量超過	69
Zhar=5: 能量遠低於	113
Zhar=7: 張貼色情圖片或	73
Zhar=8: 幸好我們發現得早	155

where *Zhar*(*S*) is defined as the number of Chinese or other characters in a sentence *S*. Note that if two different n-gram sets become the same after removing the space, their will merge into one entry with the summation of their frequencies. Simplified Chinese words were translated into Traditional Chinese in advanced.

Given a sentence *S*, let *SubStr*(*S*, *n*) be the set of all substrings in *S* whose *Zhar* values are *n*. We define ***Google string frequency*** *gsf*(*u*) of a string *u* to be its frequency data provided in the modified Chinese Web 5-gram dataset. If a string does not appear in that dataset, its *gsf* value is defined to be 0.

Equation 1 give the definition of ***averaged weighted log frequency score*** $GS_{wgt}(S)$ which sums up the logarithm of frequencies of all substrings with length *n*, averages scores at the same *n* level, and multiplies log*n*.

$$GS_{wgt}(S) = \sum_{n=2}^{12}\left(\frac{\log n}{|SubStr(S,n)|} \times \sum_{u \in SubStr(S,n)} \log(gsf(u))\right) \quad \text{Eq. 1}$$

Now the ***Google n-gram preference score*** is defined as Eq 2.

$$GS_{prf}(S_{new}, S_{org}) = \frac{GS_{wgt}(S_{new})}{GS_{wgt}(S_{old})} - 1 \quad \text{Eq. 2}$$

As the same algorithm of error detection as described in Section 2, a top-1 replacement should have a Google *n*-gram preference score no lower than the threshold 0.0002 so that it could be reported as an error correction.

4 Experimental Results

We submitted 2 formal runs this year by two different statistics-based systems. The first system checks the word-unigram, word-bigram, and POS-bigram preference scores of the top-1 sentence to decide the occurrence of a spelling error, as described in Section 2. The second system uses Google *n*-gram preference scores instead to check the occurrence of a spelling error, as described in Section 3.3.

Table 2 and 3 illustrate the evaluation results of formal runs. As we can see, the first system guesses errors more correctly but too cautiously. The second system, on the other hand, proposed more errors so it achieved a higher recall rate and a higher F-score.

5 Conclusion

It is our third time to participate in a Chinese spelling check evaluation project. Based on our previous CSC system, we further proposed three preference rules to handle three special cases: (1) Simplified Chinese characters or variants; (2) sentence-final particles, and (3) DE-particles. Moreover, a new sentence-likelihood scoring function, ***averaged weighted log frequency score***, was proposed which used Google *n*-gram frequency information.

Two formal runs were submitted this year. The first one was predicted by three *n*-gram language models trained by a large corpus ASBC. The second one was predicted by the system which used Google *n*-gram averaged weighted log frequency scores to decide the occurrence of errors. The evaluation results show the system using Google *n*-gram frequency information outperformed the traditional language models.

References

R.C. de Amorim and M. Zampieri. 2013. "Effective Spell Checking Methods Using Clustering

Algorithms," *Recent Advances in Natural Language Processing*, 7-13.

C. Blair. 1960. "A program for correcting spelling errors," *Information and Control*, 3:60-67.

A. Carlson, J. Rosen, and D. Roth. 2001. "Scaling up context-sensitive text correction," *Proceedings of the 13th Innovative Applications of Artificial Intelligence Conference*, 45-50.

A. Carlson and I. Fette. 2007. "Memory-Based Context-Sensitive Spelling Correction at Web Scale," *Proceedings of the 6th International Conference on Machine Learning and Applications*, 166-171.

C.C. Chang and C.J. Lin. 2011. "LIBSVM: a library for support vector machines," *ACM Transactions on Intelligent Systems and Technology*, 2:27:1-27.

C.H. Chang. 1994. "A pilot study on automatic chinese spelling error correction," *Journal of Chinese Language and Computing*, 4:143-149.

K.J. Chen, C.R. Huang, L.P. Chang, and H.L. Hsu. 1996. "Sinica corpus: Design methodology for balanced corpora," *Language, Information and Computation* (*PACLIC 11*), 167-176.

Q. Chen, M. Li, and M. Zhou. 2007. "Improving Query Spelling Correction Using Web Search Results", *Proceedings of the 2007 Conference on Empirical Methods in Natural Language* (*EMNLP-2007*), 181-189.

Y.Z. Chen, S.H. Wu, P.C. Yang, T. Ku, and G.D. Chen. 2011. "Improve the detection of improperly used Chinese characters in students' essays with error model," *Int. J. Cont. Engineering Education and Life-Long Learning*, 21(1):103-116.

W.C. Chu and C.J. Lin. 2014. "NTOU Chinese Spelling Check System in CLP Bake-off 2014," *Proceedings of The 3rd CIPS-SIGHAN Joint Conference on Chinese Language Processing*, 210-215.

S. Cucerzan and E. Brill. 2004. "Spelling correction as an iterative process that exploits the collective knowledge of web users," *Proceedings of EMNLP*, 293-300.

F. Damerau. 1964. "A technique for computer detection and correction of spelling errors." *Communications of the ACM*, 7:171-176.

S. Deorowicz and M.G. Ciura. 2005. "Correcting Spelling Errors by Modelling Their Causes," *International Journal of Applied Mathematics and Computer Science*, 15(2):275-285.

A. Golding and D. Roth. 1999. "A winnow-based approach to context-sensitive spelling correction," *Machine Learning*, 34(1-3):107-130.

A. Islam and D. Inkpen. 2009. "Real-word spelling correction using googleweb 1t 3-grams," *Proceedings of Empirical Methods in Natural Language Processing* (*EMNLP-2009*), 1241-1249.

M. Li, Y. Zhang, M.H. Zhu, and M. Zhou. 2006. "Exploring distributional similarity based models for query spelling correction," *Proceedings of the 21st International Conference on Computational Linguistics and 44th Annual Meeting of the ACL*, 1025-1032.

C.J. Lin, J.C. Zhan, Y.H. Chen, and C.W. Pao. 2012. "Strategies of Processing Japanese Names and Character Variants in Traditional Chinese Text," *International Journal of Computational Linguistics & Chinese Language Processing*, 17(3), 87-108.

Chuan-Jie Lin and Wei-Cheng Chu. 2015. "A Study on Chinese Spelling Check Using Confusion Sets and N-gram Statistics," *International Journal of Computational Linguistics and Chinese Language Processing*, to be appeared.

W. Liu, B. Allison, and L. Guthrie. 2008. "Professor or screaming beast? Detecting words misuse in Chinese," *The 6th edition of the Language Resources and Evaluation Conference.*

C.L. Liu, M.H. Lai, K.W. Tien, Y.H. Chuang, S.H. Wu, and C.Y. Lee. 2011. "Visually and phonologically similar characters in incorrect Chinese words: Analyses, identification, and applications," *ACM Transactions on Asian Language Information Processing*, 10(2), 10:1-39.

R. Mitton. 1996. *English Spelling and the Computer*, Harlow, Essex: Longman Group.

R. Mitton. 2008. "Ordering the Suggestions of a Spellchecker Without Using Context," *Natural Language Engineering*, 15(2):173-192.

T. Pirinen and K. Linden. 2010. "Creating and weighting hunspell dictionaries as finite-state automata," *Investigationes Linguisticae*, 21.

S. Verberne. 2002. Context-sensitive spell checking based on word trigram probabilities, Master thesis, University of Nijmegen.

C. Whitelaw, B. Hutchinson, G.Y. Chung, and G. Ellis. 2009. "Using the Web for Language Independent Spellchecking and Autocorrection," *Proceedings Of Conference On Empirical Methods In Natural Language Processing* (*EMNLP-2009*), 890-899.

S.H. Wu, Y.Z. Chen, P.C. Yang, T. Ku, and C.L. Liu. 2010. "Reducing the False Alarm Rate of Chinese Character Error Detection and Correction," *Proceedings of CIPS-SIGHAN Joint Conference on Chinese Language Processing* (*CLP 2010*), 54-61.

S.H. Wu, C.L. Liu, and L.H. Lee. 2013. "Chinese Spelling Check Evaluation at SIGHAN Bake-off

2013," *Proceedings of the 7th SIGHAN Workshop on Chinese Language Processing* (*SIGHAN'13*), 35-42.

L.C. Yu, L.H. Lee, Y.H. Tseng, and H.H. Chen. 2014. "Overview of SIGHAN 2014 Bake-off for Chinese Spelling Check," *Proceedings of the 3rd CIPS-SIGHAN Joint Conference on Chinese Language Processing* (*CLP'14*), 126-132.

L. Zhang, M. Zhou, C.N. Huang, and H.H. Pan. 2000. "Automatic detecting/correcting errors in Chinese text by an approximate word-matching algorithm," *Proceedings of the 38th Annual Meeting on Association for Computational Linguistics*, 248-254.

Topic-Based Chinese Message Sentiment Analysis: A Multilayered Analysis System

Hongjie Li Zhongqian Sun Wei Yang
Tencent Intelligent Computing and Search Lab
Nanshan District, Shenzhen P.R. China
{hongjieli,sallensun,willyang}@tencent.com

Abstract

Sentiment analysis in social media has attracted significant attention. Although researchers have proposed many methods, a single method is hard to meet requirement in industrial applications. In this paper, based on massive data of Tencent and industrial practice, we present a multilayered analysis system (MAS) on social media. The system is composed of three sub-systems, including topic correlation calculation, topic-related sentence recognition and sentence polarity classification. Each sub-system is composed of several simple models. Also, we have set up a closed-loop feature mining and model updating system, which will continuously promote performance of MAS. In addition, this offline system requires very little intervention. The system, including online and offline parts, has been applied in several practical projects and obtained the best results in the evaluation of task 2 of SIGHAN-8.

1 Introduction

The popularity of Web 2.0 applications promotes the emergence of user generated content (UGC), e.g., the comments in blogosphere, and the UGC reflects the viewpoints of web users towards a specific event or product. Scholars have carried out a series of studies around these data, especially in the research of sentiment analysis. It aims to understand the subjective opinions of characters, events and other subjects based on the analysis of the content published by users. Sentiment analysis has a wide range of applications, e.g. the social public opinions, the word of mouth analysis, potential users mining.

In this article, we focus on sentiment analysis of short-text generated by users, for example, micro blog, news comment, products comment, tweets and so on. Many researchers have proposed many methods to improve the effect of sentiment analysis.Mei (2007) introduced latent sentimatic analysis model for sentiment analysis, e.g. LDA. Si et al. first utilize a continuous Dirichlet Process Mixture model to classify tweets. A supervised sentiment classification framework was proposed by (Davidov et al., 2010). Based on KNN, they use Emoticons and hashtag to classify sentiment in tweets. Another significant effort for sentiment analysis is proposed by (Barbosa and Feng, 2010) who use polarity predicitions from three websites as noisy labels to train a SVM model. Hassan (2010) use dependency relations and part-of-speech patterns to classify the message in Usenet with Supervised Markoff model. A.Meena (2007) analyzes the impact of conjunction to the emotion analysis, but the system do not have field adaptive ability. Socher (2011) extended word representations beyond simple vectors. They merge words in sentences and create phrase representations recursively.

In industry, a single model is hard to achieve the expected performance. Based on massive data of Tencent, we propose an multilayered approach which integrates multiple simple methods. Meanwhile, we set up a closed-loop offline mining process, which optimizes the online classification results through continuously mining new features. The approach has been tested in task 2 of SIGHAN-8. And the result showed that both the precise and recall improved a lot.

2 A Multilayered Anasysis System

In this section, we first introduce online part of MAS. Then we introduce how MAS forms a closed-loop updating system. Last, we present some key points of MAS.

Proceedings of the Eighth SIGHAN Workshop on Chinese Language Processing (SIGHAN-8), pages 144–148,
Beijing, China, July 30-31, 2015.

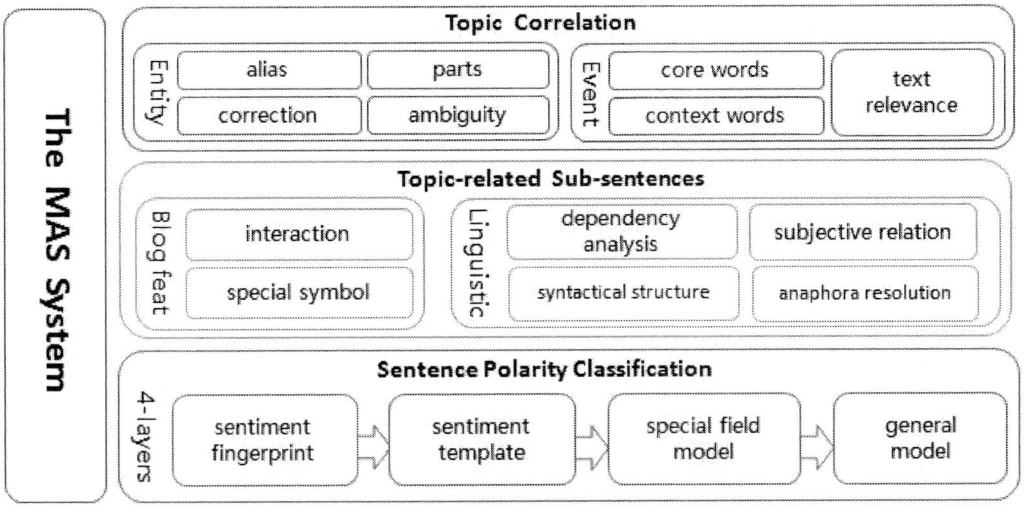

Figure 1: The online methods of MAS.

2.1 The Online Methods of MAS

As shown in Figure 1, MAS is composed of three sub-systems, including topic correlation calculation, topic-related sentence recognition and sentence polarity classification.

2.1.1 Topic Correlation Calculation

This system is used to decide whether a message is associated with the specific topic. Here, we divide topics into two types. One type is "Entity", such as "三星S6", "苹果手机" etc. The other type is "Event", such as "香港占中", "中国人疯抢日本马桶盖" etc. Different approaches are used to process the two type topics.

Entity Topic Correlation. The existing of entity name in messages determines the entity topic correlation. The difficulties of this problem is alias or varietas recognition, and word sense disambiguation. For example, topic "三星Galaxy S6" is usually expressed as "三星S6", "Galaxy S6", "samsung s6" and "三桑S6" etc. A message containing any of the expressions is regarded as a correlated message. But the simple approach is embarrassed when the entity is ambiguous. Take the topic "苹果手机" into account, "苹果" in Chinese may refer to a kind of fruit, or refer to apple cellphone. Therefore, we need eliminate this ambiguity.

We use the context of entity to solve the ambiguity. In simple terms, if "苹果" appears with "吃了", then it's more likely referring to fruits. If it is co-occurred with "屏幕", then it's more likely to be cellphone. Formally, support $D = \{d_1, ..., d_k, ..., d_m\}$ is a sentence and d_i denotes the ith word of sentence. And d_k is the specific entity. Sentence will be divided into two parts, $\{d_1, ..., d_{k-1}\}$ and $\{d_{k+1}, ..., d_m\}$. We count words appear in the two parts separately, as well as the co-occurrence of words each of which comes from the two different parts. Firstly, they are counted in a labeled dataset. Then, we statistic them in a bigger data set. Finally, using TF-IDF method, we select features as the topic's context.

We call the entity recognition and correction API of Tencent Wenzhi to solve alias or varietas problem.

Event Topic Correlation. For event type topic, we first extract the core words of events. Then, extend the words to many context words and phrase which has close relationship with event. Finally, text correlation algorithm is used to calculate the event topic correlation.

2.1.2 Topic-Related Sentence Recognition

This strategy is used to recognize sub-sentences that relate to special topic from message and get rid off non-related sub-sentences.

In this evaluation task, two kind of approaches are included. One kind is special characters of Micro-blog (e.g. replying relation), and the other approach relays on NLP technologies, such as subjective relation extracting, dependency parsing, sentence analysis (such as comparative sentence, interrogative sentence etc.) and so on.

2.1.3 Sentence Polarity Classification

In this section, we propose a 4-layer classification system. It gives the polarity of a sentence, positive, negative or neutral. Meanwhile, for each

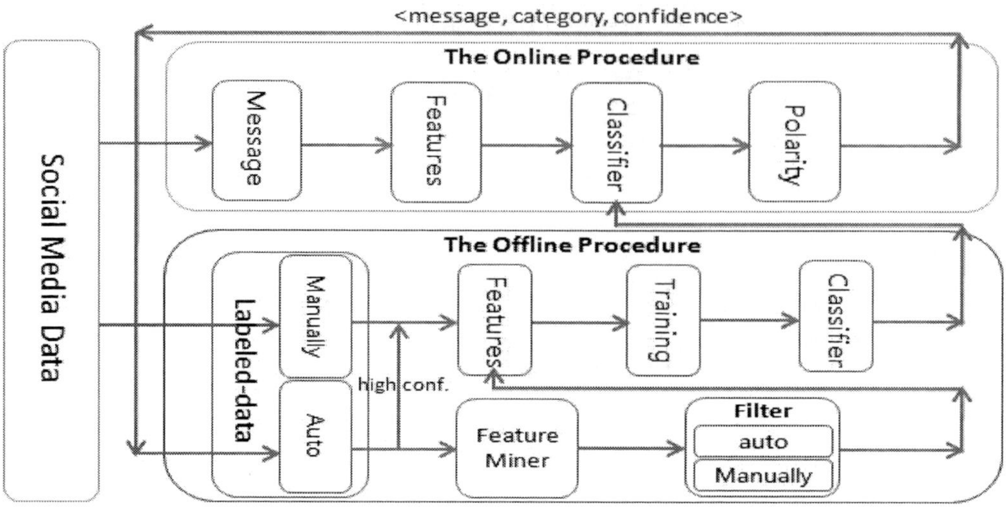

Figure 2: The online methods of MAS.

layer, it is composed of online and offline system. The offline system will continuously mine new features and updating models to promote the online system's performance.

The four layers of classification system are sentiment fingerprint layer, sentence template layer, specific field model layer and general model layer.

Sentiment Fingerprint Layer. It aims to mine the idioms and popular expressions, e.g. “人在做，天在看！”，“我也是醉了”，“人生如戏，全靠演技”. These expressions are usually hard to extract valid features for classification. In our approach, we firstly mine these expressions offline, manually label their polarities and generate a sentiment fingerprint database. When we classify a sentence, it will be looked up in our fingerprint database first.

Sentence Template Layer. It focus on lexical collocation when people express their emotions, e.g. “希望...去死”，“希望...坚强”，“没...那么差”. These lexical collocation jointly reflect people's emotion. If they are separated into single words, the sentiment may totally different. For example, “希望在苦难中挣扎的人们坚强” is positive emotion, but it is easily identified as negative due to the words “苦难” and “挣扎”. And the sentence templates can avoid it.

Special Field Model Layer. It's used to classify messages from specific field, such as movie, music, app and so on. It will use more specific features than general model. For example, in app field, “闪退” and “卡顿” are negative appraisal for app's stability. These words are very strong features for special field model. But they have little sense in general model. Therefore, in specific field, special field model usually get better performance than general model, because it can model more domain knowledge. We will present the details together with general model, as they using similar algorithms and features.

General Model Layer. It will classify messages that previous layers can't handle. It has the highest recall rate and lowest accuracy than the first three layers. It is composed of multiple algorithms and kinds of features. Formally, $g(x) = \sum_i \alpha_i f_i(x)$, where f_i is the ith model and α_i is the weight of f_i. The models are selected from a basic algorithm pool and the pool contains several different approaches, including Bayesian, SVM, Neural networks. And the weight are trained based on the training data.

2.2 The Closed-loop Updating System

In order to continuously promote the performance of MAS, we have set up a closed-loop feature mining and model updating system. And this offline system requires very little intervention. The general method is shown in Figure 2.

As shown in Figure 2, the online system processes messages from different projects and label them with confidence. Then the processed messages are sent to offline system as training data. The offline system divides data into two sets. One set contains the high confidence messages and the other contains lower confidence messages. The high confidence messages are merged to training data directly. The low confidence messages are send to human. Then they are labeled and merged to training data. The offline system process these data to mine new features and update models. It's worth mentioning that new features are firstly directly add to models without manual confirmation. And we verify new model with test data, if both recall rate and accuracy are better, the online model will be replaced by new model. Otherwise, we will manually analyse and update model.

2.3 Some Key Points of MAS

In this section, we will introduce some keypoints of MAS. Firstly, we will present algorithm used in system. Then, features in MAS are introduced. Finally, we show that how features are mined.

2.3.1 Algorithms

Naive Bayesian. Naive Bayesian is the simplest but effective classifier. Here, we use sentiment phrase as features. Because each category can be considered having the same prior probability P(c), the probability of a phrase d in category c can be expressed as likelihood $p(d|c)$. Based on independence assumption, the probability of a sentence D belonging to c can be calculated by $p(c|D) = \prod_{d \in D} p(d|c)$.

SVM. Svm is an effective classifier which can achieve good performance in high-dimensional feature space. The samples are represented as a point in space, and SVM divides these samples by a clear margin as wide as possible. In this work, libsvm[rf] are used to train a classifier. The option of probability estimation in libsvm is turned on, therefore it can produce a probability of class c given a sentence x, i.e. $P(c|x)$. For each sentence, we take N-Gram features and PMI lexicons as features.

Neural Network. Neural network is a nonlinear statistical data model. It can effectively model the relation between input and output. And it's one of the most often used algorithm for classification. In this work, we use the open source tool FANN to train a classifier. The classifier using the same features as SVM classifier.

2.3.2 Features

Word N-gram: We select N-gram (bigram and trigram) features from messages using feature selection algorithm, such as TF-IDF, X^2-Test and so on. When a certain N-gram appears in the message, the corresponding feature is set to 1, otherwise 0. The training data scale is 1.5 million and finally select 500 thousand features.

PMI bigram lexicons: Some lexicons often appear in sentences together. They determine the polarity of sentence jointly and one lexicon may express different emotion, sometimes even opposite. The features are generated base on pointwise mutual information(PMI). Then, we choose the most relevant features using the same approach with **Word N-gram**. We finally choose 50 thousand features for each category.

Sentiment Phrase: It has been shown that words with positive or negative emotions are important to sentiment classification. In this work, we believe that phrases with emotions are more useful, and we simply extend words (e.g. 喜欢) to phrase (e.g. 喜欢的不得了). Based on Tencent massive data, the words and phrases are mined automatically. Up to now, there are more than 70 thousand phrases collected.

3 Experiments

We used the dataset provided by task 2 of SIGHAN-8 to evaluate our model. The dataset contains about twenty thousand weibo comments of 20 topics. According to the official standard set, we tested performance on each topic, and the results are shown in Table 1 and Table 2.

It is shown in Table 1 that the overall performance of MAS on all given topics and the median of performance of all teams. The $F1$ value of positive and negative emotion of MAS are 60.39% and 69.38%, which are significant better than 19.15% and 36.46% of median value.

In Table 2, the best 3 and worst 3 performance of topics are chosen. The best topics, with $F1$ value around 70%, are all Entity-Topics, e.g. “12306验证码”, “陶华碧” and “美图手机”. Meanwhile, the worst topics, whose average $F1$ value is around 20%, are regard as Event-Topics, e.g. “中国政府也门撤侨”, “隆平高科超级稻” and “就业季”. In the worst cases, some Event-Topics are even classified with none message correct. For example, the $F1$ value of negative sentiment of “中国政府也门撤侨” and positive sentiment of “隆平高科超级稻” are both 0. Therefore, the MAS can deal with Entity-Topics better than Event-Topics. The main reason leading to the result is that it is difficult to determine whether a message is related to the Event-Topic then Entity-Topic. And it's an aspect that should be improved further.

	Positive			Negative		
	Precision	**Recall**	**F1**	**Precision**	**Recall**	**F1**
MAS	58.80%	62.07%	60.39%	79.17%	61.75%	69.38%
Median	19.97%	23.37%	19.15%	44.00%	34.56%	36.46%

Table 1: The overall performance of our method and the median of all teams.

Topic	**Positive**			**Negative**		
	Precision	**Recall**	**F1**	**Precision**	**Recall**	**F1**
12306验证码	62.12%	87.23%	72.57%	94.13%	78.34%	85.51%
陶华碧	91.20%	59.07%	71.70%	82.05%	86.49%	84.21%
美图手机	88.24%	54.97%	67.74%	84.21%	57.14%	68.09%
就业季	16.67%	25.00%	20.00%	85.51%	30.10%	44.53%
中国政府也门撤侨	63.64%	50.00%	56.00%	0.00%	0.00%	0.00%
隆平高科超级稻	0.00%	0.00%	0.00%	28.36%	43.18%	34.23%

Table 2: The best 3 and worst 3 performance of MAS on topics of SIGHAN-8.

4 Conclusion

In this paper, we propose a multilayered analysis approach, which is proved to be effect for sentiment analysis. In our method, the online and offline procedures are formed a closed-loop system to continuously improve approach's performance. And this system can be easily used to any classification work. However, the correlation between topic and message is still a limitation, especially between Event-topics and messages. It is one of the most important optimization in our further work.

References

Luciano Barbosa and Junlan Feng. 2010. Robust sentiment detection on twitter from biased and noisy data. In *Proceedings of the 23rd International Conference on Computational Linguistics: Posters*, pages 36–44. Association for Computational Linguistics.

Dmitry Davidov, Oren Tsur, and Ari Rappoport. 2010. Enhanced sentiment learning using twitter hashtags and smileys. In *Proceedings of the 23rd International Conference on Computational Linguistics: Posters*, pages 241–249. Association for Computational Linguistics.

Ahmed Hassan, Vahed Qazvinian, and Dragomir Radev. 2010. What's with the attitude?: identifying sentences with attitude in online discussions. In *Proceedings of the 2010 Conference on Empirical Methods in Natural Language Processing*, pages 1245–1255. Association for Computational Linguistics.

Arun Meena and TV Prabhakar. 2007. *Sentence level sentiment analysis in the presence of conjuncts using linguistic analysis*. Springer.

Qiaozhu Mei, Xu Ling, Matthew Wondra, Hang Su, and ChengXiang Zhai. 2007. Topic sentiment mixture: modeling facets and opinions in weblogs. In *Proceedings of the 16th international conference on World Wide Web*, pages 171–180. ACM.

Richard Socher, Jeffrey Pennington, Eric H Huang, Andrew Y Ng, and Christopher D Manning. 2011. Semi-supervised recursive autoencoders for predicting sentiment distributions. In *Proceedings of the Conference on Empirical Methods in Natural Language Processing*, pages 151–161. Association for Computational Linguistics.

Rule-Based Weibo Messages Sentiment Polarity Classification towards Given Topics

Hongzhao Zhou,
School of Chinese Language and Literature, Communication University of China, Beijing, China
zhzwin2011@163.com

Yonglin Teng, Min Hou,Wei He,
National Broadcast Media Language Resources Monitoring & Research Center, Communication University of China, Beijing, China
{tengyonglin,houmin,hewei}@cuc.edu.cn

Hongtao Zhu, Xiaolin Zhu and Yanfei Mu
School of Chinese Language and Literature, Communication University of China, Beijing, China
{727134880,893136856,610202467}@qq.com

Abstract

Weibo messages sentiment polarity classification towards given topics refers to that the machine automatically classifies whether the weibo message is of positive, negative, or neutral sentiment towards the given topic. The algorithm the sentiment analysis system CUCsas adopts to perform this task includes three steps: (1) whether there is an "exp" (short for "expression having evaluation meaning") in the weibo message; (2) whether there is a semantic orientation relationship between the exp and topic; (3) the sentiment polarity classification of the exp. CUCsas completes step (1) based on the sentiment lexicon and sentiment value assignment rules, completes step (2) based on the topic extraction and sentiment polarity classification rule base, and completes step (3) based on the sentiment computing rules. Taking 20 given topics and a total of 19,469 weibo messages released by SIGHAN-2015 Bake-off as the test data, the overall F value of the rule-based system CUCsas is 0.69 in the unrestricted test.

1 Algorithm Description

The locutionary subjectivity denotes the locutionary agent's self-expression of cognition, feeling or perception in the use of language (John Lyons, 1995). And the evaluation is one type of locutionary subjectivity. An evaluation discourse consists of four basic elements: E(s) = {sub, obj, exp, com}. Herein, "E(s)" represents an evaluation discourse, and "sub", "obj", "exp" and "com" refers to the subject of evaluation, the object of evaluation, an expression having evaluation meaning, and other discourse components respectively (Zhou Hongzhao et al., 2014). The study of this paper is under the condition of knowing obj (= the given topic) in the weibo message, enabling the system automatically recognize whether there is an exp in the same weibo message. If there is not, the system will output result [topic: 0]; if there is, the system will make a further identification that whether there is a semantic orientation relationship between the exp and the given topic. If there is not, the system will outputs result [topic 0]; if there is, the system will further classify the sentiment polarity of the exp. If it is positive, the system will output result [topic 1]; if it is negative, the system will output result [topic -1]; if it is neutral, the system will output result [topic 0]. Apparently, the algorithm is different from some widely used machine learning sentiment polarity classification algorithms, such as Naïve Bayes, Max Entropy, Boosted Trees and Random Forest (Amit Gupte et al., 2014). Figure 1 shows the algorithm of the the system of rule-based weibo messages sentiment polarity classification towards given topics.

Example (1) <weibo>:三星发布 Galaxy S6 和 S6 Edge，下月正式开卖。</weibo> (There is no exp in the weibo message. → Output: 0)

Proceedings of the Eighth SIGHAN Workshop on Chinese Language Processing (SIGHAN-8), pages 149–157,
Beijing, China, July 30-31, 2015.

Example (2) <weibo>:评论员手好丑,评论的也很垃圾,不看了//【视频：三星 GALAXY S6 初体验】</weibo> (There are exps “好丑” and “垃圾” in the weibo message. → But there is no semantic orientation relationship between the exps and the given topic “三星 S6”. → Output: 0)

Example (3) <weibo>:三星 s6 奇丑无比，边框还仿苹果。</weibo> (There is an exp “奇丑无比” in the weibo message. → There is a semantic orientation relationship between the exp and the given topic “三星 S6”. → The sentiment polarity of the exp is negative. → Output: -1)

Example (4) <weibo>:HTC One M9 与三星的 S6 哪个更惊艳？</weibo> (There is an exp “惊艳” in the weibo message. → There is a semantic orientation relationship between the exp and the given topic “三星 S6”. → The sentiment polarity of the exp is neutral in the weibo message context. → Output: 0)

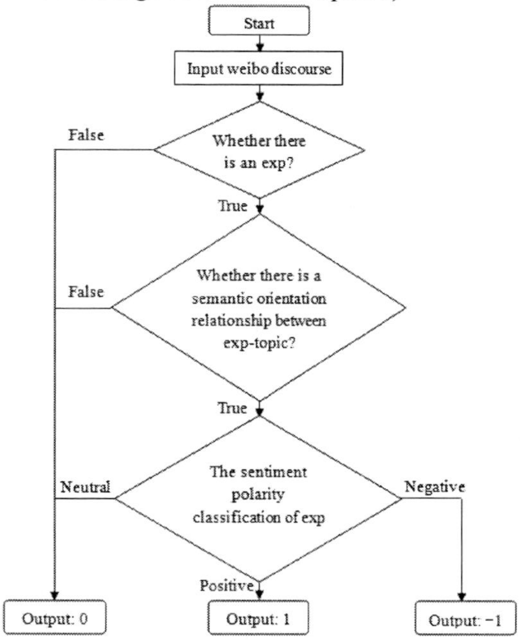

Figure 1. The Algorithm of the Weibo Topic Sentiment Polarity Classification

2 The Automatic Recognition of the Exp in the Weibo Message

From the perspective of linguistics, the exp can be divided into three broad categories, including six specific types.

(1) Category one

<1> Type one: the context-free evaluation word or phrase

Feature: Independent of context, it expresses positive or negative evaluation meaning by itself.

Sentiment marker: po or ne

Examples: 漂亮、败类、狗仗人势

Total in the sentiment lexicon: 26,042

(2) Category two: the context-sensitive evaluation word or phrase

Feature: Whether it expresses evaluation meaning or not depends on the context.

<2> Type two: the commendatory potential word

Feature: When modified by the degree word, it can express positive evaluation meaning.

Semantic marker: pxn

Examples: 规范、人道、man

Total in the semantic lexicon: 51

<3> Type three: the derogatory potential word

Feature: When modified by the degree word, it can express negative evaluation meaning.

Semantic marker: nxn

Examples: 封建、一般、2

Total in the semantic lexicon: 18

<4> Type four: the meaning-shifting noun

Feature: When modified by the affirmative word such as 有 or 具有, it expresses positive evaluation meaning; when modified by the negative word such as 没有 or 毫无, it expresses negative evaluation meaning.

Semantic marker: ypn

Examples: 诚信、效率、素质

Total in the semantic lexicon: 198

<5> Type five: the adjective of weights and measures

Feature: When combined with the product attribute or human character word, the adjective of weights and measures, such as 高、低、大、小, can express evaluation meaning.

Examples: 清晰度+高、油耗+低、辐射+大

Total in the phrase rule base: 153

(3) Category three

<6> Type six: Evaluation syntactical structure or distant collocation.

Examples: 无法和……相比；引发……问题

Total in the phrase rule base: 52

2.1 The Storage and Formal Description of Different Types of Exps

(1) Words and phrases of type one are stored in the sentiment lexicon SentiDic.txt in the form of entries. The lexicon format and entry samples are as follows:

[Word or phrase Part of speech Positive sentiment intensity value Negative sentiment intensity value]

漂亮	a	0.5	0
鄙视	v	0	0.5
败类	n	0	0.5

(2) Words and phrases of type two, three and four are stored in the semantic dictionary UsrDi1.dic first. Then, corresponding sentiment value assignment rules for them are formulated in the phrase rule base PhraseRule.txt.

The lexicon format and entry samples:

[Word or phrase Semantic marker]

规范	pxn
封建	nxn
诚信	ypn

The sentiment value assignment rule samples:

① */mopo + */pxn = #2:0.75

The left part of = is the matching condition, the right part of = is the operation result. The symbol */mopo represents a degree modifier (e.g. 很、非常、十分). The function of this rule: When there is a */mopo in front of */pxn, a 0.75 sentiment value is assigned to */pxn.

② */mone + */pxn = #2:-0.5

The symbol */mone represents a negative modifier (e.g. 没有、毫无、缺乏). The function of this rule: When there is a */mone in front of */pxn, a −0.5 sentiment value is assigned to */pxn.

(3) As to type five and six, corresponding sentiment value assignment rules are formulated in the phrase rule base PhraseRule.txt. The sentiment value assignment rule samples:

③ 质量|性能|像素|分辨率|清晰度|安全系数/% + #[*/!(w|mone)] + 高/a = #3:0.5

The symbol #[*/!(w|mone)] means that the rule can cross arbitrary segmentations here except the punctuation(w) or negative modifier(mone) .

Example (5) <weibo>:丰田车的安全系数的确是低了点。</weibo> (It satisfies the matching condition of rule ③, so a 0.5 sentiment value is assigned to the third item 低/a.)

④ 无法|没法|不能|不可能/v + 和|跟|同|与/p + #[*/!w] + 比|相比/% = #1:−0.5

Example (6) <weibo>:三星 S6 的屏幕分辨率根本无法和 iPhone6 相比。</weibo> (It satisfies the matching condition of rule ④, so a −0.5 sentiment value is assigned to the first item 无法/v.

Based on the sentiment lexicon SentiDic and sentiment value assignment rules in PhraseRule, the system CUCsas realizes the automatic recognition of whether there is an exp in the weibo discourse. Figure 2 shows the recognition procedure:

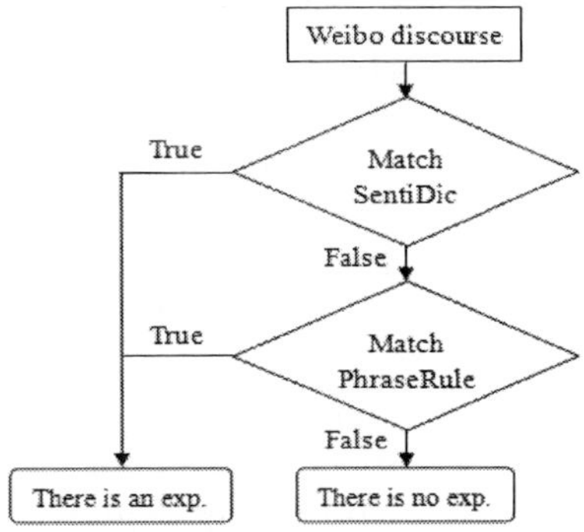

Figure 2. The Procedure of the Exp Recognition

3 The Identification of Whether There Is a Semantic Orientation Relationship between Exp-Topic

The existence of an exp in the weibo message does not imply a semantic orientation relationship between the exp and the topic. Because the evaluation object of the exp has two potential choices: topic or non-topic. The system CUCsas uses the method of combining syntactic structure and semantic features to build a topic extraction and polarity classification rule base. The essence of the rule base is using formal languages to describe the definite semantic direction relationships between exp-topic, which are induced by analyzing the training corpus by us. The topic extraction and polarity classification rule base consists of 10 rule modules with a total of 36 rules (see Table 1).

Module 1	**the exclusive method**
Explanation	When the evaluation object of the exp is non-topic, the system will assign a 0 sentiment value to the topic, so as to avoid the weibo message continuing to match the latter rule modules and cause errors.
Rule sample	QSB + #[*/!w|topic] + */(NP)&!(topic|vl) + #[*/!w|topic] + 是/% + #[*/!w] + */topic + #[*/!w] + */vl&(n|in|ln) + #[*/!w] + */w|y|e|$ = N7:0
Rule sample explanation	(1) QSB: It is a macro definition symbol (including the punctuation, conjunction, evaluation-triggering word, time word or discourse maker) used as the initial

<table>
<tr><td></td><td>item in this rule; (2) NP: It is a macro definition symbol (including the common noun or proper noun such as the name of a person, organization or product) representing a nominal element; (3) */topic: the given weibo topic; (4) */vl: an exp.</td></tr>
<tr><td>Matching example</td><td>Topic:雾霾 <weibo>:原来我一直以为汽车尾气排放是雾霾的罪魁祸首。</weibo> [output：雾霾 0]</td></tr>
<tr><td>Rule number</td><td>1-7</td></tr>
<tr><td>Module 2</td><td>the adversative compound sentence</td></tr>
<tr><td>Explanation</td><td>The content behind the adversative word is usually the semantic focus which the speaker wants to convey. Hence the rule only selects the exp appearing after the adversative word and semantically oriented to the topic as the output result, ignoring the other exps in the weibo message.</td></tr>
<tr><td>Rule sample</td><td>QSB + #[*/%] + */topic + #[!(；|;|。|.)/!NP] + ZZC/% + #[，|,/%] + #[!(,|，|；|;|。|.|？|！|、)/!NP|xjc] + */vl&!hzv + #[!(?|？|吗|呢|么)/!xjc] + JSB = N3:N8</td></tr>
<tr><td>Rule sample explanation</td><td>(1) ZZC: It is a macro definition symbol (including a total of 23 adversative words, such as 但、但是、可是、而是、然而、反而 、却); (2) =N3:N8: It means assigning the sentiment value of the eighth item */vl&!hzv to the third item */topic.</td></tr>
<tr><td>Matching example</td><td>Topic:三星 S6 <weibo>:本以为三星快不行的时候，S6 却震憾登场了。</weibo> [output：S6 1]</td></tr>
<tr><td>Rule number</td><td>8-10</td></tr>
<tr><td>Module 3</td><td>topic-exp co-occurrence in the same clause</td></tr>
<tr><td>Explanation</td><td>When the topic and the exp appear in the same clause, the rule will select the exp nearest to the topic as the one semantically oriented it.(The exception is that the topic is the subject of a sentence expressing a causing or obtaining meaning or with a “preposition + object” adverbial.) In addition, according to the Chinese pragmatic habit that the semantic focus is usually located at the end of the discourse, when exps appear both before and after the topic, i.e. exp1-topic-exp2, the rule will select exp2 only as the output result.</td></tr>
<tr><td>Rule sample</td><td>QSB + #[!(比|把)/!xjc] + */topic + #[*/!w|xjc|vl|nq] + */vl&(!hzv) + #[!(?|？|吗|呢|么)/!xjc] + JSB = N3:N5</td></tr>
<tr><td>Rule sample explanation</td><td>*/vl&(!hzv): The exp is arbitrary except for the backward-orientated sentiment verb(hzv) such as 喜爱、佩服 or 鄙视, because the evaluation object of the hzv is usually the component after it, not the topic before it.</td></tr>
<tr><td>Matching example</td><td>Topic:雾霾 <weibo>:我赞成中国雾霾问题非常严重。</weibo> [output：雾霾 -1]</td></tr>
<tr><td>Rule number</td><td>11-17</td></tr>
<tr><td>Module 4</td><td>the sentence expressing a causing or obtaining meaning</td></tr>
<tr><td>Explanation</td><td>When the topic is the subject of a sentence expressing a causing or obtaining meaning, the rule will select the last exp in the clause introduced by a word expressing a causing or obtaining meaning as the output result.</td></tr>
<tr><td>Rule sample</td><td>QSB + #[*/!vl|xjc] + */topic + #[!。/!NP|xjc] + TSC/% + #[*/!w|topic|xjc] + */vl + #[!(?|？|吗|呢|么)/!xjc] + JSB = N3:N7</td></tr>
<tr><td>Rule sample explanation</td><td>TSC: It is a macro definition symbol (including a total of 31 words expressing a causing or obtaining meaning, such as 让、使得、引起、导致、成为 or 得到).</td></tr>
<tr><td>Matching example</td><td>Topic:中国人疯抢日本马桶 <weibo>:其中最为热销的产品竟然是智能马桶盖，卖到几近断货，真是让人大跌眼镜。</weibo> [output：马桶盖 -1]</td></tr>
<tr><td>Rule number</td><td>18</td></tr>
<tr><td>Module 5</td><td>the sentence with a “preposition + object” adverbial</td></tr>
<tr><td>Explanation</td><td>When the topic is the subject of a sentence with a “preposition + object” adverbial, the rule will select the exp in the central components modified by the adverbial as the output result.</td></tr>
</table>

<table>
<tr><td>Rule sample</td><td>QSB + #[*/!vl|xjc] + */topic + #[!。/!NP|xjc] + 对|对于|为|将|给/p + #[!(；|;|。|.|？|！|：)/!topic|xjc] + */vl&!(hzv|xlv) + #[!(?|？|吗|呢|么)/!xjc] + JSB = N3:N7</td></tr>
<tr><td>Rule sample explanation</td><td>*/vl&!(hzv|xlv): The exp is arbitrary except for the backward-orientated sentiment verb(hzv) or psychological sentiment verb(xlv), because the evaluation object of the hzv or xlv is usually the object of the preposition, not the topic as the subject of the sentence.</td></tr>
<tr><td>Matching example</td><td>Topic:央行降息 <weibo>:羊年第一个周末央行再度出手降息，对券商、保险、地产等绝大多数品种构成较大利好。</weibo> [output：降息 1]</td></tr>
<tr><td>Rule number</td><td>19</td></tr>
<tr><td>Module 6</td><td>the comparative sentence</td></tr>
<tr><td>Explanation</td><td>When the topic serves as the comparative subject in the comparative sentence, its sentiment vale = the sentiment value of the exp serving as the comparative result; when the topic serves as the comparative datum in the comparative sentence, its sentiment vale = the sentiment value of the exp serving as the comparative result× (-1) (Zhou Hongzhao et al., 2014).</td></tr>
<tr><td>Rule sample</td><td>QSB + #[*/!vl|xjc] + */topic + #[!(。|：|?|？)/!vl|xjc] + 比|相比|比起|对比/p + #[!(。|！|?|？|；)/!topic|xjc] + */vl + #[!(?|？|吗|呢|么)/!xjc|vl] + JSB = N3:N7</td></tr>
<tr><td>Rule sample explanation</td><td>The */topic (N3) is located before the comparative-marker word 比|相比|比起|对比/p(N5) .So it serves as the comparative subject and its sentiment vale = the sentiment value of the exp */vl(N7) serving as the comparative result.</td></tr>
<tr><td>Matching example</td><td>Topic:三星 S6 <weibo>:个人感觉 S6 前面板一如既往三星风格，背面更是比 iPhone6 还难看。</weibo> [output：S6 -1]</td></tr>
<tr><td>Rule number</td><td>20−24</td></tr>
<tr><td>Module 7</td><td>the causation compound sentence</td></tr>
<tr><td>Explanation</td><td>In the causation compound sentence, the exp may appear in the reason clause, while its evaluation object appears in the result clause.</td></tr>
<tr><td>Rule sample</td><td>*/topic + #[!(。|？|！|；|;|：)/!xjc] + 因为/% + #[*/!w] + */vl = N1:N5</td></tr>
<tr><td>Rule sample explanation</td><td>In module 4, the topic is the reason, while the exp is the result. Here, the topic is the result, while the exp is the reason. The two rule modules complement each other.</td></tr>
<tr><td>Matching example</td><td>Topic:中国人疯抢日本马桶 <weibo>:终于明白为什么中国人都要去日本买马桶盖了，因为好用到飙泪！</weibo> [output：马桶盖 1]</td></tr>
<tr><td>Rule number</td><td>25</td></tr>
<tr><td>Module 8</td><td>The topic and the exp are distributed in different clauses or sentences. Type one: topic + exp</td></tr>
<tr><td>Explanation</td><td>The topic appears first, and then the exp appears in the clause or sentence adjacent or nonadjacent to the clause or sentence the topic in. In this case, only the weibo message satisfies certain syntactic and semantic constraints, will the rule judge that the evaluation object of the exp is the topic.</td></tr>
<tr><td>Rule sample</td><td>QSB + #[*/!vl|xjc] + */topic + #[!。/!vl|xjc] + */w + #[!。/!xjc|NP] + */vl + #1:3[!(吗|呢|么)/u|y|e] + JSB = N3:N7</td></tr>
<tr><td>Rule sample explanation</td><td>Constraints of the rule sample: (1) There is no exp appearing together with the topic in the clause; (2) There is no NP appearing before the exp in the clause; (3) The word class after the exp is only auxiliary, modal or interjection, and three interrogative words 吗、呢 and 么 are forbidden.</td></tr>
<tr><td>Matching example</td><td>Topic:油价 <weibo>:涨油价的时候也不提消费税了，流氓啊</weibo> [output：油价 -1]</td></tr>
<tr><td>Rule number</td><td>26-32</td></tr>
<tr><td>Module 9</td><td>The topic and the exp are distributed in different clauses or sentences. Type two: exp + topic</td></tr>
</table>

<table>
<tr><td>Explanation</td><td>The exp appears first, and then the topic appears in the clause or sentence adjacent or nonadjacent to the clause or sentence the exp in. In this situation, only the weibo message satisfies certain syntactic and semantic constraints, will the rule judge that the evaluation object of the exp is the topic.</td></tr>
<tr><td>Rule sample</td><td>*/^ + #[*/!nq] + */na + #[*/!w] + */vl + #[*/!nq] + */topic&nq = N7:N5</td></tr>
<tr><td>Rule sample explanation</td><td>Constraints of the rule sample: (1) */^: The initial item of the rule is the weibo start marker; (2) #[*/!nq]: The word with a semantic marker of product name is forbidden; (3) */na: A word with the semantic marker of product attribute must appear; (4) */topic&nq: The topic word must is also a product name.</td></tr>
<tr><td>Matching example</td><td>Topic:三星 S6 <weibo>:电池是唯一的小遗憾//【沉默后的爆发 三星 Galaxy S6 竞争力分析】 http://t.cn/RwQ6plU（分享自 @鲜果）</weibo> [output：S6 -1]</td></tr>
<tr><td>Rule number</td><td>33-35</td></tr>
<tr><td>Module 10</td><td>anaphora resolution</td></tr>
<tr><td>Explanation</td><td>When the referent of a pronoun is the topic, the rule will assign the sentiment value of the exp semantically orientated to the pronoun to the topic.</td></tr>
<tr><td>Rule sample</td><td>*/topic + #[*/!xjc|vl|NP] + 你|你们|这|这些|这样|这么|此举/r + #[*/m|q] + #[*/!w|xjc|vl] + */vl + #[!(?|？|吗|呢|么)/!nr|xjc] + */$ = N1:N6</td></tr>
<tr><td>Rule sample explanation</td><td>(1) #[*/m|q]: a numeral or quantifier can appear or not appear here; (2) */$: the end marker of the weibo message.</td></tr>
<tr><td>Matching example</td><td>Topic:油价 <weibo>:在未来一两年我们会看到国际油价的触底。这种状况会很好的帮助中国、日本开辟出新的机遇。</weibo> [output：油价 1]</td></tr>
<tr><td>Rule number</td><td>36</td></tr>
<tr><td colspan="2">Note:
(1) The 36 rules of the 10 rule modules are sequentially arranged, forming the topic extraction and sentiment polarity classification rule base.
(2) Matching procedure: The weibo message matches the rule base starting from the first rule. If the matching succeeds, the system will output a corresponding matching result; if fails, the weibo message will skip to the second rule to continue matching. If this matching succeeds, the system will output a corresponding matching result; or else the weibo message will skip to the next rule to continue matching……If the matching still fails at the end of the rule base (i.e. rule 36), then the system will make a judgment that there is no semantic orientation relationship between the exp and the topic in this weibo message and output a corresponding result: topic 0. The next weibo message matches the rule base in the same way……until the last weibo message in the experimental data.</td></tr>
</table>

Table 1. Topic Extraction and Sentiment Polarity Classification Rule Base

Based on the topic extraction and polarity classification rule base, the system CUCsas realizes the automatic identification of whether there is a semantic orientation relationship between the exp and the topic in the weibo message. If the weibo message matches the rule base unsuccessfully, the system will output topic 0; if successfully, the system will assign the value of the corresponding exp to the topic. If the value > 0, the system will output: topic 1; if the value < 0, the system will output: topic -1; if the value = 0, the system will output: topic 0. Figure 3 shows the general procedure:

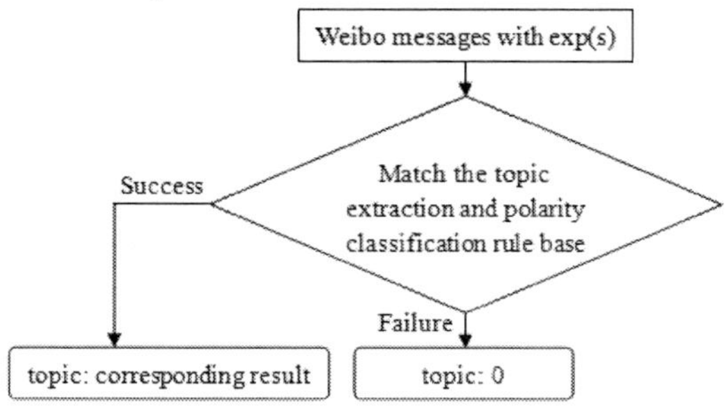

Figure 3. The Procedure of Topic Extraction and Sentiment Polarity Classification

4 The Sentiment Polarity Classification of the Exp

The term "corresponding result" in Figure 3 contains double meanings: ⅰ The "corresponding" means that there is a semantic orientation relationship between the exp and the topic. ii The "result" refers to the sentiment value and polarity of the exp in the weibo message context, not necessarily equals the value and polarity in the sentiment lexicon. i is guaranteed by 36 rules of 10 modules. ii is obtained by sentiment computing rules (see Table 2) in the PhraseRule.txt.

Type 1	**Contrary**
Description	The sentiment polarity of the exp in the weibo message context is contrary to its sentiment polarity in the sentiment lexicon.
Features	(1) The exp is modified by the word with a negative semantic marker "mone"; (2) The exp appears in a negative sentence pattern characterized by words such as 难道 or 怎么可能; (3) The exp appears in the special collocation characterized by specific words. For instance, the sentiment polarity of 美化 is positive in the sentiment lexicon, but when it collocates with 战争、侵略 or 历史, its sentiment polarity will turn negative.
Rule sample	*/mone + */po|ne = N2*N1
Matching example	(三星 S6) (看样子) (一点) (都) ([不]好用:-1) (。)
Rules total	51
Type 2	**Dissolution**
Description	The evaluation meaning of the exp is dissolved in the weibo message context.
Features	(1) The exp appears in the sentence introduced by the word with an evaluation dissolving marker "xjc" such as 如果、假如、祝愿、但愿、能否、是否—30 in all; (2) The exp appears in an evaluation dissolving sentence pattern characterized by the collocation of specific words or word classes, such as 是…还是…, exp + vv.
Rule sample	*/xjc + #[*/!w] + */po|ne = #3:0
Matching example	(三星 S6) (能否) (力挽狂澜:0) (？)
Rules total	12
Type 3	**Consistency**
Description	The polarity of the exp in the weibo message context is consistent with the sentiment lexicon. But the sentiment intensity can be unchanged, enhanced or weakened.
Features	(1) Features mentioned in type 1 and type 2 must not appear; (2) Features maintaining, enhancing or weakening the sentiment intensity of the exp, such as semantic markers or specific words can appear.
Rule sample	*/mopo + */po|ne = N2*(1+N1)
Matching example	(三星 S6) (，) (外观) (确实) ([很]漂亮:0.875) (。)
Rules total	10

Table 2. Three Types of the Exp and Corresponding Sentiment Computing Rules

Based on the sentiment computing rules stored in the PhraseRule, the system realizes the calculation of the sentiment value of the exp in the weibo message context.

5 Experimental Results and Analysis

Taking 20 given topics and a total of 19,469 weibo messages released by SIGHAN-2015 Bake-off as the test data, the experimental results of the sentiment analysis system CUCsas are as follows:

SIGHAN-2015 Bake-off (unrestricted test)	Precision	0.6937182
	Recall	0.6937182
	F	0.6937182
	Precision+	0.1839539
	Recall+	0.36024305
	F+	0.24354461
	Precision-	0.5010653
	Recall-	0.3877439
	F-	0.4371805

Table 3. The SIGHAN-2015 Bake-off (Unrestricted Test) Evaluation Result of CUCsas

Only using the sentiment lexicon resource, the experimental results are as follows:

SIGHAN-	Precision	0.46001335

2015 Bake-off (unrestricted test)	Recall	0.46001335
	F	0.46001335
	Precision+	0.12713068
	Recall+	0.62152778
	F+	0.2110849
	Precision-	0.34455307
	Recall-	0.6779335
	F-	0.45689415

Table 4. Only Using the Sentiment Lexicon

Using the sentiment lexicon together with the phrase rule base resource, the experimental results are as follows:

SIGHAN-2015 Bake-off (unrestricted test)	Precision	0.48019929
	Recall	0.48019929
	F	0.48019929
	Precision+	0.13504006
	Recall+	0.59982639
	F+	0.22044983
	Precision-	0.34286523
	Recall-	0.66556746
	F-	0.45258339

Table 5. Using the Sentiment Lexicon Together with the Phrase Rule Base

Comparing Table 4 with Table 5, we can see the introduction of the phrase rule base improved the system overall performance, but only to a small extent. Comparing Table 5 with Table 3, we can see the introduction of the topic extraction and polarity classification rule base further improved the system overall performance to a large extent.

At present, the overall F value of the system is about 0.69. Evaluation results in Table 3 suggest that the performance of the system is good in dealing with neutral sentiment weibo messages, but poor in dealing with positive sentiment weibo messages (F+≈0.24) and negative sentiment weibo messages (F-≈0.44).

Reasons and solving methods for poor Recall+ and Recall- : (1) The scale of the topic extraction and polarity classification rule base built according to the training data is small (only 36 rules). Thus, the language phenomena having not appeared in the training data can't be covered. For instance, the module 10 —anaphora resolution neglects the case that the pronoun appears ahead of the topic. In the next stage, new rules will be added to the rule base to expand its coverage. (2) The sentiment lexicon and the sentiment phrase rule base are not incomplete so that many exps in the test data can't be recognized. In the next stage, the system will improve the automatic recognition of unlisted exps.

Reasons and solving methods for poor Precision+ and Precision-: (1) Some rules in the topic extraction and polarity classification rule base do not appropriately describe the semantically orientated relationship between topic-exp, which leads to the wrong extraction of exps. In the next stage, some rules will be revised based on the errors analysis. (2) Some "exps" in the sentiment lexicon actually do not have evaluation meaning. For example, the word 激烈 is not a sentiment word. However, it is listed in the sentiment lexicon as a negative word. Therefore, the sentiment polarity output result of Topic :水货客 in <weibo>:反水货客行动越趋激烈。</weibo> is wrong -1. In the next stage, the sentiment lexicon will be checked and non-sentiment words will be removed.

6 Conclusion

In this paper, firstly, we proposed the algorithm of rule-based weibo messages sentiment polarity classification towards given topics. Then, we adopted the rule methods to implement the requirements of the algorithm procedures. Based on the sentiment lexicon SentiDic and sentiment value assignment rules in PhraseRule, the sentiment analysis system CUCsas realized the automatic recognition of the exp in weibo messages. Based on the topic extraction and polarity classification rule base, the system realized the automatic identification of whether there is a semantic orientation relationship between the exp and the topic. And based on the sentiment computing rules in PhraseRule, the system realized the sentiment value calculation and polarity classification of the exp in specific weibo message context. At present, the overall F value of the ruled-based sentiment analysis system CUCsas is about 0.69. In the future, the lexicon and rule base will be revised based on the errors analysis to improve the performance of the system.

Reference

Amit Gupte, Sourabh Joshi, Pratik Gadgul, Akshay Kadam. 2014. Comparative Study of Classification Algorithms used in Sentiment Analysis. *International Journal of Computer Science and Information Technologies (IJCSIT)*, Vol. 5 (5):6261-6264.

John Lyons. 1995. *Linguistic Semantics: An Introduction*. Cambridge University Press, Cambridge. UK.

ZHOU Hongzhao, HOU Mingwu, YAN Pengli, ZHANG Yeqing, HOU Min and TENG Yonglin. 2014. Function of Semantic Features in Opinion Target Extraction and Its Polarity Identification. *Acta Scientiarum Naturalium Universitatis Pekinensis*, 50(1):93-99.

ZHOU Hongzhao, HOU Mingwu, HOU Min and TENG Yonglin. 2014. Chinese Comparative Sentences Identification and Comparative Elements Extraction Based on Semantic Classification. *Journal of Chinese Information Processing*, 28(3):136-141.

Topic-Based Chinese Message Polarity Classification System at SIGHAN8-Task2

Chun Liao, Chong Feng, Sen Yang, Heyan Huang
School of Computer Science
and Technology, Beijing
Institute of Technology
{cliao, fengchong, syang, hhy63}@bit.edu.cn

Abstract

This paper describes the topic-based Chinese message polarity classification system submitted by LCYS_TEAM at SIGHAN8-Task2. The system mainly includes two parts: 1) a graph-based ranking model integrating local and global information is adopted to represent the classification ability of words towards different topics. In construction of graph model, a new weighting approach and a PMI-based random jumping probability selection method is proposed. 2) For sentimental features, word embedding is employed for acquiring expanded topical words and syntactic dependency is adopted for getting topic-related sentimental words. Experiment results demonstrate the effectiveness of our system.

1 Introduction

Sentiment analysis, which is to identify or determine the implied emotional orientation, attitude and opinion when people express something, is becoming more and more important for network monitoring with its application on microblog. In the traditional sentiment analysis, unsupervised methods were adopted in Ku(2005), Shen(2009), Vasileios(2000) and Turney(2002), and the limitation of such approaches based on semantic dictionary mainly is unable to solve the problem of Out-of-Vocabulary words. Supervised methods were employed with model of machine learning, such as Naive Bayes, Max Entropy, Support Vector Machine in Pang(2002), Dasgupta(2009), and Li(2011).

Hashtags, in the form of "＃topic＃", are widely used as topics in Chinese microblogs. For the topic-related work, Wang(2011) and Jakob(2010) made research on hashtag-level sentiment classification in twitter. In the traditional sentiment analysis, the object people express sentiment on is not taken into consideration. And these methods are mostly topic-ignored and cannot perform the accurate sentiment analysis in many topic-related messages. We summarize such kind of difficult cases into two categories.

1) Microblogs with multiple candidate topics

For example, "#三星 galaxy s6##华为P8##mate8#"三星 galaxy s6 真没什么亮点，华为 P8 就可以秒它了，更不用说 mate8[拜拜]". This sentence conveys negative sentiment towards topic of "三星 galaxy s6", but positive sentiment towards topic of "华为 P8" and "mate8".

2) Microblogs with topic specific sentimental words

For example, "#股票#前天刚入手一支股票，一直在升，股价越来越高" and "#三星#三星手机电量明显不够用，耗能高". The word "高" carrys positive sentiment orientation in the first sentence towards topic "股票" and negative sentiment orientation in the latter towards topic "三星".

Considering the importance of topical information in microblogs, this paper studied topic-based Chinese message polarity classification. Given a message from Chinese Weibo Platform (Such as Sina, Tencent, NetEase etc.) and a topic, classify whether the message is of positive, negative, or neutral sentiment towards the given topic. For messages conveying both a positive and negative sentiment towards the topic, whichever is the stronger sentiment should be chosen.

Proceedings of the Eighth SIGHAN Workshop on Chinese Language Processing (SIGHAN-8), pages 158–163,
Beijing, China, July 30-31, 2015. ©2015 Association for Computational Linguistics and Asian Federation of Natural Language Processing

The rest of this paper is organized as follows. In Section 2, we briefly present the topic-based Chinese message polarity classification system from two aspects of graph-based ranking feature and topic-related sentimental feature. Evaluation results are presented in Section 3. Finally, the last section summarizes this paper and describes our future work.

2 System Architecture

In topic-based Chinese message polarity classification, our system is mainly composed by two parts: topic-related keyword feature selection and topic-related sentimental feature selection. In detail, topic-related keyword feature is acquired by a novel graph-based ranking algorithm of LT-IGT, and topic-related sentimental feature is obtained by topical words expansion based on word embedding and syntactic parsing according to the expanded topical words. The architecture of our system is illustrated in Figure 1.

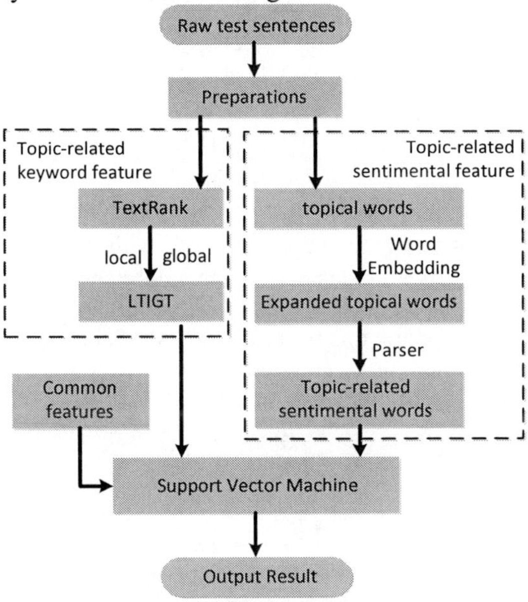

Figure 1. System architecture

2.1 Preparations

To evaluate the performance of method proposed in this paper for topic-based Chinese microblog polarity classification, we carry out experiments on dataset offered by SIGHAN8-Task 2 called Topic-Based Chinese Message Polarity Classification. This dataset is obtained from Chinese Weibo Platform, such as Sina, Tencent, NetEase etc. It contains 5*1000 manually annotated microblogs which cover 5 topics, such as "三星 S6", "央行降息", etc. In experiments, we randomly select 800 microblogs of each topic for training and 200 for testing, and finally get training set of 4000 microblogs and testing set of 1000 microblogs to perform classification.

Considering the non-standard feature of microblog, the corpus is firstly normalized by following three rules.

Rule 1: Turn over the microblog with "//" to ensure the forwarding relationship and guarantee the latter sentence is analyzed based on the front sentence.

Rule 2: Delete structures like "@+username", "http://xxx" to reduce noises caused by username and website.

Rule 3: Replace the consecutive punctuations with the first one to normalize the structure of expression.

Through filtration by these rules, this paper conducts experiments on the preprocessed dataset and accesses them with traditional Precision(P), Recall(R) and F-measure(F) under Micro-average and Macro-average.

2.2 Selection of topic-related keyword feature

Inspired by TF-IDF(Salton et al., 1975,1983), words own higher local importance and lower global importance are more significant for classification. But for topic-based Chinese message polarity classification, it is obviously insufficient to extract keywords based on frequency information merely. For example, in the sentence of "GALAXY S6一改三星此前"万年大塑料"的形象，采用了前后玻璃面板和金属框组合的机身设计，为了支撑更纤薄的机身，不惜牺牲microSD卡槽和电池更换，即使如此，仍然无法与拥有完美外观的iphone媲美。", the conventional TF-IDF method tends to extract "三星、GALAXY S6、iphone、机身、卡槽、电池、外观" as keywords, but in this topic-based task, topic-related words such as "三星、GALAXY S6、卡槽、电池、外观" are expected to be selected as the keywords feature for the topic "三星". To better solve the problem of microblogs with multiple candidate topics introduced in section 1, this paper proposes a novel LT-IGT(illustrated in Figure 2) algorithm which integrates topic, position and co-occurrence information, its function is designed as follows.

$$LTIGT = LT \times IGT = TR_{lt}(v_i) \times \frac{1}{TR_{gt}(v_i)} \quad (1)$$

where $TR_{lt}(v_i)$ and $TR_{gt}(v_i)$ represent for ranking score of vertex v_i under local and global TextRank.

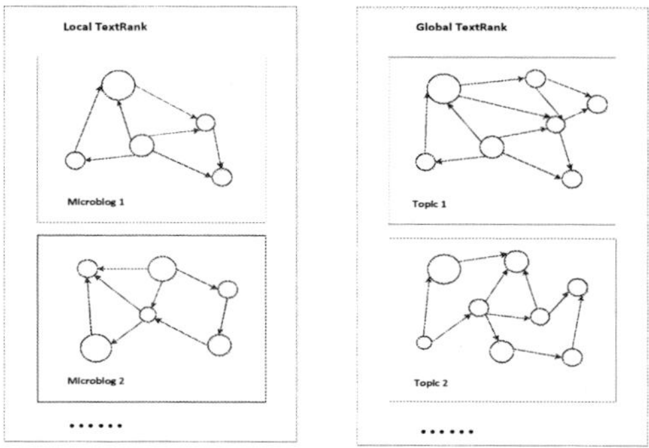

Figure 2. Graph Model of LT-IGT

The idea of TextRank(Mihalce,2004) derives from PageRank, which is achieved by dividing the text into several units to build graph model and exploiting voting mechanism for ranking. This method can model the relationship between the current word and contextual information, and the contextual related words can be recommended reciprocally. Considering the importance of a word is related to both itself and its relevant words, TextRank overcomes the independence of words in traditional "bag-of-words" model and characterizes the importance of a word more accurately.

- CST: A novel weighting method of graph-based ranking model

For each vertex in the graph, its importance ranking score benefits from adjacent nodes, and on the other hand, its own ranking score can also be transferred to the neighboring vertexes. According to the above assumptions, the indicator of vertex importance can be divided into following three parts: Coverage Importance, Semantic Similarity Importance and Topic-Related Importance. For two vertexes v_i and v_j, the influence of v_i to v_j can be transferred by the directed edge $e = < v_i, v_j >$. In this paper, we assign w_{ij} as the weight between v_i and v_j, α, β, γ as the proportions of these three indicators. Consequently, the weight value between two vertexes can be defined as follows:

$$w_{ij} = \alpha w_{cov}(v_i, v_j) + \beta w_{ss}(v_i, v_j) + \gamma w_{tr}(v_i, v_j) \qquad (2)$$

Where α+β+γ=1.

a) $w_{cov}(v_i, v_j)$ represents for coverage importance of v_i, it can be calculated by

$$w_{cov}(v_i, v_j) = \frac{1}{|\mathrm{Out}(v_i)|} \qquad (3)$$

Where $|\mathrm{Out}(v_i)|$ is the out-degree of vertex v_i. This formula expresses the coverage importance of v_i can be transmitted to its neighboring vertexes uniformly.

b) $w_{ss}(v_i, v_j)$ is regarded as semantic similarity importance from v_i to v_j. It can be expressed as

$$w_{ss}(v_i, v_j) = \frac{\mathrm{PMI}(v_i, v_j)}{\sum_{v_t \in \mathrm{Out}(v_i)} \mathrm{PMI}(v_i, v_t)} \qquad (4)$$

$$\mathrm{PMI}(v_i, v_j) = \log\left(\frac{p(v_i \,\&\, v_j)}{p(v_i)p(v_j)}\right) \qquad (5)$$

Where $\mathrm{PMI}(v_i, v_j)$ is the point mutual information between v_i and v_j. The larger the PMI value is, the higher the semantic similarity is. $p(v_i \,\&\, v_j)$ is the co-occurrence probability of v_i and v_j in sentences. $\mathrm{p}(v_i)$ and $\mathrm{p}(v_j)$ respectively represent for the independent occurrence probability of v_i and v_j. This function suggests that words with higher mutual information can substantially influence each other mutually.

c) $w_{tr}(v_i, v_j)$ shows the topic-related importance value of v_i. It can be computed by

$$w_{tr}(v_i, v_j) = \frac{\mathrm{P}(v_j)}{\sum_{v_t \in \mathrm{Out}(v_i)} P(v_t)} \qquad (6)$$

Where $\mathrm{P}(v_j)$ is the position importance score of v_j which can be designed with different strategies. Considering the importance of topical words in measuring position importance score, this paper assigns words occurring in topic or existing dependency with topical words a higher score than others. If we assign "vertex v occurring in topic or existing dependency with topical words" as X, the function is

$$\mathrm{P(v)} = \begin{cases} \lambda, & \mathrm{v} \in \mathrm{X} \\ 1, & others \end{cases} \qquad (7)$$

Where λ >1. We set λ=1.5 through investigation and evaluation in experiments.

- Selection of Random Jumping Probability

In the traditional graph model of TextRank, each vertex jumps to others randomly with an equal probability, which is shown in the function of $p_{rj}(w_i) = \frac{1}{|V|}$. But this method will bring about the problem of local optimization for its negligence of topical information. Considering the importance of topical words in charactering the main idea of an article, we assign topic-related words with a higher random jumping probability to get a larger score in ranking of graph model. Consequently, this paper adopts

PMI value between current word and topical word as the random jumping probability, and the function is as follows.

$$p_{rj}(w_i) = \frac{PMI(v_i,\text{topic})}{\sum_{j=1}^{|V|} PMI(v_j,topic)} \quad (8)$$

where $PMI(v_i, \text{topic})$ denotes the point mutual information value between current word v_i and topical word topic, $|V|$ is the number of vertexes in graph model. Moreover, the calculation of co-occurrence probability for PMI is performed in unit of sentence in global TextRank, but in unit of window in local TextRank. The size of the window is assigned as 5 through experiments.

Consequently, in the construction of graph model $G = (V, E)$, vertexes, directions and weights of the links are three important points which should be considered. In this graph model, we denote the vertexes set as $V = \{v_1, v_2, v_3 \dots \dots v_n\}$ which is combined of nouns and adjectives. Furthermore, the direction of a link between two vertexes is determined by a method of sliding window which adds links from the first word pointing to other words within the window. And the size of the sliding window is assigned as 10 through experiments. And the weight of a link is set by method of CST proposed in this paper. The basic formula of TextRank is performed for calculating the final ranking scores of each vertex. Finally, we can acquire two ranking scores for a vertex under global and local TextRank separately.

2.3 Selection of topic-related sentimental feature

In recent years, the method of word embedding based on neural network shows its outperformance in semantic expression and has attracted widespread attention paid to it(Tomas, 2013). The task of word embedding is to represent each word in corpus with a real vector, and establishing a mapping between discrete vocabulary and the feature vectors in real fields. Considering the semantic similarity between two words can be characterized by cosine value of the vectors, we propose a novel approach of topic-related sentimental word embedding which integrates syntax with semantics in this paper. This method expands topical words with word embedding first, and then performs parsing in center of these topical words to extract topical-related sentiment words based on the dependencies with them. Finally we cluster the topical-related sentiment words using K-means clustering algorithm and select the number of words belonging to a category in a microblog as the dimension values to finish the feature selection of this part.

- Expansion of Topical-words

For example, “三星S6的外观不错，但电池不行。”. Its dependency analysis result is illustrated in Figure 3 as follows.

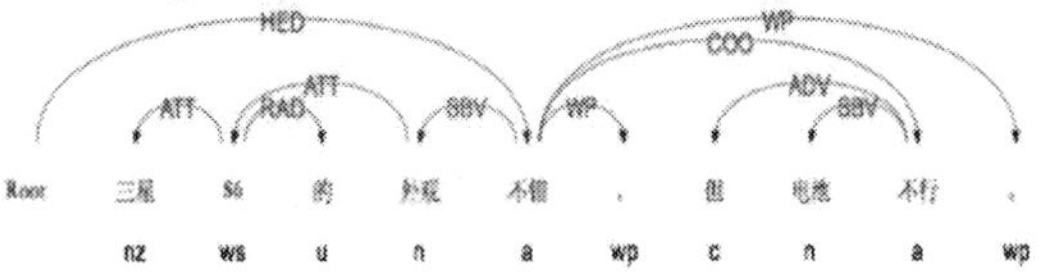

Figure 3. Example of dependency analysis result

As we can see in Figure 3, the sentimental words “不错”, “不行” do not exist dependencies with topical words “三星”, “S6”, but exist dependencies with words “外观”, “电池” of SBV(外观,不错), SBV(电池,不行). And these relationships also occupy a necessary place in topic-based sentiment analysis of Chinese microblog. So we should obtain “外观”, “电池” as the expanded topical words from topical words “三星”, “S6”.

There are many approaches to expand the topical words such as PMI(Turney, 2003), and Synonyms-based method(Wang, 2009). For its better consideration of contextual information, we adopt word embedding to calculate the semantic similarity with topical words to expand the topical words. After getting word vectors, we calculate the cosine similarity between topical words and nouns under each topic, and select the highest N words as the expansion of topical words to fulfill the expansion of topical words.

- Extraction of topic-related sentimental words

As we all know, people usually express emotions towards a specific topic or object, and the emotional words often exist dependency relationship with topics or objects in syntactic analysis. Consequently, we mainly take following three dependency relations into consideration:

1) VOB

“VOB” represents for the relation between verbs and objects. Sentimental words are verbs and topical words are the objects of verbs. For example, “我喜欢三星。”. It exits “VOB” relation between “喜欢” and “三星”.

2) SBV

“VOB” represents for the relation between subjects and predicates. Sentimental words are predicates and topical words are the subjects of sentimental words. For example, "三星很漂亮。". It exits "SBV" relation between "三星" and "漂亮".

3) ATT

"ATT" represents for the relation of attributes. Sentimental words are attributes and topical words are the modified center of sentimental words. For example, "无与伦比的三星设计！". It exits "ATT" relation between "无与伦比" and "三星".

Therefore, we design an algorithm of topical-related sentimental words extraction towards dependency analysis result of microblogs. The process of this algorithm is described as below.

Algorithm1: Topical-related Sentimental Words Extraction

Input: Dependency analysis result(DP), Expanded Topical Words(ETW)
Output: Topical-related Sentimental Words (TSW)

```
for word in DP:
    if word in ETW and word.relate in 'SBV', 'VOB', 'ATT':
        TSW+= word.parent;
    if word.parent in ETW and word.relate in 'SBV', 'VOB', 'ATT':
        TSW+= word;
return TSW
```

3 Experiments

In SIGHAN8-Task2, we select emoticons, basic sentiment lexicon, dependency relation of "SBV", "VOB", "ATT" as common features(C), LT-IGT Ranking score as topic-related keyword feature(TK) and dependency parsing of topical words with word embedding for expansion as topic-related sentimental feature(TS).

Table 1 shows the evaluation results of our system with different groups of features.

By attempting different groups of feature for topic-related Chinese microblog sentiment classification, the performance of sentiment classification is notably improved after adding topic-related keyword feature(TK) and topic-related sentimental feature(TS). This is mainly because these two features explore both the syntactic and semantic information for classification compared with the other features. Consequently, this experiment not only demonstrates the effectiveness of LT-IGT algorithm, but also reveals the importance of topical word expansion to topic-related Chinese microblog sentiment classification.

Method	Precision	Recall	F-measure
C	0.6113	0.5572	0.5830
C+TK	0.6458	0.5982	0.6211
C+TK+TS	0.6863	0.6081	0.6448

Table 1: results of topic-based Chinese message polarity classification using SVM with different groups of features

4 Conclusion

In this paper we proposed a novel method for topic-based Chinese microblog sentiment classification, and put forward two novel feature generation approaches of LT-IGT and topic-related sentimental word embedding, with other kinds of features together, for addition to SVM classifier to perform the final polarity determination. The experimental results demonstrated the effectiveness of these two proposed features, which reminds us deep processing on syntax and semantics might be helpful for traditional regarded shallow works.

To further improve the performance of our system, we will try to extend our work in the following aspects: 1) Perform phrase structure analysis on microblog to excavate the relation between topical and sentimental words; 2) Investigate the impact on other classifiers other than SVM classifier.

Acknowledgments

We would like to thank SIGHAN8 for offering the dataset. We would also acknowledge the help of HIT-IR-Lab for proving the Chinese dependency parser(Che, 2010).

References

Lun-wei Ku and Tung-ho Wu and Li-ying Lee and Hsin-hsi Chen. 2005. Construction of an Evaluation Corpus for Opinion Extraction. In *Journal of NTCIR*, pages 513--520, Taipei, Taiwan.

Yang Shen, Shuchen Li, Ling Zheng, Xiaodong Ren and Xiaolong Cheng. 2009. Emotion mining research on microblog. In *Proceedings of Computer Science & Education (ICCSE)*, pages 477-480, LanZhou, China.

Vasileios Hatzivassiloglou and Janyce M. Wiebe. 2000. Effects of Adjective Orientation and Gradability on Sentence Subjectivity. In *Proceedings of the the 18th conference on Computational linguistics - Volume 1. Association for Computational Linguistics*, pages 299-305, New York.

Turney P D. 2002. Thumbs Up or Thumbs Down? Semantic Orientation Applied to Unsupervised Classification of Reviews. In *Journal of Proc An-*

nual Meeting of the Association for Computational Linguistics,pages 417--424.

Xiaolong Wang Y and Furu Wei Z. 2011. Topic Sentiment Analysis in Twitter: A Graph-based Hashtag Sentiment Classification Approach. In *International Conference on Information & Knowledge Management Proceedings*(2011).

Pang B, Lee L, Vaithyanathan S. 2002. Thumbs up? Sentiment Classification using Machine Learning Techniques. Proceedings of Emnlp, pages: 79-86.

Dasgupta, S., & Ng, V. 2009. Mine the Easy, Classify the Hard: A Semi-Supervised Approach to Automatic Sentiment Classification. In *Meeting of the Association for Computational Linguistics*, pages 701-709.

Li F, Liu N, Jin H, et al. 2011. Incorporating Reviewer and Product Information for Review Rating Prediction. *In Proceedings of the twenty-second international joint conference on artificial intelligence*, pages 1820-1825.

Jakob N, Darmstadt T U, Gurevych I. 2010. Extracting opinion targets in a single and cross-domain setting with conditional random fields. In *Proceedings of the 2010 Conference on Empirical Methods in Natural Language Processing*, pages 427.

Salton G, Yu C T. 1975. On the construction of effective vocabularies for information retrieval. In *Proceedings of Acm Sigplan Notices*, pages 48-60.

Salton G, Fox E. 1983. Extended Boolean information retrieval. In *Journal of Communications of the Acm*, 26(11), pages:1022-1036.

Mihalcea R, Tarau P. 2004. TextRank: Bringing Order into Texts In *Proceedings of Unt Scholarly Works*.

Tomas Mikolov, Kai Chen, Greg Corrado, Jeffrey Dean. 2013. Efficient estimation of word representations in vector space.

Turney P D, Littman M L. 2003. Measuring Praise and Criticism: Inference of Semantic Orientation from Association. In *Journal of* Acm Transactions on Information Systems , 21(4), pages:315-346.

Wang S G, De-Yu L I, Wei Y J, et al. 2009. A Synonyms Based Word Sentiment Orientation Discriminating. In *Journal of Chinese Information Processing*, pages:68-74.

Wanxiang Che, Zhenghua Li, and Ting Liu. 2010. LTP: A Chinese Language Technology Platform. In Proceedings of the Coling 2010: Demonstration Volume, pages 13-16, Beijing, China.

CT-SPA: Text Sentiment Polarity Prediction Model Using Semi-automatically Expanded Sentiment Lexicon

Tao-Hsing Chang
Department of Computer Science
and Information Engineering
National Kaohsiung University of
Applied Sciences
changth@gm.kuas.edu.tw

Ming-Jhih Lin
Department of Computer Science
and Information Engineering
National Kaohsiung University of
Applied Sciences
1101108139@kuas.edu.tw

Chun-Hsien Chen
Department of Computer Science
and Information Engineering
National Kaohsiung University of
Applied Sciences
1101108103@kuas.edu.tw

Shao-Yu Wang
Department of Computer Science
and Information Engineering
National Kaohsiung University of
Applied Sciences
1101108143@kuas.edu.tw

Abstract

In this study, an automatic classification method based on the sentiment polarity of text is proposed. This method uses two sentiment dictionaries from different sources: the Chinese sentiment dictionary CSWN that integrates Chinese WordNet with SentiWordNet, and the sentiment dictionary obtained from a training corpus labeled with sentiment polarities. In this study, the sentiment polarity of text is analyzed using these two dictionaries, a mixed-rule approach, and a statistics-based prediction model. The proposed method is used to analyze a test corpus provided by the Topic-Based Chinese Message Polarity Classification task of SIGHAN-8, and the F1-measure value is tested at 0.62.

1 Introduction

The automatic text sentiment analysis method is an essential part in many big data analytics applications. For example, in opinion mining applications, the reviews for a certain movie in an online movie community are classified into positive or negative opinions (Kennedy & Inkpen, 2006). In addition, there are commercial organizations that analyze real-time social media content. When a large number of positive or negative posts on the user experience of a client's product appear suddenly in social media, these organizations automatically create an analysis report and send it to their client, thus allowing the client to gain more time for crisis response (Feldman, 2013).

There have been numerous studies on how to analyze sentiment tendency expressed in text. Most such algorithms rely on lexicon-based methods (Taboada, Brooke, Tofiloski, Voll, & Stede, 2011) that normally comprise assigning positive or negative sentiment values to words in the documents according to a sentiment dictionary, and then evaluating the sentiment orientation of the text according to different classification methods, such as weighting method and k-means. These methods can obtain very good results in certain standard tests, such as Epinions' positive and negative product review corpus. A sentiment dictionary is constructed in such a way that every word in the dictionary is assigned to a sentiment category (also called polarity), either positive or negative. Sentiment polarity labeling for these dictionaries is performed manually, semi-automatically, or automatically. Manually labeled sentiment dictionaries have been developed for many years, but most dictionaries are only labeled with polarities without polarity strength. SO-CAL, proposed by Taboada et al., is an English dictionary labeled with both polarity and strength.

In view of the restrictions associated with manually built dictionaries, several researchers have adopted semi-automatic or fully automatic methods to build sentiment dictionaries based on existing resources or large amounts of linguistic data. For example, SentiWordNet (Baccianella, Esuli, & Sebastiani, 2010) is a WordNet-based sentiment dictionary where the polarity strength of every sentiment word is labeled after analysis of the documents labeled with sentiment polarities. The Chinese dictionary NTUSD (Ku & Chen,

Proceedings of the Eighth SIGHAN Workshop on Chinese Language Processing (SIGHAN-8), pages 164–170,
Beijing, China, July 30-31, 2015.

2007) relies on an analysis of reader positive and negative opinions on the linguistic data of news to add the polarity of every word. In a previous study, we attempted to create a Chinese SentiWordNet based on the associations among ChineseWordNet, WordNet 1.6, WordNet 3.0, and SentiWordNet, but there are some restrictions on the use of SentiWordNet. For example, a word in SentiWordNet could have both a positive value of 0.3 and a negative value of 0.1 because the word is used in text with different sentiment orientations. Although this information is correct in general, it causes a problem in how to determine the value to be used in text sentiment orientation analysis. Several methods use both values, and several methods only consider the orientation with a relatively high value. These methods cause considerable estimation errors, and thus they cannot properly achieve the intended results in practical applications.

The purpose of this study is to propose a lexicon-based text sentiment analysis method called the Chinese Text Sentiment Polarity Analyzer (CT-SPA). This method uses two sentiment dictionaries from different sources: a Chinese sentiment dictionary that integrates Chinese WordNet with SentiWordNet, and a sentiment dictionary obtained by training a text corpus labeled with sentiment polarities. In this study, text sentiment polarity is analyzed using these two dictionaries, a mixed-rule approach, and a statistics-based prediction model. The content of the remaining sections is as follows. Section 2 presents a review of related studies. Section 3 describes the method for creating two sentiment dictionaries. Section 4 proposes the algorithm for predicting text sentiment using the aforementioned sentiment dictionaries. In Section 5, the proposed method is confirmed using the test corpus provided by the Topic-Based Chinese Message Polarity Classification task of ACL-SIGHAN 2015. Section 6 includes the conclusions of this study and a description of possible future study topics.

2 Related Works

Automatic text sentiment classification has been studied extensively in the last five years. The classification methods are divided into supervised learning that uses text labeled with sentiment values as training data (Moraes, Valiati, & GaviãO Neto, 2013), unsupervised learning that requires only unlabeled data (Paltoglou & Thelwall, 2012; Turney, 2002), and semi-supervised learning that combines a small amount of labeled data with a large pool of unlabeled data (Liu, Chang, & Li, 2013). The supervised learning approach delivers the best performance in classification accuracy, but collecting a large amount of labeled data in every domain is not feasible. Unsupervised learning is readily applicable to every domain, but delivers low classification accuracy. However, it is worth noting that many unsupervised learning methods rely on the characteristics of big data (for example, Paltoglou & Thelwall (2012) used a huge number of posts on social web) to improve clustering accuracy.

With regard to the content for classification, the most frequently analyzed data are posts on social networking sites, such as Twitter, Facebook (Thompson, Poulin, & Bryan, 2014; Thelwall & Buckley, 2013; Martínez-Cámara, Martínez-Valdivia, Urena-Lopez, & Montejo-Ráez, 2014), followed by long reviews, especially movie reviews (Martínez-Cámara, Martínez-Valdivia, Urena-Lopez, & Montejo-Ráez, 2006; Liu et al., 2013). It can be seen that different methods are used for different content, but most methods employ sentiment dictionaries to a certain extent.

Sentiment dictionaries can be divided into three categories according to their sources: those selected from regular dictionaries, where their sentiment polarities and strengths are defined by experts; those where the dictionaries are automatically generated through machine learning; and those where the dictionaries are semi-automatically created using manually built dictionaries as seeds or their extended definitions. There have been few studies on manually built dictionaries because creating such dictionaries is time consuming and usually results in the problem where one word can have different sentiments. However, almost all studies on automatically generated dictionaries require a comparison with manually built dictionaries, and semi-automatically generated dictionaries are considerably dependent on manually built dictionaries. Examples of well-known sentiment dictionaries include SO-CAL (Taboada, Brooke, Tofiloski, Voll, & Stede, 2011), General Inquirer (Stone, Dunphy, & Smith, 1966), and ANEW (Bradley & Lang, 1999).

Most automatic dictionary generation methods use a semantic relationship algorithm that explores the semantic relationship between two words in a large amount of text and analyzes the sentiment polarities of the words based on this relationship. For example, Turney (2002) created a dictionary that consists of adjectives and adverbs using the PMI-IR algorithm and text from the search engine AltaVista. Kilgarriff (2007) built a Google-PMI dictionary with a similar method.

Semi-automatic extension methods have been used in building most sentiment dictionaries, such as SentiWordNet (Baccianella, Esuli, & Sebastiani, 2010), SenticNet (Cambria, Speer, Havasi, & Hussain, 2010), WordNet-Affect (Strapparava, & Valitutti, 2004), and Chinese NTUSD (Ku & Chen, 2007). The most typical process is the procedure proposed by Whitelaw, Garg, & Argamon (2005). First, seed words with polarities or a small dictionary are used. Second, synonym resources (such as WordNet, HowNet, Chinese Thesaurus, and others) and extension algorithms are used to extend a small amount of sentiment data with labeled words to other words. Third, correct words are obtained through manual detection or screening. In several methods, the third step is performed using rule-based screening (for example, only retaining a few word classes), rather than manual screening.

3 Chinese SentiWordNet

We built a Chinese sentiment dictionary (CSWN) based on the relationship among four dictionaries, Academia Sinica Bilingual Ontological WordNet (BOW), WordNet1.6, WordNet 3.0, and SentiWordNet. BOW is a bilingual dictionary that corresponds to WordNet Version 1.6. SentiWordNet is an extended sentiment dictionary built on the WordNet Version 3.0 lexical database. Because there are considerable differences among different versions of WordNet and the same word does not correspond to another in different versions, we established a method for associating different versions of the same word in different WordNet versions based on several rules. For a Chinese word in BOW, its corresponding English word in SentiWordNet can be found through this association. For every Chinese word, its sentiment value can be obtained according to the given sentiment polarity and strength (hereinafter referred to as "sentiment value") of its corresponding English word in SentiWordNet, where the sentiment value of every word consists of a pair of numbers that represent positive and negative sentiment strength. It is especially worth noting that several words may have both positive and negative values because they may have different sentiment polarities in different context.

Although this method can be used to establish the sentiment values for a considerable number of Chinese words, BOW does not contain a large number of such words, and the sentiment values still have not been established for numerous Chinese words. To increase the number of Chinese words with sentiment values, the sentiment labels for the English words in E-HowNet are used, and the sentiment value of every English word in E-HowNet is assigned to its corresponding Chinese word. Meanwhile, the sentiment value of every Chinese word with sentiment value is assigned to other Chinese words without sentiment value in the synonym set through the synonym labels in E-HowNet.

The data set of Chinese words with sentiment values obtained by the aforementioned method is called Chinese SentiWordNet (CSWN). Because sometimes there might be errors in the sentiment values obtained by the aforementioned method, NTUSD is used to correct all possible errors. NTUSD is a sentiment dictionary with high labeling accuracy, but all Chinese words in the dictionary are only labeled with sentiment polarity without sentiment strength. Therefore, we use the following rules to correct the sentiment values of the Chinese words obtained previously.

Assuming a word has a positive polarity in NTUSD:

1) If both the positive and negative strengths in CSWN are greater than zero, but the positive strength is greater than the negative strength, the negative strength is adjusted to zero;

2) If both the positive and negative strengths are greater than zero, and the positive strength is equal to the negative strength, the positive strength is set to 0.125 and the negative strength is set to zero.

3) If both the positive and negative strengths are equal to zero, the positive strength is set to 0.25, and the negative strength is set to zero.

4) If both the positive and negative strengths are greater than zero, but the negative strength is greater than the positive strength, the negative strength is adjusted to zero.

5) If the negative strength is greater than zero and the positive strength is equal to zero, the positive strength is set to the average positive strength of all words with unadjusted sentiment values, and the negative strength is set to zero.

If the word has a negative polarity in NTUSD, its polarity is corrected by using rules contrary to those mentioned above.

4 Data-driven sentiment dictionary

A common method for building a sentiment dictionary is to use documents with sentimental labels. A basic prerequisite for such method is as follows: if a word appears more frequently in positive documents than negative or neutral documents, this word is prone to convey a positive sentiment, and vice versa. Therefore, we define three parameters for a corpus, All-Pos, All-Neu, and All-Neg, which represent the numbers of positive, neutral, and negative documents in a corpus, respectively. In addition, we define three parameters for a word in a corpus, Pos, Neu, and Neg, which represent the numbers of positive, neutral, and negative documents that contain the word, respectively.

Based on these six parameters, the frequency of each word occurring in different labeled documents can be calculated. Another three parameters, PosSS, NeuSS, and NegSS can be given by formula (1)-(3)

$$PosSS = Pos/All\text{-}Pos \quad (1)$$
$$NeuSS = Neu/All\text{-}Neu \quad (2)$$
$$NegSS = Neg/All\text{-}Neg \quad (3)$$

The sentiment value of a word can be determined according to the aforementioned parameters. Because the words that appear in a corpus are not necessarily contained in CSWN, the following rules are used to establish their sentiment values:

1) If a word only appears in positive and neutral documents, the positive sentiment strength is set to the y value given by formula (4), and the negative strength is set to zero.

$$y = \log(PosSS/NeuSS)*Pos/(Pos+Neu)*\alpha \quad (4)$$

where α is the strength adjustment parameter. For example, for the corpus used in the experiments for this study, if a word appears in NTUSD, α is set to 0.3343; otherwise, α is set to 0.2343.

2) If a word only appears in negative and neutral documents, the negative sentiment strength is set to the y value given by formula (5), and the positive strength is set to zero.

$$y = \log(Neg/NeuSS)*Neg/(Neg+Neu)*\alpha \quad (5)$$

where α is set similarly to the previous rule.

3) If a word only appears in positive and negative documents, the sentiment value is given by formula (6).

$$y = \log(Pos/Neg) \quad (6)$$

If y is greater than zero, the positive strength of the word is set to y and its negative strength is set to zero; if y is less than zero, the negative strength of the word is set to y and the positive strength is set to zero; and if y is equal to zero, both the positive and negative strengths are set to zero.

4) If a word appears in documents with various labels, and its PosSS value is greater than its NegSS value, the positive sentiment strength is set to the y value given by formula (7), and the negative strength is set to zero. If its PosSS value is less than the NegSS value, the negative sentiment strength is set to the y value given by formula (8), where α is the strength adjustment parameter, and the positive strength is set to zero. For example, for the corpus used in the experiments for this study, if a word appears in NTUSD, α is set to 0.7; otherwise, α is set to 0.2343.

$$y = \log(PosSS/NegSS)*Pos/(Pos+Neg+Neu)*\alpha \quad (7)$$
$$y = -\log(PosSS/NegSS)*Neg/(Pos+Neg+Neu)*\alpha \quad (8)$$

For the words contained in CSWN, the following corrective rules are used to suit the characteristics of the linguistic data. Assume that the sentimental score of a word in CSWN is G:

1) If a word only appears in neutral documents in a corpus, and its G value is greater than zero, the y value given by formula (9) is calculated. If the y value is greater than zero, the positive strength of the word is adjusted to y; otherwise, the positive strength is adjusted to zero. The negative strength is set to zero regardless of the y value. On the other hand, if the G value of the word is less than zero, the y value given by formula (9) is calculated. If the y value is greater than zero, the negative strength of the word is adjusted to y; otherwise, the negative strength is adjusted to zero. The positive strength is set to zero regardless of the y value.

$$y = (1-\log(Neu*\omega))*|G| \quad (9)$$

2) If a word only appears in positive documents in a corpus, and the number of positive documents is greater than the value of parameter δ, the positive strength is set to the y value given by formula (10), and its negative strength is set to zero.

$$y = |(1-\log(Pos*\beta))*G| \quad (10)$$

3) If a word only appears in negative documents in a corpus, and the number of negative documents is greater than the value of parameter δ, but the G value of the word in CSWN is greater than zero, the negative strength of the word is set to the y value given by formula (10), and the positive strength is set to zero.

$$y = |(1\text{-}\log(Neg*\beta))*G| \qquad (11)$$

The values of the aforementioned parameters δ, ω, and β are related to the number of documents in a corpus, and increase with the increasing number of documents. For example, for the corpus used in the experiments for this study, δ, β, and ω are set to 3, 3.3, and 1, respectively. In addition, if the y value given by any of the formulas (4) to (11) is greater than one, all these parameters are set to one.

5 Text sentiment classification method

In the method proposed herein, the difference between the positive and negative strengths for every word in the text is defined as the sentiment score of the word. A positive sentiment score means positive polarity and vice versa. The sum of the sentiment scores for all words is the sentiment score for the text. If the sentiment score for the text is a positive value greater than a threshold value, the sentiment orientation of the text is positive, and vice versa. If the sentiment score does not exceed the threshold value, the text is considered neutral. However, because sentiment words express different sentiment strengths or even opposite sentiments in different word classes and syntactic structures, the following five correction rules are used to calculate the sentiment value for the text.

First, the sentiment value shall be adjusted according to the weight of the word class. A Chinese word may appear in the text as different word classes. Several Chinese word classes impose slight or even no effect on the sentiment value of the text. Therefore, if a word appears as such word classes, its sentiment score shall be adjusted by multiplying it by a weight to obtain the new sentiment value. For example, for words of classes Nf and Neu, the weight is set to zero. The weight value can be obtained from the corpus training experiments.

Second, a weighting calculation shall be performed for words that collocate with degree adverbs. Degree adverbs may strengthen or weaken the sentiments of words. For example, "very happy" expresses stronger sentiment strength than "happy." Therefore, we select words from the word class Dfa in E-HowNet and manually screen and define the weights of degree adverbs. If a degree adverb precedes a sentiment word in a sentence, the sentiment score of the word shall be multiplied by the weight of the degree adverb to obtain the new sentiment score for this word.

Third, the sentiment scores of words in interrogative sentences and rhetorical questions shall be corrected. The sentiment of an interrogative sentence or rhetorical question is normally contrary to the sentiment score obtained. For example, in the sentence "everyone has tried their best for this. How can you still accuse who shall be blamed for his or her fault?" The "accuse" and "fault" in this sentence express negative sentiment, but their use in this interrogative sentence reverses the entire sentence to positive sentiment. Therefore, the sentiment score of interrogative sentences and rhetorical questions shall be multiplied by -1.

Fourth, the sentiment value for any word that collocates with a negative word shall be reversed to its opposite. When a negative word precedes a word, its overall sentiment polarity is normally contrary to the word. For example, the polarity of "not happy" is contrary to the polarity of "happy." Therefore, the sentiment score for a word that occurs after negative words shall be multiplied by -1.

Fifth, the sentiment value for any transition sentence shall be corrected. When a transition sentence pair with "but," "nevertheless," or "although" appears in the text, the real sentiment of the sentence pair is expressed in the sentence after, rather than before, the transition. For example, in the sentence "this way of doing things is undesirable, but the result is surprisingly good," obviously the sentiment of the entire sentence pair is identical to that of the latter sentence, but contrary to that of the former sentence. Therefore, when calculating the sentiment score of the text, the sentiment score generated by the sentence before the transition of a transition sentence pair is not considered.

6 Experiments

The Topic-Based Chinese Message Polarity Classification task of SIGHAN-8 (hereinafter referred to as SIGHAN-8) provided a corpus labeled with sentiment polarities for training. This training corpus consists of short messages classified into five different topics collected from various social networking sites. SIGHAN-8 also provided a test corpus from the same source as that for the training corpus, but includes 20 different topics. The numbers of positive, neutral, and negative documents in the two corpora are listed in Table 1. In this study, this training corpus is used to train the proposed prediction model according to the method mentioned in Section 4, and the sentiment polarities of the text in the test corpus are tested with this model.

	Positive	Negative	Neutral
Training corpus	394	538	3,973
Test corpus	1,152	3,639	14,678

Table 1 Number of documents with different polarities in the corpus provided by SIGHAN-8

Table 2 shows the predicted numbers of positive, neutral, and negative documents obtained by the proposed method. According to the SIGHAN evaluation, the prediction results of the proposed method for the test corpus are expressed by three performance indicators, recall, precision, and F1-measure, and all the three values are 0.62.

	Positive	Negative	Neutral
Predicted number of documents	993	5,054	13,422

Table 2 Number of documents with different polarities in the test corpus predicted by the proposed method

7 Discussions and future works

The experiment results show that the proposed method can predict the sentiment polarity of certain text, but results in incorrect predictions for other text. We analyzed the causes for prediction errors and made three conclusions.

First, all the test data used are short messages, with each document containing only a limited number of words. This means that whether the judgment about the sentiment value for every word is right or wrong affects the final result. The CSWN dictionary established in this study contains a large number of Chinese words, but numerous words still have not been included, such as specialized terms and unknown words. The sentiment values of these words are inputted manually, and thus developing an automatic labeling method for such words is a very important task.

Second, several prediction errors are caused by the fact that the sentiment values of the words are highly correlated to the domain of the text. Several words have strong sentiment connotations in some domains, but are neutral in other domains. Several words even exhibit a different or opposite sentiment value in the same domain under different context. Therefore, the predictive ability of a model might be improved by developing methods for solving the problem of the ambiguous sentiment value of words.

Third, there are considerable numbers of English corpora labeled with sentiment values, but very few Chinese corpora are available. Because of insufficient training corpus, combined with the short length of the document, the proposed method barely predicted the correct sentiment values for words not included in the sentiment dictionary, and many documents could not be predicted correctly. How to rapidly develop a corpus with sentiment labels through semi-automatic methods is one of the focused areas for future studies.

Acknowledgements

This work is supported in part by the Ministry of Science and Technology, Taiwan, R.O.C. under the Grants MOST 103-2511-S-151-001. It is also partially supported by the "Aim for the Top University Project" and "Center of Learning Technology for Chinese" of National Taiwan Normal University (NTNU), sponsored by the Ministry of Education, Taiwan, R.O.C. and the "International Research-Intensive Center of Excellence Program" of NTNU and Ministry of Science and Technology, Taiwan, R.O.C. under Grant MOST 104-2911-I-003-301.

References

Baccianella, S., Esuli, A., & Sebastiani, F. 2010. SentiWordNet 3.0: An Enhanced Lexical Resource for Sentiment Analysis and Opinion Mining. *Proceedings of LREC*, 10:2200-2204.

Bradley, M. M., & Lang, P. J. 1999. Affective norms for English words (ANEW): Instruction manual and affective ratings. *Technical Report C-1*, 1-45. The Center for Research in Psychophysiology, University of Florida.

Cambria, E., Speer, R., Havasi, C., & Hussain, A. 2010. SenticNet: A Publicly Available Semantic Resource for Opinion Mining. *Proceedings of AAAI Fall Symposium: Commonsense Knowledge*, 10:14-18.

Feldman, R. 2013. Techniques and applications for sentiment analysis. *Communications of the ACM*, 56(4):82-89

Kennedy, A., & Inkpen, D. 2006. Sentiment classification of movie reviews using contextual valence shifters. *Computational Intelligence*, 22(2):110-125.

Ku, L. W., & Chen, H. H. 2007. Mining opinions from the Web: Beyond relevance retrieval. *Journal of the American Society for Information Science and Technology*, 58(12):1838-1850.

Liu, C. L., Chang, T. H., & Li, H. H. 2013. Clustering Documents with Labeled and Unlabeled Documents using Fuzzy Semi-Kmeans. *Fuzzy Sets and Systems*, 221(16): 48–64.

Martínez-Cámara, E., Martínez-Valdivia, M. T., Urena-Lopez, L. A., & Montejo-Ráez, A. R. 2014. Sentiment analysis in twitter. *Natural Language Engineering*, *20*(1):1-28.

Moraes, R., Valiati, J. F., & GaviãO Neto, W. P. 2013. Document-level sentiment classification: An empirical comparison between SVM and ANN. *Expert Systems with Applications*, *40*(2), 621-633.

Paltoglou, G., & Thelwall, M. 2012. Twitter, MySpace, Digg: Unsupervised sentiment analysis in social media. A*CM Transactions on Intelligent Systems and Technology*, 3(4):66.

Stone, P. J., Dunphy, D. C., & Smith, M. S. 1966. The General Inquirer: A Computer Approach to Content Analysis.

Strapparava, C., & Valitutti, A. 2004. WordNet Affect: an Affective Extension of WordNet. *Proceedings of LREC*, 4:1083-1086.

Taboada, M., Brooke, J., Tofiloski, M., Voll, K., & Stede, M. 2011. Lexicon-based methods for sentiment analysis. *Computational linguistics*, 37(2):267-307.

Thelwall, M., & Buckley, K. 2013. Topic-based sentiment analysis for the social web: The role of mood and issue-related words. *Journal of the American Society for Information Science and Technology*, 64(8):1608-1617.

Thompson, P., Poulin, C., & Bryan, C. J. 2014. Predicting military and veteran suicide risk: Cultural aspects. Proceedings of *ACL 2014*, 1-6.

Whitelaw, C., Garg, N., & Argamon, S. 2005. Using appraisal groups for sentiment analysis. *Proceedings of the 14th ACM international conference on Information and knowledge management*, 625-631.

Chinese Microblogs Sentiment Classification using Maximum Entropy

Dashu Ye, Peijie Huang*, Kaiduo Hong, Zhuoying Tang, WeijianXie, Guilong Zhou
College of Mathematics and Informatics, South China Agricultural University,
Guangzhou 510642, Guangdong, China
dashuye4@stu.scau.edu.cn, pjhuang@scau.edu.cn, kd_hong@163.com,
tangzhy@yeah.net, tsewkviko@gmail.com, zglong2016@163.com

Abstract

This paper presents our Chinese microblog sentiment classification (CMSC) system in the Topic-Based Chinese Message Polarity Classification task of SIGHAN-8 Bake-Off. Given a message from Chinese Weibo platform and a topic, our system is designed to classify whether the message is of positive, negative, or neutral sentiment towards the given topic. Due to the difficulties like the out-of-vocabulary Internet words and emoticons, polarity classification of Chinese microblogs is still an open problem today. In our system, Maximum Entropy (MaxEnt) is employed, which is a discriminative model that directly models the class posteriors, allowing them to incorporate a rich set of features. Moreover, oversampling approach is used to hand the unbalance problem. Evaluation results demonstrate the utility of our system, showing an accuracy of 66.4% for restricted resource and 66.6% for unrestricted resource.

1 Introduction

Recent years have witnessed the tremendous growth of the online social media. In China, Weibo, a Twitter-like microblog service, attracted millions of users. Unlike traditional blogs, microblogs are comparatively short (140 words max at a time), instantaneous, and fast-spreading, which means, when some events happen, people's attitude towards them can be found on the Weibo platform (Such as Sina, Tencent, NetEase etc.) immediately. And connected by online social ties, their comments are likely to affect other users who read them or even the subsequent development of the event.

Since the enormous amount of users and its great effect, people find it necessary to take an insight look at this new form of message. Researches on microblogs fall into multiple areas, such as extraction of messages (Liu et al., 2012), extraction of opinion sentence (Ding, Liu, 2008; Liu et al., 2013), and determination of sentiment orientation (Ding, Liu, 2008; Go et al., 2009; Zhang et al., 2014). Generally speaking, researchers want to find out what people think through what they post on Weibo platform.

Weibo users share their different ideas towards a same topic, and these messages they post may be of positive, negative or neutral sentiment. By classifying the polarity of a piece of microblog, we can find out an overall attitude towards the very topic of the user who posts it. Therefore, sentiment polarity classification is undoubtedly a hotspot of microblog-based research. Nowadays, sentiment polarity of microblogs has been used in many fields, such as predicting book sales (Gruhl et al., 2005), predicting movie sales (Mishne et al., 2006), predicting future product sales (Liu et al., 2007) and investigations of the relations between breaking financial news and stock price changes (Schumakeret al., 2009). Moreover, the indirect assessment of public mood or sentiment from the results of soccer games (Edmans et al., 2007) and from weather conditions (Hirshleifer et al., 2003) have been proposed.

It is common scenery using machine learning approach such as Naïve Bayes and SVM to modeling the sentiment polarity by vectorizing the message under the technology of bag-of-words. But models can be easily suffered for the sparsity of a data matrix, especially when it comes to modeling a short text. We use Maximum Entropy (MxEnt for short) to perform

* Corresponding author

Proceedings of the Eighth SIGHAN Workshop on Chinese Language Processing (SIGHAN-8), pages 171–179,
Beijing, China, July 30-31, 2015. ©2015 Association for Computational Linguistics and Asian Federation of Natural Language Processing

satisfactory results. As a discriminative model, MaxEnt directly model the class posteriors, allowing them to incorporate a rich set of features without worrying about their dependencies on one another, which gives us a rather flexible way to construct appropriate features to cope with problem. In addition, oversampling approach is used to handling the unbalance problem. Evaluation results demonstrate the utility of the proposed method.

The rest of this paper is structured as follows. Section 2 describes the background of the task and related work. In Section 3, we briefly present the proposed CMSC system. Section 4 elaborates on the constructing of our system. Section 5 describes the experimental evaluation and the results analysis. Finally, the last section summarizes this paper and describes our future work.

2 Background and Related Work

In recent years, sentiment analysis (SA) has made a hit in the NLP research community (Jiang et al., 2011). Lots of areas are being researched, such as emotion tagging, emotional element extraction, polarity classification and so on. As to the sentiment classification area, two kinds of methods have been used for text-based sentiment classifications.

The first one is relied on rules and lexicon containing a specific sentiment (Ding, Liu, 2008). It simply accumulates the number of lexicon expressing the same emotion for a given text, independently. And output the corresponding emotion with the highest frequencies. However, the shortcoming is it relies too much on the quality of sentiment lexicon and thus hard to cover the network language arose spontaneously.

The other one is mainly based on the machine learning approach. These method have been employ in text classification and continue to be used in short-text like microblog sentiment classification. Classical model like Naïve Bayes and SVM can be found among the text mining. Turney (2002) applied unsupervised learning method on review classification. Similar work in Movie-Review domain using supervised machine learning technique is researched by Pang et al.(2002) and Go et al. (2009) who use the emoticon in twitter and build the model using MaxEnt, NB and SVM. In Chinese microblogs, abundant emoticon may be more useful in classification. Tang et al. (2014) employ deep learning (DL) method for twitter sentiment classification. Also there are some other methods being used now, e.g. KNN, RNN. However, most of the existing approaches use the bag-of-words technology. As it is known to all, microblog with a limitation of no more than 140 Chinese characters, bag-of-words technology may bring in a challenge of feature sparsity.

In our method, we utilize the flexibility of the feature function in Maximum Entropy approach to incorporate these two kinds of methods mentioned above. We use the segmentation result instead of using the word vector directly which increase dimension of the feature space obviously. In addition, we add rule-based feature which is a supplement of the feature.

3 System Overview

The flowchart of the proposed Chinese microblog sentiment classification (CMSC) system is shown in Figure 1.

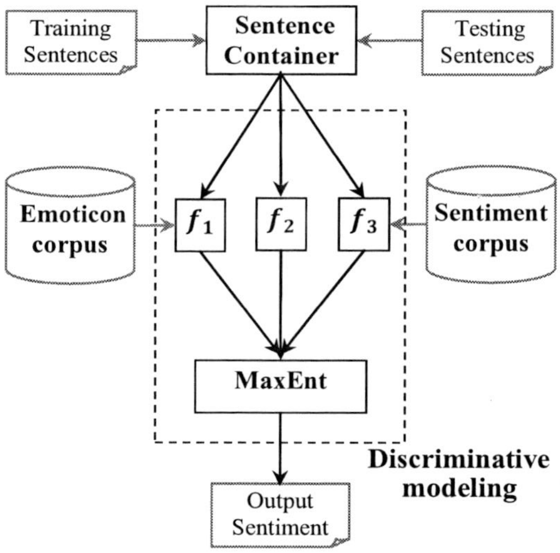

Figure 1. Flowchart of the CMSC system.

The system can be separated mainly into four parts: sentence container, language model, emoticon corpus and sentiment corpus. It performs microblogs sentiment classification as the following step:

Step 1: A given sentence is required to put into the sentence container, and only the Chinese characters and some specific notation remain in the sentence after this phase. We found that phrase containing digital number like '2014年8月15日' and punctuations like '，' or '。' do not make any sense when it comes to the predicting phase, as a result they are suggested to be deleted from the original sentence before coming to the next part.

Step 2: Extract structured feature using the feature functions. 3 feature functions were employ into the language model in current system. Feature function $f_1$compares the number of emoticon expressing the similar sentiment, f_2 makes original mircroblog message as input and yields word segmentation, feature function f_3 just like f_1 , but replaces the emoticons by sentiment words.

Step 3: In this training phase, Maximum Entropy (MaxEnt) regarded as discriminative model yields a satisfactory performance. MaxEnt, one of the most power approach in linguistics modeling, directly models the class posteriors, allowing them to incorporate a rich set of features no need for considering their independence.

Step 4: As the same as training phase, when it comes to the predicting phase, we wanted to extract the structured features among the given testing sentence, and apply them into trained MaxEnt model, to get the corresponding output sentiment.

4 Maximum Entropy based CMSC System

4.1 Maximum Entropy Modeling

Now we give a brief introduction to Maximum Entropy (MxEnt for short) for our CMSC system. MaxEnt has a wide application in real word especially in statistical modeling and pattern recognition (Berger et al., 1996).

Given a set of training data $\{(x_i, y_i)\}_{i=1}^{N}$, where where x_i represents for the contextual information and y_i stands for the corresponding target output. MaxEnt is derived from the idea that we wanted to find a most uniform distribution under the given constraints:

$$C \equiv \{p \in P | p(f_i) = \tilde{p}(f_i) for\ i \in \{1,2,...\}\}, (1)$$

where P is the whole hypothesis space, $p(f_i)$ is the expected value with respect to $p(y|x)$, namely the entire conditional probability distribution given by the model, while $\tilde{p}(f_i)$ is the expected value with respect to empirical function $\tilde{p}(x,y)$. f_i named as feature function or feature for short, describes the relation we interested in, between input x and the target output y. As usual, it can be presented in the form of:

$$f(x,y) = \begin{Bmatrix} 1 & if\ y\ and\ x\ agree\ with\ some\ relation, \\ 0 & otherwise \end{Bmatrix}, (2)$$

which act key role when making a decision. We will discuss the construction of feature function in the coming section.

To find out the most uniform distribution p*, a mathematical theory was used to measure the uniformity of conditional distribution$p(y|x)$:

$$H(p) \equiv -\sum_{x,y} \tilde{p}(x) p(y|x)\ log\ p(y|x) \quad (3)$$

With this definition in hand, we derived

$$p^* = \underset{p \in C}{argmax} H(p) \quad (4)$$

Naturally, the learning model is equivalent to optimize the following function with constrains:

$$\max_{p \in C} H(p) = -\sum_{x,y} \tilde{p}(x) p(y|x)\ log\ p(y|x). (5)$$

$$\text{s.t.} \sum_{x,y} \tilde{p}(x) p(y|x) f(x,y) = \sum_{x,y} \tilde{p}(x,y) f(x,y),$$

$$\sum_{y} p(y|x) = 1.$$

We can transform this constrain problem to unrestraint one using the Lagrange multipliers from the theory of constrained optimization. And for short, we finally get the parametric form of maximum entropy principle:

$$p_\lambda(y|x) = \frac{1}{Z_\lambda(x)} \exp\left(\sum_i \lambda_i f_i(x,y)\right). \quad (6)$$

Here $Z_\lambda(x) = \sum_y \exp(\sum_{i=1}^{n} w_i f_i(x,y))$ is called the normalizing constant, just for meeting the constrain of $\sum_y p(y|x) = 1$.

4.2 Feature Function

In this subsection, we introduce the feature construction of our CMSC system. Feature function regarded as central to the performance of MaxEnt, gives us a flexible way to express interesting evidence.

Generally speaking, feature function can broadly split into observation feature and statistical one.

For example, sentence containing positive words may convey positive sentiment. And we can roughly construct a feature function

$$f(x,y) = \begin{cases} 1 & y = 1\ and\ contain\_posi\_element(x), \\ 0 & otherwise \end{cases}. \quad (7)$$

Feature function of this kind directly finds out the interested evidence in the given sentence without any calculation.

Another kind of feature function utilizes statistic approach to dig out the latent information which may get a magical performance. For example, it can be sometimes, as easily as

$$f(x,y) = \begin{cases} 1 & y = -1\ and\ CEM(x) = 3, \\ 0 & otherwise \end{cases}, \quad (8)$$

where CEM(x) counts appearances of exclamation mark among the given sentence.

In CMSC system for about 3 feature functions were used to encoding the evidence:

$$f_1(x,y) = \begin{cases} 1 & CPE(x) > CNE(x), \\ -1 & CPE(x) < CNE(x), \\ 0 & otherwise \end{cases}, \quad (9)$$

where $CPE(x)$ calculates the number of positive emoticons, while $CNE(x)$calculates the number of negative emoticons. Emoticon is one of the most expressive elements among Chinese microblog. Not only can users type character to compose emoticon like ': p', but can also utilize the system build-in emoticon distinguished by square brackets '[微笑]', which will shows in a more lively way '☺'. For the diversification and the irregularity of character-composed emoticon, we just consider the build-in one in our CMSC system.

$$f_2(x,y) = WS(x), \quad (10)$$

where WS (x) returns a vector of words derived from the word segmentation of given sentence x. Unlike English and other language, Chinese sentences compose of single characters. As a result, word segmentation technology can split sentence into words without losing its original semantic in some way. Knowing about the shortcoming of bag-of-words technology that introduces a vast scale of zeros, we just directly use the word vector as part of input feature shrinking the feature space from ten thousands down to tens and without bringing in redundant zeros. Jieba word-segmentation tool[1] was used to enhance the performance. Jieba segmentation tool provides 3 patterns of word segmentation, including default mode, full mode and search engine mode.

$$f_3(x,y) = \begin{cases} 1 & CPW(x) > CNW(x), \\ -1 & CPW(x) < CNW(x), \\ 0 & otherwise \end{cases}, \quad (11)$$

where CPW(x) returns the appearances of positive word of a given sentence and CNW(x) counts the negative one. According to our intuition, sentences that contain much more positive word are more likely to convey positive emotion. Although sentence may contain no words conveying sentiment, it's reasonable to categorize this sentence to the group of neutral sentiment.

4.3 Sample Weighting and Validation

In this subsection we talk about parameters decision and other tricky way to enhance the system performance. From the training data we learn that the total count of sentences with a specific sentiment is 900. This may result in unbalance problem. The class imbalance problem typically occurs when, in a classification problem, there are many more instances of some classes than others. In such cases, standard classifiers can be suffered by the large classes and ignore the small ones (Chawla et al., 2004). Existing method dealing with unbalance data as sampling methods which utilize sampling techniques to balance the data set can make a satisfactory performance. Under-sampling approach randomly picks up similar size of samples from the majority one, in order to generate a relatively balanced data set. Over-sampling balances the data set by reuse minority one.

Taking our situations, which we totally get for about 5000 training message including 400 messages of positive sentiment and other 500 messages conveying negative emotion, we weight every class in the minority side, to prevent from under fitting.

Here arises a question about how much weighting is suitable for mitigating the impact bringing by the unbalance problem. Validation set was used to figure out a proper weight adding to the minority class. Though experiments, it turn

[1] github.com/fxsjy/jieba

out that by using sample weighting method our system gets significant improvement with 10%-20% performance gain.

5 Experimental Evaluations

5.1 Task Description

In task of SIGHAN-8 Bake-Off, rules of Topic-Based Chinese Message Polarity Classification is as follows: Given a message from Chinese Weibo platform (Such as Sina, Tencent, NetEase etc.) and a topic, classify whether the message is of positive, negative, or neutral sentiment towards the given topic. For messages conveying both a positive and negative sentiment towards the topic, whichever is the stronger sentiment should be chosen.

Each participant is required to submit two kinds of results based on: (1) restricted resource for fair comparison, e.g. same sentiment lexicon, corpus, etc. that will be announced together with the test data; and (2) unrestricted resource. We believe that a freely available, annotated corpus that can be used as a common testbed is needed in order to promote research that will lead to a better understanding of how sentiment is conveyed in tweets and texts.

The evaluation metrics of both kinds of results, including precision rate, recall rate and F1-score, is provided by the Topic-Based Chinese Message Polarity Classification Task group. The confusion matrix shown in Figure 2 is to measure the related indicators.

Confusion Matrix		**System Results**	
		Positive	Negative
Gold Standard	Positive	TP	FN
	Negative	FP	TN

Figure 2. Confusion matrix.

Each index measure is as follows:

$$\textit{Precision}\ (\mathrm{P}) = \mathrm{TP} / (\mathrm{TP} + \mathrm{FP}), \tag{12}$$

$$\textit{Recall}\ (\mathrm{R}) = \mathrm{TP} / (\mathrm{TP} + \mathrm{FN}), \tag{13}$$

$$\textit{F1-score} = 2 * \mathrm{P} * \mathrm{R} / (\mathrm{P} + \mathrm{R}). \tag{14}$$

Each indicator:

Precision (P): Precision rate of all sentiment Polarity Classification

Recall (R): Recall rate of all sentiment Polarity Classification

Precision+ (P+): Precision rate of positive sentiment Polarity Classification

Recall+ (R+): Recall rate of positive sentiment Polarity Classification

Precision- (P-): Precision rate of negative sentiment Polarity Classification

Recall- (R-): Recall rate of negative sentiment Polarity Classification.

5.2 Datasets

Corpus

Participants were asked to report results based on 2 kinds of resources, namely restricted resource and unrestricted resource.

The restricted resource is made up by two words set, the emotion ontology set provided by Dalian University of Technology and the sentiment words set provided by National Taiwan University (NTUSD). And we extract a vocabulary of 38553 words, 14039 words for positive sentiment, 19059 words for negative sentiment and 5376 words for neutral sentiment. We found that so many words in that file are useless since most of the people don't use that word in microblogs. We ignore such word and then construct a lexicon with the form shown as Figure 3.

```
[
    word:
    {
        Polarity:[-1,0,1]
        Intensity:[1 to 7]
    }
]
```

Figure 3. The storage form of lexicon.

It means that given a word, we bind it to its polarity and intensity.

As to unrestricted resource, we employ the sentiment analysis words set in "Hownet" (Li et al., 2002), which contains 91016 words in total. Besides, we collected 161 emoticons from training data as a emoticon lexicon, so as to solve the problem that the current corpus do not contain network language. And the construct the lexicon is as the same of the restricted ones.

Training Set and Validation Set

Original training resource and test resource of the task are messages, which fall into several given topics, extracted from the Sina Weibo platform. These messages are microblog posts on real-event topics from real users. We construct Training. By utilizing the feature function introduced above, three type of final-run training set were constructed for both restricted and unrestricted, shown in Figure 4.

Restricted Run:

Run1 = f_1

Run2=$f_1 + f_2 + f_3 + emVector$

Run3 =$f_1 + f_2 + emVector$

Unrestricted Run:

Run1=$f_1 + f_2 + f_3 + emVector$

Run2 = $f_1 + f_2 + f_3$

Run3 = $f_1 + f_2$

Figure 4. The combinations of features.

In Figure 4, f_1 is the feature function comparing the number of emoticon with different sentiment polarity which has been discussed in formulation (9), feature function f_2 takes word segmentation as input feature as show in formulation (10), feature function $f_3$constructed by formulation (11) simply compare the number of lexicon conveying different sentiments among the given sentence and *emVector* represented for a vector of emoticons which are extracted from the given sentence.

We randomly pick out 40% of microblogs from original training data for evaluating the performance by enumerating the combinations of constructed features. Through validation our model yields an acceptable result.

5.3 Experimental Setup

Word Segmentation

With a lot of word segmentation toolkits, we choose Jieba segmentation toolkit instead of ICTCLAS [2] on account of granularity and encoding problems.

The segmentation Jieba has tree mode, default mode, full mode and search mode. The differences are showed as Figure 5.

Source: "@newcomer2009 最近油价太便宜了不好过啊! "

Default Mode: "@/ newcomer2009/最近油价/太/便宜/了/不好过/啊/! "

Search Mode: "@/ newcomer2009/最近/油价/太/便宜/了/不好/不好过/啊/! "

Full Mode: "newcomer2009/最近/油价/太/便宜/了/不好/不好过/啊"

Figure 5. Different modes of word-segmentation produced by Jieba.

As shown in Figure 5, in "Default Mode" Jieba tries to separate every single Chinese character into a unique phrase on the semantic level, while in "Search Mode" long phrases generated base on "Default Mode" will be given a further segmentation. As showed in the example "不好过", "Default Mode" results in "不好" and "不好过" when it comes to "Search Mode". The shortcoming is it may bring extra noises into our system. Different from "Default Mode" and "Search Mode", "Full Mode" just extract legitimate phrase among the sentence without considering sematic validity, what's more every punctuation like "@" and "! " were left out within this mode, which may lead to a failure when modeling a strong emotion . As a result "Default mode" is adopted into our modeling system.

Using the Tool of Maximum Entropy Model

Since the sparsity of feature, we try to use Maximum Entropy model to solve this problems. In addition, we adjusted the proportion of the sample to deal with the imbalance. In order to prevent from over fitting and get a good performance, we sample the training set holding out 40% of the data for tuning out the best weight for each class. We initialize the proportion of the positive, negative and neutral sample to be 10:7:1.With the sources including restricted sources and unrestricted sources introduced above and construct the tree kind of feature and then used the maximum entropy model to train. We used the maximum entropy model toolkit of Dr. Zhang Le [3]. Since the training set were small and thus training time was short, using the general iterate scale (GIS) algorithm produced robust results and we iterated it one thousand times.

5.4 Result and Discussion

Performance on Validation Set

By playing local evaluations on validation set with enumeration among different combinations of the features, top-3 performances can be seen

[2] ictclas.nlpir.org/

[3] homepages.inf.ed.ac.uk/lzhang10/maxent_toolkit.html

from Table 1 running on restricted resources and Table 2 running on unrestricted resources. Performances in validation set best illustrate the validity of feature function we constructed. Under the combinations of Figure 4, as shown in Table 1, i.e. the restricted running performance, we learn that, a combination of different kinds of feature function is obviously superior to using a single one, and the best performance occurs when adopting the totally three types of feature functions (Run2) accompanying with an emoticon vector. We find the same when it comes to unrestricted round. By contrasting Run2 with Run3 in Table 2, 1% enhancement gains from adding feature function f_3.

Evaluation Results

The Topic-Based Chinese Message Polarity Classification task of SIGHAN8 Bake-Off 2015 attracted 13 teams who submitted their testing results. Table 3 and Table 4 show the evaluation results of the task based on restricted and unrestricted resource respectively. The "Best" indicates the highest score of each metric achieved in the task. "Run" is the evaluation score of our system. And the "Average" represents the average score of all participants. As we can see from Table 3 and Table 4, we achieve a result close to the average level, but still have a long way from the best result, especially in F1+ and F1-.

Evaluation performances on the whole constructed feature space are not as good as that in the validation phase. It boils down to the reason that topics in given training resource are totally different from the testing ones. This may causes out-of-vocabulary problems. Focusing on

	Precision	**Recall**	**F1**	**Precision+**	**Recall+**	**F1+**	**Precision-**	**Recall-**	**F1-**
Run1	0.7792	0.7792	0.7792	0.3961	0.5223	0.4505	0.4157	0.4840	0.4473
Run2	**0.8113**	**0.8113**	**0.8113**	**0.5132**	**0.4968**	**0.5049**	**0.4531**	**0.5068**	**0.4784**
Run3	0.8047	0.8047	0.8047	0.4750	0.4841	0.4795	0.4408	0.4932	0.4655

Table 1. Score on validation set of restricted resources.

	Precision	**Recall**	**F1**	**Precision+**	**Recall+**	**F1+**	**Precision-**	**Recall-**	**F1-**
Run1	**0.8108**	**0.8108**	**0.8108**	**0.5099**	**0.4904**	**0.5000**	**0.4527**	**0.5023**	**0.4762**
Run2	0.7945	0.7945	0.7945	0.4402	0.5159	0.4751	0.4408	0.4932	0.4655
Run3	0.7843	0.7843	0.7843	0.4091	0.5159	0.4563	0.4245	0.4749	0.4483

Table 2. Score on validation set of unrestricted resources.

	Precision	**Recall**	**F1**	**Precision+**	**Recall+**	**F1+**	**Precision-**	**Recall-**	**F1-**
Run1	0.6435	0.6435	0.6435	0.1431	0.2734	0.1878	0.3480	0.3366	0.3422
Run2	0.6520	0.6520	0.6520	0.1441	0.2648	0.1866	0.3648	0.3355	0.3496
Run3	**0.6640**	**0.6640**	**0.6640**	**0.1631**	**0.2813**	**0.2065**	**0.3607**	**0.3174**	**0.3377**
Average	0.6866	0.6797	0.6829	0.2037	0.2293	0.1822	0.3970	0.2867	0.3108
Best	0.8357	0.8357	0.8357	0.6258	0.5139	0.5643	0.8232	0.6048	0.5961

Table 3. Evaluation score of restricted resources.

	Precision	**Recall**	**F1**	**Precision+**	**Recall+**	**F1+**	**Precision-**	**Recall-**	**F1-**
Run1	0.6577	0.6577	0.6577	0.1367	0.2734	0.1822	0.3489	0.3122	0.3295
Run2	**0.6664**	**0.6664**	**0.6664**	**0.1626**	**0.2899**	**0.2084**	**0.3784**	**0.3237**	**0.3489**
Run3	0.6435	0.6435	0.6435	0.1500	0.2908	0.1979	0.3407	0.3471	0.3439
Average	0.7013	0.6974	0.7007	0.2030	0.2285	0.1900	0.4456	0.3475	0.3660
Best	0.8536	0.8536	0.8536	0.5880	0.6207	0.6039	0.7918	0.6175	0.6938

Table 4. Evaluation score of unrestricted resource.

the F value among the microblogs containing a specific emotion, we got slightly superior to average level, gain from utilizing the oversampling method.

5.5 Error Analysis

As is shown in the two figures, we achieved a rather robust result. But on the other hand, it is also obvious that we still have a long way from the state-of-arts, and the potential of the Maximum Entropy model method is far from the state-of-arts, and the potential of the Maximum Entropy model method is far from fully exploited. The major weakness of our system fall down to the low recall rate, which might be the result of not applying enough feature functions. Figure 6 shows some typical error examples of our current system.

Case 1:
topic: 中国政府也门撤侨
message ID: M00046783
weibo: #我有话说#【俄飞机赴也门撤侨遭阿拉伯联军阻挠 被迫折回】 这就是没有人缘的结果 http://t.cn/RAoi81S
standard polarity: 0
system polarity: -1

Case 2:
topic: 孙楠退赛
message ID: M00035167
weibo: 【张靓颖谈孙楠退赛:做什么选择必有他的道理】张靓颖谈到早前孙楠在《我是歌手 3》总决赛时突然退赛，表示孙楠是简单直接的人，他做什么选择一定有自己的道理。并且举例孙楠帮忙照顾自己和其他歌手的一些琐事，大赞孙楠没那么复杂很干脆。http://t.cn/RA67PA1
standard polarity: 1
system polarity: 0

Case 3:
topic: 隆平高科超级稻
message ID: M00048401
weibo: 超级稻的所谓高产和美的空调一晚 1 度电有的一比。//【安徽万亩"隆平稻种"减产绝收】 http://t.cn/RA67iNo
standard polarity: 0
system polarity: 1

Figure 6. Error examples.

The first case is of neutral sentiment, but our system categorizes the text as the negative size. In Our system considers "没有人缘" the negative impact on weibo.

In the second case, our system judges the polarity as neutral sentiment because the message does not contain any sentimental words of our corpus. "没那么复杂" conveys a positive emotion by double negation. What more, It is still challenge for us to cope with long distance relation.

The third case, our system judges the polarity as positive sentiment because of the message contains the words "高产" and "美的", which affect the total sentiment of the weibo by the polarity of corpus. And microblog advertising of this kind do not make any contribution to modeling the sentiment polarity, but bring in unknown noise in some way.

6 Conclusion and Future work

This paper proposes the Chinese microblog sentiment classification (CMSC) system based on MaxEnt from team of South China Agricultural University (SCAU) that participated in the SIGHAN-8 Topic-Based Chinese Message Polarity Classification task. MaxEnt enables to incorporate a rich set of features, which gives us a rather flexible way to construct appropriate features to cope with sparsity problem caused by the characters limitation of microblog. In addition, oversampling approach is used to handling the unbalance problem.

It is our first attempt on Chinese grammatical error diagnosis, and our system achieves a result close to the average level. There are many possible and promising enhancements in the coming future. More appropriate features can be added to the system for a better modeling. Besides, existing sentiment corpuses and lexicons are filled with "book words" (literary, abstract and technical terms), while microblogs are usually in much less formal forms, with a significant amount of using of colloquial phrases, network language and even emoticons and pictures. Long distance relation and adverting detection are also a challenging research topic.

Acknowledgments

This work was partially supported by National Natural Science Foundation of China under Grant No. 71472068, Science and Technology Planning Project of Guangdong Province, China under Grant No. 2013B020314013, and the

Innovation Training Project for College Students of Guangdong Province under Grant No. 201410564294.

References

Berger A, Pietra S.D, Pietra V.D. 1996. A Maximum Entropy Approach to Natural Language Processing. *Computational Linguistics,* Vol. 22, No.1, pp. 5-9.

Chawla, N.V., Japkowicz, N., and Kołcz, A., editors 2004. *SIGKDD Special Issue on Learning from Imbalanced Datasets.*

Ding, X., Liu, B., and Yu, P.S. 2008. A holistic lexicon-based approach to opinion mining. *In Proceedings of the International Conference on Web Search and Web Data Mining (WSDM'08)*, pp. 231-239.

Edmans, A, Garca, D, Norli Ø. 2007. Sports sentiment and stock returns, *The Journal of Finance*, Vol. 58, pp. 1967-1998

Go A., Bhayani R., Huang L. 2009. *Twitter sentiment classification using distant supervision.* CS224N Project Report, Stanford.

Gruhl, D, Guha, R, Kumar, R, Novak, J, & Tomkins, A. 2005. The predictive power of online chatter. *In: Proceedings of the 11th ACM SIGKDD international conference on knowledge discovery and data mining*, pp. 78–87. ACM, New York, NY, USA.

Hirshleifer, D, Shumway, T. 2003. Good Day Sunshine: Stock Returns and the Weather. *The Journal of Finance*, Vol. 58, pp.1009–1032.

Li S.J., Zhang J., Huang X., et al. 2002. Semantic computation in Chinese question-answering system. *Journal of Computer Science and Technology*, Vol. 17, No.6, pp. 933-939.

Liu N., He Y. X., He F. Y., et al. 2013. The Method of Chinese Opinion Sentence Extraction and Polarity Identification Based on Sentimental Elements, *Advanced Materials Research*, Vols. 765-767, pp. 1406-1410

Liu Y., Huang X., An A., et al. 2007. ARSA: a sentiment-aware model for predicting sales performance using blogs. *In: Proceedings of the 30th Annual International ACM SIGIR Conference on Research and Development in Information Retrieval*, pp. 607–614. ACM Press, New York

Liu Z. Y., Chen X.X., Sun M.S. 2012. Mining the interests of Chinese microbloggers via keyword extraction. *Frontiers of Computer Science in China*, Vol. 6, pp. 76-87

Jiang L., Yu M., Zhou M., et al. 2011. Target dependent Twitter Sentiment Classification. *In Proceedings of the 49th Annual Meeting of the Association for Computational Linguistics (ACL 2011)*, pp. 151-160.

Mishne G., Glance N. 2006. Predicting Movie Sales from Blogger Sentiment. *In Proceedings of the 21th National Conference on Artificial Intelligence (AAAI 2006).* Menlo Park, California, pp.155-158.

Pang B., Lee L., Vaithyanathan S. 2002. Thumbs up? Sentiment Classification Using Machine Learning Techniques. *In Proceedingsof the Conference on Empirical Methods in Natural Language Processing (EMNLP 2002)*, pp.79-86.

Schumaker R. P, Chen, H. 2009. Textual analysis of stock market prediction using breaking financial news: The azfin text system. *ACM Trans. Inf. Syst.*, Vol. 27, No. 12, pp.1– 12.

Tang D.Y., Wei F.R., Qin B., et al. 2014. A Deep Learning System for Twitter Sentiment Classification. *In Proceedings of the 8th International Workshop on Semantic Evaluation (SemEval 2014)*, pages 208–212,Dublin, Ireland, August 23-24.

Turney, P. D. 2002. Thumbs up or thumbs down? Semantic orientation applied to unsupervised classification of reviews. *In Proceedings of the 40th Annual Meeting of the Association for Computational Linguistics (ACL 2002)*, pp. 417–424.

Zhang J., Zhu B., Liang L.L., et al. 2014. Recognition and Classification of Emotions in the Chinese Microblog Based on Emotional Factor. *Acta Scientiarum Naturalium Universitatis Pekinensis*, Vol. 50, No.1, PP. 79-84 (In Chinese)

NDMSCS: A Topic-Based Chinese Microblog Polarity Classification System

Yang Wang, Yaqi Wang, Shi Feng, Daling Wang, Yifei Zhang
Northeastern University, Shenyang, China
{wangyangdm,wyqnumber1}@gmail.com,
{fengshi,wangdaling,zhangyifei}@ise.neu.edu.cn

Abstract

In this paper, we focus on topic-based microblog sentiment classification task that classify the microblog's sentiment polarities toward a specific topic. Most of the existing approaches for sentiment analysis usually adopt the target-independent strategy, which may assign irrelevant sentiments to the given topic. In this paper, we leverage the non-negative matrix factorization to get the relevant topic words and then further incorporate target-dependent features for topic-based microblog sentiment classification. According to the experiment results, our system (NDMSCS) has achieved a good performance in the SIGHAN 8 Task 2.

1 Introduction

Nowadays, people are willing to express their feelings and emotions via the microblog services, such as Twitter and Weibo. Therefore, the microblog has aggregated huge amount of sentences that contain people's rich sentiments. Extracting and analyzing the sentiments in microblogs has become a hot research topic for both academic communities and industrial companies.

The microblog usually has a length limitation of 140 characters, which leads to extremely sparse vectors for the learning algorithms. On the other hand, people are used to using a simple sentence, or even a few words to express their attitude or viewpoint toward a specific topic. Most of the existing sentiment analysis methods could classify the microblogs into positive, negative and neutral categories. However, these methods usually adopt the target-independent strategy, which may assign irrelevant sentiments to the given topic.

In this paper we develop a machine learning system for topic-based microblog polarity classification. Given a microblog and a topic, we intend to classify whether the microblog is of positive, negative, or neutral sentiment towards the given topic. For microblogs conveying both a positive and negative sentiment towards the topic, whichever is the stronger sentiment should be chosen.

To tackle challenges, firstly we use non-negative matrix factorization to find the topic relevant words. And then we propose feature selection strategy and construct vectors to convert the raw microblog text into the TFIDF feature values, combined with the linguistic features, which we then use together with the labels to train our sentiment classifier. Our approach includes an extensive usage of Python based NLP and machine learning resources for conducting word segmentation, POS tagging and classifier implementation.

We evaluate our proposed system on the test set of Topic-Based Chinese Message Polarity Classification Task in SIGHAN 8. Our system is ranked 3rd on the task test set for overall F1 value and also achieves good performance in the positive and negative F1 values. The experiment shows the effectiveness of our proposed system.

2 Non-negative Matrix Factorization

Topic based sentiment analysis task need to consider the target that sentiment words described, so we try to find the words related to the specific topic. And the topics of test set are different from the training set, so we want to use the wildcard to replace the topic words to reduce the influence of different topics. We consider using the topic modeling to discovery the hidden topic information in large collections of documents. People usually use the probabilistic methods, such as Latent Dirichlet allocation (LDA) (Blei et al., 2003), to build the topic model. However, an effective alternative is to use Non-negative Matrix Factorization (NMF) (Lee et al., 1999). NMF refers to an unsuper-

Proceedings of the Eighth SIGHAN Workshop on Chinese Language Processing (SIGHAN-8), pages 180–184,
Beijing, China, July 30-31, 2015. ©2015 Association for Computational Linguistics and Asian Federation of Natural Language Processing

vised family of algorithms from linear algebra that simultaneously performs dimension reduction and clustering.

NMF takes non-negative matrix as an input, and factorizes it into two smaller non-negative matrices *W* and *H*, each having k dimensions. When multiplied together, these factors approximate the original matrix X. It finds a decomposition of samples *X* into two matrices *W* and *H* of non-negative elements, by optimizing for the squared Frobenius norm:

$$arg \min_{W,H} \|X - WH\|^2 = \Sigma_{i,j} X_{i,j} - WH_{i,j} \quad (1)$$

We can specify the parameter k to control the number of topics that will be produced. The rows of the matrix *W* provides weights for the input documents relative to the k topics and these values indicate the strength of association between documents and topics. The columns of the matrix *H* provide weights for the terms relative to the topics. By ordering the values in a given column and selecting the top-ranked terms, we can produce a description of the corresponding topic.

NMF implements the Nonnegative Double Singular Value Decomposition(NNDSVD) which is proposed by Boutsidis et al. (2008). NNDSVD is based on two SVD processes, one approximating the data matrix, the other approximating positive sections of the resulting partial SVD factors utilizing an algebraic property of unit rank matrices. The basic NNDSVD algorithm is better fit for sparse factorization.

Once the document-term matrix *X* has been constructed, we apply NMF topic modeling as follows: First we initialize the value of k to 5 for training data and 20 for test data. We generate initial factors using the NNDSVD. Then we apply the NMF algorithm on the document-term matrix *X*, using the initial parameters from first step, for a fixed number of iterations (e.g. 1000) to produce final factors (*W*, *H*). Each row of *H* is a distribution over all terms in a vocabulary, and easily interpreted as the topics. In each topic we choose top-ranked terms as the topic words.

The data preparation and topic modeling described above can be implemented using the Python Scikit-learn[1] toolkit. We use TfidfVectorizer to create document-term matrix of size (d, t), and generate factor *W* of size (d, k) and factor *H* of size (k, t) by using NMF. Here d and t represent the number of documents and terms, and k represents the number of topics. We get the topic words in the training data as show in Table 1.

Topic ID	Topic Words
Topic 1	ssix, 三星, edge, galaxy, mnine,五千块, 给你, 还是
Topic 2	日本, 马桶盖, 中国, 杭州, 游客, 国内, 确系, 热销
Topic 3	降息, 央行, 基准利率, 下调, 百分点, 存款, 一年期, 贷款
Topic 4	油价, 令吉, 国油, 物价, 商家,公司, 调涨, 燃油
Topic 5	雾霾, 柴静, 穹顶, 之下, 调查, 视频, 同呼吸共命运, 完整版

Table 1: The topic words extracted from the document.

Because the documents carry a lot of noise and the NMF algorithm doesn't know anything about the documents, terms, or topics it contains, we manually inspect and remove the unrelated topic words. The words were discarded for various reasons: they were too generic, or irrelevant to the primary topic. In order to convert the problem to the topic independent emotion classification problem, we preprocess the microblog by replacing the topic words with TW and setting their POS tags to noun.

3 System Overview

Figure 1 gives a brief overview of our system that takes the microblogs and the corresponding labels as inputs to learn sentiment classifiers. We build a TFIDF-NMF pipeline to get the topic words after preprocessing. We use three-way classification framework in which we incorporate rich topic-dependent feature representations of the microblog text. The classifier is then used to predict test microblog sentiment labels. The proposed system basically include the module of preprocessing, topic word expansion, feature extraction and classification. In this section we discuss each module in detail.

3.1 Preprocessing

Handle Traditional Chinese Text: Some of the microblogs are written in traditional Chinese, so we first convert the traditional Chinese to the simplified Chinese based on the tool OpenCC[2], which

[1]http://scikit-learn.org/

[2]http://opencc.byvoid.com/

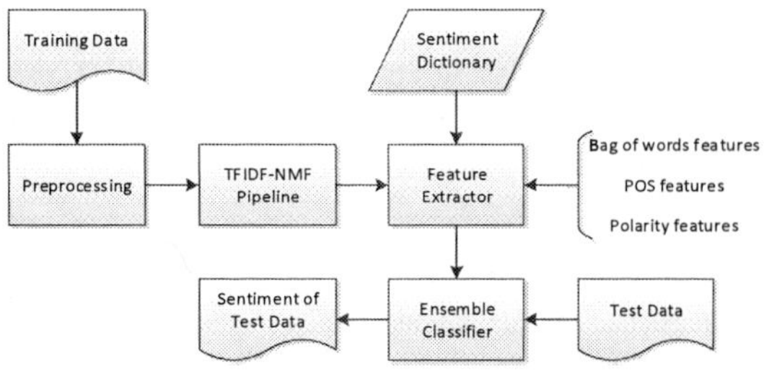

Figure 1: System Overview

is an open source project for character conversion between Traditional and Simplified Chinese.

Replace URLs: The URLs can lead the reader into the new webpages. These URLs do not carry much information about the sentiment. But they might help to identify whether the microblogs contain sentiment information. Thus we use 'http' to replace all the URLs in microblogs.

Remove Retweet Mentions: The retweet mentions in a microblog often start with '@', and are followed by people or organizations. This information is also unhelpful for the sentiment classification of the microblog. Hence they are removed.

Remove Unrelated Punctuations: Some punctuation such as single comma and colon are removed because they are unrelated to sentiment analysis. Some punctuation such as the question and exclamation mark could indicate people's sentiments, so we preserve them for further steps.

Remove numbers: Numbers are usually without any emotional information. Thus, numbers are removed in order to refine the microblog content. But there is a topic Samsung S6 in the training data, and we convert this topic to Samsung Ssix.

Text Segmentation: In the Chinese text analysis task, we need to consider the word as a unit. We use the Jieba[3] Chinese text processing tool to segment the Chinese microblogs into words. The words in sentiment lexicons are added into Jieba default dictionary, which could ensure a higher segmentation accuracy.

Remove Stop Words: Stop words are extremely common words. And stop words do not carry any sentiment information and thus are of no use.

Handle Unbalanced Data: In SIGHAN training dataset, the number of neutral microblogs is about 4 times bigger than that of the microblogs with emotions, which leads to serious unbalanced data. To tackle this problem, we oversample the microblogs with emotions to balance the dataset.

[3]https://github.com/fxsjy/jieba/

3.2 Baseline Model

SIGHAN provided two sentiment lexicon: NTUSD and DLUT Emotion Ontology. We combine the two lexicons, remove the duplicate words, and finally we get 14,828 positive words and 20,366 negative words in the new lexicon.

We first perform the preprocessing steps listed in Section 3.1 and for each sentence we count the number of positive and negative sentiment words. Simple Sentiment Word-Count Method (SSWCM) (Yuan et al., 2013) is an intuitively basic algorithm for sentiment classification. The polarity of text is determined by the number of sentiment words. If the number of positive words is larger than negative words, we will classify the text as the positive polarity. If the number of positive words is less than negative words, we will classify the text as the negative polarity. In other cases, the text is classified as the neutral polarity.

3.3 Feature Extraction

The feature extraction process is a key component for sentiment analysis. The feature vector consists of bag of words features, POS features and polarity features.

Bag of Words Features: We use unigram, bigrams and trigrams as features and the TFIDF as the weighting scheme based on the bag-of-words model. TFIDF is a term weighting scheme developed for information retrieval originally, that has also achieved good performance in document classification and clustering tasks.

Part of Speech Features: We use Jieba Part of Speech Tokenizer, which tags the POS of each word after segmentation. The feature vector uses POS tags to express of how many nouns, verbs, adjectives, hashtags, emoticons, urls and special punctuations like question marks and exclamation marks a microblog consists. These elements are normalized by the length of the microblog text.

Polarity Features: We leverage the given sentiment lexicons to increase the feature set and reflect the sentiment words of the microblog in numerical features. The feature vector consists of the following features for each sentiment lexicon: number of positive and negative sentiments words, sentiment score (number of positive words minus number of negative words), number of positive and negative emoticons, number of positive and negative sentiments words around the topic words (context 5 words).

3.4 χ^2 Feature Selection

The idea of χ^2 feature selection is similar as mutual information. For each feature and class, there is also a score to measure if the feature and the class are independent to each other. We can use χ^2 test, which is a statistic method to check if two events are independent. It assumes the feature and class are independent and calculates χ^2 value. The large score implies they are not independent. The larger the score is, the higher dependency they have. So we want keep features for each classes with highest χ^2 scores. We use the Scikit library to select features according to the k highest scores.

3.5 Classification

After pre-processing and feature extraction we feed the features into a classifier. We tried various classifiers using the Scikit library, including Linear Support Vector Classification, Logistic Regression and Random Forest.

Linear Support Vector Classification (Linear SVC) similar to SVM with parameter kernel='linear', but implemented in terms of liblinear rather than libsvm, so it has more flexibility in the choice of penalties and loss functions and should scale better to large numbers of samples.

Logistic Regression is a linear model for classification rather than regression. In this model, the probabilities describing the possible outcomes of a single trial are modeled using a logistic function.

Random Forest fits a number of decision tree classifiers on various sub-samples of the dataset and use averaging to improve the predictive accuracy and control over-fitting.

These implementations fit a multiclass (one-vs-rest) classification with L2 regularization. After experimentation it was found that Linear SVC gave the best performance. The parameters of the model were computed using grid search. The parameter search uses a 5-fold cross validation to find the maximum F-measure of different parameter values.

We implement a simple ensemble classifier that allows us to combine the different classifiers. It simply takes the majority rule of the predictions by the classifiers. The final classifier is the ensemble of linear SVC, logistic regression, random forest.

4 Experiments and Results

4.1 SIGHAN Dataset

Microblogs labeled as positive, negative or neutral were given by SIGHAN. The organizers provided us with 4,905 microblogs which contain 5 topics for training and 19,469 microblogs for the test data which contain 20 topics.

4.2 Results

We present the score and rank obtained by the system on the test dataset. There were 13 teams participated the task 2 of SIGHAN8. We compare our results with other participators using the F measure and the result is given in Table 2. The AVG and MAX represent the average and max value of the unrestricted result for all the participators. The F1+ and F1- represent the F measure for the positive and negative class respectively.

Model	F1+	F1-	F1
Baseline	0.1451	0.3943	0.3587
POS + Polarity Features	0.1551	0.3607	0.6796
POS + Polarity Features + TFIDF Weighting	0.1625	0.3888	0.7483
MAX	0.6039	0.6938	0.8535
AVG	0.1915	0.3646	0.6978

Table 2: The comparison with other participators for the classification task.

After combining POS features and polarity features with the TFIDF weighting, the model add features about the words, and the experiment result is improved.

5 Conclusion and Future Works

We present results for sentiment analysis on microblog by building a supervised system which combines TFIDF weighting with linguistic features which contain topic based features. We report the overall F-measure for three-way classification tasks: positive, negative and neutral.

At present, this system still has a lot of space to promote. Later, we will consider the following work to enhance the experiment result: Using the word vectors or neural network model for sentiment analysis tasks. More in-depth study of topics related features. For example, consider the coreference resolution technology to deal with the complicated situation refers to introducing syntax analysis.

6 Acknowledgements

This work is supported by the National Basic Research 973 Program of China under Grant No. 2011CB302200-G, the National Natural Science Foundation of China under Grant No.61370074, 61402091.

References

Dalmia A, Gupta M, Varma V. 2015. *SemEval 2015: Twitter Sentiment Analysis The good, the bad and the neutral!* SemEval 2015

Jiang L, Yu M, Zhou M, et al. 2011. *Target-dependent twitter sentiment classification*, volume 1. Association for Computational Linguistics

Blei D M, Ng A Y, Jordan M I. 2003. *Latent dirichlet allocation* the Journal of machine Learning research

Lee D D, Seung H S 1999. *Learning the parts of objects by non-negative matrix factorization* Nature

Boutsidis C, Gallopoulos E. 2008. *SVD based initialization: A head start for nonnegative matrix factorization* Pattern Recognition

Yuan B, Liu Y, Li H, et al. 2013. *Sentiment Classification in Chinese Microblogs: Lexicon-based and Learning-based Approaches* International Proceedings of Economics Development and Research (IPEDR)

Dong L, Wei F, Tan C, et al. 2014. *Adaptive recursive neural network for target-dependent twitter sentiment classification* Association for Computational Linguistics

Pang B, Lee L, Vaithyanathan S. 2002. *Thumbs up?: sentiment classification using machine learning techniques* Association for Computational Linguistics

Wang M, Liu M, Feng S, et al. 2014. *A Novel Calibrated Label Ranking Based Method for Multiple Emotions Detection in Chinese Microblogs* Natural Language Processing and Chinese Computing

Illecker M, Zangerle E. 2015. *Real-time Twitter Sentiment Classification based on Apache Storm*

Go A, Huang L, Bhayani R. 2009. *Twitter sentiment analysis* Entropy

Wasi S B, Neyaz R, Bouamor H, et al. 2014. *CMUQ@ Qatar: Using Rich Lexical Features for Sentiment Analysis on Twitter* SemEval 2014

NEUDM: A System for Topic-Based Message Polarity Classification

Yaqi Wang, Yang Wang, Shi Feng, Daling Wang, Yifei Zhang
Northeastern University, Shenyang, China
{wyqnumber1,wangyangdm}@gmail.com
{fengshi,wangdaling,zhangyifei}@ise.neu.edu.cn

Abstract

In this paper, we describe our system for the topic-based Chinese message polarity classification in SIGHAN 8 Task 2. Our system integrates two SVM classifiers which consist of LinearSVC and LibSVM to train the classification model and predict the results of Chinese message polarity in the restricted resource and the unrestricted resource, respectively. In order to assure our feature engineering effort on the task, we use some feature selection methods, such as LDA, word2vec, and sentiment lexicons including DLUT emotion ontology and NTUSD. Our system achieves the overall F1 score of 74.88% in the restricted evaluation and 74.43% in the unrestricted evaluation.

1 Introduction

With the development of social network, more and more people are actively sharing information with others and expressing their opinions and feelings on Chinese Weibo platform. Weibo has aggregated huge number of tweets that containing people's opinion about commercial products, celebrities, social event and so on. Therefore, mining people's sentiments expressed in tweets has attracted more and more attention for both research and industrial communities.

For the Chinese microblog, our task is to classify people's sentiments for a given topic as positive, negative, and neutral. Among the varieties of topics, people could express neutral, positive, and negative sentiments for them, respectively. If the topic information is ignored, it is difficult to obtain the correct sentiment for a specified target.

Topic-dependent features. The traditional learning-based methods for solving sentiment classification problem, such as (Go et al., 2009; Barbosa and Feng, 2010), basically followed (Pang et al., 2002), who utilized machine learning based classifiers for the sentiment classification of text. They worked in a topic-independent way: all the features have no relation with the topic. That is to say: the sentiment is decided no matter what the target is. Jiang et al. (2011) combined the target-independent features (content and lexicon) and target-dependent features (rules based on the dependency parsing results) together for tweet subjectivity and polarity classification.

Sparse vectors. The microblog usually has a length limitation, such as 140 characters. Therefore, the vectors formed by microblog data are extremely sparse, which sets obstacles for further classification algorithms.

To tackle these challenges, in this paper we first leverage the generative model LDA (Andrew Ng et al. 2003) to extract the top ranked topic words as topic-related features. Secondly, we count the number of positive and negative sentiment words through sentiment lexicon in the sentence and get the adjective word which only occur in the polarity sentences. Finally, we utilize the well-known deep learning word embedding tool word2vec[1] to find the top-k semantically similar words in the topic document to expand the feature representation. The used words in the word embedding tool word2vec both appear in a sentiment lexicon and the topic document. The component of feature vector can be described as follows.

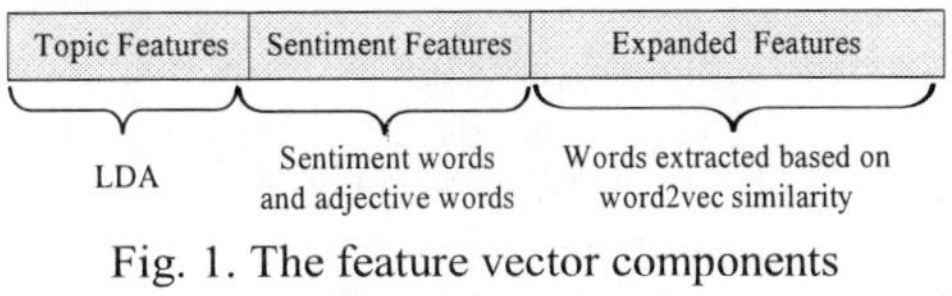

Fig. 1. The feature vector components

In Figure 1, the topic, sentiment and expanded features attempt to handle the topic-based sentiment analysis problem. The expanded features based on word2vec try to enrich the feature space and alleviate the sparse vector problem. Based on the feature vector, we can utilize off-the-shelf machine learning algorithms to train the topic-based sentiment classification model.

[1] http://code.google.com/p/word2vec/

Proceedings of the Eighth SIGHAN Workshop on Chinese Language Processing (SIGHAN-8), pages 185–189,
Beijing, China, July 30-31, 2015.

2 Related Work

The traditional sentiment classification focuses on people's sentiment expressed in text. For example, whether a product review is positive or negative (Pang, Lee, & Vaithyanathan, 2002). Different from the traditional sentiment classification, topic-based classification is more challenging. The identification of topic-based sentiment needs to extract more information.

Jiang et al. (2011) proposed to improve target-dependent Twitter sentiment classification by 1) incorporating target-dependent features; and 2) taking related tweets into consideration. More specifically, they used two-step classification method to handle target-dependent twitter sentiment classification. They classified the tweets to the subjective and objective class, and then the subjective tweets are divided into positive and negative emotion class. Finally, they get the target-dependent twitter sentiment polarity.

Li Dong et al. (2014) proposed to the Adaptive Recursive Neural Network (AdaRNN) for target-dependent Twitter sentiment classification. AdaRNN adaptively propagated the sentiments of words to target depending on the context and syntactic relationships between them.

In this paper, we present machine learning based algorithms and deep learning system for SIGHAN 8 Task 2 which has restricted resource and unrestricted resource respectively.

3 System Overview

We use two-way classification framework which is used for the restricted resource and the unrestricted resource, respectively. Figure 2 illustrates the general framework of our system that includes the module of pre-processing, feature extraction, classifier training and predicting.

3.1 Data Pre-processing

Before the Chinese message is trained and predicted for the task, it needs to process the data so that the Chinese message can be split into words (tokenization). Meanwhile, it attaches more information to each word (part-of-speech tagging).

We adopt ICTCLAS2015[2] segmentation module, which is developed by Institute of Computing Technology, Chinese Academy of Science, to segment the given Chinese message including train and test data into words and proper part-of-speech (POS) tags. In the process, we delete the stop words, punctuation characters and other necessary processing. At last, we obtain the data for further feature extraction.

Chinese message	“魅族黄章叫板三星 Galaxy S6 也不过如此！ http://t.cn/RwHsCt6 @凤凰新闻客户端”
Bag of words	“魅族 黄章 叫板 三星 Galaxy S6 也 不过如此 ！ ”
Part-of-Speech features	“魅/w 族/ng 黄/nr1 章/n 叫/vi 板/ng 三星/nt Galaxy/n S6/n 也/d 不过如此/vl ！ /wt”

Table 1: the example of ICTCLAS2015 segmentation result

3.2 Feature Extraction

The feature extraction plays very important role for the machine learning algorithms. A better feature extraction method can improve the prediction performance of the classifier, provide faster and more cost-effective classifier, and provide a better understanding of the underlying process that generated the data (Isabelle Guyon, Andre Elisseeff. 2003).

Due to the microblog can be split into many words and phrases, the overall Chinese microblog will be generate a rich set of features and may meet the curse of dimensionality problem. How to extract the appropriate features for topic-based sentiment classification is the key issue for the task. Our proposed approach of feature extraction includes:

Topic Features. Each microblog may be viewed as a mixture of various topic words. In order to obtain words and phrases which are relationship with the topic, we conduct LDA modeling for each topic collection and extract the top ranked words with higher topic generative probability.

Sentiment Features. We utilize the sentiment lexicons to select the sentiment features from Chinese microblog sentences. We calculated the number of positive emotion words and the number of negative emotion words in the Chinese microblog sentences, respectively. Then, we put the result into feature Set. The DLUT emotion ontology and NTUSD are chosen for the restricted resource setting of the SIGHAN task. For the unrestricted resource setting, we use our own sentiment lexicon. Besides the words in the lexicon, we also employ the POS tagging method to select the adjective words which only occur in the positive sentence and negative sentence as sentiment features.

Expanded features. To tackle the sparse problem of the short text in microblog, we em-

[2]www.nlpir.org

ploy the word embedding tool word2vec to enrich the feature representations. Given the topic documents *d*, *SF* is the feature set of *d*. The intersection set of sentiment lexicon and d is *ST* and $st \in ST$. Non-feature word $nw \notin SF$. Each word in the topic documents is represented as a vector based on word2vec (Dongwen Zhang et al., 2015) and then we calculate the cosine similarities between each sentiment and non-sentiment word pairs (*st*, *nw*). The *nw* with top-k similarity is added into final feature vector.

After feature selection, we utilize TFIDF method to calculate the weight of each feature in the vectors.

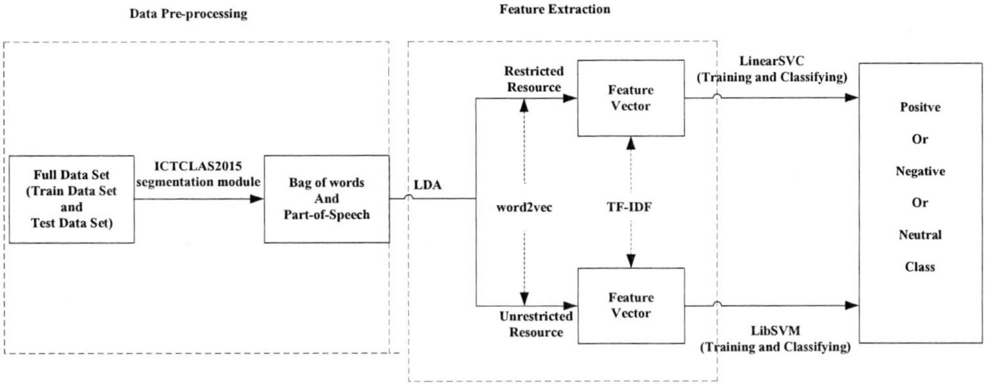

Fig. 2. The general framework of our system

3.3 Classifier

In this step, the extracted feature vectors are trained by a classifier to predict the sentiment polarity of the test data set. Lots of previous researches prove that Support Vector Machine shows substantial performance gains and is more robust in the work of sentiment classification compared with other state-of-art models (Pang et al., 2002; Tang, Tan, & Cheng, 2009). Due to this reason, SVM is adopted as the classification algorithm.

In the restricted resource, the SVM classifier is the linear support vector classification (LinearSVC) which is implemented in terms of Liblinear rather than LibSVM form the python based machine learning open source projects called Scikit-Learn[3]. In the unrestricted resource, the SVM classifier is the LibSVM which is implemented by C language. We search the best parameter c and g separately in the LibSVM for each topic dataset.

The implementation of Support Vector Classification is based on LibSVM. The fit time complexity is more than quadratic with the number of samples. Linear Support Vector Classification (LinearSVC) is similar to SVC with parameter kernel='linear'. It is implemented in terms of liblinear rather than LibSVM. The LinearSVC supports both dense and sparse input and the multiclass support is handled according to a one-vs-the-rest scheme.

4 Experiments and Results

In this section, we explain details of the data and the general settings for the different experiments we conducted. We train and evaluate our classifier for restricted resource and unrestricted resource respectively, training and testing datasets provided by SIGHAN 8 Task 2.

4.1 Dataset

The train dataset is composed of five different topics and includes 4,905 Chinese microblogs. The test dataset is composed of twenty different topics and includes 19,469 Chinese microblogs. Each topic contains approximately 1,000 Chinese microblogs. But the ratio of subjective class to objective class is four to one and the ratio of positive class to negative class is one to one in the subjective class. The serious imbalanced data set has an adverse effect on classification results. So in order to keep the train data set balanced, we adopt the sampling strategy. We do not change the neutral class data and the sum of the positive class and the negative class is resampled to be an equal number of the neutral class.

4.2 Evaluation criteria

In SIGHAN 8 task 2, we evaluate the experimental results with Precision, Recall and F1 measure. These three classic values are utilized

[3]http://scikit-learn.org/stable

to measure the performance of positive, negative, neutral class respectively.

4.3 Classifier and Result

In the Section 3.2, the process of feature extraction has been done. We use the result of feature engineering into the classifier to train the classification model. In order to transform the each topic document in the train data set and test data set to vector matrix which complies with the input format of LinearSVC classifier in the restricted resource, we use the method of TF-IDF which is often used as a weighting factor in text mining and reflect how important a word is to a document in a collection or corpus.

If the adjectives appear only in the subjective sentences, the weight of the adjectives are set to 10. It means that the adjectives are more valuable. Meanwhile, we also make the input format complied with the LibSVM in the unrestricted resource and the parameter *c* and *g* of LibSVM in the unrestricted resource is set to c=8.0 and g=0.125.

At last, we use the classifiers which consist of LinearSVC in the restricted resource and LibSVM in the unrestricted resource to train the model and predict the label of the microblogs. Table 2 shows the result of the experiments.

The results in Table 2 show that the values of Precision, Recall, F1 measure is approximately equal to 0.74 in the restricted source and unrestricted source. We have achieve good performances in overall Precision, Recall and F1 measure. However, the values of Precision+, Recall+, F1+, Precision-, Recall-, F1- are not good. It means that the problem of imbalance data need to be better solved and we may further improve Topic-Based Chinese Message Polarity Classification task by adding more topic-related linguistic features.

Restricted								
Precision	Recall	F1	Precision+	Recall+	F1+	Precision-	Recall-	F1-
0.74883145	0.74883145	0.74883145	0.31879196	0.082465276	0.1310345	0.44460857	0.082715034	0.13948101
Unrestricted								
Precision	Recall	F1	Precision+	Recall+	F1+	Precision-	Recall-	F1-
0.74436283	0.74436283	0.74436283	0.17627119	0.045138888	0.071872845	0.40792078	0.05660896	0.09942085

Table 2: the results of our system

Restricted			
	Precision	Recall	F1
NEUDM2	**0.74883**	**0.74883**	**0.74883**
TICS-dm	0.83573884	0.83573884	0.83573884
LCYS_TEAM	0.7259232	0.7259232	0.7259232
Restricted			
	Precision	Recall	F1
NEUDM2	**0.74436283**	**0.74436283**	**0.74436283**
TICS-dm	0.85356206	0.85356206	0.85356206
xk0	0.74893427	0.74893427	0.74893427

Table 3: the compare of competition results

5 Discussion

After conducting a series of experiments, in this section, we discuss the effectiveness of our method. The compare of competition results in Table 3 show that the overall F1 score of our system is good. Firstly, the noise of Data is effective removed. Secondly, the quantity of feature is sufficient through the extracting of topic features, sentiment features and expanded features, respectively. Finally, LinearSVM is better than LibSVM and it trains faster and predicts more accurate in large-scale training set. As a result, the performance of the our system proposed method for Chinese microblog polarity classification is acceptable.

6 Conclusion and future work

Different from most of the conventional methods for subjective and objective classification, our research focuses on the topic-based polarity classification. In this paper, our system relied heavily on the topic features, sentiment and expanded sentiment features. These features assure the effect of our classifiers in this task. Our system, we can achieve medium score in the SIGHAN 8 task 2.

We have a lot of work ahead of us. In the future, we would like to find more topic-related linguistic features to add in the representation vectors. We would like to extract more structured information and composition unit existing in sentences for topic features in the future work.

7 Acknowledgements

This work is supported by the National Basic Research 973 Program of China under Grant No. 2011CB302200-G, the National Natural Science Foundation of China under Grant No.61370074, 61402091.

Reference

Blei, David M.; Ng, Andrew Y.; Jordan, Michael I (January 2003). Lafferty, John, ed. "Latent Dirichlet allocation". Journal of Machine Learning Research 3 (4–5): pp. 993–1022. doi:10.1162/jmlr.2003.3.4-5.993

Alec Go, RichaBhayani, Lei Huang. 2009. Twitter Sentiment Classification using Distant Supervision.

Luciano Barbosa and Junlan Feng. 2010. Robust Setiment Detection on Twitter from Biased and Noisy Data. Coling 2010.

Long Jiang, Mo Yu, Ming Zhou, Xiaohua Liu, and Tiejun Zhao. 2011. Target-dependent twitter sentiment classification. In Proceedings of the 49th Annual Meeting of the Association for Computational Linguistics: Human Language Technologies - Volume 1, HLT '11, pages 151–160, Stroudsburg, PA, USA. Association for Computational Linguistics.

Isabelle Guyon, Andre Elisseeff. 2003. An Introdution to Variable and Feature Selection.

Dongwen Zhang, Hua Xu, Zengcai Su, Yunfeng Xu. 2015. Chinese comments sentiment classification based on word2vec andSVM^{pref}.

Pang, B., Lee, L., &Vaithyanathan, S. (2002). Senment classification using machine learning techniques.In Proceedings of the conference on empirical methods in natural language processing (pp. 79–86). Association for Computational Linguistics.

Li Dong, Furu Wei, Chuanqi Tan, Duyu Tang, Ming Zhou, Ke Xu. 2014. Adaptive Recursive Neural Network for Target-dependent Twitter Sentiment Classification.

Author Index

Association for Computational Linguistics
209 N. Eighth Street
Stroudsburg, Pennsylvania 18360

CURRAN ASSOCIATES INC.
proceedings.com

ISBN 978-1-5108-0949-9
9 781510 809499